INVESTIGATING

Christian Evidences

Bert Thompson, Ph.D.
and
Brad Harrub, Ph.D.

AP
APOLOGETICS PRESS

Apologetics Press, Inc.
230 Landmark Drive
Montgomery, Alabama 36117-2752

ISBN: 0-932859-57-7
Printed in China

Library of Congress Cataloging-in-Publication

Bert Thompson (1949 -) and Brad Harrub (1970 -)

Investigating Christian Evidences: A Study Course

Includes bibliographic references and discussion questions.

ISBN 0-932859-57-7

1. Apologetics and polemics. 2. Christian Theology. I. Title

213–dc21 2003110802

DEDICATION

God has richly blessed the authors of this book with virtuous and faithful wives who take extremely seriously their God-given responsibility of being a Christian mother, and who strive daily to diligently uphold biblical principles as an example to their children, and to the children of others around them.

One of the driving forces behind the research and writing of this book has been the innumerable requests we have received through the years from other Christian parents who want to provide information to their children that not only will assist those children in building an unwavering biblical faith, but that will help them maintain that faith in the face of the adversity and challenges that are sure to come as they grow older. Such dedicated parents are individuals who willingly, boldly, and unashamedly proclaim: "As for me and my house, we shall serve the Lord" (Joshua 24:15).

We are pleased to dedicate this volume to such parents—faithful Christians who are determined to follow the divine edict laid down in Deuteronomy 6. "And these words which I command you today shall be in your heart. And you shall teach them diligently to your children, and you shall talk of them when you sit in your house, when you walk by the way, when you lie down, and when you rise up" (vss. 6-7). It is with deep appreciation (and a heartfelt sense of camaraderie) that we offer this book to those who have made a conscientious effort to uphold the inspired Word of God before their children in every aspect of their lives. May our great God bless your efforts, and may your tribe increase.

TABLE OF CONTENTS

PREFACE

The inspired apostle Paul once said that he was "set for the defense of the gospel" (Philippians 1:16). Indeed, he was to spend the rest of his earthly existence doing just that–defending the Gospel of Jesus Christ and expounding to anyone who would listen the story of the salvation that comes through obedience to the Gospel message. He was to appear before angry mobs, the Jewish Sanhedrin, and even Agrippa the king. His situation changed often; his message never did.

Paul, and untold millions of other faithful adherents to Christianity down through the ages, served Jehovah God because they had seen, and examined, the evidences that stand incontrovertibly behind the God of the Bible and the religion He instituted through His only begotten Son, Jesus Christ.

Christianity is deeply rooted in historical fact. From the Jews of the days of Moses who were God's chosen people, to the Christians of today who are His spiritual children, the story is told of the singular God of Abraham, Isaac, and Jacob Who created the world and all that is in it, and Who loved mankind so much that He emptied heaven of its most prized possession to ensure eternal salvation for the people created "in his image" (Genesis 1:26-27).

The story told throughout the sixty-six books of the Bible is one that is verifiable. The claims that are made are backed up by the most solid kinds of evidence–from the empty tomb on the mountainside outside of Jerusalem, to the weighty manuscript evidence for the Bible as the inspired Word of God. The honest, open-minded person who, with a sincere heart, will take the time and make the effort to look, will find that there is but one option: God lives, and communicates with man through His inspired Word, which provides the truth that makes men free (John 8:32).

Investigating Christian Evidences is a study course that is intended to help a truth seeker examine the many evidences upon which historical Christianity rests, and is dedicated to explaining, and defending, the Christian system as the one and only true religion of the one and only true God. As such, it is intended to help teach and convert the non-Christian. But it also has as one of its goals strengthening the faith of the Christian.

In this volume, the reader will find lessons on God's existence, Jesus' Sonship and deity, the verbal, plenary inspiration of the Bible, the literal, historical nature of the Creation account of Genesis, what one must do to be saved, the essentiality and uniqueness of Christ's church, and much more.

This book is sent forth with the hope that you, the reader, will benefit from it, and with the prayer that: (a) if you are not a Christian, you will want to become one; or (b) if you are a Christian, you not only will have your faith strengthened by what you read, but also will use what you learn to help others find their salvation in Christ as well.

If there is any way that those of us associated with the work of Apologetics Press can assist you, please do not hesitate to call or write. We stand ready to help you in any way possible. We want you to know that we are here to serve.

Bert Thompson
Brad Harrub
September 2003

Chapter 1

THE CASE FOR THE EXISTENCE OF GOD [PART I]

One of the most basic, and most fundamental, issues that can be considered by the human mind is the question, "Does God exist?" In the field of logic, there are principles–or as they are called more often, laws–that govern human thought processes and that are accepted as analytically true. One of these is the Law of the Excluded Middle. When applied to objects, this law states that an object cannot both possess and not possess a certain trait or characteristic at the same time and in the same fashion. When applied to propositions, this law states that all precisely stated propositions are either true or false; they cannot be both true and false at the same time and in the same fashion.

The statement, "God exists," is a precisely stated proposition. Thus, it is either true or false. The simple fact is, either God exists or He does not. There is no middle ground. One cannot affirm logically both the existence and nonexistence of God. The atheist boldly states that God does not exist; the theist affirms just as boldly that God does exist; the agnostic laments that there is not enough evidence to make a decision on the matter; and the skeptic doubts that God's existence can be proven with certainty. Who is correct? Does God exist or not?

The only way to answer this question, of course, is to seek out and examine the evidence. It certainly is reasonable to suggest that if there is a God, He would make available to us evidence adequate to the task of proving His existence. But does such evidence exist? And if it does, what is the nature of that evidence?

The theist advocates the view that evidence is available to prove conclusively that God does exist and that this evidence is adequate to establish beyond reasonable doubt the existence of God. However, when we employ the word "prove," we do not mean that God's existence can be demonstrated scientifically in the same fashion that one might prove that a sack of potatoes weighs ten pounds or that a human heart has four distinct chambers within it. Such matters as the weight of a sack of vegetables, or the divisions within a muscle, are matters that may be verified empirically using the five senses. And while empirical evidence often is quite useful in establishing the validity of a case, it is not the sole means of arriving at proof. For example, legal authorities recognize the validity of a *prima facie* case, which is acknowledged to exist when adequate evidence is available to establish the presumption of a fact that, unless such fact can be refuted, legally stands proven (see Jackson, 1974, p. 13). It is the contention of the theist that there is a vast body of evidence that makes an impregnable *prima facie* case for the existence of God—a case that simply cannot be refuted. We would like to present here the *prima facie* case for the existence of God, along with a portion of the evidence upon which that case is based.

CAUSE AND EFFECT—THE COSMOLOGICAL ARGUMENT

Throughout human history, one of the most effective arguments for the existence of God has been the cosmological argument, which addresses the fact that the Universe (Cosmos) is here and therefore must be explained in some fashion. In his book, *Not A Chance*, R.C. Sproul observed:

> Traditional philosophy argued for the existence of God on the foundation of the law of causality. The cosmological argument went from the presence of a cosmos back to a creator of the cosmos. It sought a rational answer to the question, "**Why** is there something rather than nothing?" It sought a sufficient reason for a real world (1994, p. 169, emp. in orig.).

The Universe exists and is real. Atheists and agnostics not only acknowledge its existence, but admit that it is a grand effect (e.g., see Jastrow, 1977, pp. 19-21). If an entity cannot account for its own being (i.e., it is not sufficient to have caused itself), then it is said to be "contingent" because it is dependent upon something outside of itself to explain its existence. The Universe is a contingent entity since it is inadequate to cause, or explain, its own existence. Sproul has noted: "Logic requires that if something exists contingently, it must have a cause. That is merely to say, if it is an effect it must have an antecedent cause" (1994, p. 172). Thus, since the Universe is a contingent effect, the obvious question becomes, "What **caused** the Universe?"

It is here that the Law of Cause and Effect (also known as the Law of Causality) is tied firmly to the cosmological argument. Scientists, and philosophers of science, recognize laws as "reflecting actual regularities in nature" (Hull, 1974, p. 3). So far as scientific knowledge can attest, laws know no exceptions. This certainly is true of the Law of Cause and Effect. It is, indisputably, the most universal, and most certain, of all scientific laws.

This law has been stated in a variety of ways, each of which adequately expresses its ultimate meaning. Kant, in the first edition of *Critique of Pure Reason*, stated that "everything that happens (begins to be) presupposes something which it follows according to a rule." In the second edition, he strengthened that statement by noting that "all changes take place according to the law of connection of cause and effect" (see Meiklejohn, 1878, p. 141). Schopenhauer stated the proposition as: "Nothing happens without a reason why it should happen rather than not happen" (as quoted in von Mises, 1968, p. 159). The number of various formulations could be expanded almost indefinitely. But simply put, the Law of Causality states that **every material effect must have an adequate antecedent cause**.

The philosophical/theological implications of this concept –pro and con–have been argued through the years. But after the dust settles, the Law of Causality always remains intact. There is no question of its acceptance in the world of experimental science or in the ordinary world of personal experience. Many years ago, professor W.T. Stace, in his classic work, *A Critical History of Greek Philosophy*, commented:

> Every student of logic knows that this is the ultimate canon of the sciences, the foundation of them all. If we did not believe the truth of causation, namely, everything which has a beginning has a cause, and that in the same circumstances the same things invariably happen, all the sciences would at once crumble to dust. In every scientific investigation this truth is assumed (1934, p. 6).

The Law of Causality is not just of importance to science. Richard von Mises observed: "We may only add that almost all philosophers regard the law of causality as the most important, the most far-reaching, and the most firmly founded of all principles of epistemology" (1968, p. 160). Just as the Law of the Excluded Middle is true analytically, so the Law of Cause and Effect is true analytically as well. Sproul addressed this when he wrote:

> The statement "Every effect has an antecedent cause" is **analytically true**. To say that it is analytically or formally true is to say that it is true by definition or analysis. There is nothing in the predicate that is not already contained by resistless logic in the subject. It is like the statement, "A bachelor is an unmarried man" or "A triangle has three sides" or "Two plus two are four...." Cause and effect, though distinct ideas, are inseparably bound together in rational discourse. It is meaningless to say that something is a **cause** if it yields no **effect**. It is likewise meaningless to say that something is an **effect** if it has no **cause**. A cause, by definition, must have an effect, or it is not a cause. An effect, by definition, must have a cause, or it is not an effect (1994, pp. 172,171 emp. in orig.).

Effects without adequate causes are unknown. Further, causes never occur subsequent to the effect. It is meaningless to speak of a cause following an effect, or an effect preceding a cause. In addition, the effect never is qualitatively superior to, nor quantitatively greater than, the cause. This knowledge is responsible for our formulation of the Law of Causality in these words: Every material effect must have an **adequate** antecedent cause. The river did not turn muddy because the frog jumped in; the book did not fall from the table because the fly lighted on it. These are not adequate causes. For whatever effects we observe, we must postulate adequate antecedent causes–which brings us back to the original question: What **caused** the Universe?

There are but three possible answers to this question: (1) the Universe is eternal; it always has existed and always will exist; (2) the Universe is not eternal; rather, it created itself out of nothing; (3) the Universe is not eternal, and did not create itself out of nothing; rather, it was created by something (or Someone) anterior, and superior, to itself. These three options merit serious consideration.

IS THE UNIVERSE ETERNAL?

The cover of the June 25, 2001 issue of *Time* magazine announced: "How the Universe Will End: Peering Deep Into Space and Time, Scientists Have Just Solved the Biggest Mystery in the Cosmos" (see Lemonick, 2001). Comforting thought, isn't it, to know that the "biggest mystery in the Cosmos" has been figured out? But what, exactly, is that mystery? And why does it merit the front cover of a major news magazine?

The origin and destiny of the Universe always have been important topics in the creation/evolution controversy. In the past, evolutionists went to great extremes to present scenarios that included an eternal Universe, and they went to the same extremes to avoid any scenario that suggested a Universe with a beginning or end because such a scenario posed bothersome questions. In his book, *God and the Astronomers*, the eminent evolutionary astronomer Robert Jastrow, who currently is serving as the director of the Mount Wilson Observatory, put it like this:

> The Universe is the totality of all matter, animate and inanimate, throughout space and time. If there was a beginning, what came before? If there is an end, what will come after? On both scientific and philosophical grounds, the concept of an eternal Universe seems more acceptable than the concept of a transient Universe that springs into being suddenly, and then fades slowly into darkness.
>
> Astronomers try not to be influenced by philosophical considerations. However, the idea of a Universe that has both a beginning and an end is distasteful to the scientific mind. In a desperate effort to avoid it, some astronomers have searched for another interpretation of the measurements that indicate the retreating motion of the galaxies, an interpretation that would not require the Universe to expand. If the evidence for the expanding Universe could be explained away, the need for a moment of creation would be eliminated, and the concept of time without end would return to science. But these attempts have not succeeded, and most astronomers have come to the conclusion that they live in an exploding world (1977, p. 31).

What does Jastrow mean when he says that "these attempts have not succeeded"? And why do evolutionists prefer to avoid the question of a Universe with a beginning? In an interview he granted on June 7, 1994, Dr. Jastrow elaborated on this point. The interviewer, Fred Heeren, asked if there was anything from physics that could explain how the Universe first came to be. Jastrow lamented:

> No, there's not–this is the most interesting result in all of science.... As Einstein said, scientists live by their faith in causation, and the chain of cause and effect. Every effect has a cause that can be discovered by ra-

> tional arguments. And this has been a very successful program, if you will, for unraveling the history of the universe. But it just fails at the beginning.... So time, really, going backward, comes to a halt at that point. Beyond that, that curtain can never be lifted.... And that is really a blow at the very fundamental premise that motivates all scientists (as quoted in Heeren, 1995, p. 303).

Seventeen years earlier, in his book, *Until the Sun Dies*, Jastrow had discussed this very problem–a Universe without any adequate explanation for its own existence and, worse still, without any adequate cause for whatever theory scientists might set forth in an attempt to elucidate how it did originate. As Jastrow noted:

> This great saga of cosmic evolution, to whose truth the majority of scientists subscribe, is the product of an act of creation that took place twenty billion years ago [according to evolutionary estimates–BT/BH]. Science, unlike the Bible, has no explanation for the occurrence of that extraordinary event. The Universe, and everything that has happened in it since the beginning of time, are a grand effect without a known cause. An effect without a cause? That is not the world of science; it is world of witchcraft, of wild events and the whims of demons, a medieval world that science has tried to banish. As scientists, what are we to make of this picture? I do not know (1977, p. 21).

While Dr. Jastrow may not know **how** the Universe began, there are two things that he and his colleagues **do** know: (1) the Universe had a definite beginning; and (2) the Universe will have a definite ending.

Admittedly, the most comfortable position for the evolutionist is the idea that the Universe is eternal, because it avoids the problem of a beginning or ending and thus the need for any "first cause" such as a Creator. In his book, *Until the Sun Dies*, astronomer Jastrow noted: "The proposal for the creation of matter out of nothing possesses a strong appeal to the scientist, since it permits him to contemplate a Universe without beginning and without end" (1977, p. 32). Jastrow went on to remark that evolutionary scientists preferred an eternal Universe "because the notion of a world with a beginning and an end made them feel so uncomfortable" (p. 33). In *God and the Astronomers*, Dr. Jastrow explained why attempts to prove an eternal Universe had failed miserably. "Now three lines of evidence–the motions of the galaxies, the laws of thermodynamics, and the life story of the stars–pointed to one conclusion; all indicated that the Universe had a beginning" (1978, p. 111). Jastrow–who is considered by many to be one of the greatest science writers of our age–certainly is no creationist. But as a scientist who is an astrophysicist, he has written often on the inescapable conclusion that the Universe had a beginning. Consider, for example, these statements from his pen:

> Now both theory and observation pointed to an expanding Universe and a beginning in time.... About thirty years ago science solved the mystery of the birth and death of stars, and acquired new evidence that the Universe had a beginning (1978, pp. 47,105).
>
> Arthur Eddington, the most distinguished British astronomer of his day, wrote, "If our views are right, somewhere between the beginning of time and the present day we must place the winding up of the universe." When that occurred, and Who or what wound up the Universe, were questions that bemused theologians, physicists and astronomers, particularly in the 1920's and 1930's (1978, pp. 48-49).
>
> Most remarkable of all is the fact that in science, as in the Bible, the World begins with an act of creation. That view has not always been held by scientists. Only as a result of the most recent discoveries can we say with a fair degree of confidence that the world has not existed forever; that it began abruptly, without apparent cause, in a blinding event that defies scientific explanation (1977, p. 19).

The conclusion to be drawn from the scientific data was inescapable, as Dr. Jastrow himself admitted when he wrote:

> The lingering decline predicted by astronomers for the end of the world differs from the explosive conditions they have calculated for its birth, but the impact is the same: **modern science denies an eternal existence to the Universe, either in the past or in the future** (1977, p. 30, emp. added).

In her book, *The Fire in the Equations*, award-winning science writer Kitty Ferguson wrote in agreement.

> Our late twentieth-century picture of the universe is dramatically different from the picture our forebears had at the beginning of the century. Today it's common knowledge that all the individual stars we see with the naked eye are only the stars of our home galaxy, the Milky Way, and that the Milky Way is only one among many billions of galaxies. **It's also common knowledge that the universe isn't eternal but had a beginning ten to twenty billion years ago, and that it is expanding** (1994, p. 89, emp. added).

The evidence clearly indicates that the Universe had a beginning. The Second Law of Thermodynamics, as Dr. Jastrow has indicated, shows this to be true. Henry Morris correctly commented: "The Second Law requires the universe to have had a beginning" (1974b, p. 26). Indeed, it does. The simple fact is, the Universe is not eternal. It had a beginning, and it will have an ending. As Jastrow observed:

> About thirty years ago science solved the mystery of the birth and death of stars, and acquired new evidence that the Universe had a beginning.... Now both theory and observation pointed to an expanding Universe and a beginning in time (1978, p. 105).

Six pages later in *God and the Astronomers*, Dr. Jastrow concluded: "Now three lines of evidence—the motions of the galaxies, the laws of thermodynamics, the life story of the stars—pointed to one conclusion; all indicated that the Universe had a beginning" (p. 111). Earlier in that same volume, he had written: "And concurrently there was a great deal of discussion about the fact that the second law of thermodynamics, applied to the Cosmos, indicates the Universe is running down like a clock. If it is running down, there must have been a time when it was fully wound up" (1978, pp. 48-49).

Matter hardly can be eternal because, as everyone knows (and as every knowledgeable scientist readily admits), eternal things do not run down. Furthermore, there is going to be an end at some point in the future. And eternal entities have neither beginnings nor endings. In 1929, Sir James Jeans, writing in his classic book *The Universe Around Us*, observed: "All this makes it clear that the present matter of the universe cannot have existed forever.... In some way matter which had not previously existed, came, or was brought, into being" (1929, p. 316). Now, over seventy years later, we have returned to the same conclusion. As Lemonick put it in his 2001 *Time* article:

> If the latest results do hold up, some of the most important questions in cosmology–how old the universe is, what it's made of and how it will end–will have been answered, only about 70 years after they were first posed. By the time the **final chapter of cosmic history** is written–further in the future than our minds can grasp–humanity, and perhaps even biology, will long since have vanished (157[25]:56, emp. added).

The fact that *Time* magazine devoted an entire cover (and feature story to go with it) to the topic of "How the Universe Will End," and the reference to the "final chapter of cosmic history," are inadvertent admissions to something that evolutionists have long tried to avoid–the fact that the Universe had a beginning, and will have an ending. When one hears Sir James Jeans allude to the fact that "in some way matter which had not previously existed, came, or was brought, into being," the question that immediately comes to mind is: **Who** brought it into being? As Great Britain's most eminent physicist, Stephen Hawking, once remarked: "The odds against a universe like ours emerging out of something like the big bang are enormous. **I think there are clearly religious implications**" (as quoted in Boslough, 1985, p. 121, emp. added). We agree.

DID THE UNIVERSE CREATE ITSELF OUT OF NOTHING?

In the February 2001 issue of *Scientific American*, physicists Philip and Phylis Morrison wrote an article titled "The Big Bang: Wit or Wisdom?," in which they remarked: "We no longer see a big bang as a direct solution" (284[2]:95). It's no wonder. As Andrei Linde also wrote in *Scientific American* (seven years earlier) about the supporting evidences for the Big Bang: "We found many to be highly suspicious" (1994, 271[5]:48).

Dr. Linde's comments caught no one by surprise–and drew no ire from his colleagues. In fact, long before he committed to print in such a prestigious science journal the Big Bang's obituary, cosmologists had known (though they were not happy at the thought of having to admit it publicly) that the Big Bang was "scientifically brain dead."

But it was because of that very fact that evolutionists had been working so diligently to find some way to "tweak" the Big Bang model so as to possibly revive it. As David Berlinski rightly remarked:

> Notwithstanding the investment made by the scientific community and the general public in contemporary cosmology, a suspicion lingers that matters do not sum up as they should. Cosmologists write as if they are quite certain of the Big Bang, yet, within the last decade, they have found it necessary to augment the standard view by means of various new theories. These schemes are meant to solve problems that cosmologists were never at pains to acknowledge, so that today they are somewhat in the position of a physician reporting both that his patient has not been ill and that he has been successfully revived (1998, p. 30).

Scientists are desperately in search for an answer that will allow them to continue to defend at least some form of the Big Bang model. Berlinski went on to note:

> Almost all cosmologists have a favored scheme; when not advancing their own, they occupy themselves enumerating the deficiencies of the others.... **Having constructed an elaborate scientific orthodoxy, cosmologists have acquired a vested interest in its defense**.... Like Darwin's theory of evolution, Big Bang cosmology has undergone that curious social process in which a scientific theory has been promoted to a secular myth (pp. 31-32,33,38, emp. added).

Enter inflationary theory–and the idea of (gulp!) a self-created Universe. In the past, it would have been practically impossible to find **any** reputable scientist who would have been willing to advocate a self-created Universe. To hold such a view would have been professional suicide. George Davis, a prominent physicist of the past generation, explained why when he wrote: "No material thing can create itself." Further, as Dr. Davis took pains to explain, such a statement "cannot be logically attacked on the basis of any knowledge available to us" (1958, p. 71). The Universe is the created, not the Creator. And until fairly recently, it seemed there could be no disagreement about that fact.

But, once again, "that was then; this is now." Because the standard Big Bang model is in such dire straits, and because the evidence is so conclusive that the Universe had some kind of beginning, evolutionists now are actually suggesting that **something came from nothing**–that is, **the Universe literally created itself from nothing**! Edward P. Tryon, professor of physics at the City University of New York, was one of the first to suggest such an outlandish hypothesis: "In 1973," he said, "**I proposed that our Universe had been created spontaneously from nothing**, as a result of established principles of physics. This proposal variously struck people as preposterous, enchanting, or both" (1984, 101:14-16, emp. added). This is the same Edward P. Tryon who is on record as stating: "Our universe is simply one of those things which happen from time to time" (1973, 246:397). Anthony Kenny, a British evolutionist, suggested in his book, *Five Ways of Thomas Aquinas*, that something actually came from nothing (1980).

In 1981, physicist Alan Guth of MIT had published a paper titled "Inflationary Universe: A Possible Solution to the Horizon and Flatness Problems," in which he outlined the specifics of inflationary theory (see Guth, 1981). Three years later, the idea that the Universe had simply "popped into existence from nothing" took flight when, in the May 1984 issue of *Scientific American*, Guth teamed up with physicist Paul Steinhardt of Princeton to co-author an article titled "The Inflationary Universe," in which they suggested:

> From a historical point of view probably the most revolutionary aspect of the inflationary model is the notion that all the matter and energy in the observable universe may have emerged from almost nothing.... The inflationary model of the universe provides a possible mechanism by which the observed universe could have evolved from an infinitesimal region. **It is then tempting to go one step further and speculate that the entire universe evolved from literally nothing** (1984, 250:128, emp. added).

Therefore, even though principles of physics that "cannot be logically attacked on the basis of any knowledge available to us" precluded the creation of something out of nothing, suddenly, in an eleventh-hour effort to resurrect the comatose Big Bang Theory, it was suggested that indeed, the Universe simply had "created itself out of nothing." As physicist John Gribbin wrote (in an article for *New Scientist* titled "Cosmologists Move Beyond the Big Bang") two years after Guth and Steinhardt offered their proposal: "...new models are based on the concept that particles [of matter–BT/BH] can be created out of nothing at all...under certain conditions" and that "...matter might suddenly appear in large quantities" (1986, 110[1511]:30).

Naturally, such a proposal would seem–to use Dr. Tryon's words–"preposterous." [G.K. Chesterton once wrote: "It is absurd for the evolutionist to complain that it is unthinkable for an admittedly unthinkable God to make everything out of nothing, and then pretend that it is **more** thinkable that nothing should turn itself into everything" (as quoted in Marlin, et al., 1986, p. 113, emp. in orig.).] Be that as it may, some in the evolutionary camp were ready and willing to defend it–practically from the day it was suggested. One such scientist was Victor J. Stenger, professor of physics at the University of Hawaii. A mere three years after Guth and Steinhardt had published their volley in *Scientific American*, Dr. Stenger authored an article titled "Was the Universe Created?," in which he said:

> ...the universe is probably the result of a random quantum fluctuation in a spaceless, timeless void.... So what had to happen to start the universe was the formation of an empty bubble of highly curved space-time. How did this bubble form? What *caused* it? Not everything requires a cause. It could have just happened spontaneously as one of the many linear combinations of universes that has the quantum numbers of the void.... Much is still in the speculative stage, and **I must admit that there are yet no empirical or observational tests that can be used to test the idea of an accidental origin** (1987, 7[3]:26-30, italics in orig., emp. added.).

This is an interesting turn of events. Evolutionists like Tryon, Stenger, Guth, and Steinhardt insist that this marvelously intricate Universe is "simply one of those things which happen from time to time" as the result of a "random quantum fluctuation in a spaceless, timeless void" that caused matter to evolve from "literally nothing." Such a suggestion, of course, would seem to be a clear violation of the first law of thermodynamics, which states that neither matter nor energy may be created or destroyed in nature. Berlinski acknowledged this when he wrote:

> Hot Big Bang cosmology appears to be in violation of the first law of thermodynamics. The global energy needed to run the universe has come from nowhere, and to nowhere it apparently goes as the universe loses energy by cooling itself.

> This contravention of thermodynamics expresses, in physical form, a general philosophical anxiety. Having brought space and time into existence, along with everything else, the Big Bang itself remains outside any causal scheme (1998, p. 37).

But, as one might expect, supporters of inflation have come up with a response to that complaint, too. In discussing the Big Bang, Linde wrote in *Scientific American*:

> In its standard form, the big bang theory maintains that the universe was born about 15 billion years ago from a cosmological singularity—a state in which the temperature and density are infinitely high. Of course, one cannot really speak in physical terms about these quantities as being infinite. **One usually assumes that the current laws of physics did not apply then** (1994, 271[5]:48, emp. added).

Linde is not the only one willing to acknowledge what the essence of Big-Bang-type scenarios does to the basic laws of physics. Astronomer Joseph Silk wrote:

> The universe began at time zero in a state of infinite density. Of course, the phrase "a state of infinite density" is completely unacceptable as a physical description of the universe.... **An infinitely dense universe [is] where the laws of physics, and even space and time, break down** (as quoted in Berlinski, 1998, p. 36, emp. added).

But there are other equally serious problems as well. According to Guth, Steinhardt, Linde, and other evolutionary cosmologists, before the inflationary Big Bang, there was—well, **nothing**. Berlinski concluded: "But really the question of how the show started answers itself: before the Big Bang there was nothing" (p. 30). Or, as Terry Pratchett wrote in *Lords and Ladies*: "The current state of knowledge can be summarized thus: In the beginning there was nothing, which exploded" (1994, p. 7). Think about that for just a moment. Berlinski did, and then wrote:

> The creation of the universe remains unexplained by any force, field, power, potency, influence, or instrumentality known to physics—or to man. **The whole vast imposing structure organizes itself from absolutely nothing. This is not simply difficult to grasp. It is incomprehensible**.
>
> Physicists, no less than anyone else, are uneasy with the idea that the universe simply popped into existence, with space and time "suddenly switching themselves on." The image of a light switch comes from Paul Davies, who uses it to express a miracle without quite recognizing that it embodies a contradiction. **A universe that has suddenly switched itself on has accomplished something within time; and yet the Big Bang is supposed to have brought space and time into existence**.
>
> Having entered a dark logical defile, physicists often find it difficult to withdraw. Thus, Alan Guth writes in pleased astonishment that the universe really did arise from "essentially...nothing at all": "as it happens, a false vacuum patch" "[10^{-26}] centimeters in diameter" and "[10^{-32}] solar masses." **It would appear, then, that "essentially nothing" has both spatial extension and mass. While these facts may strike Guth as inconspicuous, others may suspect that nothingness, like death, is not a matter that admits of degrees** (p. 37, emp. added).

And, in their more unguarded moments, physicists and astronomers admit as much. Writing in *Astronomy* magazine on "Planting Primordial Seeds," Rocky Kolb suggested: "In a very real sense, quantum fluctuations would be the origin of everything we see in the universe." Yet just one sentence prior to that, he had admitted: "...**[A] region of seemingly empty space is not really empty, but is a seething froth** in which every sort of fundamental particle pops in and out of empty space before annihilating with its antiparticle and disappearing" (1998, 26[2]:42,43, emp. added). Jonathan Sarfati commented:

> Some physicists assert that quantum mechanics violates this cause/effect principle and can produce something from nothing.... But this is a gross misapplication of quantum mechanics. **Quantum mechanics never produces something out of nothing**.... Theories that the Universe is a quantum fluctuation must presuppose that there was something to fluctuate—their "quantum vacuum" is a lot of matter-antimatter potential—not "nothing" (1998, 12[1]:21, emp. added).

Ultimately, the Guth/Steinhardt inflationary model was shown to be incorrect, and a newer version was suggested. Working independently, Russian physicist Andrei Linde, and American physicists Andreas Albrecht and Paul Steinhardt, developed the "new inflationary model" (see Hawking, 1988, pp. 131-132). However, this model also was shown to be incorrect and was discarded. Renowned British astrophysicist Stephen W. Hawking put the matter in proper perspective when he wrote:

> The new inflationary model was a good attempt to explain why the universe is the way it is.... In my personal opinion, **the new inflationary model is now dead as a scientific theory**, although a lot of people do not seem to have heard of its demise and are still writing papers on it as if it were viable (1988, p. 132, emp. added).

Later, Linde himself suggested numerous modifications and is credited with producing what became known as the "chaotic inflationary model" (see Hawking, p. 132ff.). Dr. Hawking performed additional work on this particular model as well. But in an interview on June 8, 1994 dealing specifically with inflationary models, Alan Guth conceded:

> First of all, I will say that at the purely technical level, inflation itself does not explain how the universe arose from nothing.... Inflation itself takes a very small universe and produces from it a very big universe. But inflation by itself does not explain where that very small universe came from (as quoted in Heeren, 1995, p. 148).

After the chaotic inflationary model, came the eternal inflationary model, which was set forth by Andrei Linde in 1986. As astronomer John D. Barrow summarized it in his work, *The Book of Nothing*:

> The spectacular effect of this is to make inflation self-reproducing. Every inflating region gives rise to other sub-regions which inflate and then in turn do the same. The process appears unstoppable–eternal. No reason has been found why it should ever end. Nor is it known if it needs to have a beginning. As with the process of chaotic inflation, every bout of inflation can produce a large region with very different properties. Some regions may inflate a lot, some only a little; some may have many large dimensions of space, some only three; some may contain four forces of Nature that we see, others may have fewer. The overall effect is to provide a physical mechanism by which to realize all, or at least almost all, possibilities somewhere within a single universe.
>
> These speculative possibilities show some of the unending richness of the physicists' conception of the vacuum. It is the basis of our most successful theory of the Universe and why it has the properties that it does. Vacuums can change; vacuums can fluctuate; vacuums can have strange symmetries, strange geographies, strange histories. More and more of the remarkable features of the Universe we observe seem to be reflections of the properties of the vacuum (2000, pp. 256,271).

Michael J. Murray discussed the idea of the origin of the Universe via the Big Bang inflationary model.

> According to the vacuum fluctuation models, our universe, along with these others universes, were generated by quantum fluctuations in a preexisting superspace. Imaginatively, one can think of this preexisting superspace as an infinitely extending ocean of soap, and each universe generated out of this superspace as a soap bubble which spontaneously forms on the ocean (1999, pp. 59-60).

Magnificent claims, to be sure—yet little more than wishful thinking. For example, cosmologists speak of a particular particle—known as an "inflaton"—that is supposed to have provided the vacuum with its initial energy. Yet as scientists acknowledge, "...the particle that might have provided the vacuum energy density is still unidentified, even theoretically; it is sometimes called the inflaton because its sole purpose seems to be to have produced inflation" (see "The Inflationary Universe," 2001). In an article on "Before the Big Bang" in the March 1999 issue of *Analog Science Fiction & Fact Magazine*, John G. Cramer wrote:

> The problem with all of this is that the inflation scenario seems rather contrived and raises many unresolved questions. Why is the universe created with the inflaton field displaced from equilibrium? Why is the displacement the same everywhere? What are the initial conditions that produce inflation? How can the inflationary phase be made to last long enough to produce our universe? Thus, the inflation scenario which was invented to eliminate the contrived initial conditions of the Big Bang model apparently needs contrived initial conditions of its own (1999).

Cosmologist Michael Turner of the University of Chicago put it this way: "If inflation is the dynamite behind the Big Bang, we're still looking for the match" (as quoted in Overbye, 2001). Or, as journalist Dennis Overbye put it in an article titled "Before the Big Bang, There Was...What?" in the May 22, 2001 issue of *The New York Times*: "The only thing that all the experts agree on is that no idea works—yet" (2001). As Barrow admitted somewhat sorrowfully: "So far, unfortunately, **the entire grand scheme of eternal inflation does not appear to be open to observational tests**" (p. 256, emp. added). In his book, *The Accelerating Universe*, Mario Livio wrote in agreement:

> If eternal inflation really describes the evolution of the universe, then the beginning may be entirely inaccessible to observational tests. The point is that even the original inflationary model, with a single infla-

> tion event, already had the property of erasing evidence from the preinflation epoch. **Eternal inflation appears to make any efforts to obtain information about the beginning, via observations in our own pocket universe, absolutely hopeless** (2000, pp 180-181, emp. added).

Writing in the February 2001 issue of *Scientific American*, Philip and Phylis Morrison admitted:

> We simply do not know our cosmic origins; intriguing alternatives abound, but none yet compels. We do not know the details of inflation, nor what came before, nor the nature of the dark, unseen material, nor the nature of the repulsive forces that dilute gravity. The book of the cosmos is still open. Note carefully: **we no longer see a big bang as a direct solution. Inflation erases evidence of past space, time and matter.** The beginning–if any–is still unread (284[2]:93,95, emp. added).

The simple fact is, to quote R.C. Sproul:

> Every **effect** must have a **cause**. That is true by definition. ...It is impossible for something to create itself. The concept of self-creation is a contradiction in terms, a nonsense statement.... [S]elf-creation is irrational (1992, p. 37, emp. in orig.).

Stephen Hawking was constrained to write:

> Even if there is only one possible unified theory, it is just a set of rules and equations. What is it that breathes fire into the equations and makes a universe for them to describe? The usual approach of science of constructing a mathematical model cannot answer the question of why there should be a universe for the model to describe (1988, p. 174).

Linde himself–as the developer of the eternal inflation model –admitted that there is a chicken-and-egg problem involved here. Which came first–the Universe, or the laws governing it? He asked: "If there was no law, then how did the Universe appear?" (as quoted in Overbye, 2001). It is refreshing indeed to see that scientists of Dr. Linde's stature are willing to ask such questions.

In a chapter titled "Science and the Unknowable" in one of his books, renowned humanist author Martin Gardner followed Hawking's and Linde's lead when he wrote:

> Imagine that physicists finally discover all the basic waves and their particles, and all the basic laws, and unite everything in one equation. We can then ask, "Why that equation?" It is fashionable now to conjecture that the big bang was caused by a random quantum fluctuation in a vacuum devoid of space and time. **But of course such a vacuum is a far cry from nothing. There had to be quantum laws to fluctuate. And why are there quantum laws?**... There is no escape from the superultimate questions: Why is there something rather than nothing, and why is the something structured the way it is? (2000, p. 303, emp. added).

Barrow commented in a similar fashion when he wrote:

> **At first, the absence of a beginning appears to be an advantage to the scientific approach. There are no awkward starting conditions to deduce or explain. But this is an illusion. We still have to explain why the Universe took on particular properties**–its rate expansion, density, and so forth –at an infinite time in the past (2000, p. 296, emp. added).

Gardner and Barrow are correct. And science cannot provide the answer. Nancey Murphy and George Ellis discussed this very point in their book, *On the Moral Nature of the Universe*:

> Hence, we note the fundamental major metaphysical issues that purely scientific cosmology by itself cannot tackle–the problem of existence (what is the ultimate origin of physical reality?) and the origin and determination of the specific nature of physical laws –for these all lie outside the domain of scientific investigation. The basic reason is that there is no way that any of these issues can be addressed experimentally. The experimental method can be used to test

> existing physical laws but not to examine why those laws are in existence. One can investigate these issues using the hypothetico-deductive method, but one cannot then conduct physical, chemical, or biological experiments or observations that will confirm or disconfirm the proposed hypotheses (1996, p. 61).

Furthermore, science is based on observation, reproducibility, and empirical data. But when pressed for the empirical data that document the claim that the Universe created itself from nothing, evolutionists are forced to admit, as Dr. Stenger did, that "...there are yet no empirical or observational tests that can be used to test the idea...." Ralph Estling summarized the problem quite well when he stated: "There is no evidence, so far, that the entire universe, observable and unobservable, emerged from a state of absolute Nothingness" (1995, 19[1]:69-70). Again, we agree.

WAS THE UNIVERSE CREATED?

The Universe is not eternal. Nor did it create itself. It therefore must have been created. And such a creation most definitely implies a Creator.

Is the Universe the result of creation by an eternal Creator? Either the Universe had a beginning, or it had no beginning. But all available evidence asserts that the Universe did have a beginning. If the Universe had a beginning, it either had a cause, or it did not have a cause. One thing we know: it is correct–both scientifically and philosophically–to acknowledge that the Universe had an adequate cause, because the Universe is an effect, and as such requires an adequate antecedent cause. Nothing causeless happens. Henry Morris was correct when he suggested that the Law of Cause and Effect is "universally accepted and followed in every field of science" (1974b, p. 19). The cause/effect principle states that wherever there is a material **effect**, there must be an adequate antecedent **cause**. Further indicated, however, is the fact that no effect can be qualitatively superior to, or quantitatively greater than, its cause.

Since it is apparent that the Universe is not eternal, and since it likewise is apparent that the Universe could not have created itself, the only remaining alternative is that the Universe **was created** by something (or Someone): (a) that existed before it, i.e., some eternal, uncaused First Cause; (b) superior to it–the created cannot be superior to the creator; and (c) of a different nature since the finite, dependent Universe of matter is unable to explain itself. As Hoyle and Wickramasinghe observed: "To be consistent logically, we have to say that the intelligence which assembled the enzymes did not itself contain them" (1981, p. 139).

In connection with this, another fact should be considered. If there ever had been a time when absolutely **nothing** existed, then there would be nothing now. It is a self-evident truth that nothing produces nothing. In view of this, **since something does exist, it must follow logically that something has existed forever**! Everything that exists can be classified as either **matter** or **mind**. There is no third alternative. The argument then, is this:

1. Everything that exists is either matter or mind.
2. Something exists now, so something eternal exists.
3. Therefore, either matter or mind is eternal.

A. Either matter or mind is eternal.
B. Matter is not eternal, per the evidence cited above.
C. Thus, it is mind that is eternal.

Or, to reason somewhat differently:

1. Everything that is, is either dependent (i.e., contingent) or independent (non-contingent).
2. If the Universe is not eternal, it is dependent (contingent).
3. The Universe is not eternal.
4. Therefore, the Universe is dependent (contingent).

A. If the Universe is dependent, it must have been caused by something that is independent.

B. But the Universe is dependent (contingent).

C. Therefore, the Universe was produced by some eternal, independent (non-contingent) force.

In the past, atheistic evolutionists suggested that the mind is nothing more than a function of the brain, which is matter; thus, the mind and the brain are the same, and matter is all that exists. As the late evolutionist of Cornell University, Carl Sagan, said in the opening sentence of his television extravaganza (and book by the same name), *Cosmos*, "The Cosmos is all that is or ever was or ever will be" (1980, p. 4). However, that viewpoint no longer is credible scientifically, due in large part to the experiments of Australian physiologist Sir John Eccles. Dr. Eccles, who won the Nobel Prize in Physiology or Medicine in 1963 for his discoveries relating to the neural synapses within the brain, documented that the mind is more than merely physical. He showed that the supplementary motor area of the brain may be fired by mere **intention** to do something, without the motor cortex (which controls muscle movements) operating. Eccles explained his methodology and conclusions in several of his books, the most famous of which was *The Self and Its Brain*, co-authored with the renowned philosopher of science, Sir Karl Popper (see Popper and Eccles, 1977).

Anyone familiar with neurophysiology or neurobiology knows the name of Sir John Eccles. (One of us [BH] studied Dr. Eccles' works while earning a doctorate in neurobiology.) But for those who might not be familiar with this amazing gentleman, we would like to introduce Dr. Eccles via the following quotation, which comes from a chapter ("The Collapse of Modern Atheism") that philosopher Norman Geisler authored for the book, *The Intellectuals Speak Out About God* (which also contained a chapter by Eccles, from which we will quote shortly). Geisler wrote:

> The extreme form of materialism believes that mind (or soul) *is* matter. More modern forms believe mind is *reducible to* matter or *dependent on* it. **However, from a scientific perspective much has happened in our generation to lay bare the clay feet of materialism. Most noteworthy among this is the Nobel Prize winning work of Sir John Eccles. His work on the brain demonstrated that the mind or intention is more than physical. He has shown that the supplementary motor area of the brain is fired by mere *intention* to do something, without the motor cortex of the brain (which controls muscle movements) operating**. So, in effect, the mind is to the brain what an archivist is to a library. The former is not reducible to the latter (1984, pp. 140-141, parenthetical items and italics in orig., emp. added).

Eccles and Popper viewed the mind as a distinctly non-material entity. But neither did so for religious reasons, as both were committed Darwinians. Rather, they believed what they did about the human mind because of their own research. Eccles spent his entire adult life studying the brain-mind problem, and concluded that the two were entirely separate entities. In a fascinating book, *Nobel Conversations*, Norman Cousins, who moderated a series of conversations among four Nobel laureates, including Dr. Eccles, made the following statement: "Nor was Sir John Eccles claiming too much when **he insisted that the action of non-material mind on material brain has been not merely postulated but scientifically demonstrated**" (1985, p. 68, emp. added). Eccles himself, in his book, *The Understanding of the Brain*, wrote:

> When I postulated many years ago, following Sherrington [Sir Charles Sherrington, Nobel laureate and Eccles' mentor–BT/BH], that there was a special area of the brain in liaison with consciousness, I certainly did not imagine that any definitive experimental test could be applied in a few years. But now we have this distinction between the dominant hemisphere in liaison with the conscious self, and the minor hemisphere with no such liaison (1973, p. 214).

In an article—"Scientists in Search of the Soul"—that examined the groundbreaking work of Dr. Eccles (and other scientists like him who have been studying the mind/brain relationship), science writer John Gliedman wrote:

> At age 79, Sir John Eccles is not going "gentle into the night." Still trim and vigorous, the great physiologist has declared war on the past 300 years of scientific speculation about man's nature.
>
> Winner of the 1963 Nobel Prize in Physiology or Medicine for his pioneering research on the synapse—the point at which nerve cells communicate with the brain—Eccles strongly defends the ancient religious belief that human beings consist of a mysterious compound of physical and intangible spirit.
>
> Each of us embodies a nonmaterial thinking and perceiving self that "entered" our physical brain sometime during embryological development or very early childhood, says the man who helped lay the cornerstones of modern neurophysiology. This "ghost in the machine" is responsible for everything that makes us distinctly human: conscious self-awareness, free will, personal identity, creativity and even emotions such as love, fear, and hate. Our nonmaterial self controls its "liaison brain" the way a driver steers a car or a programmer directs a computer. Man's ghostly spiritual presence, says Eccles, exerts just the whisper of a physical influence on the computerlike brain, enough to encourage some neurons to fire and others to remain silent. Boldly advancing what for most scientists is the greatest heresy of all, Eccles also asserts that our nonmaterial self survives the death of the physical brain (1982, 90[7]:77).

While discussing the same type of conclusions reached by Dr. Eccles, philosopher Norman Geisler explored the concept of an eternal, all-knowing Mind.

> Further, this infinite cause of all that is must be all-knowing. It must be knowing because knowing beings exist. I am a knowing being, and I know it. I cannot meaningfully deny that I can know without engaging in an act of knowledge.... But a cause can communicate to its effect only what it has to communi-

> cate. If the effect actually possesses some characteristic, then this characteristic is properly attributed to its cause. The cause cannot give what it does not have to give. If my mind or ability to know is received, then there must be Mind or Knower who gave it to me. The intellectual does not arise from the nonintellectual; something cannot arise from nothing. The cause of knowing, however, is infinite. Therefore it must know infinitely. It is also simple, eternal, and unchanging. Hence, whatever it knows–and it knows anything it is possible to know–it must know simply, eternally, and in an unchanging way (1976, p. 247).

From such evidence, Robert Jastrow concluded: "That there are what I or anyone would call supernatural forces at work is now, I think, a scientifically proven fact..." (1982, p. 18). Apparently Dr. Jastrow is not alone. As Gliedman put it:

> Eccles is not the only world-famous scientist taking a controversial new look at the ancient mind-body conundrum. From Berkeley to Paris and from London to Princeton, prominent scientists from fields as diverse as neurophysiology and quantum physics are coming out of the closet and admitting they believe in the possibility, at least, of such unscientific entities as the immortal human spirit and divine creation (90 [7]:77).

In an article titled "Modern Biology and the Turn to Belief in God" that he wrote for the book, *The Intellectuals Speak Out About God*, Eccles concluded:

> Science and religion are very much alike. Both are imaginative and creative aspects of the human mind. The appearance of a conflict is a result of ignorance. **We come to exist through a divine act.** That divine guidance is a theme throughout our life; at our death the brain goes, but that divine guidance and love continues. Each of us is a unique, conscious being, a divine creation. **It is the religious view. It is the only view consistent with all the evidence** (1984, p. 50, emp. added).

And, one more time, we agree.

Our Fine-Tuned, Tailor-Made Universe

And it is not just **people** who are unique (in the sense of exhibiting evidence of design). The fact is, the Universe is "fine-tuned" in such a way that it is impossible to suggest logically that it simply "popped into existence out of nothing" and then went from the chaos associated with the inflationary Big Bang model (as if the Universe were a giant firecracker!) to the sublime order that it presently exhibits. Murphy and Ellis went on to note:

> The symmetries and delicate balances we observe in the universe require an extraordinary coherence of conditions and cooperation of laws and effects, suggesting that in some sense they have been **purposely designed**. That is, **they give evidence of intention**, realized both in the setting of the laws of physics and in the choice of boundary conditions for the universe (p. 57, emp. added).

In an article that appeared on *Nature's* August 13, 2002, on-line Science-Update ("Is Physics Watching Over Us?"), Philip Ball commented: "Our Universe is so unlikely that we must be missing something." Again, we agree. For decades now, cosmologists have been attempting to conjure up theories regarding the origin of our Universe–all the while wearing "evolutionary blinders." It appears as though some (although, admittedly, not nearly enough) cosmologists finally are removing those blinders, and actually are beginning to come to terms with their own data.

As a part of his review, Mr. Ball commented on what was at the time an upcoming research report titled "Disturbing Implications of a Cosmological Constant" (see Dyson, et al., 2002). In referring to the work being carried out by a team of researchers headed by Leonard Susskind of Stanford University, Ball wrote:

> In an argument that would have gratified the ancient Greeks, physicists have claimed that the prevailing theoretical view of the Universe is logically flawed. Arranging the cosmos as we think it is arranged, says

> the team, **would have required a miracle**. The incomprehensibility of our situation even drives Susskind's team to ponder whether an "**unknown agent**" intervened in the evolution [of the Universe] for reasons of its own (2002, emp. added).

Or, as Idit Zehavi and Avishal Dekel wrote in *Nature*: "This type of universe, however, seems to require a degree of fine tuning of the initial conditions that is in apparent conflict with 'common wisdom'" (1999, 401:252).

The idea that the Universe and its laws "have been purposely designed" has surfaced much more frequently in the past several years. For example, Sir Fred Hoyle wrote:

> A common sense interpretation of the facts suggests that **a superintellect has monkeyed with physics, as well as with chemistry and biology**, and that there are no blind forces worth speaking about in nature. The numbers one calculates from the facts seem to me so overwhelming as to put this conclusion almost beyond question (1982, 20:16, emp. added).

In his book, *Superforce: The Search for a Grand Unified Theory of Nature*, Australian astrophysicist Paul Davies made this amazing statement:

> If nature is so "clever" as to exploit mechanisms that amaze us with their ingenuity, **is that not persuasive evidence for the existence of intelligent design behind the universe**? If the world's finest minds can unravel only with difficulty the deeper workings of nature, how could it be supposed that those workings are merely a mindless accident, a product of blind chance? (1984, pp. 235-236, emp. added).

Four years later, in his text, *The Cosmic Blueprint: New Discoveries in Nature's Creative Ability to Order the Universe*, Davies went even farther when he wrote:

> There is for me powerful evidence that there is something going on behind it all.... **It seems as though somebody has fine-tuned nature's numbers to make the Universe.... The impression of design is overwhelming** (1988, p. 203, emp. added).

Another four years later, in 1992, Davies authored *The Mind of God*, in which he remarked:

> I cannot believe that our existence in this universe is a mere quirk of fate, an accident of history, an incidental blip in the great cosmic drama.... Through conscious beings the universe has generated self-awareness. This can be no trivial detail, no minor by-product of mindless, purposeless forces. **We are truly meant to be here** (1992a, p. 232, emp. added).

That statement, "We are truly meant to be here," was the type of sentiment expressed by two scientists, Frank Tipler and John Barrow, in their 1986 book, *The Anthropic Cosmological Principle*, which discussed the possibility that the Universe seems to have been "tailor-made" for man. Eight years after that book was published, Dr. Tipler wrote *The Physics of Immortality*, in which he professed:

> When I began my career as a cosmologist some twenty years ago, I was a convinced atheist. I never in my wildest dreams imagined that one day I would be writing a book purporting to show that the central claims of Judeo-Christian theology are in fact true, that these claims are straightforward deductions of the laws of physics as we now understand them. I have been forced into these conclusions by the inexorable logic of my own special branch of physics (1994, Preface).

In 1995, NASA astronomer John O'Keefe stated in an interview: "We are, by astronomical standards, a pampered, cosseted, cherished group of creatures.... If the Universe had not been made with the most exacting precision we could never have come into existence. It is my view that these circumstances indicate the universe was created for man to live in" (as quoted in Heeren, 1995, p. 200). Then, thirteen years after he published his 1985 book (*Evolution: A Theory in Crisis*), Michael Denton shocked everyone–especially his evolutionist colleagues–when he published his 1998 tome, *Nature's Destiny*, in which he admitted:

> Whether one accepts or rejects the design hypothesis...there is no avoiding the conclusion that the world **looks** as if it has been tailored for life; it **appears to have been designed**. All reality **appears** to be a vast, coherent, teleological whole with life and mankind as its purpose and goal (p. 387, emp. in orig.).

Murray noted:

> Almost **everything about the basic structure of the universe**–for example, the fundamental laws and parameters of physics and the initial distribution of matter and energy–**is balanced on a razor's edge** for life to occur.... Scientists call this extraordinary balancing of the parameters of physics and the initial conditions of the universe the "fine-tuning of the cosmos" (1999, p. 48, emp. added).

Indeed they do. And it is fine-tuning to a remarkable degree. Once more science has found itself face-to-face with yet another inexplicable, finely tuned force of nature that "somehow" must be explained by random, naturalistic forces. One would think that, after confronting **so many** of these finely tuned forces, scientists finally would admit the obvious. To use the words of evolutionist H.S. Lipson of Great Britain: "I think, however, that we must go further than this and admit that the only acceptable explanation is **creation**"(1980, 31:138, emp. in orig.).

Science is based on observation and reproducibility. But when pressed for the reproducible, empirical data that document their claim of a self-created Universe, scientists and philosophers are at a loss to produce those data. Perhaps this is why Alan Guth, co-developer of the original inflationary Universe theory, lamented: "In the end, I must admit that questions of plausibility are not logically determinable and depend somewhat on intuition" (1988, 11 [2]:76)–which is little more than a fancy way of saying, "I certainly **wish** this were true, but I could not **prove** it to you if my life depended on it." To suggest that the Universe created itself is to posit a self-contradictory position. Sproul addressed this when he wrote:

> For something to bring itself into being it must have the power of being within itself. It must at least have enough causal power to cause its own being. If it derives its being from some other source, then it clearly would not be either self-existent or self-created. It would be, plainly and simply, an effect. Of course, the problem is complicated by the other necessity we've labored so painstakingly to establish: It would have to have the causal power of being before it was. It would have to have the power of being before it had any being with which to exercise that power (1994, p. 180).

The Universe is not eternal. Nor did not create itself from nothing.

The choice is between **matter only** or **more than matter** as the fundamental explanation for the existence and orderliness of the Universe. The difference, therefore, is the difference between: (a) **time, chance, and the inherent properties of matter;** or (b) **design, creation, and the irreducible properties of organization**. There are only two possible explanations for the origin of the order that characterizes the Universe and life in the Universe: either that order was **imposed on** matter, or it **resides within** matter. If it is suggested that the order resides within matter, we respond by saying that we certainly have not seen the evidence of such.

The Law of Cause and Effect, and the cosmological argument based upon that law, have serious implications in every field of human endeavor. The Universe is here, and must have an adequate antecedent cause. In addressing this problem, R.L. Wysong commented:

> Everyone concludes naturally and comfortably that highly ordered and designed items (machines, houses, etc.) owe existence to a designer. It is unnatural to conclude otherwise. But evolution asks us to break stride from what is natural to believe and then believe in that which is unnatural, unreasonable, and... unbelievable.... The basis for this departure from what is natural and reasonable to believe is not fact, obser-

> vation, or experience but rather unreasonable extrapolations from abstract probabilities, mathematics, and philosophy (1976, p. 412, first ellipsis in orig.).

Dr. Wysong presented an interesting historical case to illustrate his point. Some years ago, scientists were called to Great Britain to study orderly patterns of concentric rocks and holes–a find designated as Stonehenge. As studies progressed, it became apparent that these patterns had been designed specifically to allow certain astronomical predictions. Many questions (e.g., how ancient peoples were able to construct an astronomical observatory, how the data derived from their studies were used, etc.) remain unsolved. But one thing is known–the **cause** of Stonehenge was intelligent design.

Now, Wysong suggested, compare Stonehenge to the situation paralleling the origin of the Universe, and of life itself. We study life, observe its functions, contemplate its complexity (which defies duplication even by intelligent men with the most advanced methodology and technology), and what are we to conclude? Stonehenge **might** have been produced by the erosion of a mountain, or by catastrophic natural forces working in conjunction with meteorites to produce rock formations and concentric holes. But what scientist or philosopher ever would suggest such an idea?

No one could ever be convinced that Stonehenge "just happened" by accident, yet atheists and agnostics expect us to believe that this highly ordered, well-designed Universe, and the complicated life it contains, "just happened." To accept such an idea is, to use Dr. Wysong's words, "to break stride from what is natural to believe" because the conclusion is unreasonable, unwarranted, and unsupported by the facts at hand. The cause simply is not adequate to produce the effect.

The central message of the cosmological argument, and the Law of Cause and Effect upon which it is based, is this: Every material effect must have an adequate antecedent cause. The Universe is here; intelligent life is here; morality is here; love is here. What is their adequate antecedent cause? Since the effect can never precede, nor be greater than the cause, it stands to reason that the Cause of life must be a living Intelligence which Itself is both moral and loving. When the Bible records, "In the beginning, God...," it makes known to us just such a First Cause.

DISCUSSION QUESTIONS

1. What are three methods by which to explain the origin of the Universe, and which is the most plausible?
2. What problems does a non-eternal Universe cause for evolutionary theory?
3. How does the very existence of the Universe provide evidence for God?
4. Can one logically claim that there was a time in the past when absolutely **nothing** existed? What are some problems with this assertion?
5. Does the existence of God somehow contradict the Law of Cause and Effect?

Chapter 2

THE CASE FOR THE EXISTENCE OF GOD [PART II]

One of the laws of thought employed in the field of logic is the Law of Rationality, which states that one should accept as true only those conclusions for which there is adequate evidence. This is sensible, for accepting as true a conclusion for which there is no evidence, or inadequate evidence, would be irrational. In discussing the *prima facie* case for God's existence, theists present–through logic, clear reasoning, and factual data–arguments that are adequate to justify the acceptance of the conclusion that God exists. The approach is intended to be positive in nature, and to establish a proposition for which adequate evidence is available.

The evidence used to substantiate the theist's proposition concerning God's existence may take many forms. This should not be surprising since, if He does exist, God would be the greatest of all realities. His existence, therefore, could be extrapolated not from just a single line of reasoning, but from numerous avenues. As one writer of the past suggested:

> The reality of such a Being can be firmly established only by concurrent reasons coming from various realms of existence, and approved by various powers of the human spirit. It is a conclusion that cannot be reached without the aid of arguments inadequate by themselves to so great a result, yet valid in their place, proving each some part of the great truth; proofs cumulative and complementary, each requiring others for its completion (Clarke, 1912, p. 104).

The various arguments presented by theists, all combined, make an ironclad case for God's existence. Where one particular argument fails to impress or convince an inquirer, another will avail. Considered cumulatively, the evidence is adequate to justify the intended conclusion. It is our purpose here to present and discuss additional evidence substantiating the proposition: God exists.

In contending for the existence of God, theists often employ the Teleological Argument. "Teleology" has reference to purpose or design. Thus, this approach suggests that where there is purposeful design, there must be a designer. The deduction being made, of course, is that order, planning, and design in a system are indicative of intelligence, purpose, and specific intent on the part of the originating cause. In logical form, the theist's argument may be presented as follows:

(1) If the Universe evinces purposeful design, there must have been a designer.

(2) The Universe does evince purposeful design.

(3) Thus, the Universe must have had a designer.

This correct form of logical reasoning, and the implications that flow from it, have not escaped the attention of those who do not believe in God. Paul Ricci, an atheistic philosopher and university professor, has written that "...it's true that everything designed has a designer..." (1986, p. 190). In fact, Mr. Ricci even conceded that the statement, " 'Everything designed has a designer,' is an analytically true statement" and thus requires no formal proof (p. 190). Apparently Mr. Ricci understands that one does not get a poem without a poet, a law without a lawgiver, a painting without a painter, or design without a designer.

He is in good company among his disbelieving counterparts. For example, atheistic evolutionist Richard Lewontin made the following admission in an article he authored for *Scientific American*:

> Life forms are more than simply multiple and diverse, however. Organisms fit remarkably well into the external world in which they live. They have morphologies, physiologies and behaviors that appear to have been carefully and artfully designed to enable each organism to appropriate the world around it for its own life. It was the marvelous fit of organisms to the environment, much more than the great diversity of forms, that was **the chief evidence of a Supreme Designer** (1978, 239[3]:213, emp. added).

To be fair to both of these authors and others like them, let us quickly point out that while they agree with the basic thrust of the theist's argument (i.e., that design leads inevitably to a designer), they do not believe that there is evidence warranting the conclusion that a Supreme Designer exists, and they therefore reject any belief in God. Their disagreement with the theist, therefore, would center on statement number two (the minor premise) in the above syllogism. While admitting that design demands a designer, they would deny that there is design in nature providing proof of the existence of a Great Designer.

A good example of such a denial can be found in a book written by British evolutionist, Richard Dawkins. During the 1800s, William Paley employed his now-famous "watch argument." Paley argued that if one were to discover a watch lying upon the ground and were to examine it closely, the design inherent in the watch would be enough to force the conclusion that there must have been a watchmaker. Paley continued his line of argumentation to suggest that the design inherent in the Universe should be enough to force the conclusion that there must have been a Great Designer. In 1986, Dawkins published *The Blind Watchmaker*, which was intended to put to rest once and for all Paley's argument. The dust jacket of Dawkins' book made that point clear:

> There may be good reasons for belief in God, but the argument from design is not one of them.... [D]espite all appearances to the contrary, there is no watchmaker in nature beyond the blind forces of physics....

> Natural selection, the unconscious, automatic, blind yet essentially nonrandom process that Darwin discovered, and that we now understand to be the explanation for the existence and form of all life, has no purpose in mind. It has no mind and no mind's eye. It does not plan for the future. It has no vision, no foresight, no sight at all. If it can be said to play the role of watchmaker in nature, it is the **blind** watchmaker (emp. in orig.).

The disagreement between the theist and atheist is not whether design demands a designer. Rather, the point of contention is whether or not there **is** design in nature adequate to substantiate the conclusion that a Designer does, in fact, exist. This is where the Teleological Argument is of benefit.

DESIGN OF THE UNIVERSE

Our Universe operates in accordance with exact scientific laws. The precision of the Universe, and the exactness of these laws, allow scientists to launch rockets to the Moon, with the full knowledge that, upon their arrival, they can land within a few feet of their intended target. Such precision and exactness also allow astronomers to predict solar/lunar eclipses years in advance or to determine when Halley's Comet can be seen once again from the Earth. Science writer Lincoln Barnett once observed:

> This functional harmony of nature Berkeley, Descartes, and Spinoza attributed to God. Modern physicists who prefer to solve their problems without recourse to God (although this seems to be more difficult all the time) emphasize that nature mysteriously operates on mathematical principles. It is the mathematical orthodoxy of the Universe that enables theorists like Einstein to predict and discover natural laws, simply by the solution of equations (1959, p. 22, parenthetical item in orig.).

The precision, complexity, and orderliness within the Universe are not in dispute; writers such as Ricci, Dawkins, and Lewontin acknowledge as much. But while atheists willingly concede complexity, and even order, they are not prepared to concede design because the implication of such a concession would demand a Designer. Is there evidence of **design**? The atheist claims that no such evidence exists. The theist, however, affirms that it does, and offers the following information in support of that affirmation.

We live in a tremendously large Universe. While its outer limits have not been measured, it is estimated to be as much as 20 billion light years in diameter. [A light-year is the distance that light travels in a vacuum in one year at a speed of slightly more than 186,000 miles per second. Distances expressed in light-years give the time that light would take to cross that distance.] There are an estimated one billion galaxies in the Universe (Lawton, 1981), and an estimated 25 **sextillion** stars. The Milky Way galaxy in which we live contains over 100 billion stars, and is so large that even traveling at the speed of light would require 100,000 years to cross its diameter. Light travels approximately 5.88×10^{12} miles in a single year; in 100,000 years, that would be 5.88×10^{17} miles, or 588 **quadrillion** miles just to cross the diameter of a single galaxy. Without doubt, this is an extremely impressive Universe. As the psalmist stated: "The heavens declare the glory of God, and the firmament [sky] shows His handiwork" (Psalm 19:1). Indeed they do! The writer of the book of Hebrews remarked: "Every house is builded by some one; but he that built all things is God" (3:4). And just one verse prior to that, he wrote: "He that built the house hath more honor than the house" (3:3). Deity's activities of day four of the Creation week show that He certainly is due more honor than the Universe He created, regardless of how impressive that Universe is.

Yet while the size itself is impressive, the inherent design is even more so. The Sun is like a giant nuclear engine. It gives off more energy in a single second than mankind has produced since the Creation. It converts 8 million tons of matter into energy **every single second**, and has an interior temperature of more than 20 million degrees Celsius (see Lawton,

1981). The Sun also produces intense radiation, which, in certain amounts, can be deadly to living things. The Earth, however, is located at exactly the correct distance from the Sun to receive the proper amount of heat and radiation to sustain life as we know it. We should be grateful that we live so far from the Sun, because the 93 million miles of empty space between the Earth and the Sun help stop the destructive pressure waves given off by the Sun as it converts matter to energy. If the Earth were much closer to the Sun, human life could not survive because of the horrible heat and pressure. If the Earth were moved just 10% closer to the Sun (about 10 million miles), far too much radiation (and heat) would be absorbed. If the Earth were moved just 10% farther from the Sun, too little heat would be absorbed. Either scenario would spell doom for life on the Earth.

Humans receive some protection from the Sun's radiation, however, because in one of the layers of the atmosphere (referred to as the mesosphere–about 12 to 18 miles above the Earth), there is a special form of oxygen known as ozone, which filters out most of the ultraviolet rays from the Sun that would be harmful, or fatal, in larger amounts. In addition, the Sun constantly sends out an invisible wind that is composed of protons and electrons. These particles approach the Earth from outer space at an extremely high speed, and could be very dangerous to humans. Fortunately, most of these protons and electrons are reflected back into space because God created the Earth like a giant magnet that pushes away the solar wind and makes life on Earth both possible and comfortable.

The Earth is rotating on its axis at 1,000 miles per hour at the equator, and moving around the Sun at 70,000 miles per hour (approximately 19 miles per second), while the Sun and its solar system are moving through space at 600,000 miles per hour in an orbit so large it would take over 226 million years just to complete a single orbit. This rotation provides periods of light and darkness–a phenomenon necessary for sustaining life as we know it. If the Earth rotated much faster, fierce cyclones would stir over the Earth like a kitchen food-mixer. If the Earth turned significantly slower, the days and nights would be impossibly hot or cold. Venus, for example, turns only once every 243 days, which accounts in part for the fact that daytime temperatures can reach as high as 500 degrees Celsius (remember: water boils at 100 degrees Celsius). The Earth's orbital speed and tilt are "just right." Just by accident? The Earth completes its orbit once every 365.25 days—the time period we designate as a year. This, together with the fact that the Earth is tilted on its axis, allows for what we refer to as seasons.

The Earth's orbit is not a perfect circle, however, but is elliptical. This means that sometimes the Earth is closer to the Sun than at other times. In January, the Earth is closest to the Sun; in July, it is farthest away. When it is closer, the Earth "speeds up" to avoid being pulled into the Sun; when it is farther away, it "slows down," so that it remains in a position in space that is "just right." How does the Earth "know" to do all of this?

Interestingly, as the Earth moves in its orbit around the Sun, it departs from a straight line by only one-ninth of an inch every eighteen miles. If it departed by one-eighth of an inch, we would come so close to the Sun that we would be incinerated; if it departed by one-tenth of an inch, we would find ourselves so far from the Sun that we would all freeze to death (see *Science Digest*, 1981). What would happen if the rotation rate of the Earth were cut in half, or doubled? If it were halved, the seasons would be doubled in their length, which would cause such harsh heat and cold over much of the Earth that it would be difficult, if not impossible, to grow enough food to feed the Earth's population. If the rotation rate were doubled, the length of each season would be halved, and again it would be difficult or impossible to grow enough food to feed the Earth's population.

The Earth is tilted on its axis at exactly 23.5 degrees. If it were not tilted, but sat straight up in its orbit around the Sun, there would be no seasons. The tropics would be hotter, and the deserts would get bigger. If the tilt went all the way over to 90 degrees, much of the Earth would switch between very cold winters and very hot summers.

The Earth is poised some 240,000 miles from the Moon. This, too, is just right. The Moon helps control the movement of the oceans (tides). This movement is very beneficial to the Earth, because it provides a cleansing of shorelines, and helps ocean life to prosper. Tides are an important part of ocean currents. Without these currents, the oceans would stagnate, and the animals and plants living in the oceans and seas soon would perish. Our existence as humans depends upon the Moon's tides, which help to balance a delicate food chain in nature. If the Moon were moved closer to the Earth by just a fifth, the tides would be so enormous that twice a day they would reach 35-50 feet high over most of the Earth's surface.

The Earth's oceans are another good example of perfect design. Water covers about 72% of the Earth's surface, which is good because the oceans provide a reservoir of moisture that constantly is evaporating and condensing. Eventually, this causes rain to fall on the Earth. It is a well-known fact that water heats and cools at a much slower rate than a solid land mass, which explains why desert regions can be blistering hot in the daytime and freezing cold at night. Water, however, holds its temperature longer, and provides a sort of natural heating/air-conditioning system for the land areas of the Earth. The Earth's annual average temperature (56°F; 13.3°C) is closely maintained by the great reservoir of heat found within the waters of the oceans. Temperature extremes would be much more erratic than they are, were it not for the fact that approximately four-fifths of the Earth is covered with water. In addition, humans and animals inhale oxygen and exhale carbon dioxide. On the other hand, plants take in carbon dioxide and give off oxygen. We depend upon the world of botany for our oxygen supply, yet we often fail to realize that approximately 90% of our oxygen comes from microscopic plants in the seas (see Asimov, 1975, 2:116). If our oceans were appreciably smaller, we soon would be out of air to breathe.

Wrapped around the Earth is a protective blanket we know as the atmosphere. It is composed of nitrogen (78%), oxygen (21%), and carbon dioxide (0.03%), in addition to water vapor and small levels of other gases. The proper balance of these gases is essential to life on the Earth. The atmosphere of Venus is too thick to sustain life; that of Mars is too thin. But the Earth's atmosphere does several things. It scatters light waves to that you can read the words on this page. It captures solar heat so that it does not escape too rapidly. Without atmosphere, the heat would escape as soon as the Sun set each day, and nights would be unbearably cold. Frequently, meteors fall from space. Were it not for the fact that most of them burn up (from friction) when they strike the atmosphere, the Earth would be pounded almost daily by these unwelcome visitors. And, electronically charged particles called "ions" in the upper atmosphere (known as the ionosphere) help make radio communications on the Earth possible. The Earth has an atmosphere that is "just right." Just by accident?

Can a rational person reasonably be expected to believe that these exacting requirements for life as we know it have been met "just by accident"? The Earth is exactly the right distance from the Sun; it is exactly the right distance from the Moon; it has exactly the right diameter; it has exactly the right atmospheric pressure; it has exactly the right tilt; it has exactly the right amount of oceanic water; it has exactly the right weight and mass; and so on. Were this many requirements to be met in any other essential area of life, the idea that they had been provided "just by accident" would be dismissed immediately as ludicrous. Yet atheists, agnostics, skeptics, and infidels suggest that the Universe, the Earth, and life on the Earth are all here as a result of fortuitous accidents.

Physicist John Gribbin (1983), writing on the numerous specific requirements necessary for life on our planet, emphasized in great detail both the nature and essentiality of those requirements, and then, somewhat curiously chose to title his article, "Earth's Lucky Break"–as if all of the precision, orderliness, and intricate design in the Universe could somehow be explained by postulating that the Earth simply received, in a roll of the cosmic dice, a "lucky break."

Yet atheist Richard Dawkins of Oxford University has admitted: "The more statistically improbable a thing is, the less we can believe that it just happened by blind chance. Superficially, **the obvious alternative to chance is an intelligent Designer**" (1982, 94:130, emp. added). Except for the fact that they do not believe it to be "superficial," that is the very conclusion theists have drawn from the available evidence. The statistical improbability of the Universe "just happening by blind chance" is staggering. Nobel laureate Arno Penzias put it this way: "Astronomy leads us to a unique event, a universe which was created out of nothing, one with the very delicate balance needed to provide exactly the conditions required to permit life, and one which has an underlying (one might say 'supernatural') plan" (as quoted in Margenau and Varghese, 1992, p. 83, parenthetical item in orig.). Who designed the Universe with "the very delicate balance needed to provide exactly the conditions required to permit life"? The answer, of course, is the Intelligent Designer described in the Bible–God.

DESIGN OF THE HUMAN BODY

Many years ago, the ancient scholar Augustine observed that "men go abroad to wonder at the height of mountains, at the huge waves of the sea, at the long course of the rivers, at the vast compass of the ocean, at the circular motion of the stars; and they pass by themselves without wondering." Indeed, while we stand in amazement at so many stunning scenes from our unique Universe, we often fail to stand equally amazed at the marvelous creation of man. According to those who do not believe in God, the human body is little more than the result of a set of fortuitous circumstances credited to that mythical lady, "Mother Nature." Yet such a suggestion does not fit the actual facts of the case, as even evolutionists have been forced to recognize from time to time. The late George Gaylord Simpson of Harvard once suggested that in man one finds "the most highly endowed organization of matter that has yet appeared on the earth..." (1949, p. 293). Another evolutionist observed:

> When you come right down to it, the most incredible creation in the universe is you—with your fantastic senses and strengths, your ingenious defense systems, and mental capabilities so great you can never use them to the fullest. Your body is a structural masterpiece more amazing than science fiction (Guinness, 1987, p. 5).

Can one reasonably be expected to conclude that the "structural masterpiece" of the human body—with its "ingenious" systems and "highly endowed organization"—is the result of blind chance operating over eons of time in nature as atheism suggests? Or would it be more in keeping with the facts of the matter to suggest that the human body is the result of purposeful design by a Master Designer?

One scientist wrote: "Where do I start? The human body is so amazing and so detailed that one of the hardest aspects of teaching about it is deciding where to begin" (Wile, 2000, p. 267). For organizational purposes, the human body may be considered at four different levels (see Jackson, 1993, pp. 5-6). First, there are cells, representing the smallest unit of life. Second, there are tissues (muscle tissue, nerve tissue, etc.), which are groups of the same kind of cells carrying on the same kind of activity. Third, there are organs (heart, liver, etc.), which are groups of tissues working together in unison. Fourth, there are systems (reproductive system, circulatory system, etc.), which are composed of groups of organs carrying out specific bodily functions. An investigation of these various levels of organization, and of the human body as a whole, leads inescapably to the conclusion that there is intelligent design at work. As Wayne Jackson noted: "It is therefore quite clear...that the physical body has been marvelously designed and intricately organized, for the purpose of facilitating human existence upon the planet Earth" (1993, p. 6). In light of the following facts, such a statement certainly is justified.

The Body's Cells

A human body is composed of over 250 different kinds of cells (red blood cells, white blood cells, muscle cells, fat cells, nerve cells, etc.–Baldi, 2001, p. 147), totaling approximately 100 trillion cells in an average adult (Fukuyama, 2002, p. 58). These cells come in a variety of sizes and shapes, with different functions and life expectancies. For example, some cells (e.g., male spermatozoa) are so small that 20,000 would fit inside a capital "O" from a standard typewriter, each being only 0.05 mm long. Some cells, placed end-to-end, would make only one inch if 6,000 were assembled together. Yet all the cells of the human body, if set end-to-end, would encircle the Earth over 200 times. Even the largest cell of the human body, the female ovum, is unbelievably small, being only 0.01 of an inch in diameter.

Anatomist Ernst Haeckel, Charles Darwin's chief supporter in Germany in the mid-nineteenth century, once summarized his personal feelings about the "simple" nature of the cell when he wrote that it contained merely "homogeneous globules of plasm" that were

> composed chiefly of carbon with an admixture of hydrogen, nitrogen, and sulfur. These component parts properly united produce the soul and body of the animated world, and suitably nursed became man. With this single argument the mystery of the universe is explained, the Deity annulled, and a new era of infinite knowledge ushered in (1905, p. 111).

Voilà! As easy as that, simple "homogeneous globules of plasm" nursed man into existence, animated his body, dispelled the necessity of a Creator, and ushered in a new era of "infinite knowledge." In the end, however, Haeckel's simplistic, naturalistic concept turned out to be little more than wishful thinking. As Lester and Hefley put it:

> We once thought that the cell, the basic unit of life, was a simple bag of protoplasm. Then we learned that each cell in any life form is a teeming micro-universe of compartments, structures, and chemical agents–and each human being has billions of cells... (1998, pp. 30-31).

Billions of cells indeed! In the section he authored on the topic of "life" for the *Encyclopaedia Britannica*, the late astronomer Carl Sagan observed that a single human being is composed of what he referred to as an "ambulatory collection of 10^{14} cells" (1997, 22:965). He then noted: "The information content of a simple cell has been established as around 10^{12} bits, comparable to about a hundred million pages of the *Encyclopaedia Britannica*" (22:966). Evolutionist Richard Dawkins acknowledged that the cell's nucleus "contains a digitally coded database larger, in information content, than all 30 volumes of the *Encyclopaedia Britannica* put together. And this figure is for **each** cell, not all the cells of a body put together" (1986, pp. 17-18, emp. in orig.). Dr. Sagan estimated that if a person were to count every letter in every word in every book of the world's largest library (approximately 10 million volumes), the total number of letters would be 10^{12}, which suggests that the "simple cell" contains the information equivalent of the world's largest library (1974, 10:894)! Rational people recognize that not one of the books in such a library "just happened." Rather, each and every one is the result of intelligence and painstaking **design**. Stephen C. Meyer suggested:

> Since the late 1950s advances in molecular biology and biochemistry have revolutionized our understanding of the miniature world within the cell. Mod-

> ern molecular biology has revealed that living cells—the fundamental units of life—possess the ability to store, edit and transmit information and to use information to regulate their most fundamental metabolic processes. Far from characterizing cells as simple "homogeneous globules of plasm," as did Ernst Haeckel and other nineteenth-century biologists, modern biologists now describe cells as, among other things, "distributive real-time computers" and complex information processing systems (1998, pp. 113-114).

So much for the "simple" cell being a lump of albuminous combination of carbon, as Haeckel once put it.

Cells have three major components. First, each cell is composed of a cell membrane that encloses the organism. The lipoprotein cell membrane (lipids/proteins/lipids—known as a bilipid membrane) is approximately 0.06-0.08 of a micrometer thick, yet allows selective transport into, and out of, the cell. Evolutionist Ernest Borek has observed: "The membrane recognizes with its uncanny molecular memory the hundreds of compounds swimming around it and permits or denies passage according to the cell's requirements" (1973, p. 5).

Second, inside the cell is a three-dimensional cytoplasm—a watery matrix containing specialized organelles. Inside the cytoplasm, there are over 20 different chemical reactions occurring at any one time, with each cell containing five major components for: (1) communication; (2) waste disposal; (3) nutrition; (4) repair; and (5) reproduction. Within this watery matrix there are such organelles as the mitochondria (over 1,000 per cell, in many instances) that provide the cell with its energy. The endoplasmic reticulum is a "...transport system designed to carry materials from one part of the cell to the other" (Pfeiffer, 1964, p. 13). Ribosomes are miniature protein-producing factories. Golgi bodies store the proteins manufactured by the ribosomes. Lysozomes within the cytoplasm function as garbage disposal units. Vacuoles aid in intracellular cleaning processes. And so on.

Third, within the cytoplasm is the nucleus, which contains most of the genetic material, and which serves as the control center of the cell. The nucleus is the control center of the cell, and is separated from the cytoplasm by a nuclear membrane. Within the nucleus is the genetic machinery of the cell (chromosomes and genes containing deoxyribonucleic acid–DNA). The DNA is a supermolecule that carries the coded information for the replication of the cell. If the DNA from a single human cell were removed from the nucleus and unraveled (it is found in the cell in a spiral configuration), it would be approximately six feet long, and would contain approximately 3.1 billion base pairs (Watson, 2003, p. 204). It has been estimated that if all the DNA in an adult human were placed end-to-end, it would reach to the Sun and back (186 million miles) 400 times.

It also should be noted that the DNA molecule does something that we as humans have yet to accomplish: it stores coded information in a chemical format, and then uses a biologic agent (RNA) to decode and activate it. As Darrel Kautz has stated: "Human technology has not yet advanced to the point of storing information **chemically** as it is in the DNA molecule" (1988, p. 45, emp. in orig.; see also Jackson, 1993, pp. 11-12). If transcribed into English, the DNA in the human genome (i.e., in a spermatozoon or ovum) would fill a 300-volume set of encyclopedias of approximately 2,000 pages each (Baldi, p. 21). Yet just as amazing is the fact that all the genetic information needed to reproduce the entire human population (about six billion people) could be placed into a space of about one-eighth of a cubic inch. In comparing the amount of information contained in the DNA molecule with a much larger computer microchip, evolutionist Irvin Block remarked: "We marvel at the feats of memory and transcription accomplished by computer microchips, but these are gargantuan compared to the protein granules of deoxyribonucleic acid, DNA" (1980, p. 52).

The Genetic Code–Its Design and Function

Faithful, accurate cellular division is critically important, of course, because without it life could not continue. But neither could life sustain itself without the existence and continuation of the extremely intricate genetic code contained within each cell. Scientific studies have shown that the hereditary information contained in the code found within the nucleus of the living cell is universal in nature. Regardless of their respective views on origins, all scientists acknowledge this. Evolutionist Richard Dawkins observed: "The genetic code is universal.... The complete word-for-word universality of the genetic dictionary is, for the taxonomist, too much of a good thing" (1986, p. 270). Creationist Darrel Kautz agreed: "It is recognized by molecular biologists that the genetic code is universal, irrespective of how different living things are in their external appearances" (1988, p. 44). Or, as Matt Ridley put it in his 1999 book, *Genome:*

> Wherever you go in the world, whatever animal, plant, bug or blob you look at, if it is alive, it will use the same dictionary and know the same code. **All life is one**. The genetic code, bar a few tiny local aberrations, mostly for unexplained reasons in the ciliate protozoa, is the same in every creature. We all use exactly the same language.
>
> **This means–and religious people might find this a useful argument–that there was only one creation, one single event when life was born**.... The unity of life is an empirical fact (pp. 21-22, emp. added).

It is the genetic code which ensures that living things reproduce faithfully "after their kind," exactly as the principles of genetics state that they should. Such faithful reproduction, of course, is due both to the immense complexity and the intricate design of that code. It is doubtful that anyone cognizant of the facts would speak of the "simple" genetic code. A.G. Cairns-Smith has explained why:

> Every organism has in it a store of what is called **genetic information**.... I will refer to an organism's genetic information store as its **Library**.... Where is the Library in such a multicellular organism? The answer is everywhere. With a few exceptions every cell in a multicellular organism has a complete set of all the books in the Library. As such an organism grows, its cells multiply and in the process the complete central Library gets copied again and again.... The human Library has 46 of these cord-like books in it. They are called chromosomes. They are not all of the same size, but an average one has the equivalent of about 20,000 pages.... Man's Library, for example, consists of a set of construction and service manuals that run to the equivalent of about a million book-pages together (1985, pp. 9,10, emp. in orig.).

Wilder-Smith concurred with such an assessment when he wrote:

> Now, when we are confronted with the genetic code, we are astounded at once at its simplicity, complexity and the mass of information contained in it. One cannot avoid being awed at the sheer density of information contained in such a miniaturized space. When one considers that the entire chemical information required to construct a man, elephant, frog, or an orchid was compressed into two minuscule reproductive cells, one can only be astounded. **Only a sub-human could not be astounded**. The almost inconceivably complex information needed to synthesize a man, plant, or a crocodile from air, sunlight, organic substances, carbon dioxide and minerals is contained in these two tiny cells. If one were to request an engineer to accomplish this feat of information miniaturization, one would be considered fit for the psychiatric line (1976, pp. 257-259, emp. in orig.).

It is no less amazing to learn that even what some would call "simple" cells (e.g., bacteria) have extremely large and complex "libraries" of genetic information stored within them. For example, the bacterium *Escherichia coli*, which is by no means the "simplest" cell known, is a tiny rod only a thousandth of a millimeter across and about twice as long, yet "it is an indication of the sheer complexity of *E. coli* that its Library runs to a thousand page-equivalent" (Cairns-Smith, p. 11). Biochemist Michael Behe has suggested that the amount of DNA in a cell "varies roughly with the complexity of the organism" (1998, p. 185). There are notable exceptions, however. Humans, for example, have about 100 times more of the genetic-code-bearing molecule (DNA) than bacteria, yet salamanders, which are amphibians, have 20 times more DNA than humans (see Hitching, 1982, p. 75). Humans have roughly 30 times more DNA than some insects, yet less than half that of certain other insects (see Spetner, 1997, p. 28).

It does not take much convincing, beyond facts such as these, to see that the genetic code is characterized by orderliness, complexity, and adeptness in function. The order and complexity themselves are nothing short of phenomenal. But the **function** of this code is perhaps its most impressive feature, as Wilder-Smith explained when he suggested that the coded information

> ...may be compared to a book or to a video or audiotape, with an extra factor coded into it enabling the genetic information, under certain environmental conditions, to read itself and then to execute the information it reads. It resembles, that is, a hypothetical architect's plan of a house, which plan not only contains the information on how to build the house, but which can, when thrown into the garden, build entirely of its own initiative the house all on its own without the need for contractors or any other outside building agents.... Thus, it is fair to say that the **technology** exhibited by the genetic code is orders of magnitude higher than any technology man has, until now, developed. What is its secret? The secret lies in its ability to store and to execute incredible magnitudes of conceptual information in the ultimate molecular miniaturization of the information storage and retrieval system of the nucleotides and their sequences (1987, p. 73, emp. in orig.).

This "ability to store and to execute incredible magnitudes of conceptual information" is where DNA comes into play. In their book, *The Mystery of Life's Origin*, Thaxton, Bradley, and Olsen discussed the DNA-based genetic code elucidated by Crick and Watson.

> According to their now-famous model, hereditary information is transmitted from one generation to the next by means of a simple code resident in the specific sequence of certain constituents of the DNA molecule.... The breakthrough by Crick and Watson was their discovery of the specific key to life's diversity. It was the extraordinarily complex yet orderly architecture of the DNA molecule. They had discovered that there is in fact a code inscribed in this "coil of life," bringing a major advance in our understanding of life's remarkable structure (1984, p. 1).

How important is the "coil of life" represented in the DNA molecule? Wilder-Smith concluded: "The information stored on the DNA-molecule is that which controls totally, as far as we at present know, by its interaction with its environment, the development of all biological organisms" (1987, p. 73). Professor E.H. Andrews summarized how this can be true:

> The way the DNA code works is this. The DNA molecule is like a template or pattern for the making of other molecules called "proteins." ...These proteins then control the growth and activity of the cell which, in turn, controls the growth and activity of the whole organism (1978, p. 28).

Thus, the DNA contains the information that allows proteins to be manufactured, and the proteins control cell growth and function, which ultimately are responsible for each organism. The genetic code, as found within the DNA molecule, is vital to life as we know it. In his book, *Let Us Make Man*, Bruce Anderson referred to it as "the chief executive of the cell in which it resides, giving chemical commands to control everything that keeps the cell alive and functioning" (1980, p. 50). Kautz followed this same line of thinking when he stated:

> The information in DNA is sufficient for directing and controlling all the processes which transpire within a cell including diagnosing, repairing, and replicating the cell. Think of an architectural blueprint having the capacity of actually building the structure depicted on the blueprint, of maintaining that structure in good repair, and even replicating it (1988, p. 44).

Likely, many people have not considered the exact terminology with which the genetic code is described in the scientific literature. Lester and Bohlin observed:

> The DNA in living cells contains coded information. It is not surprising that so many of the terms used in describing DNA and its functions are language terms. We speak of the genetic **code**. DNA is **transcribed** into RNA. RNA is **translated** into protein.... Such designations are not simply convenient or just anthropomorphisms. They accurately describe the situation (1984, pp. 85-86, emp. in orig.).

Kautz thus concluded:

> The information in the DNA molecule had to have been imposed upon it by some outside source just as music is imposed on a cassette tape. The information in DNA is presented in **coded** form as explained previously, and codes are not known to arise spontaneously.... Further, consider that human beings have learned to store information on clay tablets, stone, papyrus, paper, film, magnetic media such as audio and video cassettes, microchips, etc. Yet human technology has not yet advanced to the point of storing information **chemically** as it is in the DNA molecule (1988, pp. 44,45, emp. in orig.).

How, then, did this complex chemical code arise? What "outside source" imposed the information on the DNA molecule? The intricate and complex nature of the DNA molecule–combined with the staggering amount of chemically coded information that it contains–speaks unerringly to the fact that this "supermolecule" simply could not have come into existence as a result of blind chance and random natural forces operating through eons of time, as evolutionists have claimed. This is not an adequate explanation for the inherent complexity of the DNA molecule. Andrews was correct when he stated:

> It is not possible for a code, of any kind, to arise by chance or accident.... A code is the work of an intelligent mind. Even the cleverest dog or chimpanzee could not work out a code of any kind. It is obvious then that chance cannot do it.... This could no more have been the work of chance or accident than could the "Moonlight Sonata" be played by mice running up and down the keyboard of my piano! Codes do not arise from chaos (1978, pp. 28-29).

Indeed, codes do not arise from chaos. Obvious design demands a designer. And that is the very point the theist is stressing: an intelligent Designer is demanded by the available evidence.

The Body's Tissues

In the human body, there are numerous tissues (e.g., muscle tissues, nerve tissues, etc.). In fact, a single human has nearly 700 muscles (containing about six billion muscle fibers), composing about 40% of the body's weight (Gillen, 2001, p. 47). I.M. Murray, professor of anatomy at the State University of New York, once referred to muscles as the body's "engines" that provide the power for movement (1969, p. 22). Some muscles are tiny, such as those regulating the amount of light entering the eye, while others, like those in the legs, are massive.

Muscles may be classified either as "voluntary" (i.e., under the control of the human will), or "involuntary" (i.e., not under control of the will). The voluntary muscles of the arms, for example, are attached to the bones by tough cords of connective tissue called tendons. One must "think" in order to move these muscles. The involuntary muscles are those whose contraction and relaxation cannot be controlled consciously (e.g., the heart and intestines). Some muscles are both voluntary and involuntary (e.g., the muscles controlling the eyelids, and the diaphragm). There are three types of muscle tissue: (1) skeletal (voluntary muscles that generally are attached to bones); (2) cardiac (red-colored involuntary muscles that are fast-acting and powerful); and (3) smooth (involuntary muscle cells that are found in walls of blood vessels, the digestive tract, etc. and that are slow-acting). All muscles, in one way or another, are regulated by the nervous system.

Muscles work by contracting (tightening). When they contract, they shorten, thereby exerting a "pull" (muscles do not "push"). Frequently, muscles work in pairs or groups, with the overall function of muscles being motion. The biceps in the upper arm pulls the forearm forward, whereas the triceps moves the forearm downward. While one works, the other rests. These groups of muscles power all actions of the body, ranging from the delicate threading of a needle to the lifting of a heavy object like a piano. The design inherent in such tissues is utterly amazing.

Some muscles, like those attached to the skeleton, are analogous to strong steel cables. Each muscle is constructed of long cells combined in small bundles called fibers. These bundles are bound together, making larger bundles of which the whole muscle consists. Muscle fibers vary in size from a few hundred-thousandths of an inch, to an inch or inch-and-a half in length. Each muscle has its own stored supply of high-grade fuel, especially sugar (glycogen), which the body has manufactured from food that has been consumed. This analogy may be helpful. In an automobile engine, the spark ignites vaporized gasoline, the piston moves, and keeps moving in response to a series of explosions. "A muscle performs the functions of both the spark and the piston; the cell itself splits a molecule of fuel and also exerts the resulting physical power" (Miller and Goode, p. 23). If it is clear that an automobile engine was intelligently designed, why is it not reasonable to draw the same conclusion with reference to muscles? Lenihan, even though an evolutionist, wrote: "The body's engines [muscles–BT/BH]...demonstrate some surprisingly modern engineering ideas" (1974, p. 43). The question is: Who initiated these "modern engineering ideas"? The answer, of course, is the Great Engineer, God.

Connected to the skeletal muscle is a nerve that conveys a signal, telling the muscle when to contract or relax. Obviously, there must be precise orchestration between the skeletal muscle system and the nervous system. Without doubt, their cooperative nature was planned. Some muscles, like those in the stomach, are stimulated to work by means of chemicals known as hormones.

Furthermore, there is a precisely integrated relationship between muscles and bones. Here is just one such example. "As certain muscles increase in strength, they pull harder than before on the bones to which they are attached. With this as a stimulus, bone-forming cells build new bone to give internal reinforcement where necessary" (Shryock, 1968, p. 27). Would this not indicate design?

In his book, *Human Design*, evolutionist William S. Beck hardly could contain himself when he wrote of "the intricate structural organization" of the muscles and tendons in the hand, which are capable of such a wide variety of actions. But "intricate structural organization" indicates design. Beck characterized this phenomenon as "one of evolution's most remarkable achievements" (1971, p. 691). Remarkable indeed! A number of years ago, an article on the human hand appeared in the magazine, *Today's Health*, published by the American Medical Association. Although saturated with evolutionary concepts (e.g., the hand is alleged to have evolved from a fish's fin), the article nevertheless conceded:

> ...If the most gifted scientists cudgeled their brains they probably could not come up with a stronger or more perfect tool for grasping and delicate manipulation than the human hand. And seen **from an engineering standpoint**, the loveliest hand is a highly complex mechanical device composed of muscle, bone, tendon, fat, and extremely sensitive nerve fibers, capable of performing thousands of jobs with precision (Wylie, 1962, p. 25, emp. added).

But something "engineered" requires an **engineer**. That is just sound logic. Alan Gillen wrote concerning the design inherent in the human hand:

> The movement of the hand and fingers of a concert pianist is an awesome sight. The necessity of coordination, timing, and order to play Beethoven's "Fifth Symphony" or Bach's "Jesu–Joy of Man's Desire" is a feat that is not accomplished by chance. There is marvelous skill not only in playing the music, but also in the 70 (35 in each hand) separate muscles contributing to the hand movement on the keyboard. The hand has been described as the most sophisticated "tool" in the body. It looks like it was crafted for maximum dexterity and strength in movement. The hand is capable of 58 distinct movements. These movements allow for dexterity and power for a diversity of actions ranging from piano playing and threading of a needle to holding a jackhammer. This amazing diversity of functions is accomplished with the help of muscles in the forearm and wrist. The fingers have no muscles in themselves; the tendons transfer force from muscles in the forearm and palm.... Orthopedic surgeons could write many manuals suggesting various ways to repair hands that have been injured. Yet, there has never been a surgical technique that succeeded in improving the movement of a healthy hand. It frequently takes over a dozen muscles and tendons working together with the opposable thumb to accomplish one movement (2001, p. 52).

Little wonder that Sir Isaac Newton once remarked: "In the absence of any other proof, the thumb alone would convince me of God's existence."

While many living organisms share common muscle activity, there are some muscle movements that are unique to man. These forcefully demonstrate that the human being is not some kind of "evolved animal." Rather, he is a creature "fearfully and wonderfully made" by a Creator. Observe the following quotation from two evolutionists, which no doubt reveals more than these authors intended. Then, ask yourself how scientists can echo these sentiments and still ignore the evidence of design in nature that demands a Designer.

> Only man can combine muscle with intelligence and imagination, plan and purpose, to plow and plant a field, to create a museum masterpiece or the "Gettysburg Address." And only man trains to perform the most highly coordinated forms of bodily motion for their own sake, in the expressive and athletic arts. We applaud this skill in our species every time we clap our hands for a ballerina or a circus aerialist (Miller and Goode, p. 21).

The Body's Organs

The Skin

The skin, which is the largest single organ of the human body, consists of three areas: (a) the skin layers; (b) the glands; and (c) the nails. There are two skin layers. The outer layer (the epidermis) consists of rows of cells about 12 to 15 deep, and is between 0.07 and 0.12 millimeters thick. The uppermost layers are dead, and are being replaced constantly with newly formed living cells. It would be an interesting question to ask: What manmade house replaces its own covering? The epidermis contains a pigment called melanin, which gives the skin its distinctive color.

The lower layer (the dermis), which consists mainly of collagen-rich connective tissue, is a spongy, leathery area with a thickness of between one and two millimeters. It serves to protect and cushion the body, and also contains hair follicles, sweat glands, sebaceous glands, and nerve endings, as well as capillaries and lymphatic vessels. It is joined to the epidermis by a corrugated surface that contains nerves and blood vessels.

Receptors (from the Latin *receptor*, meaning "recorder") are the ends of nerve fibers that can detect stimuli and convert them into neural impulses to be sent to the brain via the central nervous system. Incredible amounts of information can be detected by the receptors. The physiological term for the transmission of information by means of receptors is "sensibility" (from the Latin *sensibilis*, meaning "observable"). Huge numbers of receptors are located in the skin, in structures like muscles and skeletal joints, and in internal organs. Although we "touch" with our epidermis, it is in the dermis that the sense of touch actually is recorded and passed on to the central nervous system.

The skin, as turns out, is a very busy place. In his book, *The Wonder of Man*, Werner Gitt described one square centimeter of skin as containing the following: 6,000,000 cells, 100 sweat glands, 10 sebaceous glands, 5,000 sensory corpuscles, 200 pain points, 25 pressure points, 12 cold-sensitive points, and 2 heat-sensitive points (1999, p. 41). If the skin of a 150-pound man were spread out, it would cover approximately 20 square feet of space, and would make up about one-sixth of a person's average body weight. Human skin is one of the body's most vital organs. Its value may be summarized as follows.

(1) The skin is a protective fortification that keeps harmful bacteria from entering the human system.

(2) It is a waterproof wall that holds in the fluids of the body (our bodies are about 75% fluids).

(3) It protects the interior parts of the body from cuts, bruises, etc.

(4) With its pigment, melanin, it shields the body from harmful rays arriving on the Earth from the Sun. Beck referred to melanin as "an epidermal light filter" (1971, p. 745). Do light filters invented by man require intelligence?

(5) The skin's many nerve endings make it sensitive to touch, cold, heat, pain, and pressure. Thus, it is a major sense organ.

(6) The sweat glands help eliminate waste products and also function in cooling the skin.

(7) The oil glands lubricate the skin and help keep it soft–while at the same time providing a waterproofing system. Though soft, the skin is quite durable. When a 2,000-year-old Egyptian mummy was fingerprinted, the ridges were found to be perfectly preserved (Guinness, 1987, p. 132).

(8) About one-third of the body's blood circulates through the skin. The blood vessels, by contracting and expanding, work to regulate body temperature. If body temperature increases by 7 or 8 degrees, and remains there for any length of time, a person almost always will die. The skin is thus a radiator system (see Brand and Yancey, 1980, p. 154). Does a radiator happen by accident?

(9) The skin absorbs ultraviolet rays from the Sun, and uses them to convert chemicals into vitamin D, which the body needs for the utilization of calcium. The skin is therefore a chemical-processing plant for the entire body.

(10) And, as odd as it may sound, skin also performs a respiratory function, handling between one and two percent of the gas exchange of the body.

The ends of the fingers and toes are protected by a horn-like substance, usually referred to as the fingernail or toenail. Actually, most of the nail is dead; only the lower, crescent-shaped, white portion is living. The fingernails grow about three times as fast as the toenails, which is certainly evidence of good design, considering the respective functions of the hands and feet. The skin of the underside of the fingers, the palms, and the soles of the feet have a special friction surface, and no hair. These areas, like the knurling on a tool handle or the tread of a tire, have been designed specifically for gripping.

Hair has several functions. It is a part of the body's sentry system. Eyelashes warn the eyes to close when foreign objects strike them. Body hairs also serve as levers, connected to muscles, to help squeeze the oil glands. Hair acts as a filter in the ears and nose. Hair grows to a certain length, falls out, and then, in most instances, is replaced by new hair. Hair is "programmed" to grow only to a certain length. But who provided the "program"? Compared to most mammals, man is relatively hairless. But why is this the case? A strong case can be made for the fact that the best explanation is to be found "in the design of the human body with personhood in view" (Cosgrove, 1987, p. 54). In fact, it has been estimated that touching is ten times as strong as verbal or emotional contact. Strong emotions can be aroused via the sense of touch. A tender kiss or caress at a romantic moment, a gentle hug during a time of grief, or a slap in the face, all have the ability to arouse various emotions. And, of course, in the end, if the sense of touch were not pleasant, procreation would not occur.

Skin is a highly responsive sense organ that can detect a large number of stimuli at once, all the while keeping them separate and distinct. The softness of a rabbit's fur, the roughness of a masonry brick, the smoothness of a piece of glass, the warmth of a sauna, the thorns of a rose, or the searing pain associated with a burn are all things that the skin can detect and identify. Man has yet to develop a durable material that can perform the many functions that the skin carries out on a daily basis. Does it make sense to suggest that the skin "just happened"? We think not.

The Eye

One of the most forceful evidences of design within the human body is the eye. Even Charles Darwin struggled with the problem of an organ so complex as the eye evolving via naturalistic processes. In *The Origin of Species* he wrote:

> To suppose that the eye with all its inimitable contrivances for adjusting the focus to different distances, for admitting different amounts of light, and for the correction of spherical and chromatic aberration, could have been formed by natural selection, seems, I freely confess, absurd in the highest sense (1859, p. 170).

However, in spite of his misgivings, Darwin went on to argue that the eye had, in fact, been produced by natural selection through an evolutionary process. Darwin, of course, is not the only one to be troubled by what appears to be obvious evidence of design in the eye. Evolutionist Robert Jastrow once wrote:

> The eye is a marvelous instrument, resembling a telescope of the highest quality, with a lens, an adjustable focus, a variable diaphragm for controlling the amount of light, and optical corrections for spherical and chromatic aberration. **The eye appears to have been designed; no designer of telescopes could have done better**. How could this marvelous instrument have evolved by chance, through a succession of random events? (1981, pp. 96-97, emp. added).

Though Dr. Jastrow argued that "the fact of evolution is not in doubt," he nonetheless confessed: "...there seems to be no direct proof that evolution can work these miracles.... **It is hard to accept the evolution of the eye as a product of chance**" (1981, pp. 101,97,98, emp. added).

Considering how extremely complex the mechanism of the eye is known to be, it is easy to understand why Dr. Jastrow would make such a comment. Although it accounts for only one four-thousandth of the average adult's body weight, it processes approximately 80% of the information received from the outside world. In fact, the eyes can handle 500,000 messages simultaneously. In an average day, the eye moves about 100,000 times, using muscles that, milligram for milligram, are among the body's strongest. The body would have to walk 50 miles to exercise the leg muscles an equal amount. Interestingly, the eyes are kept clear by tear ducts that produce exactly the right amount of fluid to cleanse both eyes simultaneously in one five-hundredth of a second.

The eye can be divided functionally into two distinct parts. The first is the physical "dioptric" mechanism (from the Greek *dioptra*, meaning something through which one looks), which handles incoming light. The second is the receptor area of the retina where the light triggers processes in the nerve cells. To form an image, the incoming light rays (arriving at approximately 186,000 miles per second) must be refracted (bent) and focused sharply on the retina. The retina itself is a masterpiece of engineering design. As Gitt noted:

> One single square millimetre of the retina contains approximately 400,000 optical sensors. To get some idea of such a large number, imagine a sphere, on the surface of which circles are drawn, the size of tennis balls. These circles are separated from each other by the same distance as their diameter. In order to accommodate 400,000 such circles, the sphere must have a diameter of 52 metres, nearly, three times as large as the hot air balloons used for advertising promotions (1999, p. 15).

The cornea takes care of most of the refraction, and the lens serves to focus items seen at varying distances as it changes its curvature. The iris and the pupil work together (like the light-meter and diaphragm of a camera) to let in just the right amount of light. There are two opposing sets of muscles that regulate the size of the aperture (the opening, or pupil) according to the brightness or dimness of the incoming light. The images move through a lens that focuses the "picture" (in an inverted form) on the retina (which covers less than a square inch) at the rear of the eyeball. The image is then picked up by some 137 million light-sensitive receptor cells that convey the message (at over 300 miles per hour) to the brain for processing. Those cells [130 million rods (that allow the eye to see in black and white) and 7 million cones (that allow the eye to see in full color)] convert light into chemical (and subsequently into chemical) signals, which then travel along the optic nerve to the brain.

This "dioptric mechanism" produces miniaturized and upside-down images, which, as it turns out, also are left-right inverted. But the optic nerves from both eyes split up and cross each other in such a way that the left halves of the images of both eyes are received by the right hemisphere of the brain, and the right halves end up in the left hemisphere. Each half of the observer's brain receives information from only one half of the image. As Gitt went on to explain:

> Note that, although the brain processes the different parts of the image in various remote locations, the two halves of the field of vision are seamlessly re-united, without any trace of a joint–amazing! This process is still far from being fully understood (p. 17).

Amazing indeed! Little wonder that secular writers are prone to speak of "the miraculous teamwork of your eye and your brain" (Guinness, 1987, p. 196). In fact, the vocabulary of such writers becomes rather unguarded when contemplating this phenomenon. Bioengineer John Lenihan has suggested: "The eye is an exceptionally sensitive optical instrument **displaying many striking features of design** and performance; even the windscreen washers and wipers have not been forgotten" (1974, p. 75, emp. added). Since Dr. Lenihan is an evolutionist, his terminology cannot be dismissed as some kind of creationist jargon.

It is no wonder that the eye frequently is compared to a camera. Evolutionists Miller and Goode suggested: "The living camera of the eye photographs fleeting images by the thousands, between one moment and the next, and it makes its own adjustments, automatically and precisely, with each change in distance light, and angle" (1960, p. 315). The eye does indeed photograph "fleeting images by the thousands." It can take and develop approximately half a million pictures a day (Gardner, 1994, p. 105). The eye is infinitely more complex than any manmade camera. Actually, the camera was patterned after the eye–a fact admitted even by evolutionists. The Time-Life science series volume, *The Body*, spoke of the camera as a "manmade eye" and conceded that this optical instrument was "modeled" after the design of the eye (Nourse, 1964, p. 154). Indeed, the eye does display many striking features of design (see chart on next page).

THE EYE	THE CAMERA
Eyelid	Lens cover
Lens	Lens
Close-up	Close-up
Wide-angle	Wide-angle
Telephoto	Telephoto
Ciliary muscle + lens	Autofocus
Iris + pupil	Light meter
Retina	Film
Rods	Black and white
Cones	Color
Brain	Processing

If the function of the camera demands that it was "made," does it not stand to reason that the more complex human camera, the eye, also must have had a Maker? As the ancient proverb says: "There is none so blind as those who will not see."

The Ear

Another incontrovertible evidence of design within the human body is the ear, which is composed of three areas: outer, middle, and inner. Sound waves enter the outer ear (at a speed of 1,087 feet per second) and pass along a tube to the middle ear. Stretched across the tube is a thin membrane, the eardrum. The sound waves hit this tissue and cause it to vibrate. The resulting vibrations then are passed on by three tiny bones (the smallest in the human body, connected and operated by miniature muscles)–the malleus, incus, and stapes (bones popularly known as the hammer, anvil, and stirrup, respectively, because of their shapes).

These bones, which one authority says "are **designed** to transmit even very faint sounds," (Sedeen, 1986, p. 280, emp. added), are connected to another membrane called the oval window. As the oval window vibrates, it generates movement within a small spiral passage, the cochlea, which is filled with a highly viscous liquid known as endolymph. The vibrations within the cochlea are picked up by some 25,000 auditory receptors and transferred as electrical impulses, by means of the auditory nerve (with its 30,000 nerve fibers) to the brain. The brain receives these vibrations (up to 25,000 per second) and interprets them as voice, thunder, music (more than 1,500 separate musical tones), or as the thousands of other sounds that humans hear on a daily basis. The complexity of this integrated system is nothing short of phenomenal. One writer noted: "Amazingly, the inner ear, although no bigger than a hazelnut, contains as many circuits as the telephone system of a good-sized city" (Guinness, 1987, p. 208). Would anyone suggest that a city's telephone system could design itself? Dr. Lenihan even went so far as to remark that the "level of sensitivity" within the human ear is "far beyond the achievement of any microphone" and "represents the ultimate limit of performance" (1974, p. 87).

There are two additional tubes on either side of the cochlear duct, which are partially filled with a somewhat less viscous fluid (known as perilymph). Nerve endings from these canals are connected to the brain, which, in cooperation with the muscle system, helps us maintain our equilibrium. The balancing ability of the auditory system has been compared to the "inertial system used in missiles and submarines" (Lenihan, p. 90). Thus, the ear mechanism actually is designed to accomplish two functions–hearing and balance. This feature of the body demonstrates incredible planning. In the words of Lenihan, "The combination, in such a small space, of the hearing and balancing systems of the body **represents a remarkable achievement of biological engineering**" (p. 94, emp. added). Does "blind nature" have the ability to carry out such "remarkable achievements of biological engineering"?

The psalmist affirmed that God "planted the ear" and "formed the eye" (Psalm 94:9). Hearing and seeing are not developments of an eons-long evolutionary process. "The hearing ear, and the seeing eye, Jehovah has made even both of them" (Proverbs 20:12). "Our eyes and ears are transformers. They sense the light and sounds around us and turn them into electrical impulses that the brain can interpret. **Each organ is designed** to handle its own medium" (Sedeen, 1986, p. 276, emp. added). Designed indeed! And such design speaks eloquently of a Grand Designer.

The Body's Systems

The Skeletal System

The average adult has 206 bones in his body (an infant can have more than 300, but many of these fuse during the maturation process). The human skeleton accounts for about 15% of the body's weight, and works in tandem with 600 muscles and 100 joints. [Tendons that anchor the muscles to bones have been known to withstand a stress of eight tons per square inch! Blanchard, 2000, p. 312.]

There are two major classifications of bones. **Axial bones** are the 80 bones that lie along the central, vertical axis of the body and that support and protect the head and torso. They include the skull and the spinal column. **Appendicular bones** include the 126 bones that comprise the appendages, including the shoulders, hips, arms, legs, hand, feet, fingers, and toes. There are four major classification groups in regard to the shape of bones: (1) **long bones** (such as the radius, humerus, and femur); (2) **short bones** (like the carpals and tarsals); (3) **flat bones** (such as the sternum and skull bones); and (4) **irregular bones** (like the vertebrae).

Bones serve several important functions.

(1) Bones provide a rigid support system for the organs and tissues of the body. They are like the interior framework of a house. The skeletal system is "something of an **engi-**

neering marvel, strong enough to support weight and carry burdens, yet flexible to cushion shocks and allow for an extraordinary variety of motion" (Miller and Goode, p. 25, emp. added). Who was the engineer responsible for the marvel known as the skeletal system?

(2) Bones function as protective devices for many of the softer parts of the anatomy. For example, certain sections of the skull, which are independent in infancy but have grown together in the adult, offer protection for the fragile brain. The 12 pairs of ribs form a cage to shield the heart and lungs. The backbone (called the spinal column) is made up of 33 block-like bones that are ingeniously designed to allow movement, yet these bones protect a major feature of the nervous system–the spinal cord.

(3) Bones also serve as levers. In his book, *Body by Design*, Alan Gillen remarked:

> Our skeletal frames are more than just scaffolding that holds us erect; they serve as the structures upon which we hang all that we are. Our bones are the anchors to which muscles attach, and they act as the levers and fulcrums for our daily activities (2001, p. 41).

Miller and Goode noted:

> When our muscles move us about, they do it by working a series of articulated levers that make a most efficient use of every ounce of muscular motive power. The levers are the bones of the body's framework, fitted together with the neatness of jigsaw pieces and hinged by joints that must win the admiration of any mechanic (p. 25).

(4) Bones even have a metabolic function. Gillen commented: "Bones are far from rigid, lifeless structures. Nerves etch their surfaces; blood vessels interweave them. Bones bustle with metabolic activity. Break one and you will immediately understand how sensitive they can be" (p. 41). Part of each major bone is dense, and part (the marrow) is spongy. Until fairly recently, it was assumed that bones were inert tissue. However, studies have revealed that they are "constantly

being remodeled" (Beck, 1971, p. 626). They provide a reservoir of essential minerals (99% of the calcium and 88% of the phosphorus, plus other trace elements), which must be rebuilt continuously. For example, without calcium, impulses could not travel along the nerves, and blood would not clot. Too, red blood cells (180 million of which die every minute), certain white blood cells, and platelets (that help the blood to clot) arise in the marrow of the bones (the marrow produces one trillion red blood cells daily; see Gardner, 1994, p. 108). Incredibly, when a bone is broken, it immediately begins to repair itself. And, after the repair process is complete, it will be even stronger than it was before. Brand and Yancey commented:

> Perhaps an engineer will someday develop a substance as strong and light and efficient as bone, but what engineer could devise a substance that, like bone, can grow continuously, lubricate itself, require no shutdown time, and repair itself when damage occurs? (1980, p. 91).

In order for the skeletal system to be effective, it must have several attributes, among which are strength, elasticity, and lightness of weight. Amazingly, the bones possess all of these characteristics. A cube of bone 1 square inch in surface will bear, without being crushed, a weight of more than 4 tons. Ounce for ounce, bone is stronger than solid steel. And yet, a piece of bone will stretch 10 times as much as steel. A steel frame comparable to the human skeleton would weight 3 times as much. The long bones in the arms and legs have a lengthwise hollow in the shaft that gives strength without adding extra weight. Alexander Macalister, former professor of anatomy at Cambridge University, suggested: "Man's body is a machine formed for doing work. Its framework is the most suitable that could be devised in material, structure, and arrangement" (1886, 7:2).

As a specific example of bone design, consider the bones of the foot. One-fourth of all the body's bones are in the feet. Each human foot contains 26 bones. The feet have been designed to facilitate a number of mechanical functions. They **support**, using arches similar to those found in an engineered bridge. They operate as **levers** (as in those occasions when one presses an automobile accelerator peddle). They act like **hydraulic jacks** when a person tiptoes. They **catapult** a person as he jumps. And feet act as a **cushion** for the legs when one is running. All of these features are quite helpful–especially in view of the fact that an average person will walk about 65,000 miles in his/her lifetime (equivalent to traveling around the world more than two-and-a-half times). Brand and Yancey observed:

> Even when a soccer player subjects these small bones to a cumulative force of one thousand tons per foot over the course of a match, his living bones endure the stress, maintaining their elasticity.... Our body weight is evenly spread out through architecturally perfect arches which serve as springs, and the bending of knees and ankles absorbs stress (1980, p. 70).

The skeletal system demonstrates brilliant design, to be sure. The conclusion is inescapable that there must have been a brilliant Designer behind it. Jay Wile put it like this:

> ...[D]espite the amazing technology that can be designed and created by us today, we cannot make a machine that can do even a fraction of what you can do with your own body! Nevertheless, if you do not believe in God, you have to assume that this incredible machine that we call the human body–a machine that far surpasses anything our best applied scientists can build–had to have been the result of **random chance**. After all, without God, you have to believe that the human body is the product of evolution, and evolution occurs by random chance. If our greatest applied scientists cannot build anything that comes anywhere close to performing the functions of the human body, how likely is it that the human body evolved by chance? In my opinion, the answer is "no chance whatsoever" (2000, pp. 268-269, emp. in orig.).

The Circulatory System

The circulatory system consists of the heart, blood, and arteries, vessels, and capillaries, and has several important functions. First, the circulatory system transports digested food particles to the various parts of the body. Second, it takes oxygen to the cells for burning food, thereby producing heat and energy. Third, it picks up waste materials and carries them to the organs that eliminate refuse from the body as a whole.

The heart is a small muscle (or, as some would say, two muscles connected in tandem) in the upper chest cavity. Renowned heart surgeon Michael DeBakey once called it a "busy machine" that pumps blood to all parts of the body (1984, 9: 132a). In the adult male human, the heart weighs about 11 ounces, and is about the size of a large fist; a woman's heart is slightly smaller. Miller and Goode have described this marvelous muscle as a "pump with a **built-in** motor" (p. 63, emp. added). The question comes to mind: Is it not the case that something **built** always has a **builder**?

The heart is the strongest muscle in the body. Normally it beats (in an adult) at about 70 to 80 times per minute. When the body needs an extra supply of blood (e.g., during vigorous exercise), it can beat 150 to 180 times a minute—an automatic regulating feature that clearly indicates design. Note this unwitting testimony from an evolutionist.

> The heart and blood vessels do more than speed or slow our blood flow to meet [the body's] needs. They carry the scarlet stream to different tissues under differing pressures to fuel different actions. Blood rushes to the stomach when we eat, to the lungs and muscles when we swim, to the brain when we read. To satisfy these changing metabolic needs, the cardiovascular system **integrates information as well as any computer, then responds as no computer can** (Schiefelbein, 1986, p. 124, emp. added).

The heart can exert tremendous force. It can squirt a stream of blood about 10 feet into the air. In the span of a single hour, the heart generates enough energy to lift a medium-sized car

3 feet off the ground (Avraham, 1989, p. 13). It beats about 100,000 times a day, or nearly 40,000,000 times in a year. It pumps approximately 1,800-2,000 gallons of blood a day (enough to fill over 40 bathtubs!), or about 680,000 gallons a year (see Gillen, 2001, p. 70). In a lifetime, a heart will pump some 600,000 metric **tons** of blood! Physicians have suggested that if it were kept healthy and not abused, a human heart could beat for 120 years without structural failure.

The heart is a high-capacity pump that also is self-lubricating. A tough sac called the pericardium sheaths the heart. Membranes within the pericardium secrete a lubricating fluid that permits the pericardium to slide smoothly against the heart's surface as the cardiac muscles contract and relax. Interestingly, although the heart itself is continually filled with blood, it nevertheless requires its own blood supply to provide oxygen and nutrients to the hard-working cardiac muscles. Located on the surface of the heart, the branches of the coronary arteries penetrate its wall. The coronary veins collect blood from the capillaries in the heart muscles, and carry it back to be used again–a circulatory route that happens to be the shortest in the entire body.

But what causes the heart to "pump" or "beat"? It contains a small patch of tissue called the sinus node, or cardiac pacemaker. Somehow, about every 8/10 of a second, it produces an electrical current (a sort of "jump-start") to certain nerve fibers that stimulate the muscular contractions that send the blood flowing (at up to 10 miles per hour) throughout the body. To accomplish its varied tasks, the atria and ventricles must contract and relax using a highly regulated and strictly coordinated series of actions known as the "cardiac cycle." Nerves stemmed from the medulla oblongata automatically control this cycle. The stage of the cardiac cycle where the heart relaxes and fills with blood is known as diastole, while the pumping and contracting stage is known as systole. Each cardiac cycle is perceived as a "heartbeat," which is regulated by autonomic (i.e., involuntary) control. The heart is not only self-lubricating, but also self-regulating. The blood requirements for the body's tissues and organs are not constant, but depend on activity levels, overall health, amount of stress, state of consciousness (i.e., awake or asleep), etc. Accelerator nerves link the heart to the central nervous system, and transmit signals to heart's pacemaker, which can increase the heart rate as needed.

To look at it, the heart appears somewhat like a rounded-off cone, the base of which is known as the cardiac base. The septum separates the two halves of the heart, the right half serving the pulmonary circulation, while the left half independently pumps blood all over the body. Oxygen-depleted blood from the body is received by the right half of the heart and passed on to the lungs where it is oxygenated. It then flows to the left side of the heart where it is pumped in various directions to the rest of the body.

Obviously, there are numerous impressive design features within the heart. But few of them are as impressive as the system of valves put in place to prevent back-flow of blood in the heart. These valves work flawlessly to keep blood flowing in the right direction. The two main valves are known as the bicuspid valve (or mitral valve) and the tricuspid valve, which are held in position by strong tendinous cords that are attached to the ventricle walls by cone-shaped papillary muscles. These cords keep the cuspid valves from everting (think of how an umbrella is blown "inside out" in a strong gust of wind). Known collectively as the atrioventricular valves (or A-V valves), these valves separate the atria and the ventricles of the heart.

And how is the blood able to make its way, against gravity, back up the veins to the heart? The veins, it turns out, also contain their own one-way valves with open ends that face the heart–analogous to the valves in an automobile engine (Miller and Goode, p. 71). The blood is pushed partially upward by force from the heart, but it also is propelled by muscle movements that massage the veins, pushing the blood forward through the valves.

Blood is being continuously pumped into, and out of, the heart with its rhythmic beating. The difference between arteries and vessels is not determined by the quality or quantity of blood they carry, but by its flow direction to or away from the heart. Arteries carry blood **from** the heart; veins carry blood **to** the heart. A human adult has between 60,000 and 100,000 miles' worth of various types of blood vessels. Capillaries are the smallest yet most abundant of the blood vessels, being microscopic in size. It has been estimated that it would take ten of them tied together to equal the thickness of a single human hair, and about 120 short capillaries to measure 3 inches. All of them laid end-to-end, however, would circle the equator twice (Avraham, p. 40). Some ten billion capillaries snake through the tissues and, although they contain at any given time less than 5% of the body's entire blood supply, they bring blood within the reach of every one of the 120 trillion cells that compose a normal adult. The blood is pumped into the capillaries with a force sufficient to drive the plasma and its rich cargo through the porous walls of these tiny vessels, thus re-nourishing the surrounding cells. This procedure requires a very "precise balance of pressures between the blood flowing within their walls and the fluid in and around the body's cells" (Schiefelbein, p. 114). Capillaries have thin walls (a mere one-cell thick!), across which gases and waste products also are exchanged. Gillen described the process as follows:

> As blood flows through the capillaries in the lungs, it changes from venous blood to arterial blood by diffusing carbon dioxide out and oxygen in. The color of blood changes in the process from a deep crimson to a bright scarlet. As blood flows through tissue capillaries, it changes back from arterial blood to venous blood. The oxygen leaves the blood to enter cells, and carbon dioxide and other wastes leave the cells and enter the blood. Capillaries converge to form venules and then further converge to form veins (2001, p. 72).

The system is so efficient that the entire process of circulation, "during which every cell in the body is serviced, takes only a total of 20 seconds" (Avraham, p. 41). The body's skillfully constructed transportation system clearly evinces design, hence a Designer. Lenihan confessed: "The circulation is an example of a multipurpose system, often found in the body but **generally beyond the capability of the engineering designer**" (p. 5, emp. added). In describing the heart, Werner Gitt observed:

> The focal point of circulation, it responds to every demand, even from the most distant corners of the body. The larger blood vessels, arteries, and veins are the main roads carrying the necessary volumes of blood, but the capillaries provide the actual nourishment. In this **cleverly designed network**, the arteries branch repeatedly and supply the entire capillary network with blood. These capillaries in turn combine to form larger and larger veins (1999, p. 54, emp. added).

Notice the phraseology used by scientists to describe the heart and circulatory system. Gitt described it as a "cleverly designed network." Evolutionists Miller and Goode conceded that "for a pump that is keeping two separate circulatory systems going in perfect synchronization, **it is hard to imagine a better job of engineering**" (p. 68, emp. added). They likewise admitted that it is "hard to describe as anything short of a **miracle**" (p. 64, emp. added). Is "nature" an "engineer" that performs "miracles"? Hardly. Medical authorities have observed that the heart's efficiency (i.e., the amount of useful work in relation to fuel expended) is about twice that of a steam engine (see Lenihan, p. 131). If intelligence was required to invent the steam engine, does it not stand to reason that intelligence lies behind the human heart? Gitt acknowledged: "The human heart is morphologically and functionally a masterpiece of its Creator" (p. 54). Indeed it is. The question is: Who is the Creator?

The Nervous System

Consider this simple test. Read the following sentence: *Mom had hot apple cider ready for us on that cold snowy day.* In the seconds that were required for you to complete the sentence, your brain already had carried out a multitude of tasks. Initially, your eyes focused on the piece of paper on which the sentence was written, and then transmitted the visual stimuli chemically via your optic nerve to your brain. The brain received that chemical signal, and immediately recognized the symbols on the page as English letters. It then compiled those letters into an entire sentence (using rules that you learned long ago in elementary school), which it analyzed and comprehended. In addition, your brain also may have painted a mental image of this snowy day and your mother. You may even have found yourself suddenly craving a mug of hot apple cider. Also during that short span, your ears reported any unusual sounds and your nose constantly was sampling the air for new odors. All the while, your brain was keeping your body at homeostasis–that is, it signaled your heart to beat and your lungs to respire, it measured hormone levels in your blood stream (and made adjustments as needed), and relayed any pain or sensation that you might be feeling during those few short seconds. And all of this is merely the proverbial "tip of the iceberg." The brain, and the nerves associated with it, carry out countless physiological functions, most of which we understand at only a very basic level. Again, truth be told, we have yet to understand exactly how this unique organ can perform all of these functions simultaneously and with such marvelous precision.

And therein lies the enigma surrounding the brain. How can we take three pounds of matter, and in that small space cram all of our education, memories, communication skills, emotions, likes, and dislikes–yet, all the while it is those same three pounds of matter that keep our heart beating, cause our lungs to respire, and give us a detailed internal map of the position of our arms or legs? How is it that a certain smell instantaneously can carry us back to a period in our childhood, offering us crystal clear images of that particular time in our life? Exactly how is it that we can distinguish between a banana and an orange, just by using our nose? What chemical reactions occur to tell us which one is an orange? **Where** is that memory stored, and how long will that memory **remain** stored? What part of our brain controls our emotions? Where do we hold feelings such as love and hate? How is it that the sound of one voice can bring tears of joy, while sounds from another can cause our blood pressure to begin to climb? In fact, why is it that humans love at all?

As vexing as these questions are, they are even more troubling for individuals who espouse that the brain arrived here by Darwinian mechanisms. Evolutionists would like us to believe that the brain is nothing more than an advanced computer–it receives input (via the senses), and after the input makes its way through various neuronal circuits, output is the end result. Input equals output. In their book, *The Amazing Brain*, Robert Ornstein and Richard Thompson speculated: "What exists as only a few extra cells in the head of the earthworm, handling information about taste and light, has evolved in us humans into the incredibly complex and sophisticated structure of the human brain" (1984, p. 22). These sentiments no doubt are shared by thousands of individuals who stand in utter awe of the brain, yet who chalk up its existence to pure happenstance. Is the brain merely the product of evolution, or were humans created differently than animals?

The nervous system is the "communication center" of the body, and consists of: (1) the **brain**; (2 the **spinal cord**; and (3) the **nerves**, which spread out from the brain and spinal cord to all parts of the body, somewhat like the root system of a tree. The nervous system has many functions. It regulates the actions of organs like the muscles, liver, kidneys, etc. It monitors the senses, such as seeing, hearing, feeling, etc. It also controls our thinking, learning, and memory capabilities.

The specialized nerve receptors in the sensory organs receive information from the environment. To chose just one example, in the skin there are some 3 to 4 million structures sensitive to pain. There are a half-million touch detectors and more than 200,000 temperature gauges. These tiny receptors, plus those in the eyes, ears, nose, tongue, etc., constantly send data to the brain. This information is transmitted (at up to 45 feet per second, or 30 miles per hour), via the nerve fibers to the brain. The transmission involves both electrical and chemical energy. The brain analyzes the data and determines the appropriate action to be taken. Noted science writer, John Pfeiffer, an evolutionist, has called the nervous system "the most elaborate communications system ever devised" (1961, p. 4). **Who** devised it? A number of years ago, the prestigious journal, *Natural History*, contained this statement: "The nervous system of a single starfish, with all its various nerve ganglia and fibers, is more complex than London's telephone exchange" (Burnett, 1961, p. 17). If that is true for the nervous system of the lowly starfish, what could be said about the infinitely more complex nervous system of the human?

Those three pounds of "matter" in the brain represent literally billions of interconnected nerve cells and millions of protective glial cells–which, according to evolutionists, arose by the effects of time, natural law, and chance from nonliving matter. The brain has been estimated to contain 100 billion (10^{11}) neurons (Kandel, 1991, p. 18), each a living unit within itself. While most neurons share similar properties, they can be classified into "perhaps as many as 10,000 different types" (p. 18). Over 100 thousand billion electrical connections are estimated to be present throughout the human brain, which has been said to be more than "all the electrical connections in all the electrical appliances in the world." In describing this awesome organ, R.L. Wysong wrote:

> The human brain weighs about three pounds, contains ten billion neurons with approximately 25,000 synapses (connections) per neuron. Each neuron is made up of 10,000,000,000 macromolecules. The human mind can store almost limitless amounts of information (a potential millions of times greater than the 10^{15} bits of information gathered in a lifetime), compare facts, weigh information against memory,

> judgment and conscience and formulate a decision in a fraction of a second (1976, p. 340, parenthetical item in orig.).

The brain, arguably, is the most unique organ in the entire body–not merely because of its physical make-up, but because of **what** it does and **how** it does it. As evolutionist George Bartelmez put it many years ago: "Only a single fundamental organ has undergone great specialization in the genus *Homo.* This is the brain" (1926, p. 454). Today, from an evolutionary perspective, that assessment still is viewed as correct. As Johanson and Edgar noted seventy years later: "This change in both size and shape represents one of the most remarkable morphological shifts that has been observed in the evolutionary history of any mammal, for it entailed both an enhanced cranial capacity and a radical reorganization of brain proportions" (1996, p. 83).

We believe that the brain deserves a great deal more respect than evolutionists are willing to afford it. The late evolutionist Isaac Asimov characterized the human brain as "the most complex and orderly arrangement of matter in the universe" (1970, p. 10). When Paul Davies, professor of mathematics and physics at the Universe of Adelaide, referred to it as "the most developed and complex system known to science" (1992b, 14[5]:4), he did not overstate the case. Sherwin Nuland, in *The Wisdom of the Body*, wrote in regard to the human brain:

> Though the three pounds represent a mere 2 percent of the body weight of a 150-pound person, the quartful of brain is so metabolically active that it uses 20 percent of the oxygen we take in through our lungs. To supply this much oxygen requires a very high flow of blood. Fully 15 percent of the blood propelled into the aorta with each contraction of the left ventricle is transported directly to the brain. Not only does the brain demand a large proportion of the body's oxygen and blood but it also begins its life requiring an equivalent share, or even more, of its genes. Of the total of about 50,000 to 100,000 genes in *Homo sapi-*

> *ens*, some 30,000 code for one or another aspect of the brain. Clearly, a huge amount of genetic information is required to operate the human brain.... From all of this emerges the brain's overarching responsibility–it is the chief means by which the body's activities are coordinated and governed (1997, pp. 328,346).

James Trefil addressed the brain's complexity when he wrote:

> The brain is a physical system. **It contains about 100 billion interconnected neurons–about as many neurons as there are stars in the Milky Way galaxy**.... In the end, by mechanisms we still haven't worked out (but we will do so!), these signals are converted, by neurons in different parts of the brain, into the final signals that produce images or smells or sounds... (1996, pp. 217-218, parenthetical item in orig., emp. added).

Notice Trefil's admission that the brain works "by mechanisms we still haven't worked out." Ian Tattersall, in his book, *Becoming Human*, wrote in a similar fashion in describing the brain's marvelous sophistication–while admitting that "there's a huge amount that we don't know."

> [T]he brain is an extremely power-hungry mechanism that, because of its size, monopolizes some 20 percent of our entire energy intake.... But the matter doesn't rest there, for sheer brain size is far from the full story. **The organization–the structure–of our brains is also unique, and it is this that appears to hold the ultimate key to our remarkable cognitive powers**. There's a huge amount, of course, that we don't know about how the brain works and especially about how a mass of chemical and electrical signals can give rise to such complex effects as cognition and consciousness (1998, pp. 69,70, emp. added).

The point in Dr. Tattersall's last sentence is well taken. There is a "**huge amount that we don't know**"–including (among other things) how "a mass of chemical and electrical signals can give rise to such complex effects as cognition and consciousness." [Pardon us if we are a bit skeptical of Trefil's exuberant suggestion, "but we will do so!" On this topic, we agree wholeheartedly with Robert Jastrow of NASA, who admitted:

> Is it possible that man, with his remarkable powers of intellect and spirit, has been formed from the dust of the earth by chance alone? It is hard to accept the evolution of the human eye as a product of chance; it is even harder to accept the evolution of human intelligence as the product of random disruptions in the brain cells of our ancestors.... Among the organs of the human body, none is more difficult than the brain to explain by evolution. The powers that reside in the brain make man a different animal from all other animals (1981, pp. 98-99,104).]

In spite of the fact that "neuroscience is said to be awash with data about what the brain does, but virtually devoid of theories about how it works" (Lewin, 1992, p. 163), there are some things we **do** know.

> The brain, although being **the most complex structure existing on Earth—and perhaps in the Universe**—is a well-defined object: it is a material entity located inside the skull, which may be visualized, touched and handled. It is composed of chemical substances, enzymes and hormones which may be measured and analyzed. Its architecture is characterized by neuronal cells, pathways and synapses. Its functioning depends on neurons, which consume oxygen, exchanging chemical substance through their membranes, and maintaining states of electrical polarization interrupted by brief periods of depolarization (Cardoso, 1997/1998, emp. in orig.).

> The brain is a helmet-shaped mass of gray and white tissue about the size of a grapefruit, one to two quarts in volume, and on average weighing three pounds (Einstein's brain, for example, was 2.75 pounds). Its surface is wrinkled like that of a cleaning sponge, and its consistency is custardlike, firm enough to keep from puddling on the floor the brain case, soft enough to be scooped out with a spoon.... **The human genome database accumulated to 1995 reveals that the**

> **brain's structure is prescribed by at least 3,195 distinctive genes, 50 percent more than for any other organ or tissue**... (Wilson, 1998, p. 97, parenthetical item in orig., emp. added).

> Some overall descriptions of the properties of the human brain are instructive. For instance, **10 billion neurons are packed into the brain, each of which, on average, has a thousand links with other neurons, resulting in more than sixty thousand miles of writing. Connectivity on that scale is beyond comprehension**, but undoubtedly it is fundamental to the brain's ability to generate cognition. Although individual events in an electronic computer happen a million times faster than in the brain, **its massive connectivity and simultaneous mode of activity allows biology to outstrip technology for speed**. For instance, the fastest computer clocks up a billion or so operations a second, which pales to insignificance beside the 100 billion operations that occur in the brain of a fly at rest.... To say that the brain is a computer is a truism, because, unquestionably, what goes on in there is computation. But so far, no man-made computer matches the human brain, either in capacity or design.... Can a computer think? And, ultimately, can a computer generate a level of consciousness... (Lewin, 1992, pp. 160,163, emp. added).

> The human brain's increase in neurons is due to its greater size, not to greater density, since humans have only about 1.25 as many neurons per cubic centimeter as chimpanzees do. There are approximately 146,000 neurons per square millimeter of cortical surface. The human brain has an area of about 2,200 square centimeters and about 30 billion neurons (more than assumed until quite recently). The chimpanzee and the gorilla have brains of about 500 square centimeters, and with about 6 billion neurons (Ornstein, 1991, p. 63, parenthetical item in orig.).

Can anyone—after reading descriptions (and admissions!) such as these—really believe that the human brain is "only another organ" as Michael Lemonick claimed in *Time* magazine (2003, 161[3]:66)? Not without denying the obvious! In the January 16, 1997 issue of *Nature*, Sir Francis Crick's close collaborator, Christof Koch, wrote: "The latest work on information processing and storage at **the single cell (neuron) level reveals previously unimagined complexity and dynamism**" (385:207, parenthetical item in orig., emp. added). His concluding remarks were: "As always, we are left with a feeling of awe for the amazing complexity found in Nature" (385:210). Amazing complexity indeed!

A case in point is British evolutionist Richard Dawkins. In the preface to his book, *The Blind Watchmaker*, he discussed the brain's incredible complexity and "apparent design," and the problem posed by both.

> The computer on which I am writing these words has an information storage capacity of about 64 kilobytes (one byte is used to hold each character of text). The computer was consciously designed and deliberately manufactured. The brain with which you are understanding my words is an array of some ten million kiloneurones. Many of these billions of nerve cells have each more than a thousand "electric wires" connecting them to other neurons. Moreover, at the molecular genetic level, every single one of more than a trillion cells in the body contains about a thousand times as much precisely coded digital information as my entire computer. **The complexity of living organisms is matched by the elegant efficiency of their apparent design. If anyone doesn't agree that this amount of complex design cries out for an explanation, I give up** (1986, p. ix, emp. added).

It is no wonder that Dr. Dawkins was tempted to "give up" trying to explain the intricate design found in nature. It is that very design that is so incredibly evident in the brain.

The human brain consists of three main areas. The cerebrum is the thinking/learning center. It deciphers messages from the sensory organs and controls the voluntary muscles. Evolutionist William Beck spoke of the "architectural plan" characteristic of this region (1971, p. 444). Does not an "architectural plan" require an architect? The maintenance of equilibrium and muscle coordination occurs in the cerebellum. Finally, there is the brain stem, which has several components that control the involuntary muscles–regulating heartbeat, digestion, breathing, etc.

Let us consider several aspects of the brain's uncanny abilities. [Incidentally, human beings, unlike animals, are the only creatures who think about their brains!] The brain's memory storage capacity is incredible. It has been compared to a vast library. Evolutionist Carl Sagan of Cornell University wrote:

> The information content of the human brain expressed in bits is probably comparable to the total number of connections among the neurons–about a hundred trillion, 10^{14} bits. If written out in English, say, that information would fill some twenty million volumes, as many as in the world's largest libraries. The equivalent of twenty million books is inside the heads of every one of us. The brain is a very big place in a very small space (1980, p. 278).

It has been suggested that it would take a bookshelf 500 miles long–from San Francisco, California, to Portland, Oregon–to house the information stored in the human brain. Would anyone actually contend that this kind of information content "just happened"? Evolutionists do. A popular science journal employed this analogy.

> The brain is an immense computer with 1^{10} circuits and a memory of perhaps 10^{20} bits, each of these being five to ten orders of magnitude more complex than any computer yet built. It is still more fascinating that the brain performs this work, using only 20 to 25 watts compared to the six and ten kilowatts used by our large computers (Cahill, 1981, 89[3]:105).

One writer has suggested that "many researchers think of the brain as a computer. This comparison is inadequate. Even the most sophisticated computers that we can envision are crude compared to the almost infinite complexity and flexibility of the human brain" (Pines, 1986, p. 326). The Cray-2 supercomputer has a storage capacity about 1,000 times less than that of a human brain. One authority stated that "problem solving by a human brain exceeds by far the capacity of the most powerful computers" (*Encyclopaedia Britannica*, 1989, 2:189).

Walk into any office, hospital, or even grocery store, and you will find yourself in the presence of computers. Computers have become an integral part of everyday life–they even played a part in getting this book to you. But most intelligent individuals will agree that computers did not arrive on this planet by time, natural law, and chance. Computers are designed and manufactured, and they constantly are being improved to increase their speed and capabilities. But the computer fails miserably in comparison to the human brain. When is the last time a computer grabbed a pencil to compose a sonnet, a short story, or a poem? How many computers are capable of taking a piece of wood, fashioning it in the shape of a violin, and then sitting down to play Barber's *Adagio for Strings.* And yet evolutionists insist that the human brain–an object far more complex, and with far more capabilities than a computer –"evolved" in order to provide us with memories, emotions, the ability to reason, and the ability to talk.

Other individuals like to "simplify" the human brain down to the level of modern-day computers. They rationalize that, like computers, the human brain can rapidly process, store, and recall bits of information. Also, some scientific investigators compare neuronal connections to the wiring found within computers. However, the inner workings of a computer always can be reduced to one thing–electronics. The basic function of computers always involves the movement of an electrical charge in a semiconductor. The brain, on the other hand, operates purely on electrochemical reactions. The transmission of nerve signals involves chemicals known as neurotransmitters. Once a neuron is caused to fire, it moves these neurotransmitters into the tiny space between itself and the neighboring neurons (at the synapse) in order to stimulate them.

Additionally we know that the human brain can reason and think–i.e., we possess self-awareness. Computers have the ability to carry out multiple tasks, and they even can carry out complex processes–but not without the programming and instruction they receive from humans. Furthermore, computers do not possess the ability to reason. When asked to translate into Russian the sentence–"the spirit is willing but the flesh is weak"–one computer came up with words that meant "the vodka is fine, but the meat is tasteless" (Allan, 1989, p. 68)–which is a far cry from the original meaning. Nor are computers self-aware. In comparing a modern-day computer to the awesome power of the human brain, astrophysicist Robert Jastrow admitted: "The machine would be a prodigious artificial intelligence, but it would be only a clumsy imitation of the human brain" (1981, p. 143).

It has been estimated that if we learned something new every second of our lives, it would take three million years to exhaust the capacity of the human brain (Weiss, 1990, p. 103). Plainly put, the brain is not just an advanced computer. All those convolutions and neuronal networks are the result of an intelligent Creator. If we are able to rationalize that a computer found in the middle of the Sahara Desert did not just "happen" by random chance, then why are so many willing to believe that a far more complex human brain occurred in such a fashion?

No rational person subscribes to the notion that the computer "just happened by chance" as the result of fortuitous accidents in nature. The computer obviously was designed, and that demands a designer. Nobel laureate Sir John Eccles, an evolutionist, conceded the design evinced by the brain's amazing memory capacity when he wrote:

> We do not even begin to comprehend the functional significance of this richly complex **design**.... If we now persist in regarding the brain as a machine, then we must say that it is by far the most complicated machine in existence (1958, pp. 135,136, emp. added).

In *The Blind Watchmaker*, Dawkins admitted: "Darwinism seems more in need of advocacy than similarly established truths in other branches of science" (1986, p. xi). In other words, whereas in genuine science, certain truths/laws are demonstrable, and thus evident to the unbiased mind, such is not the case when it comes to evolution, which must have **special pleading** to make it appear legitimate. Dawkins even went so far as to say (with obvious frustration): **"It is almost as if the human brain were specifically designed to misunderstand Darwinism, and to find it hard to believe"** (p. xi, emp. added). That is absolutely correct, for the human brain was designed to think **logically**, and evolutionary theory is **not logical**. It is not reasonable to assume that chaos gave rise to order, that the nonrational produced the rational, that nonliving evolved into the living, that nonconscious became conscious, that amoral developed morality, etc.

In addition to its phenomenal memory capacity, the brain also exhibits extraordinary ability in its orchestration of muscular movements. Suppose you decide that you want to pick up a pen and some paper from your desk. Your brain will have to send signals to your hands, wrists, arms, and shoulders, which will direct the manipulation of 60 different joints and more than 100 muscles. In addition to moving the muscles directionally, the brain regulates the exact force needed for a particular task. Opening the car door of your classic 1937 Chevrolet requires 400 times more torque (turning force) than dialing a rotary-style telephone. Picking up a paper clip requires only a fraction of an ounce of force, whereas pulling on your socks and shoes necessitates about 8 to 12 pounds of force. The brain compensates for multiplied thousands of these kinds of variables in daily life. Too, it does its work efficiently in terms of energy use. One scientist observed that "half a salted peanut provides sufficient calories for an hour of intense mental effort" (Pfeiffer, 1961, p. 102).

One of the astounding features of the brain is its ability to process and react to so many different circumstances at once. While an artist is working on a painting (using his voluntary muscles at the behest of this brain), he can: smell food cooking and know whether it is turnip greens or steak; hear a dog barking and determine if it is his dog or a neighbor's; feel a breeze upon his face and sense that rain is near; and be reflecting on a warm friendship of the past. Even while all of this is taking place, the brain is regulating millions of internal bodily activities that the person never even "thinks" about.

Logical contemplation of these facts can only lead one to agree with prominent brain surgeon, Robert White, who wrote: "I am left with no choice but to acknowledge the existence of a Superior Intellect, responsible for the design and development of the incredible brain-mind relationship–something far beyond man's capacity to understand" (1978, p. 99). Jastrow himself even admitted: "It is not so easy to accept that theory [Darwin's theory of evolution by natural selection–BT/BH] as the explanation of an extraordinary organ like the brain" (1981, p. 96).

The precision and complexity of our brain, and the manner in which it is able to interact with our mind, clearly point to an intelligent Designer. Writing in the *Bulletin of Atomic Scientists*, professor Roger Sperry, a psychologist at the California Institute of Technology, observed:

> Before science, man used to think himself a free agent possessing free will. Science gives us, instead, causal determinism wherein every act is seen to follow inevitably from preceding patterns of brain excitation. Where we used to see purpose and meaning in human behavior, science now shows us a complex biophysical machine composed entirely of material elements, all of which obey inexorably the universal laws of physics and chemistry.... I find that my own conceptual working model of the brain leads to inferences that are in direct disagreement with many of the foregoing; especially I must take issue with that whole general materialistic-reductionist conception of human nature and mind that seems to emerge from the currently prevailing objective analytic approach in

> the brain-behaviour sciences. When we are led to favour the implications of modern materialism in opposition to older, more idealistic values in these and related matters, **I suspect that science may have sold society and itself a somewhat questionable bill of goods** (1966, pp. 2-3, emp. added)

We suspect so, too. Ornstein and Thompson summed it up well when they stated: "After thousands of scientists have studied it for centuries, the only word to describe it remains **amazing**" (1984, p. 21, emp. in orig.).

And it is not just the brain that is "difficult to explain by evolution." Were space to permit, we could examine numerous other body systems (e.g., digestive, reproductive, etc.), each of which provides clear and compelling evidence of design. Atheistic philosopher Paul Ricci has suggested that "Although many have difficulty understanding the tremendous **order and complexity** of functions of the human body (the eye, for example), **there is no obvious designer**" (1986, p. 191, emp. added). The only people who "have difficulty understanding the tremendous order and complexity" found in the Universe are those who have "refused to have God in their knowledge" (Romans 1:28). Such people can parrot the phrase that "there is no obvious designer," but their arguments are not convincing in light of the evidence at hand.

DISCUSSION QUESTIONS

1. Discuss why design in nature is a strong argument for the existence of God.
2. The brain has been described as the "most complex and orderly arrangement of matter in the Universe." What are some other examples of design in the human body?
3. Does the Big Bang Theory explain the complex design we see around us today?
4. Can a faithful Christian believe in the Big Bang Theory?
5. How is it that scientists can accurately predict the appearance of comets, years before their arrival?
6. If the brain–the most complex matter in the Universe–simply evolved, then how do we account for our system of morality?

Chapter 3

THE CASE FOR THE EXISTENCE OF GOD [PART III]

Rape. Murder. Adultery. These words conjure up ghastly images of actions that humans have deemed unacceptable. But ask yourself this: Why do humans possess a sense of moral law–right and wrong? Have we evolved morals, or were humans, in fact, created in the image of God? The late, eminent evolutionist of Harvard University, George Gaylord Simpson, stated that although "man is the result of a purposeless and materialistic process that did not have him in mind," nonetheless "good and evil, right and wrong, concepts irrelevant in nature except from the human viewpoint, become real and pressing features of the whole cosmos as viewed morally because **morals arise only in man**" (1967, p. 346, emp. added).

The past several decades have seen the emergence of a new discipline that now is being taught in many universities–a discipline formed specifically to combat the idea that **God** set forth a certain moral "code" for humans to follow. When college freshmen look through their course catalogs, they now find courses such as evolutionary psychology or sociobiology. Regardless of the name used to describe the class, the goal is still the same–to explain human behavior in Darwinian terms, and thus remove any biblical implications. College students now sit at the feet of professors who attempt to address–using evolutionary presuppositions–why humans rape, murder, and commit adultery.

On March 16, 2001, a biology professor of the University of New Mexico, Randy Thornhill, delivered a lecture at Simon Fraser University at Harbour Centre in Vancouver, Canada. His transcript stated that "rape is evolutionary, biological, and natural." He further argued that "rape itself is an adaptation, a product of direct selection for rape in the past. Our male ancestors became ancestors in part because they conditionally used rape" (Thornhill, 2001). In his new book, *A Natural History of Rape* (coauthored by Craig T. Palmer), Dr. Thornhill characterized rape as an "adaptive reproductive strategy" (2000). The authors contend that rape is a sexual act that has its origins in what could be called the "Darwinist imperative"–i.e., the desire to reproduce and pass on one's genes.

But the excuses for evil do not end there. In a now-famous (some would say infamous) article that he penned for the *New York Times Magazine,* MIT professor of psychology Steven Pinker argued that a civilized society should not treat mothers who kill their newborn children in the same manner that it treats those who kill either older children or adults. That's because, in Pinker's estimation, those women who murder their newborn babies may not be mad or evil, but instead are merely obeying (perhaps unconsciously) some sort of "primeval instinct" that compels them to sacrifice their children for the good of the tribe (1997).

Once organic evolution has been accepted as the correct explanation for humankind's origin, such a sad assessment becomes practically inevitable. As a result of such thinking, college professors like Thornhill and Pinker expound that murder, rape, and adultery are "natural responses" to our ancient evolutionary heritage.

The simple fact is that morals and ethics **are** important. Even those who eschew any belief in God, and consequently any absolute standard of morality/ethics, concede that morality and ethics play a critical role in man's everyday life. In his book, *Ethics Without God,* atheist Kai Nielsen admitted that to ask, "Is murder evil?," is to ask a self-answering question (1973, p. 16). While Simpson and his evolutionary cohorts of the past and present may personally believe, and want others to believe, that "man is the result of a purposeless and materialistic process that did not have him in mind," the real truth of the matter is that "purposeless and materialistic processes" are completely incapable of producing anything close to what we recognize as the undeniable traits of human morals and ethics. Thomas C. Mayberry summarized humanity's condition quite accurately when he wrote: "There is broad agreement that lying, promise breaking, killing, and so on are generally wrong" (1970, 54:113).

MORALITY AND ETHICS

If such concepts as "good and evil, right and wrong" are, in fact, "real and pressing features," how, then, should moral and ethical systems be determined? Morals and ethics are universally accepted traits among the human family. Their origin, therefore, must be explained. Simply put, there are but two options. Either morality and ethics are **theocentric**–that is, they originate from the mind of God as an external source of infinite goodness, or they are **anthropocentric**–that is, they originate from man himself (see Geisler and Corduan, 1988, pp. 109-122).

The person who refuses to acknowledge the existence of God does indeed have "little latitude of choice." Simpson was forced to conclude: "Discovery that the universe apart from man or before his coming lacks and lacked any purpose or plan has the inevitable corollary that the workings of the universe cannot provide any automatic, universal, eternal, or absolute ethical criteria of right and wrong" (1967, p. 346). Since man is viewed as little more than the last animal among many to be produced by the long, meandering process of organic evolution, this becomes problematic. In their book, *Origins*, Richard Leakey and Roger Lewin wrote: "There is now a critical need for a deep awareness that, no matter how special we are **as an animal**, we are still part of the greater balance of nature..." (1977, p. 256, emp. added). Charles Darwin declared: "There is no fundamental difference between man and the higher mammals in their mental faculties" (as quoted in Francis Darwin, 1898, 1:64). A lion is not plagued by guilt after killing a gazelle's infant offspring for its noon meal. A dog does not experience remorse after stealing a bone from one of its peers.

In 1986, British evolutionist Richard Dawkins [who has described himself as "a fairly militant atheist, with a fair degree of hostility toward religion" (see Bass, 1990, 12[4]:86)] authored a book titled *The Selfish Gene* in which he set forth his theory of genetic determinism. In summarizing the basic thesis of the book, Dawkins said: "You are for nothing. You are here to propagate your selfish genes. There is no higher purpose in life" (Bass, 12[4]:60).

Matter–by itself–is completely impotent to "evolve" any sense of moral consciousness. If there is no purpose in the Universe, as Simpson and others have asserted, then there is no purpose to morality or ethics. But the concept of a "purposeless morality," or a "purposeless ethic," is irrational. Unbelief therefore must contend, and does contend, that there is no ultimate standard of moral/ethical truth, and that morality and ethics, at best, are relative and situational. That being the case, who could ever suggest, correctly, that someone else's conduct was "wrong," or that a man "ought" or "ought not" to do thus and so? The simple fact of the matter is that infidelity cannot explain the origin of morality and ethics.

Whether the unbeliever is willing to admit it or not, if there is no God, man exists in an environment where "anything goes." Morals and ethics without God is not a pretty picture, as the following investigation of these various systems documents all too well. **Relativism**, for example, suggests that there are no universal, objective criteria for determining morals and ethics. Since all value systems are considered to be "culturally derived," all such systems are equally valid; no one system has the right to claim that it is the "correct" system by which men should determine their actions and judge their choices based on those actions.

What have been the consequences of this kind of thinking? Sexually transmitted diseases are occurring in epidemic proportions. Teenage pregnancies are rampant. Babies are born already infected with deadly diseases such as AIDS because their mothers contracted the diseases during their pregnancies and passed them on to their unborn offspring. In many places divorces are so common that they equal or outnumber marriages. Jails are filled to overflowing with rapists, stalkers, and child molesters. What else, pray tell, will have to go wrong before it becomes apparent that attempts to live without God are futile?

Utilitarianism is the edifice that stands upon the foundation of hedonism. As advocated by J.S. Mill, Jeremy Bentham, and others, it suggests that "good" is that which ultimately gives the greatest amount of pleasure to the greatest number of people. The proof of such a point, oddly enough, comes from an intriguing book written by Katherine Tait, the only daughter of renowned British agnostic, Bertrand Russell. In *My Father, Bertrand Russell*, Mrs. Tait described what it was like to live in the Russell household with her brothers. She commented, for example, that her father firmly believed that parents should teach a child "with its very first breath that it has entered into a moral world" (1975, p. 59). But as any evolutionist would, her father had great difficulty in defending such a position. Mrs. Tait recounted in her book the fact that as a child she would say "I don't want to; why should I?" when her father told her that she "ought" to do something. She noted that a normal parent might say, "Because I say so," or "because your father says so," or "because God says so." Admittedly, however, Bertrand Russell was not your "normal" parent. He would say to young Katherine, "Because more people will be happy if you do than if you don't." "So what!" she would scream. "I don't care about other people!" "Oh, but you should," her father would reply. In her youthful naïveté, Katherine would ask, "But why?" To which her father would respond: "Because more people will be happy if you do than if you don't." In the end, however, Mrs. Tait wrote: "We felt the heavy pressure of his rectitude and obeyed, but the reason was not convincing–neither to us nor to him" (pp. 184-185). Would it be convincing–for any rational human being who possessed even a smattering of common sense?

Situationism teaches that something is "right" because the **individual** determines it is right on a case-by-case basis, thus invalidating the concept of common moral law applied consistently. The atheistic authors of *Humanist Manifesto II* bluntly affirmed that "moral values derive their source from human experience. Ethics is autonomous and situational, needing no theological or ideological sanction. Ethics stems from human need and interest" (see *Humanist Manifestos*, 1973, p. 17). If a sane man therefore decided it was "right" to kill his business competitors, upon what basis could we (justifiably) ask someone (e.g., the police) to stop him without denying his autonomy and thus violating (and ultimately invalidating) the very principle upon which this ethic is supposed to work? If humans are merely "matter in motion," if no one piece of matter is worth more than any other piece of matter, if we are autonomous, if the situation warrants it, and if we can further our own selfish interests by doing so, could we not lie, steal, maim, or murder at will? Yes indeed. But who would want to live in such a society?

Determinism is the idea that man is not responsible for his actions. In its early stages, the concept flowed from the teachings of John Watson (1878-1958), a psychologist who taught at Johns Hopkins University. He believed that the long evolutionary process had imbued mankind with certain habits, from which flowed both personality and conduct. Later, psychologist B.F. Skinner of Harvard would inherit the mantle of Watson and become the primary proponent of what was known as "behavioral determinism." Ultimately, said Skinner, the concept of "human responsibility" was so much nonsense since no one was "responsible" in the true sense of the word. In more recent times, Harvard entomologist E.O. Wilson, in his book, *Sociobiology: The New Synthesis*, has suggested that determinism can be documented and studied via the concept known as "sociobiology." This attempted amalgamation between certain of the social sciences and biology propagates the view that man has been "programmed" by his genetics to act as he does. Instead of the refrain that was made popular in the 1970s by talented comedian Flip Wilson (in character as the hilarious, loud-mouthed "Geraldine"), "The devil made me do it," the mantra for the 1990s became "My genes made me do it!"

THE PRACTICAL IMPACT OF MORALS AND ETHICS WITHOUT GOD

When Martin Gardner wrote on "The Relevance of Belief Systems" in his book, *The New Age: Notes of a Fringe Watcher*, and observed that **what a person believes profoundly influences how a person acts**, he could not have been more right (1988, pp. 57-64). Nowhere has this been more true than in regard to the effect of incorrect beliefs concerning morality and ethics. And what a price we as humans have paid! In the evolutionary scheme of things, man occupies the same status as animals. He may be more knowledgeable, more intellectual, and more scheming than his counterparts in the animal kingdom. But he is still an animal. And so the question is bound to arise: Why should man be treated any differently when his life no longer is deemed worth living? Truth be told, there is no logical reason that he should. From cradle to grave, life–from an evolutionary vantage point–is completely expendable.

As an example, consider the position of the late atheist Carl Sagan and his wife, Ann Druyan. In an article on "The Question of Abortion" that they co-authored for *Parade* magazine, these two humanists contended for the ethical permissibility of human abortion on the grounds that the fetus, growing within a woman's body for several months following conception, is not a human being. Their conclusion, therefore, was this: the killing of this tiny creature is not murder (see Sagan and Druyan, 1990).

Once those who are helpless, weak, and young become expendable, who will be next? Will it be the helpless, weak, and old? Will it be those whose infirmities make them "unfit" to survive in a society that values the beautiful and the strong? Will it be those who are lame, blind, maimed? Will it be those whose IQ falls below a certain point or whose skin is a different color? Some in our society already are calling for such "cleansing" processes to be made legal, using euphemisms such as "euthanasia" or "mercy killing." After all, they shoot horses, don't they?

MORALITY, ETHICS, AND THE EXISTENCE OF GOD

When George Gaylord Simpson commented that "morals arise only in man" (1967, p. 346), he acknowledged (whether or not he intended to) the fact that morality is something unique to humankind. No two apes ever sat down and said, "Hey, I've got a good idea. Today let's talk about morals and ethics." On the same page of his book, Simpson thus was forced to admit that "the workings of the universe cannot provide any automatic, universal, eternal, or absolute ethical criteria of right and wrong."

And civilization is indeed in a "muddle" identified by a definite "decline in morality." With guns blasting, children (some as young as 10 or 11 years old) bearing a grudge or desiring to settle a score, walk into school hallways, classrooms, and libraries, shoot until they have emptied every round from all chambers, and watch gleefully as shell casings, teachers, and classmates alike fall silently at their feet. Then parents, administrators, and friends congregate amidst the bloody aftermath and wonder what went wrong. Yet why are we shocked or enraged by such conduct? Our children have been taught they are nothing more than "naked apes"–and they are intelligent enough to figure out exactly what that means. As Guy N. Woods lamented, "Convince a man that he came from a monkey, and he'll act like one!" (1976, 118[33]:514). Children have been taught that religion is an outward sign of inner weakness –a crutch used by people who are too weak and cowardly to "pull themselves up by their own boot straps." Why, then, should we be at all surprised when they react accordingly (even violently!)? After all, "nature," said the famed British poet Alfred Lord Tennyson, "is red in tooth and claw."

The truth of the matter is that only the theocentric approach to this problem is consistent logically and internally; only the theocentric approach can provide an objective, absolute set of morals and ethics. But why is this the case? True morality is based on the fact of the unchanging nature of Almighty God. He is eternal (Psalm 90:2; 1 Timothy 1:17), holy (Isaiah 6:3; Revelation 4:8), just and righteous (Psalm 89:14), and forever consistent (Malachi 3:6). In the ultimate sense, only He is good (Mark 10:18). Furthermore, since He is perfect (Matthew 5:48), the morality that issues from such a God is good, unchanging, just, and consistent–i.e., exactly the opposite of the relativistic, deterministic, or situational ethics of the world.

When Newman suggested that we as humans "feel responsibility," it was a recognition on his part that there is indeed within each man, woman, and child a sense of moral responsibility which derives from the fact that God is our Creator (Psalm 100:3) and that we have been fashioned in His spiritual image (Genesis 1:26-27). As the potter has sovereign right over the clay with which he works (Romans 9:21), so our Maker has the sovereign right over His creation since in His hand "is the soul of every living thing" (Job 12:10). As the patriarch Job learned much too late, God is not a man with whom one can argue (Job 9:32).

Whatever God does, commands, and approves is good (Psalm 119:39,68; cf. Genesis 18:25). What He has commanded results from the essence of His being–Who He is–and therefore also is good. In the Old Testament, the prophet Micah declared of God: "He showed thee, O man, what is good; and what doth Jehovah require of thee, but to do justly, and to love kindness, and walk humbly with thy God" (Micah 6:8). In the New Testament, the apostle Peter admonished: "As he who called you is holy, be ye yourselves also holy in all manner of living; because it is written, 'Ye shall be holy: for I am holy'" (1 Peter 1:15).

The basic thrust of God-based ethics concerns the relationship of man to the One Who created and sustains him. God Himself is the unchanging standard of moral law. His perfectly holy nature is the ground or basis upon which "right" and "wrong," "good" and "evil" are determined. The Divine will–expressive of the very nature of God–constitutes the ultimate ground of moral obligation. Why are we to pursue holiness? Because God is holy (Leviticus 19:1; 1 Peter 1:16). Why are we not to lie, cheat, or steal (Colossians 3:9)? Because God's nature is such that He cannot lie (Titus 1:2; Hebrews 6:18). Since God's nature is unchanging, it follows that moral law, which reflects the divine nature, is equally immutable.

While there have been times in human history when each man "did that which was right in his own eyes" (Judges 17:6), that never was God's plan. He has not left us to our own devices to determine what is right and wrong because He knew that through sin, man's heart would become "exceedingly corrupt" (Jeremiah 17:9). Therefore, God "has spoken" (Hebrews 1:1), and in so doing He has made known to man His laws and precepts through the revelation He has provided in written form within the Bible (1 Corinthians 2:11ff.; 2 Timothy 3:16-17; 2 Peter 1:20-21). Thus, mankind is expected to act in a morally responsible manner (Matthew 19:9; Acts 14:15-16; 17:30; Hebrews 10:28ff.) in accordance with biblical laws and precepts. In addressing this point, Wayne Jackson commented that the Bible "contains many rich **principles** which challenge us to develop a greater sense of spiritual maturity and to soar to heights that are God-honoring.... Our Creator has placed us 'on our honor' to grow to greater heights.... [Biblical] morality runs deep into the soul; it challenges us to get our hearts under control" (1984, 4:23, emp. in orig.).

David Lipe, speaking as both a philosopher and a theist, has suggested that for quite some time, certain philosophers and theologians generally have "turned away from" standard textbook arguments for the existence of God, not because the doctrines were weak or had been disproved, but because "morality has furnished the main support" (1987, 7:26). Indeed it has.

Miethe and Habermas were correct when they suggested that "naturalism is not even close to being the best explanation for the existence of our moral conscience" (1993, p. 219). Man's moral and ethical nature, as Newman proclaimed, "implies that there is One to whom we are responsible...a Supreme Governor, a Judge, holy, just, powerful" (1887, pp. 105,106). Eventually, each of us will meet "the righteous judgment of God, who will render to every man according to his works" (Romans 2:5-6). It therefore behooves us to "live soberly, righteously, and godly in this present age" (Titus 2:12) for, as Carnell put it:

> Death is the one sure arch under which all men must pass. But if death ends all–and it very well may unless we have inerrant revelation to assure us to the contrary–what virtue is there in present striving? Job...expressed [that] man lives as if there is a sense to life, but in the end, his mortal remains provide but a banquet for the worms, for man dies and "The worm shall feed sweetly on him" (Job 24:20).... The only full relief man can find from the clutches of these "tiny cannibals" is to locate some point of reference outside of the flux of time and space which can serve as an elevated place of rest. In Christianity, and in it alone, we find the necessary help, the help of the Almighty, He who rules eternity (1948, pp. 332,333).

CONCLUSION

So where did man learn to differentiate right from wrong? The Bible clearly demonstrates that whatever God does, commands, and approves is good (Psalm 119:39,68; cf. Genesis 18:25). What He has commanded results from the essence of His being–Who He is–and therefore also is good. In the Old Testament, the prophet Micah declared of God: "He showed thee, O man, what is good; and what doth Jehovah require of thee, but to do justly, and to love kindness, and walk humbly with thy God" (Micah 6:8). In the New Testament, the apostle Peter admonished: "As he who called you is holy, be ye yourselves also holy in all manner of living; because it is written, 'Ye shall be holy: for I am holy'" (1 Peter 1:15).

The basic thrust of God-based ethics concerns the relationship of man to the One Who created and sustains him. **God Himself is the unchanging standard of moral law**. His perfectly holy nature is the ground or basis upon which "right" and "wrong," "good" and "evil" are determined. Neither evolution-based ethics nor humanistic based ethics can provide an **absolute** moral standard. Only God-based ethics can do that.

DISCUSSION QUESTIONS

1. Discuss the difference between **theocentric** and **anthropocentric** systems of morality. Why does the anthropocentric position leave evolutionists in such a quandary when it comes to explaining the existence of morality in humans?
2. If humans are little more than advanced ape-like creatures, then why would it be wrong for us to rape, steal, or kill—especially if we are merely trying to survive and further our genealogical line (survival of the fittest)?
3. Discuss why the following statement is self-contradictory: "Ethics is both situational and autonomous."
4. How does evolutionary theory account for human consciousness? How would creationists account for the fact that humans are "self-aware"?
5. Why do most evolutionists want to reduce everything to purely materialistic causes?

Chapter 4

WHAT ABOUT EVIL, PAIN, AND SUFFERING?

The images have now been forever etched into the recesses of our minds. A generation never will forget the pictures of that hijacked plane purposefully nose-diving into the south tower of the World Trade Center on September 11, 2001. Then, before we had time to catch our breath and fully comprehend what was happening, both towers imploded and careened toward the ground–leaving everything for miles around covered in a morose gray ash. As our brains began to calculate the horror of this tragedy, we quickly learned that there were, in fact, other hijacked planes and more victims subjected to flaming rubble. In the blink of an eye, countless individuals lost their lives–some choosing to do so in a calculated attempt to cripple the United States. But the majority were innocent men, women, and children–men, women, and children who started that fateful day by going about their normal routines, never expecting to take that final step into eternity on that tragic day of September 11.

As news crews scrambled to provide us with the most shocking images and the most heart-rending stories some of us have ever seen or heard, a quiet but detectable uncertainty began to ripple throughout communities in light of these tragic events: "Where was God, and why did He let this happen to so many innocent people?" Had we been forgotten? A semblance of these questions was echoed thousands of years ago by King David, who desperately asked: "Why standest thou afar off, O Lord? Why hidest thou thyself in times of trouble?" (Psalm 10:1). The Israelite Gideon lamented: "Oh my lord, if Jehovah is with us, why then is all this befallen us?" (Judges 6:13). During tragedies like the attacks on the World Trade Center towers in New York and the Pentagon outside of Washington, D.C., questions similar to these are heralded not only from street corners in front of news cameras, but also whispered through sobs and tears in the dark recesses of private bedroom closets.

The appeal is simple enough to understand: "If there really is a God, then why did so many people die?" Evolutionists often phrase it this way: "If God is a loving God, then why do bad things happen to good people?" This simple question frequently becomes a stumbling block for some individuals–who end up making a conscientious decision not to believe in God. Many rationalize it this way: if God can prevent evil, but won't, then He is not good; or if He wants to prevent evil, but cannot, then He is not all-powerful. Unfortunately, all too often it is during pain and suffering that we forget that God is in the same place now that He was when His own Son was being maliciously nailed to an old rugged cross almost two thousand years ago. And how thankful we should be that on **that** grim day, God **did** remain in heaven as the sin of all humanity was placed on His Son's back and nailed to that cross. Had Christ not died for our sins, we would have no hope of inheriting heaven (1 Corinthians 15).

Thanks to God's incredible love (1 John 4:8), humanity has been endowed with free will (see Genesis 2:16-17; Joshua 24:15; Isaiah 7:15; John 5:39-40; 7:17; Revelation 22:17). God loves us enough to allow us freedom of choice. Thus, all of those responsible for the savage attack upon the World Trade Center toward and the Pentagon woke up that Tuesday morning with the freedom to choose what they wanted to do or where they wanted to go, for we know that God is "no respecter of persons" (Acts 10:34).

Evolutionists are quick to ask why, then, didn't God reach down and save those innocent people? Why didn't He just stretch out His almighty arm and cradle those thousands of innocent lives in the palm of His hand? As odd as it may sound at first, God did not act in such a fashion because He loves us! We live in a world regulated by natural laws that were established at the creation of this world. For example, the laws of gravity and motion behave consistently. Thus, if you step off the roof of a fifteen-story building, gravity will pull you to the pavement beneath and you will die. If you step in front of a moving bus, the laws of motion will keep that bus in motion, even though it will result in your death. But individuals still ask, "Why?" Why could not God intervene to prevent such disasters? Think for just a moment what sort of world would this be if God directly intervened, suspending His natural laws, every time a human encountered a life-threatening situation. This would cause indescribable chaos and confusion all over our planet. This chaotic, haphazard system would argue more for atheism than it would for theism!

Where was God when that plane full of innocent passengers slammed into the south tower of the World Trade Center? He was right where He has always been–in heaven, on His holy mountain (Psalm 15:1), with Christ at His side (Mark 16:19), in a place where there is no suffering. We must remember that while we may not understand every facet of human suffering in the here and now, we can explain enough to negate the charge that misery is incompatible with the existence of God. And we must yearn with every fiber of our being to make our permanent abode in those heavenly mansions (John 14:1-3) where "the wicked cease from troubling and there the weary are at rest" (Job 3:17) God did not forget us on September 11th, just as He did not forget Christ when He hung on that cruel cross of Calvary.

WHY DOES GOD ALLOW SUFFERING?

But why does God allow human suffering? As we answer that question, let us make it clear that the Word of God must be used as the main source in this discussion; after all, both the problem and the solution can be found within its pages. Think with us: Where does the idea originate that God is all-powerful? It does not come from science or philosophy. Rather, the idea derives from passages within the Bible such as Genesis 17:1 where God said, "I am Almighty God," or Matthew 19:26 where Jesus said, "With men this is impossible, but with God all things are possible." And the same principle applies to the idea that God is all-loving (1 John 4:8,16).

Unfortunately, when we appeal to the Bible for an answer to the problem of evil, pain, and suffering, some people object. They say that we should not use the Bible, but they do not realize that **they** used the Bible to formulate the problem. After all, if the Bible did not teach that God is all-loving and all- powerful, then this problem would not exist in the first place. Therefore, we can and must use the Bible to find the solution to the problem.

One important point that must not be overlooked is this: **after God had finished creating everything, it was very good** (Genesis 1:31). However, Adam and Eve sinned against God, and as a result brought pain and suffering into the world. God always has given human beings the right to make their own decisions. He did not create us as robots that have no choice. In Psalm 32:9, King David wrote: "Do not be like the horse or like the mule, which have no understanding, which must be harnessed with bit and bridle, else they will not come near you." God never has **forced** (and never will force) humans to obey Him. He does not want us to be like the horse or mule that must be forced into His service. Instead, He graciously allows humans to make their own decisions. Much of the suffering present in the world today is a direct result of the misuse of the freedom of choice of past generations. Paul wrote in Romans 5:18: "Therefore, as through one man's offense judgment came to all men." Mankind–not God–is to blame for the suffering in this world.

But do not think that **all** the pain and suffering in this world can be blamed on past generations. Each one of us makes wrong decisions and incorrect judgments, and in doing so, we frequently inflict pain and suffering upon ourselves and upon others. The young man who decides to "sow his wild oats" eventually will learn that every person reaps what he sows (Galatians 6:7).

Many destitute people have awakened in a gutter because they freely chose to get drunk the night before. Many teenage girls have become pregnant out of wedlock due to poor decisions and lack of will power. And many drunk drivers have killed themselves, their passengers, and innocent victims, because they chose not to relinquish the keys.

All of us must understand that actions have consequences! What we do today can (and often does) determine what our life will be like tomorrow. God will allow us to be forgiven of our sins, but He will not always remove the painful consequences of our actions. Let's face it: **much of the pain and suffering that we experience in this world is our own fault!**

In addition, as we mentioned earlier, God created a world that is ruled by natural laws. If a man steps off the roof of the Empire State Building, gravity will pull him to his death below. If a boy steps in front of a moving freight train, the momentum of the train most likely will kill the child. All of nature is regulated by natural laws set in place by God. They are the same for everyone (believer and unbeliever alike). In Luke 13:2-5, Jesus told the story of eighteen people who died when the tower of Siloam fell on them. Did they die because they were more wicked or more deserving of death than others around them? No, they died because of natural laws that were in effect. Fortunately, natural laws are constant so that we can study them and benefit from them. We are not left to sort out some kind of random system that works one day but not the next.

Furthermore, there are times when suffering is beneficial. Think of the man whose chest begins to throb as he begins to have a heart attack, or the woman whose side starts to ache at the onset of appendicitis. Pain often sends us to the doctor for prevention or cure. Also, tragedy can help humans develop some of the most treasured traits known to mankind–bravery, heroism, and self-sacrifice–all of which flourish in less-than-perfect circumstances. Yet those who exhibit such qualities usually are said to have gone "above and beyond the call of duty." Wasn't that the point Christ was making in John 15:13 when He said, "Greater love has no one than this, than to lay down one's life for his friends"?

But sometimes there seems to be no logical explanation for the immense suffering that a person is experiencing. Take the Old Testament character of Job as an example. He lost ten children and all of his wealth in a few short hours. Yet the Bible describes him as upright and righteous. Why would God allow such a man to suffer? James 1:2-3 helps us see the answer: "My brethren, count it all joy when you fall into various trials, knowing that the testing of your faith produces patience." Jesus Christ was the only truly innocent individual ever to live, yet even He suffered immensely. The fact is, pain and suffering have benefits that we sometimes cannot see and therefore do not appreciate. But God knows what is best for us in the long run.

Instead of blaming God for pain, or denying His existence, we should be looking to Him for strength, and let tragedies remind us that this world never was intended to be our final home (read Hebrews 11:13-16). James 4:14 instructs us regarding the fact that our time on this Earth is extremely brief. The fact that even the Son of God was subjected to incredible evil, pain, and suffering (Hebrews 5:8; 1 Peter 2:21ff.), proves that God does love and care for His creation. He could have abandoned us to our own sinful devices, but instead, "God demonstrates His own love toward us, in that while we were still sinners, Christ died for us" (Romans 5:8).

Surely, it can be said without fear of contradiction that one of the most frequent, and thus one of the most important, causes of unbelief is the existence of evil, pain, and suffering in the world. But before we explore this concept, let us take a momentary diversion to separate the **genuine** problem from the **counterfeit**. When an individual claims not to believe in God because of the problem of evil, pain, and suffering, the person **making** such a claim may mean something entirely different than what the person **hearing** the claim thinks he means. Allow us to explain.

Admittedly, some people have difficulty believing in God because of what they consider to be **real intellectual obstacles** to such a belief. An *ex nihilo* (from nothing) creation, a virgin birth, or the bodily resurrection of Christ from the dead cause some to consider belief in God on par with belief in the Tooth Fairy or Santa Claus. Such concepts represent insurmountable barriers to the acceptance of God's existence.

Other people, however, face no such intellectual obstacles. Instead, they simply do not want to have to deal with the issue of the ultimate existence of a transcendent God. Their refusal to believe is not based necessarily on "this" barrier or "that" barrier. Rather, belief in God simply is inconvenient at best, or bothersome at worst. In a chapter titled "What Keeps People from Becoming Christians?" in his timely book, *Intellectuals Don't Need God*, Alister McGrath exerted considerable effort in an attempt to separate the claims of these two types of individuals when he wrote:

> "I could never be a Christian because of the problem of suffering" can mean two quite different things: (a) Having thought the matter through carefully, it seems to me that there is a real problem posed to the intellectual coherence of the Christian faith because of the existence of human suffering; (b) I don't want to get involved in a discussion about Christianity, which could get very personal and threatening. But I don't want to admit this, as it might seem to imply that I lack intellectual courage, stamina, or honesty. I can

> save face by letting it be understood that there are good grounds for my rejection of Christianity. So let me select a problem...suffering will do very nicely. Anyway, it will stall the efforts of this guy who's trying to convert me.
>
> For some, then, throwing intellectual problems at the Christian evangelist is like a warplane ejecting flares to divert heat-seeking missiles. It is a decoy meant to divert a deadly attack. But intellectual difficulties nevertheless constitute a real problem for some people, and answers must be given to their difficulties (1993, pp. 64-65, ellipsis in orig.).

It is not our intention here to deal with those in the second category who use the problem of evil, pain, and suffering merely as a ruse to hide their own cowardice in the face of overwhelming evidence regarding the existence of God. Likely, no evidence ever could convince them. Rather, we would like to discuss the unbelief of those who fall into the first category–i.e., people who view the co-existence of God and moral evil as an intellectual inconsistency that is incapable of being solved. Their number is legion, and their tribe is increasing.

For example, consider the following assessments offered by a variety of writers that runs the gamut from a Nobel laureate to a former well-known televangelist. The Nobel laureate is Steven Weinberg, author of *Dreams of a Final Theory*, which includes a chapter titled "What About God?" Within that chapter these comments can be found.

> I have to admit that sometimes nature seems more beautiful than strictly necessary. Outside the window of my home office there is a hackberry tree, visited frequently by a convocation of politic birds: blue jays, yellow-throated vireos, and, loveliest of all, an occasional red cardinal. Although I understand pretty well how brightly colored feathers evolved out of a competition for mates, it is almost irresistible to imagine that all this beauty was somehow laid on for our benefit. **But the God of birds and trees would have to be also the God of birth defects and cancer**....

> Remembrance of the Holocaust leaves me unsympathetic to attempts to justify the ways of God to man. **If there is a God that has special plan**s for humans, then He has taken very great pains to hide His concern for us (1993, pp. 250-251, emp. added).

The former well-known televangelist is Charles B. Templeton, a high school dropout who, according to one writer, has "the natural flare and fluidity of a salesman" (Lockerbie, 1998, p. 228). He served for many years as the pulpit minister for the Avenue Road Church (Toronto, Ontario, Canada) where his ubiquitous "Youth for Christ" rallies in the late 1940s were extremely popular. Eventually he became a world-renowned evangelist with the Billy Graham Crusade. Then, one day, he quit. He abandoned it all–not just the Billy Graham Crusade, but belief in God, belief in Christ, belief in the Bible, belief in heaven–everything! He explained why in his book, *Farewell to God.*

> I was ridding myself of archaic, outdated notions. I was dealing with life as it is. There would be an end to asking the deity for his special interventions on my behalf because I was one of the family.... If there is a loving God, why does he permit–much less create–earthquakes, droughts, floods, tornadoes, and other natural disasters which kill thousands of innocent men, women, and children every year? How can a loving, omnipotent God permit–much less create–encephalitis, cerebral palsy, brain cancer, leprosy, Alzheimer's and other incurable illnesses to afflict millions of men, women, and children, most of whom are decent people? (1996, pp. 221,230).

It is not our intention here to provide an in-depth response to these (or similar) accusations. These matters have been dealt with elsewhere in detail (see: Jackson, 1988; Major, 1998; Thompson, 1990, 1993; Thompson and Jackson, 1992). Instead, we merely would like to document the role that evil, pain, and suffering have played, and still continue to play, as an important cause of man's unbelief.

Many have been those who, through the ages, have abandoned their belief in God because of the presence of evil, pain, and suffering in their lives or in the lives of those close to them. Charles Darwin abandoned once and for all any vestige of belief in God after the death of his oldest daughter, Annie (see Desmond and Moore, 1991, pp. 384,386-387). But Darwin was not the only one so affected. Nine years later, on September 15, 1860, Thomas Huxley was to watch his oldest son, four-year-old Noel, die in his arms from scarlet fever. In their massive, scholarly biography, *Darwin,* Desmond and Moore wrote that the tragedy of Noel's death brought Huxley "...to the edge of a breakdown. Huxley tried to rationalize the 'holy leave-taking' as he stood over the body, with its staring blue eyes and tangled golden hair, **but the tragedy left a deep scar**" (1991, p. 503, emp. added).

At Noel's funeral, the minister briefly referred to 1 Corinthians 15:14-19 in his eulogy. When he quoted the passage from that section of Scripture which mentions, "if the dead be not raised," Huxley was outraged. Eight days after Noel's death, on September 23, he wrote to his close friend, Charles Kingsley, about the minister's words: "I cannot tell you how inexpressibly they shocked me. [The preacher–BT/BH] had neither wife nor child, or he must have known that his alternative involved a blasphemy against all that was best and noblest in human nature. I could have laughed with scorn" (see Leonard Huxley, 1900, 1:151-152). In the equally scholarly (and equally massive) companion biography that he authored, *Huxley,* Adrian Desmond wrote of the man known as "Darwin's Bulldog" on the day of his son's death:

> He sat in the study facing the tiny body. His emotions were unleashed as he looked back to that New Year's Eve 1856, when he had sat at the same desk and pledged on his son's birth to give "a new and healthier direction to all Biological Science." He had found redemption on his son's death. There was no blame, **only submission to Nature**, and that brought its own catharsis (1997, p. 287, emp. added).

"Submission to Nature" became Huxley's watchword. Belief in God–however feeble it may have been prior to Noel's death –now had evaporated completely. All that remained was to give "a new and healthier direction to all Biological Science." And so it was to "Nature" that Huxley devoted the remainder of his life.

But not all such events have occurred in centuries long since gone. Modern-day parallels abound. Samuel Langhorne Clemens (a.k.a. Mark Twain) became implacably embittered against God after the death, in 1896, of his favorite daughter, Suzy. Famed English novelist, W. Somerset Maugham, recounted in his autobiography, *The Summing Up*, how that as a youngster he had prayed to God one night that he might be delivered from the terrible speech impediment that afflicted him. The next day he arose, only to find that the impediment still was present. So profound was his grief and disappointment at the failure of God to cure him overnight that from that point forward he pledged never to believe in God again.

In the mid-1960s, a devoutly religious young man from Chattanooga, Tennessee was a role model for all of his classmates. He led a prayer group, and planned to become a foreign missionary–until his sister died of leukemia and his father committed suicide. The boy's belief in God collapsed, and he subsequently became one of America's most outspoken unbelievers, humanists, and pro-abortion advocates. That boy's name?–Ted Turner, founder of world-famous CNN, the Turner Broadcasting System, and other well-known media enterprises.

Time and space would fail us if we were to attempt merely to enumerate, much less discuss, all those who have abandoned belief in God because of evil, pain, and suffering in their lives or in the lives of those close to them. In the end, however, the most important question is not, "Why did 'this' or 'that' happen to me?," but instead, "How can I understand what has happened, and how am I going to react to it?" As McGrath put it:

> The sufferings of this earth are for real. They are painful. God is deeply pained by our suffering, just as we are shocked, grieved, and mystified by the suffering of our family and friends. But that is only half of the story. The other half must be told. It is natural that our attention should be fixed on what we experience and feel here and now. But faith demands that we raise our sights and look ahead to what lies ahead. We may suffer as we journey–but where are we going? What lies ahead? (1993, pp. 105-106).

Instead of blaming God because evil, pain, and suffering exist, we should turn to Him for strength, and let tragedies, of whatever nature, remind us that this world never was intended to be a final home (Hebrews 11:13-16). Our time here is temporary (James 4:14), and with God's help, we are able to overcome whatever comes our way (Romans 8:35-39; Psalm 46:1-3). With Peter, the faithful believer can echo the sentiment that God, "who called you unto his eternal glory in Christ, after that ye have suffered a little while, shall himself perfect, establish, strengthen you" (1 Peter 5:10).

The unbeliever, for reasons known only to himself, either is unable, or unwilling, to concede the love of God. That–not the current evil, pain, or suffering that he currently endures–is the greatest tragedy of his life.

DISCUSSION QUESTIONS

1. In the first century, what was a major opinion concerning the cause of pain and death (John 9:1-3; Luke 13:1-5)? In what two ways did Jesus alter the popular opinion on the issue?

2. Jesus taught that a person's suffering is not always the result of his or her sinful behavior (John 9:1-3). Many righteous people suffer while, on the other hand, some very sinful people prosper. How, then, do we explain such biblical statements as those found in Proverbs 10:6 and 12:7? (Note that the entire book of Job deals with this issue.)

3. Discuss some instances in which pain actually can be beneficial. Use both physical and spiritual examples. James 1:1-5, 2 Corinthians 7:8-10, and Proverbs 13:24 can help.

4. Even though all suffering is not a result of individual sin, some is. Discuss ways that people bring suffering on themselves. How do passages such as Romans 1:27, Hebrews 12:4-11, and Proverbs 23:29-35 enter into this discussion?

5. Think about the suffering that may have occurred in your life. What suffering did you bring upon yourself? What have you learned from it? How can you use what you have learned to help others?

Chapter 5

IS THE BIBLE FROM GOD?

With the existence of God established, it becomes reasonable to think that such a Creator-God would wish to communicate with His creation. Mankind shows evidence of high intelligence, kindness, goodness, justice, and many other unique characteristics. Since it is inconceivable that the Creator could be inferior to His creation in any fashion, and since the effect never is greater than the cause, it is inevitable that God would exhibit infinite intelligence, kindness, goodness, justice, etc. Therefore, some form of personal communication between the intelligent Creator and His intelligent creature would be expected. Else, how could mankind ever come to know, or appreciate, certain aspects of the Creator, or understand what the Creator might possibly require of the beings He had created?

Lacking adequate revelation from God, we would have no accurate way of understanding what we needed to know regarding God, His Son, our place in the creation, and many other topics of ultimate importance to humanity. We would have no objective standard upon which to base ethics and morals. We would know little of the ministry and message of Jesus of Nazareth. We would have no information regarding the theological purpose of His crucifixion and resurrection—namely, that they were essential ingredients in God's plan to offer ruined man a way of escape from the devastating consequences of his sin (Matthew 20:28; 26:28). We would know nothing of how to enter that sacred body of saved souls, the church (Ephesians 5:23; 1 Corinthians 12:13), or how, once we had entered, to worship God correctly. Without God's revelation, we would know utterly nothing about these important spiritual matters that impact our eternal destiny. Truly, we should be grateful to God for providing us with a revelation that could be retained in a permanent form, studied faithfully, and used profitably by all of mankind.

A revelation from God might take almost any form. God could choose to communicate with His creation directly via word of mouth, through messengers (e.g., angels), or through dreams and visions. For that matter, He could choose any means that suited the occasion. Seemingly, however, the most appropriate medium for long-term results would be one that ensured permanence. That is to say, it would withstand the test of time and could be passed faithfully from generation to generation throughout human history. One possible way to accomplish such a goal would be to produce the revelation in a written form that could be duplicated and distributed as needed, thus benefiting the whole of mankind across the ages.

The question then becomes: Is there any evidence that mankind possesses such a revelation? And the answer to that question is: Yes, evidence does exist to establish the claim that God has given mankind His revelation in the written form known as the Bible. B.C. Goodpasture, the distinguished editor of the *Gospel Advocate* for almost forty years (1939-1977), wrote:

> The nature and contents of the Bible are such that the rank and file of its readers in all generations have recognized God as its author. Man would not have written such a book, if he could; and could not, if he would. It moves on a superhuman plane in design, in nature, and in teaching. It caters not to worldly desire and ambition. It condemns much which men in the flesh highly prize, and commends much which they despise. Its thoughts are not the thoughts of men (1970, p. 54).

WHAT DOES THE BIBLE CONTAIN?

The fact that the Bible exists in the first place brings to mind the question: What does the Bible contain? It contains two things: (1) known facts; and (2) revelation. What is the difference between the two?

When we say that the Bible contains "known facts," we mean that it contains information known to the people of that time and place. For example, if the Bible mentions people known as Hittites (Exodus 23:28), then historical records could verify their existence. If the Bible mentions that the Roman emperor, Caesar Augustus, commanded that a census be taken at a certain time (Luke 2:1), then we could set about corroborating the truthfulness of such a statement.

But to say that the Bible "contains" known facts implies that it also contains something else. That "something else" is revelation. By definition, revelation designates the unveiling of facts and truths to man by God–facts and truths that man, on his own, otherwise could not have known. Revelation has reference to the communication of information.

Compare and contrast the following. When Moses wrote in the book of Numbers about Israel's wilderness wanderings, he did not need revelation from God to do so. He was their leader during that period, and simply wrote what he observed as an eyewitness. When Luke penned the book in the New Testament that bears his name, he did not need revelation from God to do so. He acknowledged as much when he said: "It seemed good to me also, **having traced the course of all things accurately from the first**, to write unto thee in order, most excellent Theophilus" (Luke 1:3, emp. added). Luke had been on certain of the missionary journeys, and thus was able to write from firsthand experience.

On the other hand, notice Moses' statement in Deuteronomy 29:29: "The secret things belong unto Jehovah our God; but **the things that are revealed** belong unto us and to our children for ever, that we may do all the words of this law" (emp. added). As an illustration of this fact, we may observe that Moses would have had absolutely no way to know the details of the Creation week (Genesis 1:1ff.) unless God Himself had revealed those details to Moses. Nor could the apostle John have described in such a beautiful panorama the splendors of heaven (as he did within the book of Revelation), unless God first described to John the splendors of heaven.

On occasion, the various Bible writers could, and did, place into print what they saw, or what they had been told by credible witnesses. When they penned such matters, they had no need of revelation from God, since they wrote from firsthand experience. At times, however, they wrote about things they neither had experienced nor had been told by others. When they did so, it was God's revelation that provided them the information they needed (Amos 3:7; Daniel 2:28; Ephesians 3:3-5).

THE BIBLE'S CLAIMS FOR ITS OWN INSPIRATION

Imagine, if you can, that somehow you could have access to every religious book that has ever been written. Imagine, also, that you could run those books through some sort of a sieve, to winnow out only those volumes that claimed to be a creed book, by which you should pattern and live your life. That, admittedly, would be a tough test and one that, likely, very few books could pass. Then, imagine further that you could take the books that passed this test, and run them through a second sieve. This time you would winnow out only those books that claimed to be both a creed book for regulating your life **and inspired of God**. Interestingly, you could count that number on the fingers of two hands.

The claim of inspiration at the hand of God is rare indeed. Sadly, misguided devotees of various religions clamor about, defending this book or that book as allegedly being "inspired of God," when, in fact, the books themselves do not even make such a claim. So, the first question that should be asked of any volume for which inspiration is touted is this: Does the **book itself** claim to be inspired?

When it comes to the Bible, that question can be answered in the affirmative. In his first letter to his coworker, Timothy, Paul stated: "All scripture is given by inspiration of God, and is profitable for doctrine, for reproof, for correction, for instruction in righteousness: That the man of God may be perfect, throughly furnished unto all good works" (2 Timothy 3: 16-17). Peter wrote: "Knowing this first, that no prophecy of scripture is of private interpretation. For no prophecy ever came by the will of man: but men spake from God, being moved by the Holy Spirit" (2 Peter 1:20-21). When he wrote his first epistle to the Christians at Corinth, Paul reminded them:

> But we received, not the spirit of the world, but the spirit which is from God; that we might know the things that were freely given to us of God. Which things also we speak, not in words which man's wisdom teacheth, but which the Spirit teacheth; combining spiritual things with spiritual words (1 Corinthians 2:12-13).

Furthermore, statements such as "God said..." or "these are the words of the Lord..." appear thousands of times in both the Old and New Testaments. Moses wrote in Exodus 20:1: "And God spake all these words...." The psalmist wrote in 119:89: "For ever, O Jehovah, Thy word is settled in heaven." In Matthew 22:31, the Lord asked: "Have ye not read that which was spoken unto you by God?" In fact, "[t]here are 2,700 such statements in the Old Testament alone, all of which make direct claim that the Bible is the Word of God" (Ridenour, 1967, p. 2).

When the Bible claims to be "inspired," what is meant by that term? The English term "inspiration" derives from the Latin *inspirare*, which means "to breathe upon or into something." The five English words, "given by inspiration of God," in the King James Version of 1611 actually are translated from the single Greek adjective, *theopneustos*, which is derived from two Greek root words (*theos*–God, *pneo*–to blow or breathe). *Pneuma*, meaning "spirit," comes from the verb *pneo*. *Pneustos*, then, might mean "spirited," and *theopneustos* would mean God-spirited, God-breathed, filled with the breath of God, the product of the divine breath (or Spirit), or given by God through the Spirit. The word implies an influence from without producing effects that are beyond natural powers. "Inspiration," then, is used for the condition of **being directly under divine influence**. Paul's point was that every scripture is "God breathed." [The word "scripture" in 2 Timothy 3:16 refers primarily to the Old Testament Scriptures. However, as the New Testament was written, it, too, was referred to as "scripture." Peter, for example, referred to Paul's epistles as authoritative "scripture" (2 Peter 3:15-16). Thus, "all scripture" refers to both testaments.]

One searches in vain in the Bible for an exact statement containing the details of **how** God related to the apostles and others in the production of the words they spoke or wrote. We know that the Spirit spoke by men, and that His word was on their tongues (2 Samuel 23:2). We know the Holy Spirit spoke by the mouth of men (Acts 1:16). We know the things spoken were in words taught by the Holy Spirit (1 Corinthians 2:12-13). But no one knows the exact details of how the Spirit guided, superintended, guaranteed, and produced the end result. There are hidden details here that we may not presume to know. Holy men of God spoke as they were moved by the Spirit (2 Peter 1:20-21), guaranteeing that all Scripture is inspired of God (2 Timothy 3:16-17). But one must be content with these and similar statements. God simply has not spelled out the details of exactly how His Spirit entered into the minds of the writers, or how He worked with their hands as they wrote. The point is that the work produced was God's Word, not man's. As such, it bears His divine stamp.

When Peter wrote in 2 Peter 1:20-21 that "men spake from God, being **moved** by the Holy Spirit," he employed the Greek word *pheromenoi*, which literally means "borne along." His point was that the Bible writers did not speak from themselves, but were "borne along" by God's Holy Spirit to write what they did. The Bible writers never credited their words to mere human reason. Both Old and New Testament passages bear this out. In 2 Samuel 23:2 it is written: "The Spirit of Jehovah spake by me, And his word was upon my tongue."

In Acts 1:16, Luke observed that "the Holy Spirit spake before by the mouth of David." Likely, however, the best explanatory passage regarding inspiration is Paul's commentary in 1 Corinthians 2:12-13, wherein he affirmed that the information the Bible writers received came not from human wisdom, but directly from God. Further, that wisdom was not expressed in man's choice of words, but via words guided by the Holy Spirit.

The correct view of inspiration holds that men wrote exactly what God wanted them to write, without errors or mistakes, yet with their own personalities in evidence in their writings. Such inspiration is referred to as "verbal, plenary" inspiration. By "verbal," we mean that every word in the Bible is there because God permitted it by the direction of the Holy Spirit. By "plenary" (from the Latin, *plenus*–full), we mean that **each and every part** of the Bible is inspired, with nothing having been omitted.

In other words, by employing what we today refer to as verbal (word-for-word), plenary (full) inspiration, God ensured that the writings were correct and consistent with His will. This view holds that men wrote exactly what God wanted them to write, without errors or mistakes, yet with their own individual characteristics in evidence. While the various books of the Bible reflect the writers' personalities as expressed in the human element that often is so evident (type of language used, fears expressed, prayers offered, etc.), it was only by verbal, plenary inspiration that God could convey–objectively and accurately–His Word to mankind.

There is compelling evidence from within the Bible itself about the nature of its inspiration. Immediately after His baptism, Christ went into the wilderness for a crucial confrontation with Satan. When the devil suggested that He convert stones into bread to stay His hunger after a lengthy fast, the Savior replied by quoting Deuteronomy 8:3: "It is written, 'Man shall not live by bread alone, but by every word that proceeds out of the mouth of God'" (Matthew 4:4). Twice more

He stopped the devil's mouth with "It is written...," citing Deuteronomy 6:13,16. In declaring, "It is written," Jesus employed the Greek perfect tense, denoting completed action with abiding results. He thus declared that God's words were written–and remain so.

Jesus endorsed the whole Old Testament at least a dozen times, using such designations as: the Scriptures (John 5:39); the law (John 10:34); the law and the prophets (Matthew 5:17); the law, the prophets, and the psalms (Luke 24:44); or Moses and the prophets (Luke 16:29). In addition, the Son of God quoted, cited from, or alluded to incidents in at least eighteen different Old Testament books. But to what degree did Christ believe in inspiration? The following references document beyond doubt that the Lord affirmed **verbal, plenary** inspiration. In Matthew 5:17-18, Christ exclaimed:

> Think not that I came to destroy the law and the prophets: I came not to destroy, but to fulfill. For verily I say unto you, Till heaven and earth pass away, one jot or one tittle shall in no wise pass from the law, till all things be accomplished.

The "jot" was the smallest Hebrew letter, and the "tittle" was the tiny projection on certain Hebrew letters. When He employed these specific terms as examples, the Lord affirmed the minutest accuracy for the whole of the Old Testament.

In the midst of His discussion with the Sadducees about their denial of the resurrection of the dead (Matthew 22:23-33), Jesus referred to Exodus 3:6 wherein God said to Moses: "I am the God of Abraham, and the God of Isaac, and the God of Jacob." When God spoke these words, Abraham had been dead almost 400 years, yet He still said, "I **am** the God of Abraham." As Jesus correctly pointed out to the Sadducees, "God is not the God of the dead, but of the living" (Matthew 22:32). Thus, Abraham, Isaac, and Jacob must have been living. The only way they could be living was if their spirits continued to survive the death of their bodies. That kind of conscious existence implies a future resurrection of the body

–the very point Christ was attempting to make. Of interest is the fact that His entire argument rested on the **tense** of the verb!

In addition to these examples from Christ, there are other clear indications of the recognition of verbal inspiration. David once said, "The Spirit of Jehovah spake by me, and His word was upon my tongue" (2 Samuel 23:2). Observe that the king did not say God's "thoughts" or "concepts" were upon his tongue, but that Jehovah's **word** was upon his tongue. If that is not verbal inspiration, one would be hard pressed to know how verbal inspiration would be expressed.

In the first letter of Paul to the Corinthians, the apostle declared that the things of God were revealed to men by the Spirit. Then, concerning the divine messages, he said, "which things we speak, not in words which man's wisdom teacheth, but which the Spirit teacheth; combining spiritual things with spiritual words" (1 Corinthians 2:13). The words of divine revelation are Spirit-directed words, not words of mere human wisdom. That is **verbal, plenary** inspiration.

The same kind of reliance on a single word was expressed by Paul (as he referred to Genesis 22:18) in Galatians 3:16: "Now to Abraham were the promises spoken, and to his seed. He saith not, 'And to seeds,' as of many; but as of one, 'And to thy **seed**, which is Christ' " (emp. added). The force of his argument rested on the number of the noun (singular, as opposed to plural). In John 8:58, Jesus said: "...I say unto you, Before Abraham was born, I **am.**" He was attempting to impress upon the Jews His eternal nature, and to do so, He once again based His entire argument on the tense of the verb.

We should note, however, that this inspiration process applied only to the original documents as penned by each writer. While Bible writers were inspired, the scribes, translators, and others who followed were not. This does not mean, as some have suggested, that we do not have God's Word in an accurate form today. The text of the Bible we possess can be trusted.

EVIDENCE OF THE BIBLE'S INSPIRATION

Evidence to substantiate the Bible's claims of its own inspiration can be drawn from two general sources. **External** evidences for inspiration include such things as historical documentation of biblical people, places, and events, or archaeological artifacts that corroborate biblical statements or circumstances. These will be covered in the next chapter. **Internal** evidences are part of the warp and woof of the actual biblical fabric itself. These are self-authenticating phenomena from within the Sacred Volume that bear singular testimony to the fact that the very existence of the Holy Scriptures cannot be explained in any other way except to acknowledge that they are the result of an overriding, superintending, guiding Mind.

When the evidences for the Bible's inspiration are allowed to speak for themselves, the story they tell is totally in accord with the Bible's claims for its own inspiration. Consider, for example, the following.

The Unity of the Bible

The Bible exhibits a unity that–on purely human terms–is quite simply inexplicable. In order to appreciate that unity, one first must come to terms with how The Book was put together. The Bible was written by more than forty different men from practically every walk of life. Nehemiah was a royal cupbearer. Peter was a fisherman. Luke was a physician. Matthew was a tax collector. Solomon was a king. Moses was a shepherd. Paul was a tentmaker. Furthermore, these men wrote from almost every conceivable human condition. David wrote from heights of joy on the rolling, grassy hills of Judea. Paul wrote from pits of despair caused by Roman incarceration. They wrote in three languages (Hebrew, Aramaic, and Greek), from at least two continents (Europe and Asia), over a period of time that spanned approximately sixteen centuries (1500 B.C. to A.D. 100). And they covered topics as diverse as eschatology, soteriology, theology, psychology, geography, history, medicine, and many others.

All this being true, one might expect that so diverse a group of men, writing on so varied a group of subjects, over such a lengthy span of time, would have produced a book that would be a tangled mishmash of subjects more often than not marred by an incredible number of inconsistencies, errors, and incongruities. Yet this hardly is the case. In fact, quite the opposite is true. The Bible exhibits such astounding harmony, such consistent flow, and such unparalleled unity that it defies any purely naturalistic explanation. It is as if the Bible were a magnificent symphony orchestrated by a single Conductor. The "musicians" each may have played a different instrument, in a different place, at a different time. But when the talented Maestro combined the individual efforts, the end result was a striking masterpiece.

Consider this analogy. Suppose you assembled forty contemporary scholars with the highest academic training possible in a single field of study (e.g., forty academicians with terminal Ph.D. degrees in world history). Suppose, further, that you placed them in a room, and asked them to write a twenty-page paper on a single topic–the causes of World War II. What kind of consensus would be exhibited when all of their treatises were completed? Likely, the forty scholars would be unable to agree on all but a few points; their compositions would be recognized more for the **dis**agreements they contained than for the agreements. The Bible writers, by contrast, generally were not contemporaries. They worked independently, and the majority never even met another biblical writer. Most were not highly trained, and what training they did have certainly was not in the same field of study. Nor were they allowed to write on a single topic in which they already had an interest. Yet they produced a book that is unified from beginning to end. The books of 1 and 2 Chronicles and 1 and 2 Kings corroborate one another in numerous historical events. Joshua 1 verifies Deuteronomy 34. Judges 1:1 verifies Joshua 24:27-33. Ezra 1 verifies 2 Chronicles 36:22-23. Daniel refers to Jeremiah (Daniel 9:2). Ezekiel refers to Daniel (Ezekiel 28:3.

And so on. This kind of unity, which is in evidence throughout the Sacred Volume, attests to the fact that there was a Superintending Intelligence behind it. So many writers, over so many years, covering so many themes, simply could not have been so harmonious by mere coincidence.

Each book of the Bible complements the others in a single unified **theme**. From Genesis to Revelation there is a marvelous unfolding of the general theme of man's fall from his holy estate, God's plan for his redemption (as carefully worked out across the centuries), the sinless life and atoning death of Jesus Christ, and the ultimate victory of the Christian system. In essence, the Bible is the story of one problem–sin–with one solution, Jesus Christ.

Each book of the Bible complements the others in a single, unified **plan**. In Genesis, there is the record of humanity's pristine origin and covenant relationship with God, followed by its tragic fall into a sinful state. But, a specific family line (the Hebrew nation) was selected to provide a remedy for this disaster (Genesis 12:1ff.; 22:18). Man needed to learn precisely what sin is, thus the books of Exodus through Deuteronomy document the giving of the law of God to Moses. Via a set of ordinances, sin would be defined, and humanity would be illuminated regarding the price of rebellion against God (Romans 7:7,13; Galatians 3:19). The historical books of the Old Testament revealed mankind's inability to keep perfectly God's law system (Galatians 3:10), and therefore underscored the need for a Justifier–Someone to do for man what he could not do for himself. The prophets of the Old Testament heralded the arrival of that Savior (Luke 24:44); more than 300 prophecies focus on the promised Messiah.

After four silent centuries (the "inter-biblical era"), four gospel writers described in great detail the arrival, and life's work, of the Justifier–Jesus of Nazareth. The books of Matthew, Mark, Luke, and John are carefully crafted accounts of the birth, life, death, and ultimate resurrection of the Son of God (John 20:30-31). Each emphasized different parts of

Christ's ministry in order to relate the "good news" to Jews or Gentiles. Matthew directed his record primarily to the Jewish nation. Mark stressed the works of Jesus. Luke, being the only Gentile writer of a Bible book (except possibly the author of Job), wrote to Gentiles. John's primary purpose in writing was to produce faith.

The book of Acts was written to convey the means by which mankind was to appropriate God's saving grace. It is a historical record that instructs a person on how to become a Christian. It also teaches about how the church of Christ was established in Jerusalem, and how that same church flourished throughout the Roman Empire of the first century. The various epistles that follow the book of Acts in the English Bible were directions to individuals and churches on how to obtain, and maintain, spiritual maturity. Finally, the book of Revelation predicted (in symbolic fashion) the ultimate triumph of good over evil–acknowledging that Christians would win, and Satan would lose. To the careful reader, the unity of both theme and plan in the Bible are apparent.

The Factual Accuracy of the Bible

The Bible claims to be the inspired Word of God. Therefore, it should be accurate in whatever subject(s) it discusses, since God is not the Author of confusion and contradiction (1 Corinthians 14:33), but of truth (John 17:17). The factual accuracy of the Bible proves that it **is** accurate. Time and again the Bible's facts have withstood the test.

For example, some Bible critics have suggested that Luke misspoke when he designated Sergius Paulus as proconsul of Cyprus (Acts 13:7). Their claim was that Cyprus was governed by a propraetor (also known as a consular legate), not a proconsul. Upon further examination, such a charge can be seen to be completely vacuous, as Thomas Eaves has documented.

> As we turn to the writers of history for that period, Dia Cassius (*Roman History*) and Strabo (*The Geography of Strabo*), we learn that there were two periods of Cyprus' history: first, it was an imperial province gov-

> erned by a propraetor, and later in 22 B.C., it was made a senatorial province governed by a proconsul. Therefore, the historians support Luke in his statement that Cyprus was ruled by a proconsul, for it was between 40-50 A.D. when Paul made his first missionary journey. If we accept secular history as being true we must also accept Biblical history for they are in agreement (1980, p. 234).

In his classic text, *Lands of the Bible*, J.W. McGarvey remarked:

> A fictitious narrative, located in a country with which the writer is not personally familiar, must either avoid local allusions or be found frequently in conflict with the peculiarities of place and of manners and customs. By this conflict the fictitious character of the narrative is exposed (1881, p. 375).

McGarvey then documented numerous instances in which the facts of the Bible can be checked, and in which it always passes the test. Are compass references accurate? Is Antioch of Syria "down" from Jerusalem, even though it lies to the north of the holy city (Acts 15:1)? Is the way from Jerusalem to Gaza "south" of Samaria (Acts 8:26)? Is Egypt "down" from Canaan (Genesis 12:10)? McGarvey noted that "in not a single instance of this kind has any of the Bible writers been found at fault" (p. 378). Further, as Wayne Jackson has commented:

> In 1790, William Paley, the celebrated Anglican scholar, authored his famous volume, *Horae Paulinae* (*Hours with Paul*). In this remarkable book, Paley demonstrated an amazing array of "undesigned coincidences" between the book of Acts and the epistles of Paul, which argue for the credibility of the Christian revelation. "These coincidences," said Paley, "which are often incorporated or intertwined in references and allusions, in which no art can be discovered, and no contrivance traced, furnish numerous proofs of the truth of both these works, and consequently that of Christianity" (1839 edition, p. xvi). In 1847, J.J. Blunt of Cambridge University released a companion volume titled, *Undesigned Coincidences in the Writings of*

> *Both the Old Testament and New Testament.* Professor Blunt argued that both Testaments contain numerous examples of "consistency without contrivance" which support the Scriptures' claim of a unified origin from a supernatural source, namely God (1884, p. vii) [1991, 11:2-3].

A sampling of the information within Paley's and Blunt's books provides startling evidence of the fact that the writers simply could not have "contrived" their stories. Often the writers were separated from one another by centuries, yet their stories dovetail with astounding accuracy, and provide additional proof of the Bible's inspiration.

When Joseph was seventeen years old, he was sold into Egyptian slavery by his brothers. While serving in the house of an Egyptian named Potiphar, Joseph found himself the object of affection of Potiphar's wife, whose advances he rejected. Her anger aroused, she fabricated a story that resulted in Joseph's being thrown into prison where the king's captives were "bound" (Genesis 39:20). In the context of this passage, the word "bound" is of critical importance because hundreds of years after the fact, the psalmist would state of Joseph: "His feet they hurt with fetters: He was laid in chains of iron" (Psalm 105:18). Contrivance–or consistency?

When Pharaoh stubbornly refused to release the Israelites from bondage, God rained down plagues on the Egyptian monarch and his people, including a plague of hail that destroyed the **flax** in the fields (Exodus 9:31). Eventually, the Israelites were released, traveled to the wilderness of Sinai, were found faithless in God's sight, and were forced to wander for four decades while everyone over the age of twenty perished (except for the houses of Joshua and Caleb–Numbers 14:29-30). Finally, however, the Hebrews were allowed to enter the promised land of Canaan. The arrival of the younger generation was exactly forty years after Moses had led them out of Egypt (Joshua 4:19), and thus shortly before the anniversary of that eighth plague which destroyed the flax.

The book of Joshua mentions that their entrance into Canaan was near harvest time (3:15). Interestingly, when spies were sent to investigate the city of Jericho, the Bible notes that they were concealed by Rahab under drying stalks of **flax** upon the rooftop of her house (Joshua 2:6). Coincidence–or concordance?

In Exodus 1:11, the story is told of how the Israelites were forced to build the treasure cities of Pithom and Raamses for the Egyptian ruler. Exodus 5 records that, initially, the slaves made bricks containing straw, but later were forced to use stubble because Pharaoh ordered his taskmasters not to provide any more straw. Excavations at Pithom in 1883 by Naville, and in 1908 by Kyle, discovered that the lower layers of the structures were made of bricks filled with good, chopped straw. The middle layers had less straw with some stubble. The upper layers contained bricks that were made of pure clay, with no straw whatsoever (see Pfeiffer, 1966, p. 459). Contrivance–or correctness?

The Tell-el-Armarna Tablets (c. 1450 B.C.) record the custom of bowing down seven times when meeting a superior. Thus the statement in Genesis 33:3–"And he [Jacob] himself passed over before them, and bowed himself to the ground **seven times**, until he came near to his brother [Esau]"–is confirmed as an act of respect. Coincidence–or consistency?

On one occasion during His earthly ministry, Jesus miraculously provided a meal for more than 5,000 people. Mark records that the Lord seated the people upon the "green grass" (6:39). Such a statement agrees completely with John's reference to the fact that this event occurred near the time of the Passover (6:44), which occurs in the spring–exactly the time in Palestine when the grass should be green. Coincidence–or correctness?

In his second letter to Timothy, Paul admonished the young man by stating that "from a babe thou hast known the sacred writings which are able to make thee wise unto salvation through faith which is in Christ Jesus" (2 Timothy 3:15). The reference to the "sacred writings" is an allusion to the Old Testament. Since Timothy had known those writings from his earliest days, certainly it would be safe to suggest that his background was Jewish. As a matter of fact, the book of Acts states Timothy was "the son of a Jewess that believed, but his father was a Greek" (Acts 16:1). Of further interest is the fact that when Paul commended Timothy for his strong faith (2 Timothy 1:5), he alluded to the spirituality of both the young man's mother and grandmother, yet made no mention of Timothy's father. Coincidence–or concordance?

When Jesus died, His disciples desired to prepare His body for burial by embalming it. In his gospel, John declared that the Jewish ruler, Nicodemus, brought a hundred pounds of spices (myrrh and aloes) for this purpose (19:39). It would be safe to conclude, therefore, that large quantities of these kinds of spices would be required for the embalming process. It is an undisputed fact of secular history that the Egyptians were experts in embalming. When Jacob died, the physicians of Egypt embalmed him (Genesis 50:2). Likewise, Joseph was embalmed upon his demise (50:26). The Egyptians required vast quantities of spices–like myrrh–for their embalming purposes. Not surprisingly, then, the Old Testament teaches that myrrh was imported by camel caravans into Egypt (Genesis 37:24). Contrivance–or inspiration?

In their book, *A General Introduction to the Bible*, Geisler and Nix wrote: "Confirmation of the Bible's accuracy in factual matters lends credibility to its claims when speaking on other subjects" (1986, p. 195). Indeed it does!

CONCLUSION

Those who have set their face against God have railed against the Bible for generations. King Jehoiakim took his penknife, slashed the Old Testament Scriptures to pieces, and tossed them into a fire (Jeremiah 36:22-23). During the Middle Ages, attempts were made to keep the Bible from the man on the street. In fact, those caught translating or distributing the Scriptures often were subjected to imprisonment, torture, and even death. Centuries later, the French skeptic Voltaire boasted that "within fifty years, the Bible no longer will be discussed among educated people." His braggadocio notwithstanding, the Bible still is being discussed among educated people, while the name of Voltaire languishes in relative obscurity.

Like the blacksmith's anvil–which wears out many hammers but itself remains unaffected–the Bible wears out the skeptics' innocuous charges, all the while remaining unscathed. John Clifford (1836-1923), a Baptist minister and social reformer, once wrote:

Last eve I passed beside a blacksmith's door,
And heard the anvil ring the vesper chime;
Then looking, I saw upon the floor,
Old hammers, worn with beating years of time.
"How many anvils have you had," said I,
"To wear and batter all these hammers so?"
"Just one," said he, and then with twinkling eye;
"The anvil wears the hammers out, ye know."
And so, thought I, the anvil of God's Word,
For ages skeptic blows have beat upon;
Yet though the noise of falling blows was heard
The anvil is unharmed...the hammers gone.

Governments come and go. Nations rise and fall. People live and die. Jesus warned that "heaven and earth shall pass away" (Matthew 24:35), but went on to note that "my words shall not pass away." Isaiah wrote: "The grass withereth, the flower fadeth; but the word of our God shall stand forever" (40:8). Yes, it shall.

DISCUSSION QUESTIONS

1. Discuss why, at first glance, some verses in the Bible may appear to be contradictory.
2. Give some examples to illustrate the degree to which Jesus Christ acknowledged the inspiration of the Holy Scriptures.
3. What is the single unified theme that runs throughout the Bible, and how does it affect Christians today?
4. Discuss what verbal, plenary inspiration means, and how, even though they are inspired, the four gospel narratives could contain different information.
5. Just because the Bible **claims** to be the Word of God does not necessarily make it so. We must provide evidence to prove its inspiration. How is that similar to the life of a Christian? What things can one use to "prove" his or her Christianity? Refer to John 13:35, James 1:27, 2:14-26, and 1 John 3:18.
6. Why can it be said with accuracy that the Bible exhibits amazing unity? What is the main theme of the Bible? Who are some of the main characters (mentioned in several books), and what do they have or not have in common?

Chapter 6

SCIENTIFIC FOREKNOWLEDGE IN THE BIBLE

Among the many intriguing proofs of the Bible's inspiration is its unique scientific foreknowledge. From anthropology to zoology, the Bible presents astonishingly accurate scientific information that the writers, on their own, simply could not have known. Henry Morris has suggested: "One of the most arresting evidences of the inspiration of the Bible is the great number of scientific truths that have lain hidden within its pages for thirty centuries or more, only to be discovered by man's enterprise within the last few centuries or even years" (1969, p. 5). In her book, *Science in the Bible,* Jean S. Morton commented:

> Many scientific facts, which prove the infallibility of Scripture, are tucked away in its pages. These proofs are given in nonscientific language; nevertheless, they substantiate the claims of authenticity of the Holy Scriptures.... In some cases, scientific concepts have been known through the ages, but these concepts are mentioned in a unique manner in Scripture. In other cases, scientific topics have been mentioned hundreds or even thousands of years before man discovered them (1978, p. 10).

Space limitations prohibit an in-depth examination of the Bible's scientific foreknowledge, but we would like to mention a few of the more prominent examples.

FROM THE FIELD OF ASTRONOMY

1. Isaiah, in speaking of God, stated (40:22), "It is he who sitteth upon the circle of the earth." The Hebrew word Isaiah used for "circle" is the word *khug*, which means literally something with "roundness," a "sphere." But, of course, the people of Isaiah's day thought the Earth was flat. And that was the concept of the many generations of people who followed Isaiah. Later, of course, it was discovered that the Earth was not flat; rather it was a *khug* (circle). Isaiah had been correct all along, even when the people of his day emphatically stated the opposite. How did Isaiah know the Earth to be a sphere? Just a lucky guess?

[NOTE: In recent years some have suggested that Isaiah's statement contains no foreknowledge since in chapter 40 he is dealing solely with the subject of God's sovereignty, and it therefore was not his intent to teach "scientific truths" (cf. England, 1983, pp. 135ff.). We repudiate such a claim. There can be no doubt that Isaiah's treatise is dealing with the sovereign nature of the Israelite God. Chapter 40 is, in fact, one of the most beautiful and stirring passages in the Bible dealing with that very subject. At the same time, however, Isaiah did set forth a "scientific truth" while acknowledging an important "spiritual truth." One does not preclude the other. Isaiah made two points: (1) God **is** sovereign and; (2) the Earth **is** a sphere (*khug*). How could Isaiah have known either, unless God had revealed them both?]

2. Psalm 19:5-6 contains several interesting scientific facts. In speaking of the Sun, the psalmist suggested that "his going forth is from the end of the heaven, and his circuit unto the ends of it; and there is nothing hid from the heat thereof." For years, Bible critics scoffed at Bible believers, stating that this verse taught the false concept of geocentricity (i.e., the Sun revolves around the Earth). Then it was discovered that the Sun, not the Earth, was the center of our solar system. People subsequently felt that the Sun was stationary, with the Earth revolving around it.

Only recently has it been discovered that, rather than being fixed in space, the Sun actually is in an orbit of its own. In June of 1999, astronomers focused on a star at the center of the Milky Way, and measured precisely for the first time how long it takes the Sun to circle its home galaxy. The answer: 226 million years. In fact, it is estimated to be moving through space at the rate of 600,000 miles per hour. How did the psalmist portray such accurate statements—when we didn't know the "rest of the story" until just a few short years ago? And, by the way, there is another gem packed away in these two verses. The psalmist hinted at the fact that the Sun is the source of energy for the Earth ("and there is nothing hid from the heat thereof"). An amazing statement, is it not, considering when it was written and by whom?

3. Concerning light and darkness, the Lord asked Job: "Where is the way to the dwelling of the light? And as for darkness, where is the place thereof?" (38:19). Light is said to travel in a "way" (Hebrew, *derek*), which is literally a traveled path or road (cf. Genesis 16:7), whereas darkness is said to be a "place" (Hebrew, *maxim*) which means a place, a spot, as standing (cf. Genesis 1:9; 28:11). Until the seventeenth century, it was believed that light was transmitted instantaneously. Then Sir Isaac Newton suggested that light is composed of small particles that travel in a straight line. Christian Huygens proposed the wave theory of light, and Olaus Roemer measured the velocity of light as evinced by its delay while traveling through space. Scientists now know that light is a form of energy called radiant energy, and that it travels in electromagnetic waves in a straight line at the speed of over 186,000 miles per second (660 million miles per hour). For example, it takes about eight minutes for light to travel its "path" from the Sun to the Earth.

Scientists use the speed of light to measure distances in our vast Universe. Our solar system is said to be about 26,000 light-years from the edge of our galaxy (i.e., it would take 26,000 years, traveling at the speed of light, to reach our solar system, starting at the edge of the Milky Way Galaxy). Some evolutionists, who deny the chronological data found in the Bible, have suggested that light, which spans the distances from stars to us, proves the Universe is billions of years old. They overlook, of course, the fact that God created the heavenly lights already in place (Genesis 1:14-16) to serve as a "witness" of His infinite power and for man's benefit (Psalm 19:1). God, in making His perfect, mature Universe, formed the stars so that their light could be seen on Earth.

Jehovah also inquired of Job? "By what way is light parted?" (38:24). The word "parted" is from the Hebrew *halaq*, meaning to divide, allot, apportion (cf. Numbers 26:53). Though the Lord simply may have been asking the patriarch if he knew how light is distributed on Earth, nonetheless it is an amazing scientific fact that light literally can be parted. When a narrow beam of sunlight passes at a slant into a triangular, transparent prism, the sunlight is broken into a band of seven colored lights called a spectrum. Sir Isaac Newton eventually discovered this, yet the writer of the book of Job knew it first.

FROM THE FIELD OF OCEANOGRAPHY

1. Long ago, Solomon wrote, "All the rivers run into the sea, yet the sea is not full; unto the place whither the rivers go, thither they go again" (Ecclesiastes 1:7). This statement, considered by itself, may not seem profound at first glance. But when considered with additional evidence and other biblical passages, it becomes all the more remarkable. For example, the Mississippi River, when moving at normal speed, dumps approximately **6,052,500 gallons** of water **per second** into the Gulf of Mexico. And that is just one river! Where, pray tell, does all that water go? The answer, of course, lies in the hydrologic cycle so well illustrated in the Bible. Ecclesiastes 11:3a states that "if the clouds be full of rain, they empty themselves upon the earth." Amos 9:6b tells us that "He...calleth for the waters of the sea, and poureth them out upon the face of the earth; the Lord is His name." The idea of a complete

water cycle was not fully understood or accepted until the sixteenth and seventeenth centuries. The first substantial evidence came from experiments of Pierre Perrault and Edme Mariotte. These scientists demonstrated that the flow of the Seine River could be accounted for by precipitation. Astronomer Edmund Halley also contributed valuable data to the concept of a complete water cycle. More than 2,000 years prior to their work, however, the Scriptures had indicated a water cycle. How?

2. There is hook-like bay on southernmost tip of Maui that locals call La Perouse–named after the Frenchman who discovered it. Imagine scientists' surprise when they learned that, up until just a few years ago, natives from this village got their fresh water from the ocean water in this bay–without a desalinization factory. To get to the fresh water, the ancient Hawaiians (knowing that salt water was warmer and more dense than the cold, fresh water) learned how to use gourds to collect fresh water from the deep-sea springs. In fact, if you were to travel there today, you would find surfing spots on the Big Island where surfers and children dive into the fresh-water springs before getting out of the water, thus saving them the trouble of having to shower later.

Yet thousands of years earlier, Job was asked by God (38: 16), "Hast thou entered into the springs of the sea? Or hast thou walked in the recesses of the deep?" The Hebrew word for "recesses" (or "trenches") refers to that which is "hidden, and known only by investigation." What were these "recesses of the deep" (the Hebrew word for "deep" is the word for seas or oceans)? Man, in previous centuries, considered the seashore as nothing but a shallow, sandy extension from one continent to another. Then, in 1873 a team of British scientists working in the Pacific Ocean found a "recess" 5½ miles deep. Later, another team of researchers discovered another trench 35,800 feet deep (over 6 miles down). Trenches now are known to exist in all three major oceans, but the Pacific Ocean is unique in that it has a semi-continuous peripheral belt of trenches and deep-sea troughs. Extensive studies have now been conducted on the Marianas Trench off the coast of Guam. The bathyscaph *Trieste* has traveled down almost seven miles into that trench. The best-known trench is perhaps the one off the coast of Puerto Rico, with its deepest point known as the Milwaukee Depth. How did Job know about these "recesses in the deep," when we didn't discover them for centuries? A lucky guess?

3. God told Noah (Genesis 6:15) to build an ark that measured 300 cubits in length, 50 cubits in width, and 30 cubits in height. This is a ratio of 30 to 5 to 3, length to breadth to height. Until approximately 1858 the ark was the largest seagoing vessel of which we have any written record. Using the most conservative estimate available for a cubit (approximately 17½ to 18 inches), the ark would have been roughly 450 feet long (a football-field-and-a-half) and would have contained approximately 1.5 million cubic feet of space. In 1844, when Isambard K. Brunnel built his giant ship, the *Great Britain*, he constructed it to almost the exact dimensions of the ark–30:5:3. As it turns out, these dimensions are the perfect ratio for a huge boat build for seaworthiness and not for speed. Obviously the ark was not built for speed–it had nowhere to go! In fact, shipbuilders during World War II used that 30:5:3 ratio to build a boat (the *S.S. Jeremiah O'Brien*) that eventually was nicknamed "the ugly duckling"–a huge, barge-like ship (with the same ratio as the ark) built to carry tremendous amounts of cargo. How did Noah know the perfect seagoing ratio to use in building the ark? Upon whose knowledge did he draw? Brunnel and others like him had many generations of shipbuilding knowledge upon which to draw, but Noah's craft literally was the first of its kind.

FROM THE FIELD OF PHYSICS

1. Moses (Genesis 2:1) stated, "And the heavens and the earth were finished, and all the host of them." This is an extremely interesting assessment of the situation, because Moses chose the Hebrew past definite tense for the verb "finished," indicating an action completed in the past, never to

occur again. Moses stated that the creation was "finished"– once and for all. That is exactly what the First Law of Thermodynamics states. This Law (often referred to as the Law of Conservation of Energy/Matter) states that neither matter nor energy can be created or destroyed. It was because of this Law that the late Sir Fred Hoyle's "Steady State" (or "Continuous Creation") Theory was discarded several years ago. Hoyle stated that at points in the Universe called "irtrons" matter was being created constantly. But the First Law states just the opposite. The Bible says that God "ended His work which He had made" (Genesis 2:2). As Henry M. Morris has suggested: "This is the most universal and certain of all scientific principles and it states conclusively that, so far as empirical observation has shown, there is **nothing** now being created anywhere in the known universe" (1974a, p. 235, emp. in orig.).

It is because God has finished His creation that nothing now is being created. But, as a corollary to that, why is it that nothing is being destroyed? This is the second half of the statement of the Law. Matter and/or energy may change form, but the total amount of energy in the Universe remains the same. Nothing is being destroyed, even though its form may change. Once again, the answer can be found in the science of the Bible. Nehemiah provided a portion of the answer when he stated: "Thou hast made heaven, the heaven of heavens, with all their host, the earth, and all things that are therein, the seas, and all that is therein, and thou preservest them all" (9:6). Hebrews 1:3 points out that God "upholds all things by the word of His power." If God is upholding it, then man will not destroy it. Other verses make that clear in this regard (cf. Isaiah 40:26, Ecclesiastes 3:14, and 2 Peter 3:7). Thus, we see that the biblical writers penned accurate scientific statements long before such statements were even known to be scientific. How? Just a lucky guess?

2. In three places in the Bible (Hebrews 1:11; Isaiah 51:6; Psalm 102:26) the indication is given that the Earth, like a garment, is wearing out. This, of course, is exactly what the

Second Law of Thermodynamics states. This Law, also known as the Law of Increasing Entropy, governs all processes; there is not a single known exception. The Law states that as time progresses, entropy increases. Entropy is the scientific word which simply means that things become more disorderly, more random, more unstructured. In other words, a flower blooms, fades, and dies. A child grows into adolescence, adulthood, senility, and dies. The house we build today, in 250 years will be a heap of junk. The car we buy today, given 30 or 40 years, will rust and fall apart. Everything is running down. Everything is wearing out. Energy is becoming less available for work. Eventually then (theoretically speaking) the Universe, left to itself, will experience a "heat death" when no more energy is available for use. We did not discover these laws of physics until fairly recently, yet the Bible writers portrayed them accurately thousands of years ago. What was the source of their knowledge?

FROM THE FIELD OF MEDICINE

1. Moses told the Israelites (Leviticus 17:11-14) that "the life of the flesh is in the blood." He was correct. Because the red blood cells can carry oxygen (due to hemoglobin in the cells) life is made possible. In fact, the human red blood cells carry, for example, approximately 270,000,000 molecules of hemoglobin per cell (see Perutz, 1964, pp. 64-65).

If there were any less, there would not be enough residual oxygen to sustain life after, say, a hard sneeze or a hefty pat on the back. We know today that the "life of the flesh is in the blood." But we didn't know that in George Washington's day. How did the "father of our country" die? We bled him to death (see Havron, 1981, p. 62). People felt that the blood was where evil "vapors" were found, and that getting rid of the blood would make a person well again. Today, of course, we know that is not true. Think of how often blood transfusions have made life possible for those who otherwise would have died. Today we know the truth of the matter. How did the biblical writer know it?

2. Genesis 3:15 teaches plainly that both the male and the female possess the "seed of life." This was not the commonly held position in Moses' day, however. Nor was it the commonly held position just a few centuries ago. Several writers of days gone by, including some of Moses' day, felt that only the male possessed the seed of life, and that the woman actually was little more than a "glorified incubator." One writer even suggested that the male seed could be deposited in warm mud, and the end result would be the same as placing it in the woman's womb. But Moses spewed forth no such nonsense. Rather, he stated the truth of the matter. But how did he know? Upon whose knowledge of such facts did he draw?

3. Leviticus 17:15 teaches that an animal that has died **naturally** is not to be eaten. Moses obviously was highly trained in public health procedures, for he certainly knew that of which he spoke. Today it is against local, state, and federal public health laws to take an animal that has died naturally to a slaughterhouse in order to be prepared for human consumption. What if the animal died of rabies, anthrax, brucellosis, or a similar disease? Obviously, it would not be suitable for human consumption because if the animal died, something was wrong. Even today this practice is one of our basic public health standards. But how did Moses possess such knowledge?

4. While the Old Testament placed no restrictions on the eating of fruits and vegetables, severe limitations were given for the eating of certain meats. Among land animals, only those that had a split hoof and chewed the cud were approved as edible (Leviticus 11:3). Of the water-living animals, only those with fins and scales were acceptable (Leviticus 11:9; of interest is the fact that poisonous fish have no scales). Birds of prey were prohibited, as were almost all insects. But perhaps the best known among these biblical injunctions was eating the meat of a pig. To the Jew, pork was considered unclean, and thus was inedible.

Today, we know there is good scientific reasoning behind such a prohibition. The pig is a scavenger, and will eat almost anything. In so doing, on occasion it ingests the parasite,

Trichinella spiralis, which is the cause of trichinosis in humans. Left untreated, this disease can be debilitating and even deadly. Pigs also are known carriers (as intermediate hosts) of the tapeworm *Taenia solium*, and of the parasite *Echinococcus granulosis*, which causes tumors in the liver, lungs, and other parts of the body. Raw or undercooked pork can be quite dangerous when consumed by humans. Pigs can provide safe meat if they are fed properly and if the muscle tissue is cooked correctly. But such conditions often did not prevail in ancient times.

Were the Israelites "ahead of their times" in regard to their extensive public health and personal hygiene laws? Archaeologists admit that they have yet to find civilizations as ancient as the Israelites with rules and regulations that could rival those of the Jewish people in regard to complexity and scientific accuracy. The Egyptians, for example, were brilliant in many respects when it came to their medical technology. Yet the Jews had access to this kind of information (and much more) that not even the Egyptians possessed. Interestingly, even today in some countries (like Germany) raw pork is considered a delicacy–in spite of the knowledge we possess about the potential dangers of eating it.

5. In Deuteronomy 23:12-14, Moses instructed the Israelites always to bury human waste products. Today, of course, with centuries of experience behind us, we know that this is an excellent sanitary hygienic practice. But the common course of action in Moses' day, and for centuries to follow, was to dump waste products in any convenient place. History has recorded the folly of this kind of action.

In Europe, during the Middle Ages, "Black Plague" swept over the continent on two different occasions, slaughtering more than 13 million people in the process. Europeans routinely dumped waste of all kinds out their windows and into the public streets where decomposition took place and microorganisms flourished.

One of those microorganisms–the one we know today as *Yersinia pestis*–grew in the waste products and contaminated the fleas associated with those waste products. The fleas, using rats as their hosts, subsequently traveled into the people's houses. Once inside a dwelling, the fleas then jumped from the rats onto the humans, biting them and infecting them with the plague organism. As this cycle was repeated over and over, millions perished. Yet if the people simply had obeyed God's injunction, as given by Moses to the Israelites, all of the death and horror of two separate epidemics could have been avoided. How did Moses know to instruct the Israelites regarding such public health hygiene laws, when none of the nations surrounding God's people enlisted such practices–and would not for centuries?

6. In Genesis 17:12, God commanded Abraham to circumcise newborn males on the **eighth** day. But why day eight? In humans, blood clotting is dependent upon three factors: (a) platelets; (b) vitamin K; and (c) prothrombin. In 1935, professor H. Dam proposed the name "vitamin K" for the factor that helped prevent hemorrhaging in chicks. We now realize that vitamin K is responsible for the production (by the liver) of prothrombin. If the quantity of vitamin K is deficient, there will be a prothrombin deficiency and hemorrhaging may occur.

Interestingly, it is only on the fifth to seventh days of a newborn's life that vitamin K (produced by the action of bacteria in the intestinal tract) is present in adequate quantities. Vitamin K–coupled with prothrombin–causes blood coagulation, which is important in any surgical procedure. A classic medical text, *Holt Pediatrics*, corroborates that a newborn infant has

> ...peculiar susceptibility to bleeding between the second and fifth days of life.... Hemorrhages at this time, though often inconsequential, are sometimes extensive; they may produce serious damage to internal organs, especially to the brain, and cause death from shock and exsanguination (Holt and McIntosh, 1953, pp. 125-126).

Obviously, then, if vitamin K is not produced in sufficient quantities until days five through seven, it would be wise to postpone any surgery until sometime after that. But why did God specify day **eight**?

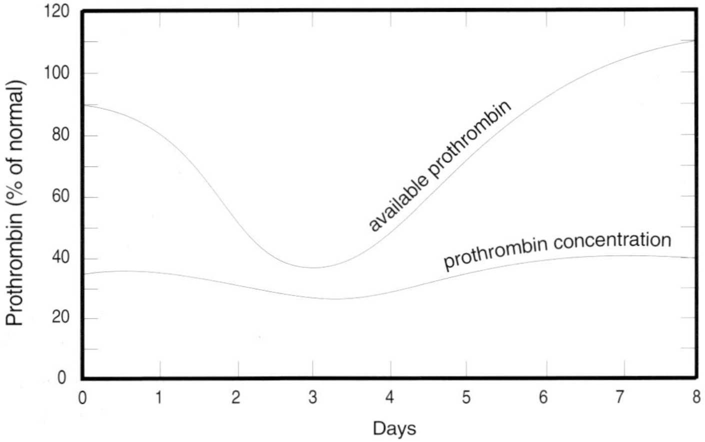

On the eighth day, the amount of prothrombin present actually is **elevated above 100 percent of normal**. In fact, day eight is the only day in the male's life in which this will be the case under normal conditions. If surgery is to be performed, day eight is the perfect day to do it. S.I. McMillen, the renowned medical doctor who authored *None of These Diseases*, wrote concerning this information:

> ...as we congratulate medical science for this recent finding, we can almost hear the leaves of the Bible rustling. They would like to remind us that four thousand years ago, when God **initiated** circumcision with Abraham, He said "And he that is eight days old shall be circumcised...." Abraham did not pick the eighth day after many centuries of trial-and-error experiments. Neither he nor any of his company from the ancient city of Ur in the Chaldees had ever been circumcised. It was a day picked by the Creator of vitamin K (1963, p. 21, emp. in orig.).

The medical information employed by Abraham, and confirmed by Moses, was accurate scientifically then, and still remains so to this very day. No culture around the Israelites possessed such scientific acumen, which, by the way, was far ahead of its time. How, then, did Abraham and Moses come to know the best time for circumcision, unless, of course, this particular fact was revealed to them by God, and recorded in His Word through inspiration?

FROM THE FIELD OF BIOLOGY

1. Moses stated (Genesis 1:11,12,21,24) that things reproduce "after their kind." This, of course, is no surprise to us today because we understand genetics and the laws of heredity which ensure that things do indeed reproduce "after their kind." If a farmer plants corn seed, he knows full well that he will not be harvesting wheat. If he breeds a bull to a heifer, he knows that the end result will not be a baby colt. Corn produces corn; cows produce cows. Why? Because all living things reproduce "after their kind." Even today, in nature these things hold true. But how did Moses know–long years before the science of genetics (which came into existence only around 1900) was discovered?

2. Paul stated that it is God who giveth all life (Acts 17:25). For centuries, men have been trying to "create life" through processes of spontaneous generation. Even though men like Spallanzani, Redi, Pasteur and hundreds of others have proven time and again that spontaneous generation is impossible, evolutionists still keep on trying. But, to date, no one ever has "created" life. They do well, in fact, even to get one of the simplest "building blocks"–amino acids. Paul knew long ago that it was God who gives life. Just a lucky guess?

3. Paul also stated that there are **four** fleshes–those of men, beasts, birds and fishes (1 Corinthians 15:39). Today even evolutionists accept this fact of science. These fleshes are indeed different in their biochemical make-up. But how did Paul, an itinerant preacher of the first century A.D., know this?

FROM THE FIELD OF ARCHAEOLOGY

The science of archaeology has outdone itself in verifying the Scriptures. Famed archaeologist William F. Albright wrote: "There can be no doubt that archaeology has confirmed the substantial historicity of the Old Testament tradition" (1953, p. 176). Nelson Glueck, himself a pillar within the archaeological community, said: "It may be stated categorically that no archaeological discovery has ever controverted a Biblical reference. Scores of archaeological findings have been made which conform in clear outline or exact detail historical statements in the Bible" (1959, p. 31).

1. The Hittites are mentioned over forty times in Scripture (Exodus 23:28; Joshua 1:4; et al.), and were so feared that on one occasion they caused the Syrians to flee from Israel (2 Kings 7:6). Yet critics suggested that Hittites were a figment of the Bible writers' imaginations, since no evidence of their existence had been located. But in the late 1800s, A.H. Sayce discovered inscriptions in Syria that he designated as Hittite. Then, in 1906, Hugh Winckler excavated Boghazkoy, Turkey and discovered that the Hittite capital had been located on that very site. His find was all the more powerful because of the more than 10,000 clay tablets that were found in the ancient city's library and that contained the society's law system—which eventually came to be known as the Hittite Code. Thus, Ira Price wrote of the Hittites:

> The lack of extra-biblical testimony to their existence led some scholars about a half-century ago to deny their historicity. They scoffed at the idea of Israel allying herself with such an unhistorical people as the Hittites, as narrated in 2 Kings vii.6. But those utterances have vanished into thin air (1907, pp. 75-76).

2. The Moabite Stone, found in 1868 by a German missionary, was cut in 850 B.C., in the reign of Mosha, king of Moab. It tells of his being subjected to the Israelites. It also mentions that Omri, the captain of the Israelite host, was made king in that day. The Scriptures speak of that very event in 1

Kings 16:16. With every scoop of dirt that the spade overturns, archaeology proves biblical statements to be factual.

3. The Bible plainly speaks of a king by the name of Belshazzar (Daniel 5:22; 7:1; 8:1). It was common practice for Bible critics to ridicule the Bible regarding its references concerning Belshazzar, because secular records never had been found that substantiated what the Bible said. Then, in 1876, Sir Henry Rawlinson discovered more than 2,000 tablets concerning Babylon. They disclosed records of a man named Belshazzar who, in the absence of his father Nabonidus, became king. The Bible had been right all along.

4. In days of yore, detractors accused Isaiah of having made a historical mistake when he wrote of Sargon as king of Assyria (Isaiah 20:1). For years, this remained the sole historical reference–secular or biblical–to Sargon having been linked with the Assyrian nation. Thus, critics assumed Isaiah had erred. But in 1843, Paul Emile Botta, the French consular agent at Mosul, working with Austen Layard, unearthed historical evidence that established Sargon as having been exactly what Isaiah said he was–king of the Assyrians. At Khorsabad, Botta discovered Sargon's palace. Pictures of the find may be found in *Halley's Bible Handbook* (1962, p. 289). Apparently, from what scholars have been able to piece together from archaeological and historical records, Sargon made his capital successively at Ashur, Calah, Nineveh, and finally at Khorsabad, where his palace was constructed in the closing years of his reign (c. 706 B.C.). The walls of the palace were adorned quite intricately with ornate text that described the events of his reign. Today, an artifact from the palace–a forty-ton stone bull (slab)–is on display at the University of Chicago's Oriental Institute ("weighty" evidence of Sargon's existence). Isaiah had been correct all along. And the critics had been wrong–all along.

The incredible accuracy of the Bible's science is yet another example of God's superintending guidance, and one that provides an impressive proof of its inspiration.

DISCUSSION QUESTIONS

1. How do scientific accuracies found in the Bible strengthen the fact of inspiration? Can you think of any additional examples of scientific foreknowledge in the Bible?

2. Job 26:7 states: "He stretcheth out the north over the empty place, and hangeth the earth upon nothing." After looking at the context and realizing who is talking, why is this **not** a good example of scientific foreknowledge?

3. The Second Law of Thermodynamics states that everything is increasing in entropy (disorder). What problems does this law pose for evolutionists who ascribe to the belief that we arrived here as the result of a "Big Bang"-type explosion?

4. Many individuals believe that the Bible and science cannot be reconciled. If God created the Universe, and if He inspired the Bible, then shouldn't the two agree? Why are some reasons that scientific theories might not always coincide with biblical teaching?

5. The Law of Biogenesis states that life comes only from other life of its kind. Paul recorded that it was God Who gave all life (Acts 17:28). How do evolutionists try to circumvent this fact of science? What was the Harold Urey and Stanley Miller experiment of 1953 trying to prove?

Chapter 7

JESUS CHRIST—LORD AND SAVIOR

On Tuesday, prior to the Christ's crucifixion the following Friday, Jesus engaged in a discussion with the Pharisees, who made no secret of their hatred for Him. When Matthew recorded the scene in his gospel, he first commented on an earlier skirmish the Lord had with the Sadducees: "But the Pharisees, when they heard that he had put the Sadducees to silence, gathered themselves together" (22:34).

Jesus–with penetrating logic and an incomparable knowledge of the Old Testament Scriptures–had routed the Sadducees completely. No doubt the Pharisees thought they could do better. Yet they were about to endure the same embarrassing treatment.

In the midst of His discussion with the Pharisees, Jesus asked: "What think ye of the Christ? Whose son is he?" (Matthew 22:42). They were unable to answer the questions satisfactorily because their hypocrisy prevented them from comprehending both Jesus' nature and His mission. The questions the Lord asked on that day, however, are ones that every rational, sane person must answer eventually.

The two questions were intended to raise the matter of Christ's deity. The answers–had the Pharisees' spiritual myopia not prevented them from responding correctly–were intended to confirm it. Today, these questions still raise the spectre of Christ's identity. Who is Jesus? Is He, as He claimed to be, the Son of God? Was He, as many around Him claimed, God incarnate? Is He, as the word "deity" implies, of divine nature and rank?

CHRIST AS A HISTORICAL FIGURE

The series of events that eventually would lead to Jesus' becoming the world's best-known historical figure began in first-century Palestine. There are four primary indicators of this fact. First, when Daniel was asked by king Nebuchadnezzar to interpret his wildly imaginative dream, the prophet revealed that God would establish the Messianic kingdom during the time of the Roman Empire (viz., the fourth kingdom represented in the king's dream; see Daniel 2:24-45). Roman domination of Palestine began in 63 B.C. and continued until A.D. 476.

Second, the Christ was promised to come before "the scepter" departed from Judah (Genesis 49:10). Bible students recognize that this prophecy has reference to the Messiah ("Shiloh") arriving before the Jews lost their national sovereignty and judicial power (the "scepter" of Genesis 49). Thus, Christ had to have come prior to the Jews' losing their power to execute capital punishment (John 18:31). When Rome deposed Archelaus in A.D. 6, Coponius was installed as Judea's first procurator. Interestingly, "the...procurator held the power of jurisdiction with regard to capital punishment" (Solomon, 1972, 13:117). Therefore, Christ was predicted to come sometime prior to A.D. 6 (see also McDowell, 1972, pp. 176-178).

Third, Daniel predicted that the Messiah would bring an end to "sacrifice and offering" before the destruction of Jerusalem (cf. Daniel 9:24-27 and Matthew 24:15; see also Jackson, 1997a). History records that the Temple was obliterated by the Romans in A.D. 70.

Fourth, the Messiah was to be born in Bethlehem of Judea (Micah 5:2). It also is a matter of record that Jesus was born in Bethlehem while Palestine was under Roman rule, before Judah lost her judicial power, and before the destruction of Jerusalem (see also Matthew 2:3-6; Luke 2:2-6).

In an excellent, thought-provoking article titled "The Historical Christ–Fact or Fiction?," Kyle Butt examined the hostile testimony from both Romans and Jews that inadvertently (yet powerfully!) documented Christ's historicity. In commenting on the records available to us from secular sources, he remarked:

> Interestingly, the first type of records comes from what are known commonly as "hostile" sources–writers who mentioned Jesus in a negative light or derogatory fashion. Such penmen certainly were not predisposed to further the cause of Christ or otherwise to add credence to His existence. In fact, quite the opposite is true. They rejected His teachings and often reviled Him as well. Thus, one can appeal to them without the charge of built-in bias.... Even a casual reader who glances over the testimony of the hostile Roman witnesses who bore testimony to the historicity of Christ will be struck by the fact that these ancient men depicted Christ as neither the Son of God nor the Savior of the world. They verbally stripped him of His Sonship, denied His glory, and belittled His magnificence. They described Him to their contemporaries, and for posterity, as a mere man. Yet even though they were wide of the mark in regard to the truth of **Who** He was, through their caustic diatribes they nevertheless documented **that** He was. And for that we are indebted to them.... Faced with such overwhelming evidence, it is unwise to reject the position that Jesus Christ actually walked the streets of Jerusalem in the first century (2000, 20:1,3,6, emp. in orig).

CHRIST IN THE OLD TESTAMENT

The Old and New Testaments portray a portrait of Christ that presents valuable evidence for the person desiring to answer the questions, "What think ye of the Christ?," and "Whose son is he?" In Isaiah 7:14, for example, the prophet declared that a virgin would conceive, bear a son, and name him "Immanuel," which means "God with us" (a prophecy that was fulfilled in the birth of Christ; Matthew 1:22-23). Later, Isaiah referred to this son as "Mighty God" (9:6). In fact, in the year that king Uzziah died, Isaiah said he saw "the Lord" sitting upon a throne (see Isaiah 6:1ff.). Overpowered by the scene, God's servant exclaimed: "Woe is me,...for mine eyes have seen the King, Jehovah of hosts" (6:5). In the New Testament, John wrote: "These things said Isaiah, because he saw His [Christ's–BT/BH] glory; and he spake of him" (John 12:41).

Isaiah urged God's people to sanctify "Jehovah of hosts" (8:12-14), a command applied to Jesus by Peter (1 Peter 3:14-15). Furthermore, Isaiah's "Jehovah" was to become a stone of stumbling and a rock of offense (8:14), a description that New Testament writers applied to Christ (cf. Romans 9:33, 1 Peter 2:8). Isaiah foretold that John the Baptizer would prepare the way for the coming of **Jehovah** (40:3). It is well known that John was the forerunner of **Christ** (cf. Matthew 3:3; John 1:23).

Isaiah pictured Christ not only as a silent "lamb" (53:7), but as a man Who "a bruised reed will he not break, and a dimly burning wick will he not quench" (42:3; cf. Matthew 12:20). J.W. McGarvey explained the imagery in these verses as follows:

> A bruised reed, barely strong enough to stand erect... a smoking flax (a lamp wick), its flame extinguished and its fire almost gone, fitly represent the sick, and lame, and blind who were brought to Jesus to be healed. ...he would heal their bruises and fan their dying energies into a flame (1875, p. 106).

Other Old Testament writers illuminated Christ in their writings as well. The psalmist suggested He would be known as zealous for righteousness (Psalm 69:9), that He would be hated without cause (Psalm 22), and that He would triumph over death (Psalm 16:8-11). Daniel referred to His coming kingdom as one that would "stand forever" (12:44). The prophets' portrait of Christ was intended not only to foreshadow His coming, but to make Him all the more visible to the people in New Testament times as well (see Bromling, 1991b).

CHRIST IN THE NEW TESTAMENT

The New Testament is equally explicit in its commentary regarding the Christ, and offers extensive corroboration of the Old Testament declarations concerning Him. The prophets had portrayed the Messiah's demise as unjust, painful, and vicarious (Isaiah 53:4-6; Psalm 22). In the New Testament, Paul reiterated that fact (Romans 5:6-8). The prophets predicted that He would be betrayed by a friend (Psalm 41:9) for a mere thirty pieces of silver (Zechariah 11:12), and He was (Luke 22:47-48; Matthew 26:15). They said that He would be mocked (Psalm 22:7-8), spat upon (Isaiah 50:6), numbered among common criminals (Isaiah 53:12), pierced through (Zechariah 12:10), and forsaken by God (cf. Psalm 22:1), and He was (Luke 23:35; Matthew 26:67; Matthew 27:46; Mark 15:27-28; John 19:37; John 20:25; Mark 15:34). Without any explanation, an inspired prophet predicted that the suffering servant's hands and feet would be pierced (Psalm 22:16). Later revelation reveals the reason for such a statement: He was nailed to a cross (Luke 23:33).

The prophets had said that He would be raised from the dead so that He could sit upon the throne of David (Isaiah 9:7). This occurred, as Peter attested in his sermon on Pentecost following the resurrection (Acts 2:30). He would rule, not Judah, but the most powerful kingdom ever known. As King, Christ was to rule (from heaven) the kingdom that "shall never be destroyed" and that "shall break in pieces and consume all these [earthly] kingdoms, and... shall stand forever" (Daniel 2:44). The New Testament establishes the legitimacy of His kingdom (Colossians 1:13; 1 Corinthians 15:24-25). The subjects of this royal realm were to be from every nation on Earth (Isaiah 2:2), and were prophesied to enjoy a life of peace and harmony that ignores any and all human distinctions, prejudices, or biases (cf. Isaiah 2:4 and Galatians 3:28). This King would be arrayed, not in the regal purple of a carnal king, but in the humble garments of a holy priest (Psalm 110:4; Hebrews 5:6). Like Melchizedek, the Messiah was to be both Priest and King (Genesis 14:18), guaranteeing that His subjects could approach God without the interference of a clergy class. Instead, as the New Testament affirms, Christians offer their petitions directly to God through their King–Who mediates on their behalf (cf. Matthew 6:9; John 14:13-14; 1 Timothy 2:5; Hebrews 10:12,19-22). It would have been utterly impossible for the New Testament writers to provide any clearer answers than they did to the questions that Christ asked the Pharisees.

CHRIST AS A MAN

The Scriptures teach that Jesus possessed two natures–divine and human. As an eternal Being (Isaiah 9:6; Micah 5:2; John 1:1ff.), He was God; yet, He became man (1 Timothy 2:5), made in the likeness of sinful flesh (Romans 8:3), though without sin (Hebrews 4:15). Isaiah observed that Christ would be "a **man** of sorrows, and acquainted with grief" Who would **grow up** "as a tender plant, and as a root out of dry ground" (Isaiah 53:2-3).

As a human, the prophets had said, Christ was to be the seed of woman (Genesis 3:15), and a descendant of Abraham, Isaac, Jacob, and David (Genesis 22:18; 26:4; 28:14; 2 Samuel 7:12-13). The New Testament confirms that indeed, He was born of a woman (Galatians 4:4) who was a virgin (Matthew 1:23), and that He was the descendant of Abraham, Isaac, Jacob, and David (Matthew 1:1ff.). The apostle John stated that He had become flesh and had dwelt among men (John 1:14). Paul wrote that Christ was recognized "in fashion as a man" (Philippians 2:7-8). From his position as a physician, Luke wrote that Christ "advanced in wisdom and stature, and in favor with God and men" (Luke 2:52). He was able to learn

(Hebrews 5:8). He experienced hunger (Matthew 4:2), thirst (John 19:28), weariness (John 4:6), anger (Mark 3:5), frustration (Mark 9:19), joy (John 15:11), sadness (John 11:35), and grief (Luke 19:41; Hebrews 5:7). He was "in all points tempted as we are, yet without sin" (Hebrews 4:15). But most significantly, He was able to die (Mark 15:44). In every respect, He was as human as you and I, which is why He could, and did, refer to Himself as the "Son of Man" (see Matthew 1:20; 9:6; et al.).

But the impact He had on the world was not due to His physical appearance. In fact, Isaiah foretold that He would have "no form nor comeliness; and when we see Him, there is no beauty that we should desire Him" (Isaiah 53:2). Rather, it was His nature and His character that made Him so intriguing, so commanding a figure, and so worthy of honor, respect, and worship. Here we see a man–but no mere man, for He is the only man ever to be born of a virgin (Isaiah 7:14; Matthew 1:18), and to whom the inspired prophets dared to apply the revered name of "Jehovah" (Isaiah 40:3).

Why do the Scriptures place importance upon the **human** nature of Christ? Wayne Jackson has suggested:

> If Christ had not become a man, He could not have died. Deity, as pure Spirit-essence, possesses **immortality** (1 Tim. 6:16–the Greek word denotes deathlessness). The writer of Hebrews makes it wonderfully plain that Christ partook of "flesh and blood" that "through death he might bring to nought him that had the power of death, that is, the devil" (Heb. 2:14). If Christ had not died, there would have been no atonement, no forgiveness of sins–the human family would have been hopelessly lost forever! Thank God for Christ's humanity (1979, p. 66, emp. in orig.).

CHRIST AS GOD

The Scriptures do not speak of Christ as **just** a man, however. They also acknowledge His divine nature. In most of its occurrences, the name "Jehovah" is applied to the first person of the Godhead (i.e., the Father–Matthew 28:19). For example: "Jehovah said unto my Lord, Sit thou at my right hand, until I make thine enemies thy footstool" (Psalm 110:1). Jesus later explained that this verse pictures the Father addressing the Christ (Luke 20:42).

Yet the name "Jehovah" also is used on occasion to refer to Christ. For example, Isaiah prophesied concerning the mission of John the Baptizer: "The voice of one that crieth, 'Prepare ye in the wilderness the way of Jehovah; make level in the desert a highway for our God'" (Isaiah 40:3; cf. Matthew 3:3, Mark 1:3, Luke 3:4). John was sent to prepare the way for Jesus Christ (John 1:29-34). But Isaiah said that John would prepare the way of **Jehovah**. Clearly, Jesus and Jehovah are the same.

The writer of Hebrews quoted the Father as addressing His Son in this way: "Thou, Lord [Jehovah–Psalm 102:25], in the beginning did lay the foundation of the earth, and the heavens are the works of thy hands" (Hebrews 1:10). This verse not only applies the word "Jehovah" to Jesus, **but actually attributes the quotation to the mouth of God**. Again, Jesus and Jehovah are used synonymously (see Bromling, 1991a).

Furthermore, Jesus spoke and acted like God. He affirmed that He was "one" with the Father (John 10:30). He forgave sins–a prerogative of God alone (Mark 2:5,7). He accepted the worship of men (John 9:38), which is due only to God (Matthew 4:10), and which good angels (Revelation 22:8-9) and good men (Matthew 4:10) refuse.

In addition, Jesus plainly is called "God" a number of times within the New Testament. In John 1:1, regarding Him "Who became flesh and dwelt among men" (1:14), the Bible says that "the Word was God." And in John 20:28, one of the disciples, Thomas, upon being confronted with empirical evidence for the Lord's resurrection, proclaimed: "My Lord and my God!" Significantly (and appropriately), Christ accepted the designation. Additional passages that reveal Christ as God include Philippians 2:5ff., 2 Corinthians 4:4, Colossians 1:15, and many others.

CHOICES REGARDING CHRIST'S DEITY

When Jesus was put on trial before the Sanhedrin, the Jewish high priest asked: "Are you the Christ, the Son of the Blessed?" To that question Christ replied simply, "I am" (Mark 14:62). In view of the exalted nature of such a claim, and its ultimate end results, there are but three possible views one may entertain in reference to Christ's claim of being deity: (1) He was a liar and con-artist; (2) He was a madman; or (3) He was exactly Who He said He was.

In his book, *Evidence that Demands a Verdict*, Josh McDowell titled one chapter: "The Trilemma–Lord, Liar, or Lunatic?" His purpose was to point out that, considering the grandiose nature of Christ's claims, He was either a liar, a lunatic, or the Lord. McDowell introduced his chapter on Christ's deity with a quotation from the famous British apologist of Cambridge University, C.S. Lewis, who wrote:

> I am trying here to prevent anyone saying the really foolish thing that people often say about Him: "I'm ready to accept Jesus as a great moral teacher, but I don't accept His claim to be God." That is the one thing we must not say. A man who was merely a man and said the sort of things Jesus said would not be a great moral teacher. He would either be a lunatic–on a level with the man who says he is a poached egg–or else he would be the Devil of Hell. You must make your choice. Either this man was, and is, the Son of God: or else a madman or something worse. You can shut Him up for a fool, you can spit at Him and kill Him as a demon; or you can fall at His feet and call Him Lord and God. But let us not come up with any patronising nonsense about His being a great human teacher. He has not left that open to us. He did not intend to (1952, pp. 40-41).

Was Christ a Liar?

Was Christ a liar? A charlatan? A "messianic manipulator"? In his book, *The Passover Plot*, Hugh J. Schonfield claimed that He was all three. Schonfield suggested that Jesus manipulated His life in such a way as to counterfeit the events described in the Old Testament prophecies about the Messiah. At times, this required "contriving those events when necessary, contending with friends and foes to ensure that the predictions would be fulfilled" (1965, p. 7). Schonfield charged that Jesus "plotted and schemed with the utmost skill and resourcefulness, sometimes making secret arrangements, taking advantage of every circumstance conducive to the attainment of his objectives" (p. 155). He further asserted that Jesus even planned to fake His own death on the cross. Unfortunately, however, Jesus had not counted on having a Roman soldier pierce His side with a spear. Thus, instead of recovering from His stupor, Jesus died unexpectedly. On Saturday night, His body was moved to a secret place so that His tomb would be empty on the next day, thus leaving the impression of His resurrection and, simultaneously, His deity (pp. 161, 165). One writer has asked, however:

> But does this reconstruction of the life of Christ ring true? Even if a charlatan **could** beguile a few followers into believing that he had fulfilled a few of the prophecies (either by coincidence, or by contrivance), how could he possibly fulfill those which were beyond his control? How could an impostor have planned his betrayal price? How could he have known the money would be used to buy the potter's field (cf. Zechariah 11:13, Matthew 27:7)? How could he have known that men would gamble for his clothing (cf. Psalm 22:17-18, Matthew 27:35-36)? Yet, these are just a few of the prophecies over which he would have no control. Jesus fulfilled every single one of them (Bromling, 1991b, 11:47, parenthetical items and emp. in orig.).

In considering the possibility that Christ was little more than an accomplished liar, renowned biblical historian Philip Schaff wrote:

> How in the name of logic, common sense, and experience, could an impostor—that is a deceitful, selfish, depraved man—have invented, and consistently main-

> tained from the beginning to end, the purest and noblest character known in history with the most perfect air of truth and reality? How could he have conceived and successfully carried out a plan of unparalleled beneficence, moral magnitude, and sublimity, and sacrificed his own life for it, in the face of the strongest prejudices of his people and ages? (1913, pp. 94-95).

Further, the question must be asked: What sane man would be willing to **die** for what he **knows** is a lie? As McDowell summarized the matter: "Someone who lived as Jesus lived, taught as Jesus taught, and died as Jesus died could not have been a liar" (1972, p. 106).

Was Christ a Lunatic?

Was Jesus merely a psychotic lunatic Who sincerely (albeit mistakenly) viewed Himself as God incarnate? Such a view rarely has been entertained by anyone cognizant of Christ's life and teachings. Schaff inquired:

> Is such an intellect–clear as the sky, bracing as the mountain air, sharp and penetrating as a sword, thoroughly healthy and vigorous, always ready and always self-possessed–liable to a radical and most serious delusion concerning His own character and mission? Preposterous imagination! (1913, pp. 97-98).

Would a raving lunatic teach that we should do unto others as we would have them do unto us? Would a lunatic teach that we should pray for our enemies? Would a lunatic teach that we should "turn the other cheek," and then set an example of exactly how to do that–even unto death? Would a lunatic present an ethical/moral code like the one found within the text of the Sermon on the Mount? Hardly! Lunacy of the sort ascribed to Christ by His detractors does not produce such genius. Schaff wrote:

> Self-deception in a matter so momentous, and with an intellect in all respects so clear and so sound, is equally out of the question. How could He be an enthusiast or a madman who never lost the even bal-

> ance of His mind, who sailed serenely over all the troubles and persecutions, as the sun above the clouds, who always returned the wisest answer to tempting questions, who calmly and deliberately predicted His death on the cross, His resurrection on the third day, the outpouring of the Holy Spirit, the founding of His Church, the destruction of Jerusalem–predictions which have been literally fulfilled? A character so original, so completely, so uniformly consistent, so perfect, so human and yet so high above all human greatness, can be neither a fraud nor a fiction. The poet, as has been well said, would be in this case greater than the hero. It would take more than a Jesus to invent a Jesus (1910, p. 109).

Was Christ Deity?

If Jesus was not a liar or a lunatic, then the questions that Jesus asked the Pharisees still remain: "What think ye of the Christ? Whose son is He?" Was Jesus, in fact, exactly Who He claimed to be? Was He God incarnate? The evidence suggests that, indeed, He was.

EVIDENCE FOR THE DEITY OF CHRIST

In Mark 10, an account is recorded concerning a rich young ruler who, in speaking to Christ, addressed Him as "Good Teacher." Upon hearing this reference, Jesus asked the man: "Why callest thou me good? None is good, save one, even God" (Mark 10:17).

Was Christ suggesting that His countryman's loyalty was misplaced, and that He was unworthy of being called "good" (in the sense that ultimately only God merits such a designation)? No. In fact, Christ was suggesting that He **was worthy** of the appellation. He wanted the ruler to understand the significance of the title he had used. R.C. Foster paraphrased Jesus' response as follows: "Do you know the meaning of this word you apply to me and which you use so freely? There is none good save God; if you apply that term to me, and you understand what you mean, you affirm that I am God" (1971, p. 1022).

What evidence establishes Christ's deity? Among other things, it includes Christ's fulfillment of Old Testament prophecies, His confirmation of His Sonship via the miracles He performed, His crucifixion and subsequent resurrection, and His post-resurrection appearances.

Fulfillment of Old Testament Prophecies

Scholars have documented over 300 messianic prophecies in the Old Testament (Lockyer, 1973, p. 21). From Genesis through Malachi, the history of Jesus is foretold in minute detail. Bible critics who wish to disprove Christ's deity, must refute fulfilled prophecy. To accomplish this, one would have to contend that Jesus did not fulfill the prophecies **genuinely**; rather, He only **appeared** to fulfill them. Yet with over 300 prophecies relating to Christ–none of which can be dismissed flippantly–this is an impossible task (see Bromling, 1989).

Could Christ have fulfilled 300+ prophetic utterances **by chance**? P.W. Stoner and R.C. Newman selected eight specific prophecies and then calculated the probability of one man fulfilling only those eight. Their conclusion was that 1 man in 10^{17} could do it (1976, p. 106). The probability that a single man could fulfill–by chance–**all** of the prophecies relating to Christ and His ministry would be practically incalculable, and the idea that a single man did so would be utterly absurd.

Performance of Genuine Miracles

Christ also backed up His claims by working miracles. Throughout history, God had empowered other people to perform miracles. But while their miracles confirmed they were **servants** of God, Jesus' miracles were intended to prove that He **is** God (John 10:37-38; cf. John 20:30-31).

While in prison, John the Baptizer sent his followers to ask Jesus: "Art thou he that cometh, or look we for another?" (Matthew 11:3). Jesus' response was: "Go and tell John...the blind receive their sight and the lame walk, the lepers are cleansed, the deaf hear, and the dead are raised up, and the poor have good tidings preached to them" (Matthew 11:4-5).

> Over seven hundred years earlier, the prophet Isaiah predicted that those very things would be done by the Messiah (Isaiah 35:5-6; 61:1). Jesus wasn't merely saying, "Look at all the good things I am doing." He was saying: "I am doing **exactly what the Coming One is supposed to do**!" (Bromling, 1995, 15:19, emp. added).

When Peter addressed the very people who had put Jesus to death, he reminded them that Christ's unique identity had been proved "by mighty works and wonders and signs which God did by him in the midst of you, even as ye yourselves know" (Acts 2:22). The key phrase here is "even as ye yourselves know." The Jews had witnessed Christ's miracles occurring among them on practically a daily basis. And, unlike the pseudo-miracles allegedly performed by today's "spiritualists," Jesus' miracles were feats that truly defied naturalistic explanation. In the presence of many witnesses, the Nazarene not only gave sight to the blind, healed lepers, fed thousands from a handful of food, and made the lame to walk, but also calmed turbulent seas and raised the dead! Although not overly eager to admit it, Jesus' critics often were brought face-to-face with the truth that no one could do what Jesus did unless God was with Him (John 3:2; see also John 9).

The Resurrection, and Post-Resurrection Appearances

Likely, however, the most impressive miracle involving Jesus was His resurrection. In agreement with Old Testament prophecy, and just as He had promised, Christ came forth from the tomb three days after His brutal crucifixion (Matthew 16:21; 27:63; 28:1-8). His resurrection was witnessed by the soldiers who had been appointed to guard His tomb. In the end, those soldiers had to be bribed to change their story so that the Jewish leaders would not lose credibility, and in order to prevent the Jewish people from recognizing their true Messiah (Matthew 28:11-15). It is a matter of history that Christ's tomb was empty on that Sunday morning almost 2,000 years ago. If Jesus was not raised from the dead, how came His guarded and sealed tomb to be empty?

That Christ had been raised from the dead was witnessed by many different types of people: the soldiers who guarded His tomb; the women who came early in the morning to anoint Him with spices; eleven apostles; and more than 500 other witnesses (1 Corinthians 15:4-8). When they saw the living, breathing Jesus–days after His death–they had concrete proof that He was Who He claimed to be all along! Even His detractors could not deny successfully the fact, and significance, of the empty tomb.

Thousands of people go annually to the graves of the founders of the Buddhist and Muslim religions to pay homage. Yet Christians do not pay homage at the grave of Christ–for the simple fact that **the tomb is empty**. A dead Savior is no good! For those who accept, and act upon, the evidence for Christ's deity provided by the resurrection, life is meaningful, rich, and full (see Paul's discussion in 1 Corinthians 15). For those who reject the resurrection, the vacant tomb will stand forever as eternity's greatest mystery, and one day will serve as their silent judge.

CONCLUSION

Who is Jesus of Nazareth? He had no formal rabbinical training (John 7:15). He possessed no material wealth (Luke 9:58; 2 Corinthians 8:9). Yet, through His teachings, He turned the world upside down (Acts 17:6). Clearly, as the evidence documents, He was, and is, both the Son of Man and the Son of God. He lived, and died, to redeem fallen mankind. He gave Himself a ransom (Matthew 20:28). He is God, Who predates, and will outlast, time itself (Philippians 2:5-11).

DISCUSSION QUESTIONS

1. Why did the soldiers who guarded the tomb of Jesus claim that His body had been stolen?
2. What are three different ways we can establish the deity of Christ?
3. What are some secular historical documents that mention Jesus, and what is the value of their testimony?
4. Describe the differences between the miracles Jesus performed, and acts of magic or sorcery that occur even today.
5. What part does prophecy play in proving Christ was the Messiah? List several Old Testament messianic prophecies.

Chapter 8

GENESIS 1-11: MYTHICAL OR HISTORICAL?

On November 24, 1859, J.M. Dent & Sons of London released for distribution Charles Darwin's book, *The Origin of Species*–a volume that would change forever the perceptions held by many people regarding their ultimate origin. However, long before Darwin wrote his book, he had seen his own perceptions of origins change as well. When he was but a young man, his parents sent him to Cambridge University to become a minister. In fact, somewhat ironically, the only earned degree that Charles Darwin ever held was in theology. But while studying theology, he also was studying geology and biology. After his graduation, and a subsequent five-year voyage at sea aboard the *H.M.S. Beagle*, Darwin's attitudes and views had changed drastically.

In 1959, Nora Barlow edited Darwin's autobiography, and included additional material that previously had been unavailable. In that volume, this amazing statement can be found:

> I had gradually come, by this time, to see that the Old Testament from its manifestly false history of the world and from its attributing to God the feelings of a revengeful tyrant, was no more to be trusted than the sacred books of the Hindoos [sic], or the beliefs of any barbarian (pp. 85-86).

Before Darwin could give himself over wholly to the doctrine of evolution, he first had to abandon all confidence in the historicity of the Old Testament and any belief in its teachings on origins. That accomplished, he then was able to imbibe evolutionary scenarios without obvious discomfort.

"If evolution is accepted, Adam and Eve go out! That story, that Bible fable, is interesting **mythology** but it doesn't present the true picture of the origin of man." This was the assessment of Woolsey Teller, second president of the American Association for the Advancement of Atheism, when he debated James Bales of Harding University on the existence of God (Bales and Teller, 1947, p. 54, emp. added). Equally as harsh are these words from Dorsey Hager regarding those who accept the Genesis account as being literal and historical:

> The most important responsibility of the geologist involves the effect of their [sic] findings on the mental and spiritual lives of mankind. Early geologists fought to free people from the myths of Biblical creation. Many millions still live in mental bondage controlled by ignorant ranters who accept the Bible as the last word in science, and accept Archbishop Ussher's claim that the earth was created in 4004 B.C.... Man's rise from the simple life forms, even today, causes much controversy among "fundamentalists" who cling to a literal belief in the Bible (1957, p. 12).

The idea set forth by these two men is that the Genesis account of creation is to be regarded as nothing more than "interesting mythology." That such an attitude should be expressed by atheists like Teller and Hager hardly is surprising. What is surprising, however, is the fact that some who profess to be Bible believers agree with this viewpoint. For example, the editor of the popular *Westminster Dictionary of the Bible* wrote: "The recital of the facts of creation is obviously not a literal, historical record" (see Davis, 1944, p. 119). The March 9, 1961 issue of *The United Church Herald* boldly stated: "The Biblical **myths** that Christians deal with are familiar: the Paradise story, Adam and Eve, the Fall, the Flood, the Tower of Babel, the miracles, the resurrection, and Ascension. These are myths to be solved for a myth is a combination of symbols pointing to an ultimate concern" (p. 15, emp. added). John L. McKenzie, in an article, "Myth and the Old Testament," in *The Catholic Biblical Quarterly*, wrote: "It is not a tenable view that God in revealing Himself also revealed directly and in detail the truth about such things as creation and the fall of man; the very presence of so many mythical elements in their traditions is enough to eliminate such a view" (1959, 21:281).

In 1981, Neal Buffaloe (professor of biology at the University of Central Arkansas in Conway, Arkansas) and N. Patrick Murray (Rector, All Saints' Episcopal Church, Russellville, Arkansas), co-authored a small volume titled *Creationism and Evolution.* In that book, they stated concerning the Genesis creation account:

> In other words, the Genesis poems are significant not because they tell us how things **were**, or the way things happened long ago. Rather, they are talking about man's situation **now**–the eternal importance of man's relationship to God, and the primordial disruption of that fellowship that lies at the root of human nature and history. When we read the ancient Hebrew accounts of the creation–Adam and Eve, the Garden of Eden, man's "fall" by listening to the seductive words of a serpent, and God's Sabbath rest–we must understand...that "these things never were, but always are.... The stories are told and retold, recorded and read and reread not for their **wasness** but for their **isness**" (1981, p. 8, emp. in orig.).

How much clearer could it be stated? The first chapters of Genesis are about things that "never were." They are not literal, historical writings, but poems, allegories, or myths.

In Exodus 20:11, Moses wrote: "For in six days Jehovah hath made heaven and earth, the sea, and all that in them is, and rested the seventh day...." However, in his publication, *Does God Exist?,* John N. Clayton of South Bend, Indiana stated that the acceptance of Exodus 20:11 as literal history is "a very shallow conclusion" that is "inconsistent with the Genesis record as well as other parts of the Bible" (1976, 3[10]:5). Clayton also has gone on record as stating that "Exodus 20: 11 is a quote of Genesis 2 and Genesis 2 **is not a historical account**" (1979, 7[4]:3, emp. added).

Is the material in Genesis 1-11 to be accepted at face value as literal history? Or, are statements such as the ones above correct in suggesting that the information contained in these chapters is mythological in nature?

IS GENESIS 1-11 LITERAL AND HISTORICAL?

Genesis 1-11 should be accepted as a literal, historical account, and should not be relegated to the status of a myth or "poem" for the following reasons.

(1) The style of these early chapters of Genesis does not suggest a mythical, allegorical, or poetical approach. Noted scholar Edward J. Young declared:

> Genesis one is not poetry or saga or myth, but straightforward, trustworthy history, and, inasmuch as it is a divine revelation, accurately records those matters of which it speaks. That Genesis one is historical may be seen from these considerations: (1) It sustains an intimate relationship with the remainder of the book. The remainder of the book (i.e., The Generations) presupposes the Creation Account, and the Creation Account prepares for what follows. The two portions of Genesis are integral parts of the book and complement one another. (2) The characteristics of Hebrew poetry are lacking. There are poetic accounts of the creation and these form a striking contrast to Genesis one (1975, p. 105).

The cautious reader will be completely unable to detect differences in style and syntax between Genesis 1-11 and Genesis 12-50. There is no striking difference between the type of literature or style of writing within these two sections of the book. The same type of narrative is to be found in Genesis 1-11 as in Genesis 12-50. As Thomas H. Horne stated in his classical *Introduction to the Scriptures*: "The style of these chapters, as indeed, of the whole book of Genesis, is strictly historical, and betrays no vestige whatever of allegorical or figurative description; this is so evident to anyone that reads with attention, as to need no proof" (1970, 2:205).

(2) The Genesis narrative is to be accepted as literal history because that is the view entertained by our Lord. Henry Morris observed:

> Especially significant is the fact that the Lord Jesus Christ Himself frequently quoted from Genesis. In one instance He used a quotation from both Genesis 1 and Genesis 2 (Matthew 19:4-6), thus stamping these chapters as both historically accurate and divinely inspired. Thus, one cannot legitimately question the historicity of the creation record without questioning the judgment or veracity of the Apostles and of Christ Himself. And this, of course, is an option which is not open to any consistent Christian (1967, p. 57).

John Whitcomb suggested:

> ...It is the privilege of these men to dispense with an historical Adam if they so desire. But they do not at the same time have the privilege of claiming that Jesus Christ spoke the truth. Adam and Jesus Christ stand or fall together, for Jesus said: "If ye believed Moses, ye would believe me. But if ye believe not his writings, how shall ye believe my words?" (John 5: 46-47). Our Lord also insisted that "till heaven and earth pass away, one jot or one tittle shall in no wise pass from the law (and this includes Genesis) till all things be accomplished" (Matthew 5:18). If Genesis is not historically dependable, then Jesus is not a dependable guide to all truth, and we are without a Savior (1972, p. 111).

Christ referred to the literal and historical events of Genesis 1-11 on more than one occasion. For example, Jesus spoke of the Flood of Noah as a real, historical event (Matthew 24: 37ff.). He referred to Abel as a real, historical character (Matthew 23:35). He spoke the truth on marriage and divorce in Matthew 19 (cf. Mark 10), using a command of God from Genesis 2:24 as a the historical background. Jesus called Satan the "father of lies" (John 8:44), referring back to the historical account of Genesis 3:4. Other similar examples could be given, but these should be sufficient to prove Jesus' support of the historical nature of Genesis. As Morris has stated: "...[D]enying the historical validity of the Creation account also undermines the authority of the New Testament and of Christ Himself" (1966, p. 92).

(3) The Genesis narrative is to be accepted as literal and historical because the inspired writers of the New Testament not only referred often to the narrative, but also made doctrinal arguments that depended upon the historical validity of the Genesis record. Every New Testament writer made allusions to, or quoted from, the book of Genesis. In fact, all books of the New Testament except Philemon, 2 John, and 3 John contain allusions to Genesis. Of the fifty chapters in Genesis, only seven (20,24,34,36,40,43,44) are not quoted or cited in the New Testament. Each of the first eleven chapters of Genesis is quoted or cited; none is omitted. There are two hundred references to Genesis used by the New Testament writers, more than half of which are from the first eleven chapters. Sixty-three of those references are to the first three chapters of Genesis, while fourteen are from the Flood story, and fifty-eight are related to Abraham.

Paul stated that woman is **of** (*ek*–a Greek preposition meaning "out of") man (1 Corinthians 11:8,12). He called Adam and Eve by name (1 Timothy 2:13), and considered Adam as historical as Moses (Romans 5:14) and Christ (1 Corinthians 15:45-47). He labeled Adam as the first man (1 Corinthians 15:45). He also stated that "the serpent deceived Eve by his craftiness" (2 Corinthians 11:3). Peter used the Flood to make an analogy to our salvation (1 Peter 3), and referred to the emerging, created Earth as something that had actually taken place (2 Peter 3:5b). Other examples are far too numerous to give here. Morris has commented:

> Many people have tried to explain away the record of this chapter by calling it an allegory, or hymn, or myth. But this is impossible without simultaneously undermining the integrity of all the rest of the Bible. This first chapter of Genesis fits perfectly into the his-

> torical record of the rest of the book of Genesis, which in turn is foundational to the entire Bible (1967, pp. 56-57).

(4) The Genesis narrative is to be accepted as literal and historical because of its relation to human redemption. Ed Wharton, and in his book, *Redemption is Planned, Needed, Provided*, correctly pointed out:

> A rejection of the biblical record of man's fall and of God's redemptive acts as historically factual has severe implications relative to the necessity and reliability of redemptive Christianity. When the Old Testament is not viewed as reliable history, the New Testament naturally comes under suspicion. For if the Genesis account of man's fall is not accepted as a reality, what can make redemption through Christ a **necessity**? If mankind did not actually fall through sin, from what would he need saving? The Old Testament presents the origin of man, his fall, and his inability to redeem himself and so educates him to his need for salvation. The New Testament presents Christ as the satisfaction of that need. Thus both testaments form a unity of narrative and of purpose. Their accounts are so interrelated that they cannot be separated and at the same time maintain that redemption is a human necessity.... **If therefore Genesis is not literally true, then Jesus as presented in the gospels is simply not necessary** (1972, pp. 10-11, emp. added).

Whitcomb agreed when he wrote that "the full historicity of the Genesis account of Adam and Eve is absolutely crucial to the entire God-revealed plan of salvation" (1972, p. 111).

(5) The Genesis narrative is to be accepted as literal and historical because of the importance it plays in presenting and tracing the Messianic seed-line through history. If the Genesis account of man's origin and fall is viewed as mythical, then mankind obviously cannot be viewed as fallen and in need of salvation. So why would God feel the need to preserve the Messianic seed-line from Adam through the rest of

his future descendants (Noah, Abraham, David, et al.)? For what purpose would the seed-line need to be preserved?

If, however, man is in desperate need of salvation from sin (as the Bible indicates that he is), then at some point in his history, he actually must have sinned against God. Genesis records the occurrence of that sin, and then provides a factual account of God's promise of redemption through the seed of mankind (3:1-15). The remainder of the Old Testament reveals the providential preservation of the seed-line, and its eventual culmination in the person of Christ. When man's fall through Adam—as clearly revealed in the first chapters of Genesis—is regarded as factual and true, then the Messianic seed-line promised in Genesis 3:15 must somehow be historically traceable from Adam to Christ. As Wharton went on to note:

> A discounting of the early chapters of Genesis as historically true must eventually lead to a discounting of the supernatural Christ and the salvation which he supernaturally attained for us through his death and resurrection. Any view of these chapters in Genesis other than authentic history will necessarily regard the genealogies and the tracing of the Messianic seed-line as unhistoric and unimportant. This will eat away at trust in God's word and cause faith's fire to go out (1972, pp. 11-13, emp. in orig.).

Thomas Whitelaw, writing on "Genesis" in the *Pulpit Commentary*, remarked:

> If we are to listen to many expositors of no mean authority, we must believe that what seems so clearly defined in Genesis—as if very great pains had been taken that there should be no possibility of mistake—is not the meaning of the text at all.... A person who is not a Hebrew scholar can only stand aside and admire the marvelous flexibility of a language which admits of such diverse interpretations (n.d., 1:4).

In other words, how is it possible to have so much evidence—in a language as specific as Hebrew—and still have people claim that "it does not mean what it says"? If we are unwilling to accept Genesis 1-11 as historical, how, then, will we be able to accept: (a) any biblical concept of man's origin; (b) the unifying concept of both the Old and New Testaments (i.e., the need for a coming Redeemer): (c) God's personally designed plan of salvation; (d) the Sonship of Christ; (e) the truthfulness of the Old and New Testament writers; or (f) the overall authority of the Scriptures as the inspired Word of God? [NOTE: For an in-depth treatment of these, and other, arguments supporting the literal, historical nature of Genesis 1-11, see Thompson, 2000a, pp. 133-161.]

G. Richard Culp correctly observed: "One who doubts the Genesis account will not be the same man he once was, for his attitude toward Holy Scripture has been eroded by false teaching. Genesis is repeatedly referred to in the New Testament, and it cannot be separated from the total Christian message" (1975, pp. 160-161). John Whitcomb's words form a fitting conclusion to this portion of our study.

> Surely the words of rebuke given by our Lord to the two on the road to Emmaus must be applicable to many Christians today: "O fools and slow of heart to believe all that the prophets have spoken" (Luke 24:25). Our basic problem today in the question of origins is not so much that we are ignorant of the theories and speculations of men. Our problem too often is that we neither know the Scriptures nor the power of God, and therefore deeply err in communicating God's message to modern man (1972, p. 111).

CAN A FAITHFUL CHRISTIAN BELIEVE IN BOTH CREATION AND EVOLUTION?

The thesis of this chapter is that compromises of the Genesis account of creation not only are unnecessary, but also wrong. While they may not always spring from ill motives, in the end they all produce the same unpleasant results. Christ said that "every good tree bringeth forth good fruit; but the corrupt tree bringeth forth evil fruit" (Matthew 7:17). One verse before that, He also said that "by their fruits ye shall know them." In this day and age, Bible believers desperately need to be more active "fruit inspectors." The compromises offered in place of the historical account of creation as recorded in Genesis 1, and as confirmed by writers in both the Old and New Testaments, are the "corrupt trees" of which Jesus spoke. The damage that such compromises have inflicted, and continue to inflict, is the evil fruit. Perhaps if more Christians could see those fruits, they would not be so quick to compromise.

Did Man Fall or Rise?

Surely one of the most serious problems with theistic evolution and similar compromises is the theological doctrine of the fall of man into sin. Once again those who are so willing to compromise the text would do better simply to admit that they do not believe the biblical record of origins.

> If evolution is true and if a man evolved from lower forms of life, whether through a mechanical process as Darwin proposed or through acts of God in accordance with theistic evolution, there was no first man who stood distinctly separate from the animal kingdom, but merely a gradual blending from animal to man. Without an Adam and Eve, it follows that there was no fall of man as recorded in Genesis. But the atonement of Christ is based upon the fall of man as a real historic event. If evolution is true, then, whether mechanistic or theistic, no historic fall of man occurred, and thus no Redeemer is needed to save us from our sins. If we are not a fallen people, unable to save ourselves, but a product of our animal ancestry, gradually improving and moving toward perfection, Christ was only a martyr, a good man ahead of His time but not the Saviour, the Redeemer (Davidheiser, 1973, 3:50-51).

Lindsell asked:

> The evolutionary approach forces us into a hermeneutic which regards the creation account as saga or myth rather than history and fact. This in turn does gross violence to even didactic portions of the Bible in both the Old and New Testaments and creates other problems for which there are no answers. The Apostle Paul builds his theology of redemption in Romans around the first and the second Adams. Jesus for Paul is the second Adam. The first Adam was the inhabitant of the Garden of Eden, our first ancestor through whom...sin with all of its consequences came. And it was the first man's sin that made necessary the second Adam's sacrifice on the cross of Calvary. To argue that the first Adam was a mythical figure while holding that the second Adam was true man boggles the imagination and turns the Scripture on its head. Moreover, if there was no first Adam, whence did...sin come? (1977, pp. 17-18).

The Problem with Eve

Theistic evolution and its counterparts should be rejected because they cannot explain Eve. The Bible teaches that from the beginning there were male and female (Matthew 19:4) with capability of reproduction (Genesis 1:28). Theistic evolution contends that the sexes evolved. Wilder-Smith addressed this contradiction.

> But surely it is going to be very difficult to honestly interpret the biblical account of origins in a consistently evolutionary context, in spite of all the heroic efforts of sincere theistic evolutionists. Is not the account of Eve's miraculous surgical origin from Adam's side sufficient to prove that the Bible is not describing here any natural evolutionary chance process modified by natural selection through millions of years? Eve was taken during sleep direct from Adam's side, which is surely not, by any stretch of the imagination, a description of the evolutionary process....
>
> The account of Eve's arrival on the scene, if we take the Bible seriously, surely cuts out the possibility of any "natural" evolutionary process over millions of

> years as the total explanation of man's origin. The biblical account is that of a plainly miraculous and nonuniformitarian origin, of woman at least. It represents a complete break with normal methods of reproduction in the whole higher animal kingdom. Evolutionary processes cannot by any stretch of the imagination be called upon to explain it (1975, pp. 41,42).

After discussing the inconsistencies between various compromises and the actual creation account in regard to the creation of woman, Davidheiser wrote: "A theistic evolutionist should honestly admit, 'I do not believe the creation account,' for when he attempts to inter-relate the two positions, he necessarily finds evolution incompatible with Scripture" (1973, 3:50).

Dr. Davidheiser was right when he urged theistic evolutionists to admit that they do not believe the Genesis account of creation. One cannot consistently believe both the biblical record of origins and the evolutionary position.

Turning the Savior into a Liar

One of the first things students learn in freshman philosophy classes is that any doctrine that implies a false doctrine is itself false. This is true in every area of life. Each of the compromises discussed in this book should be rejected on that account alone. Each of these compromises not only postulates an unscriptural old-Earth scenario, but has man appearing as the end product of some sort of long, meandering "creation process." During His earthly tenure, Christ discussed human origins, and commented that man and woman had been here "since the beginning of the creation" (Mark 10:6). If the compromising theories are correct, Jesus is not. Being a member of the Godhead, He is omniscient. Therefore, He had to have known the truth of the matter. But instead of revealing it, He lied. Yet Peter spoke of Jesus as One Who "did no sin" (1 Peter 2:22). The writer of Hebrews reiterated that point (4:15). The compromising theories, whether they intend to or not, accuse Christ of lying. Such an accusation, however, is false.

And any doctrine that implies a false doctrine is itself false. The late Gus Nichols once wrote:

> Since Jesus endorsed the Genesis record of the miraculous creation of man and woman, this record is true. If it is not, Jesus is a false Christ. Thus, theistic evolution overthrows faith in Christ, and thereby overthrows faith in Christianity.... Yes, the theory that God created the world by means of organic evolution rejects the Bible account of creation in Genesis, and rejects Christ who endorsed these writings, and in so doing makes Christ an ignoramus and the Christian religion a false religion. It is a fact that theistic evolution is more dangerous and misleading, more deceptive, and overthrows the faith of more people, than avowed atheistic evolution and atheism (1972, p. 24).

Robert R. Taylor also commented on this point.

> For years we have been warning young people what an espousal of theistic evolution does to Jesus Christ. Jesus went on record as accepting the fact that man and woman were made at the beginning.... Evolution does not believe humanity was made but slowly evolved through long eons of time. Jesus said humanity existed from the beginning and Mark has his affirmation of man's having existed from the beginning of creation. Evolution does not believe humanity has existed from the beginning. If evolution be true, Jesus is proved to be an unreliable witness of truthfulness in Matthew 19:4 and Mark 10:6 (1974, 116[1]:6).

No Bible believer ever should accept, or ask others to accept, a doctrine that impugns the sinless nature of the Savior, and turns Him into a liar.

"Either...or," not "Both...and"

Were Christians to be made aware of the logical implications of their belief in evolution, we are convinced that most would retreat post-haste from such a belief. The problem appears to be that many Christians are not aware that it is an "either...or" situation when it comes to belief in creation and evolution–not a "both...and." That dichotomy is the topic of the material that follows.

It would take a veritable encyclopedia to list the many contradictions between evolutionary theory and the Genesis account of origins. While it is impossible to discuss each, we would like to offer the following list, which has been combined from a variety of sources (Culp, 1975, pp. 154-155; Thompson, 1977, pp. 109-123,215-235; Niessen, 1980, pp. 17-22; Overton, 1981, pp. 117-118; Morris, 1984, pp. 119-120; Hayward, 1985, p. 14; Jackson, 1987, pp. 127-129; Kautz, 1988, pp. 24-25).

1. The Genesis narrative states that light existed before the Sun was made (Genesis 1:3,16), while evolution contends that the Sun was Earth's first light.

2. Moses declared that the waters existed before dry land ever appeared (Genesis 1:2,6,9). Evolution alleges that Earth's first waters gradually seeped out of its interior to form the vast oceans.

3. Scripture teaches that the first biological forms of life upon the Earth were plants (Genesis 1:11), whereas evolution argues that the initial life forms were marine organisms (see Sagan, 1980, p. 30; Fortey, 1997, pp. 3-28).

4. The Bible teaches that fruit-bearing trees existed before fish were created (Genesis 1:11,20), but evolution contends that fish evolved long before fruit-bearing trees (see Sagan, 1980, p. 33).

5. Genesis states that plants came into being before the Sun was made (Genesis 1:11,14ff.), whereas evolution suggests that the Sun was burning millions of years before the first plants.

6. Moses taught that birds were made on the fifth day of the creation week, and that "creeping things" (which would include both insects and reptiles) were brought into existence on the sixth day (Genesis 1:21,24); evolution asserts that birds developed long after both insects and reptiles (see Fortey, 1997, pp. 222-237,261-288).

7. The Genesis account reveals that living creatures were created according to individual groups, and thereafter each reproduced after its own "kind" (Genesis 1:11,12,21,24,25).

According to evolutionary theory, all living organisms derive from a common, primitive life-source (see Sagan, 1980, pp. 30-31; Ridley, 1999, pp. 21-22).

8. The biblical record teaches that man was fashioned from the dust of the ground (Genesis 2:7; 3:19; 1 Corinthians 15:45; 2 Corinthians 5:1), but evolution suggests that humans ultimately descended from ape-like creatures (see Johanson, et al., 1994).

9. The Bible teaches that the first humans were made with distinctive sexual characteristics–male and female (Genesis 1:27; 2:7,22; Matthew 19:4); evolution suggests that sexes "evolved" approximately two billion years ago in a process that "must have been agonizingly slow" (Sagan, 1980, p. 31).

10. The Bible is plain in its teaching that mankind has existed on Earth "from the beginning of the creation" (Matthew 19:4; Mark 10:6; Romans 1:20), thus virtually "from the foundation of the world" (Isaiah 40:21; Luke 11:50-51). Conversely, evolutionists teach that man is a "Johnny-come-lately" to the planet (cf. Sagan, 1980, p. 33; Fortey, 1997, p. 16–"Imagine that the history of the world is represented by a clockface, say, then the appearance of 'blue green' bacteria in the record happened at about two o'clock, while invertebrates appeared at about ten o'clock, and mankind, like Cinderella suddenly recalling the end of the ball, at about one minute to midnight.").

11. Genesis declares that man was appointed to exercise dominion over "every living thing that moveth upon the earth" (Genesis 1:28), but evolution argues that multiplied millions of creatures already had lived and become extinct eons before man ever set foot upon the Earth, hence before he had opportunity to have dominion over them.

12. Moses affirmed that God's work of creation was "finished" with the completion of the sixth day (Genesis 2:1-2). Evolution, on the other hand, requires that some sort of creative process has continued, hammering out new forms of living organisms across the many eons of time since life first

began. [The famous evolutionist of Harvard, Kirtley F. Mather, wrote that evolution is "not only an orderly process, it is a continuing one. Nothing was finished on any seventh day; the process of creation is still going on. The golden age for man–if any–is in the future, not in the past" (1960, pp. 37-38).]

13. The Word of God teaches that man has a soul that will live forever (1 Corinthians 15:35-58; cf. Thompson, 2000b); evolution teaches that man is wholly mortal (cf. Huxley, 1960, 3:252-253–"The earth was not created; it evolved. So did all the animals and plants that inhabit it, including our human selves, mind and soul as well as brain and body. So did religion." Cf. also Mather, pp. 37-38–"The spiritual aspects of the life of man are just as surely a product of the processes called evolution as are his brain and nervous system.").

14. Adam, according to the Bible, was to name the animals (Genesis 2:19); evolutionary geologists contend that most of the animals were extinct long before man appeared on Earth.

15. Genesis 1:31 records that God surveyed everything He had created and called it "very good." Evolutionists claim that most of these things did not even survive to that point, and the groaning world that did survive until man's appearance was far from perfect (cf. Hull, 1991, 352:486; Russell, 1961, p. 73).

16. The Genesis account speaks of the early Earth as having been designed specifically for man's habitation; evolutionary theory postulates an early Earth endowed with a reducing atmosphere that provided no free oxygen (see Thaxton, et. al., 1984, pp. 14-41,69-98).

17. The Bible speaks of mankind as being created with a moral nature (Genesis 1:26-27, et al.; cf. Thompson, 2000c, pp. 157-181); according to evolution, mankind is by nature amoral. [Famed British evolutionist Richard Dawkins commented: "You are for nothing. You are here to propagate your selfish genes. There is no higher purpose in life" (as quoted in Bass, 1990, 124[4]:60); American evolutionist George Gaylord Simpson described "good and evil, right and wrong" as "concepts irrelevant in nature" (1967, p. 346).]

18. The Scriptures portray early civilizations as producing sophisticated musical instruments (Genesis 4:21) and refining alloys (Genesis 4:22), as well as building such structures as the ark of Noah (Genesis 6:14-16) and the Tower of Babel (Genesis 11:3-6). Evolution, contrariwise, presents early man as primitive and technologically immature (cf. Birdsell, 1972, pp. 192-363).

19. According to Genesis, Adam was endowed with language from the first day of his creation; evolutionary theory postulates that language evolved slowly over long periods of time as man struggled to develop means of communication (cf. Birdsell, 1972, pp. 335-336; Diamond, 1992, pp. 141-167).

20. The biblical record is clear that Adam's responsibility was to tend the Garden of Eden (Genesis 2:9,15-16); Abel, his son, was a farmer by occupation (Genesis 4:2). Evolutionary theory, however, asserts that agriculture developed late in man's history (cf. Diamond, 1992, pp. 180-191).

21. Throughout Scripture, there are events that God has orchestrated (e.g., the Flood, the long day of Joshua, et al.) that cannot be called in any sense of the word "uniformitarian" in nature. Yet one of the cardinal tenets of evolutionary dogma (and the one that is the foundation of almost all evolutionary-based dating systems) is uniformitarianism. [Geologist Charles Felix wrote: **"Uniformitarianism is the great underlying principle of modern geology!** ...Uniformitarianism endures, partly because it seems reasonable and the principle is considered basic to other fields of study, but it also persists because **this is the only way to arrive at the enormous time-frame required for placement of slow evolutionary processes.** It is probably correct to state that evolution depends on the unqualified acceptance of Uniformitarianism! (1988, pp. 29,30, emp. in orig.); cf. Eiseley, 1961, p. 115.]

22. According to Genesis, the creation took place in six literal, 24-hour days; evolution is alleged to have taken place over billions of years.

CONCLUSION

For generations, biblical creationism has adopted a historical approach to the first eleven chapters of Genesis, and for good reason–**these chapters discuss real, literal, historical events**. There is nothing in the biblical record that suggests Genesis 1-11 should be viewed as containing mythical or allegorical material. And such a claim is supported quite adequately by the available evidence.

From the biblical perspective, the Mosaic affirmation–that in six days Jehovah made the heavens, the earth, the seas, and everything in them (Exodus 20:11)–is a clear, historical reference to Genesis 1. If Genesis 1-11 is not historical, these questions are appropriate.

(1) Did God literally form Adam from the dust of the ground?

(2) Was Eve a real person?

(3) Was the Garden of Eden a real, historical place?

(4) Was there an actual tree of knowledge of good and evil?

(5) Did Adam really name all the animals?

(6) Did Adam and Eve really sin?

If Genesis 2 is not historical, none of these questions can be answered with certainty. Yet the Bible answers each of them in an affirmative fashion–which clearly indicates that Genesis 1-11 is, in fact, both literal and historical. We should accept it as such.

DISCUSSION QUESTIONS

1. The Bible and evolution cannot both be true. Why? Some people say that both can be true, so how do they fit the two together?
2. According to the Gap Theory, what is responsible for many of the fossils found in the Earth? Where does the Gap Theory propose to fit the billions of years necessary for evolution to take place?
3. Numerous verses in the Bible can be used to refute false ideas like the Gap Theory. Which verse is one of the most damaging to the theories that attempt to fit evolution into the biblical account? Why?
4. What does the Day-Age Theory teach? Sometimes 2 Peter 3:8 is used to try to justify this theory. Why will that not work? How does Genesis 1:14 fit into this discussion?
5. Why do you think that many people have tried to fit evolution into the Bible? Do you think it is due to the fact that the text of the Bible points them that way, or is it more likely because of what "current scientific theory" teaches? If God is all-powerful, why would He need to use evolution to create the Universe?

WALKING AMIDST THE DINOSAURS

The numbers were staggering! Some time ago at a camp for Christian young people, a short, three-question quiz was given to the teenagers in attendance–most of whom were from homes with Christian parents (and many of whom already had made the decision to become a Christian themselves). The first question asked simply, "How long ago did the dinosaurs live?," and provided four possible answers. Over 70% of those present answered that dinosaurs had walked this Earth millions of years ago. People enamored with the type of material normally found within the pages of *Time* magazine or *National Geographic*, or those who watch CNN and the *Discovery* channel, probably would not find that answer alarming. But try to harmonize the idea that dinosaurs existed millions of years ago–long before man is supposed to have arrived–with the Genesis account of creation. It simply cannot be done.

These youngsters were not atheists or agnostics from some "intellectually elite" university; they were children who had been reared and nurtured in the church, and who believed that Jesus Christ is the divine Son of God Who lived and died for them. And yet, by the time many had reached their teens, they already had discounted the words of the Bible in favor of an evolutionary timeline that, from their vantage point at least, is dominated by the most amazing creatures ever to have lived –the dinosaurs.

Ask an average 10-year-old boy or girl when the dinosaurs existed, and see what response you get. Follow up that question with one about whether or not men lived with the dinosaurs, and watch how quickly that same 10-year-old's brow wrinkles in quizzical shock at the very idea of such. Chances are, that excited little face–which belongs to a child who could share a veritable plethora of dinosaur trivia with you–will change into a puzzled look that is accompanied by a troubling frown. For, you see, we live in a world where our children are taught that dinosaurs evolved, and became extinct, millions and millions of years ago–long before man arrived on the scene. And so, those precious little souls march off to school, where they will learn about the "terribly great lizards"–completely unaware of the fact that what they are learning is thoroughly at odds with the biblical account of creation.

One thing on which both creationists and evolutionists agree is that dinosaurs make marvelous teaching tools. Rare is the adult–and even more rare is the child–who does not have a keen interest in dinosaurs. These magnificent beasts with the polysyllabic names capture our attention as we fixate on their massive size, their lizard-like skin, or the terror they apparently were able to create as they roamed the planet. From kindergarten through graduate school, dinosaurs frequently are used as a tool to indoctrinate students regarding the "fact" of organic evolution. In most public school, college, and university settings, whenever dinosaurs are discussed, it is in the context of their evolutionary origin, development, and extinction. Additionally, students are told about how the dinosaurs evolved into what we now know as birds.

What effect does this kind of teaching have on young minds? If the correspondence we receive at Apologetics Press on a regular basis via telephone calls, e-mail, and regular mail is any indication, the evolution-based teaching regarding dinosaurs may be pulling more of our children away from the church than any other single concept. Because practically all youngsters have a fascination with dinosaurs, and because teachers are among the most trusted of all adults, children often accept without question evolutionary dogma and its accompanying concept of an ancient Earth. With what results?

If testimony from many of the evolutionists themselves is taken at face value, the study of dinosaurs was the deciding factor in their conclusion to abandon their belief in God and to accept in its place organic evolution. Evolutionists like the late paleontologist Stephen Jay Gould of Harvard, the famed dinosaur hunter, Robert Bakker, and others are on record as stating that it was the study of dinosaurs, at a very young age, which set them on their lifelong path as evolutionists. Dr. Bakker even commented on this fact in the preface to his immensely popular book on dinosaurs (1986, p. 9). Edward O. Wilson, the father of the discipline known as sociobiology, once commented that when he was fifteen years old, he had "great fervor and interest in the fundamentalist religion; I left at seventeen when I got to the University of Alabama and heard about evolutionary theory" (1982, p. 40). Henry M. Morris, former professor and department head at Virginia Polytechnic Institute, observed that he "spent over twenty-eight years teaching in secular universities and saw this sad tale repeated in many lives" (1984, p. 113). Because dinosaurs are fascinating to children, because they are such an effective teaching aid, and because they generally are used to teach evolution, these creatures represent a formidable tool to be used in robbing students of all ages of their faith in God and His Word. This makes the controversy over dinosaurs most important.

DID DINOSAURS REALLY EXIST?

One of the worst mistakes we can make as parents, grandparents, and teachers is to suggest that dinosaurs never existed. While such a response may appear, at first glance, to be a simple and quick solution to "the dinosaur dilemma," in reality, it is a response that becomes impossible to defend when our children visit a museum and come face to face with a two-story-tall *Tyrannosaurus rex* skeleton. Children cannot be expected to deny such tangible, forceful evidence, and at the same time believe a well-meaning but very wrong parent. Did dinosaurs really exist? Most certainly! We have discovered their fossilized remains on all seven continents–from North America to the Antarctic. As a matter of fact, great dinosaur graveyards have been discovered in places like Tanzania, Africa, and at the Dinosaur National Monument on the Colorado/Utah border in the United States. Literally tons of fossilized dinosaur bones have been recovered from all over the globe. In 1993, Mike Hammer even unearthed a fossilized dinosaur (from the Hell Creek formation in northwestern South Dakota) that was said to still possess the ancient creature's heart. Plus, of course, paleontologists have unearthed numerous caches of fossilized dinosaur eggs.

The first discovery of the dinosaurs, as far as "recent" times is concerned, occurred in the spring of 1822. Gideon Mantell, a country doctor in England with a lifelong passion for fossil hunting, set off in horse and buggy to visit a patient. His wife, Mary Ann, accompanied him on the trip. While Dr. Mantell tended to his ill patient, Mrs. Mantell took a stroll. As she walked, she came across a pile of stones that had been placed alongside the road to be used in filling ruts caused by the spring rains. Amidst those stones, she discovered what appeared to be very large fossil teeth. She took the fossils back to her husband (a well-known, amateur paleontologist in his own right), who was amazed, never having seen such huge teeth before. He went to the nearby rock quarry from which the stones were cut, and found more teeth like those that his wife had discovered. He presented the teeth to several scientists, but none agreed with him that they were from some type of heretofore-unknown creature. He, however, was stubbornly sure that they were. In 1825, he named the long-dead owner of the teeth, *Iguanodon* ("iguana-tooth"), since the teeth were similar to those of an iguana, but much larger. Several years later, more teeth like these were discovered in a different quarry. Now, no one doubted that *Iguanodon* had once existed. Meanwhile, huge bones of another creature (which came to be known as *Megalosaurus*) had been dug up farther away in Oxfordshire. By 1842, enough of these kinds of fossils had been uncovered to convince the leading British anatomist, Sir Richard Owen of the British Museum of Natural History, that an entire tribe of huge, lizard-like reptiles had lived in the distant past. Based on his studies, he named them "dinosaurs" (from the Greek words *deinos* and *sauros*, translated by him as "fearfully great lizards")–known to us today as "terribly great lizards."

Soon, American fossil hunters joined in the search. The climax came in March of 1877, when two schoolmasters–Arthur Lakes and O.W. Lucas–separately stumbled onto colossal fossil bones projecting from the rocks in different parts of the state of Colorado. Lakes showed his find to the well-known paleontologist, Othniel Marsh. Lucas showed his find to Marsh's bitter rival, Edward Cope. Marsh and Cope became the most famous of all the "dinosaur hunters." All told, Cope named nine new genera of dinosaurs, while Marsh named nineteen. Now, no one who bothered to keep up with the times doubted the existence of the dinosaurs.

WHEN DID DINOSAURS EXIST?

The question no longer was, "did the dinosaurs exist?," but "**when** did the dinosaurs exist?" Today, an important controversy exists between evolutionists and creationists regarding the matter of exactly when the dinosaurs lived. In fact, a chasm exists between these two groups that never will be bridged–so long as each side maintains its present view. Evolutionists advocate that dinosaurs evolved from some ancient reptile 200 million years ago, and that they became extinct roughly 65-70 million years ago. Man (in one form or another) allegedly evolved approximately 2-3 million years ago, and thus was separated from the dinosaurs by some 65 million years of geologic time.

Creationists who accept Genesis 1-2 as an accurate, historical record of God's creative activity, oppose such claims, and maintain instead that the dinosaurs were created by God within the six literal days described in the biblical record. Genesis informs us that **all** creatures were created during the Creation week (cf. also Exodus 20:11 and 31:17). Genesis also instructs us regarding the fact that dinosaurs, as land-dwelling animals, were formed on day six–the same day on which man was created. Thus, the inescapable conclusion is that dinosaurs and man would have lived together on the Earth as contemporaries.

Truth be told, dinosaurs and men **did** coexist as contemporaries. There is no other conclusion that respects the clear, compelling statements of the inspired Word of God. For some people, however, such a conclusion simply is not acceptable, and they have gone to incredible lengths in order to avoid the import and implications of the Bible's teaching on this subject. Consider, to choose just one example, the following statements from John N. Clayton of South Bend, Indiana:

> (1) If dinosaurs existed 200 million years before Adam and Eve it does not present any problem to a literal understanding of the Genesis record (1968b, p. 16).
>
> (2) I have no way of telling where man's beginning should be on the chart [of geological time–BT/BH]. Clearly man has become the dominant form of life on the Earth only in modern times, but where Adam and Eve fitted into this picture is unclear (1968b, p. 35).
>
> (3) Birds, mammals and man are mentioned; and all of these are recent additions to the Earth geologically (1977, p. 151).
>
> (4) Man is a very recent newcomer to this planet (1968a, lesson 8).

> (5) Genesis 1:1 simply says, "In the beginning God created the Heaven and the Earth." The verse is undated, untimed, and without details as to how this was done. Tradition has said that the first verse is an instantaneous event and that verses 2-31 detail how it was done. It does not seem to this writer that this interpretation is consistent with the flow of the language and the message.... Could not dinosaurs and many other forms have been involved in the production of an Earth ready for man? I further submit for your consideration that some time may be involved in this verse and that natural processes may have been used as well as miraculous ones to prepare the Earth for man (1982, pp. 5-6).

Contrast such statements ("Man is a very recent newcomer to this planet") with statements from Jesus Christ Himself: "But **from the beginning of the creation**, male and female made he them" (Mark 10:6; cf. Matthew 19:4, emp. added). Further contrast such statements ("all of these are recent additions to the earth geologically") to statements of the inspired apostle Paul:

> For the invisible things of him **since the creation of the world** are clearly seen, being perceived through the things that are made, even his everlasting power and divinity; that they may be without excuse (Romans 1:20, emp. added).

The term "perceived" is from the Greek *noeo*, a word used for rational **human** intelligence. Paul, speaking by inspiration, stated that someone human was "perceiving." What, exactly, were they perceiving? The things God had made. How long had they perceived those things? **Since the creation of the world!** Who, from a human vantage point, was doing the "perceiving"? Adam (1 Corinthians 15:45; Romans 5:14) and Eve (1 Timothy 2:13). The apostle's point was that Adam and Eve had been present since the creation of the world (i.e., as a part of the six-day creative activity of God), perceiving the things that were made. And that includes the dinosaurs!

EVIDENCE THAT HUMANS AND DINOSAURS COEXISTED

An article in the January 1993 *National Geographic* boldly proclaimed: "No human being has ever seen a live dinosaur" ("Age of the Dinosaurs," 1993, 183[1]:142). The evidence, however, reveals an entirely different story. Consider the following:

The Doheny Expedition

In the late 1800s, Samuel Hubbard, honorary curator of archaeology at the Oakland, California, Museum of Natural History, was excavating ancient Indian dwellings in the Hava Supai Canyon in Arizona. On the walls of the canyon where the Indians' ancestors once lived, Dr. Hubbard found elegant drawings of an elephant, an ibex, a dinosaur, and other animals. He stated concerning the dinosaur drawing: "Taken all in all, the proportions are good." He further suggested that the huge reptile is "depicted in the attitude in which man would be most likely to see it–reared on its hind legs, balancing with the long tail, either feeding or in fighting position, possibly defending itself against a party of men" (as quoted in Verrill, 1954, pp. 155ff.). Hubbard also noted:

> The **fact** that some prehistoric man made a pictograph of a **dinosaur** on the walls of this canyon upsets completely all of our theories regarding the antiquity of man.... The fact that the animal is upright and balanced on its tail would seem to indicate that the prehistoric artist must have seen it alive (1925, pp. 5,7, emp. in orig.).

Nearby, Dr. Hubbard and his team of archaeologists discovered dinosaur tracks preserved in strata identified as Triassic–alleged by evolutionists to be more than 165 million years old. Question: How could Indians have known how to draw such a perfect picture of an animal (the dinosaur) that they never had seen (or had described to them by someone who had seen it)?

According to the belief commonly held by evolutionists, no advanced mammals were present during the "age of the dinosaurs." Artists' reconstructions generally show the huge reptiles living in swamps, surrounded only by other species of dinosaurs. The late evolutionary paleontologist George Gaylord Simpson suggested that the only mammals that had evolved up to that point in time (even at the very end of the Cretaceous period) were supposedly "small, mostly about mouse-sized, and rare" (Simpson, et al., 1957, p. 797). In his book, *Wonderful Life: The Burgess Shale and the Nature of History*, Stephen Jay Gould addressed the same issue when he wrote:

Left: *Edmontosaurus* (courtesy of Paul S. Taylor, Eden Communications).
Right: Petroglyph discovered by Dr. Samuel Hubbard in Havai Supai Canyon (courtesy of www.bible.ca).

> Mammals evolved at the end of the Triassic, at the same time as dinosaurs, or just a tad later. Mammals spent their first hundred million years–two-thirds of their total history–as small creatures living in the nooks and crannies of a dinosaur's world. Their sixty million years of success following the demise of the dinosaurs has been something of an afterthought (1989, p. 318).

It thus is completely unthinkable, in evolutionary terms, that dinosaurs and advanced mammals (like elephants or giraffes) could have co-existed. Again, however, Dr. Hubbard's discoveries have "thrown a monkey wrench" into the evolutionary timescale.

> Another highly important feature of Dr. Hubbard's report is the discovery of fossil footprints of both the **three-toed carnivorous dinosaurs and the imperial elephants in the same locality**. If, as it appears, both of these creatures left their footprints in the river's sand or mud at approximately the same period, then we must assume that the dinosaurs continued to survive for millions of years later than scientists would have us believe, or else that the imperial elephants appeared on earth millions of years before their supposed arrival. But **it seems highly preposterous, and entirely contrary to all known laws of evolution**, to assume that these highly developed pachyderms were inhabiting the earth long ages before more primitive types of mammals (Verrill, p. 162, emp. added).

To complicate matters, researchers reported in the April 18, 2002 issue of *Nature* (one of the premier science journals in the world) that they now have determined that the "last common ancestor of extant primates" existed (as dated by evolutionary dating methods) **85 million years ago** (Tavaré, et al., 2002). Since dinosaurs are supposed to have died out 65 million years ago, that means the primate would have lived with the dinosaurs for at least 20 million years. One of the co-authors of the *Nature* paper, Christophe Soligo of London's Natural History Museum, stated in regard to the find: "What we demonstrate is that modern orders of mammals appeared well before dinosaurs disappeared..." (see "Primate Ancestor Lived with Dinos," 2002). So much for the belief that mammals evolved "just a tad later" than the dinosaurs.

Ica Burial Stones

Javier Cabrera Darquea came into possession of his first burial stone (from the Ica section of the country of Peru) when he was given one as a paperweight for his birthday. Ironically, he could recall his own father also possessing similar oddly carved stones that his family found in their fields in the 1930s. Dr. Darquea sought out the origin of his unique gift, in an effort to amass a collection of these unique stones, and eventually assembled over 11,000 of them. The rocks turned out to be ancient burial stones that the Inca Indians placed with their dead. Almost one-third of the stones depicted specific types of dinosaurs (such as *Triceratops* and *Stegosaurus*) and various pterosaurs. The type of art form represented by these stones, and their location, dated them to the time of the Inca Culture, c. A.D. 500-1500. How could these ancient Indians have known the anatomy of these creatures if they never had witnessed them firsthand?

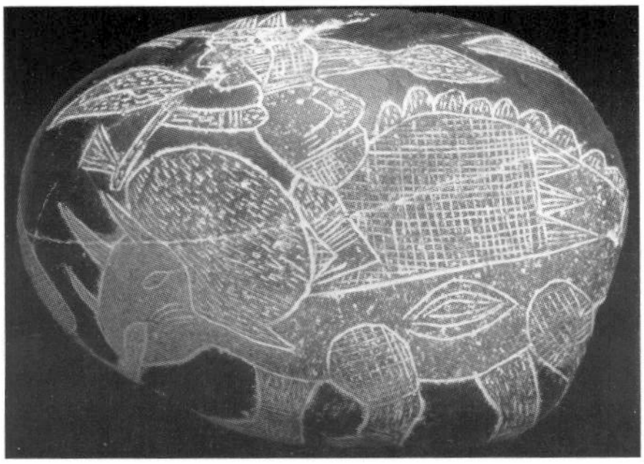

Image courtesy of www.bible.ca

Validation of these stones comes from a full understanding of their history. In the 1570s, the Indian historian and chronicler of the Incas, Juan de Santa Cruz Llamgui, wrote about the engraved stones. He noted that Conquistadors had taken some of the stones back to Spain, and wrote that at the time of the Inca Pachachuti, many carved stones had been found in the kingdom of Chinca, in Chinchayunga. On October 3, 1993, the *OJO, Lima Domingo*, a major newspaper based in Lima, Peru, reported a Spanish priest traveling in the area of Ica in 1525, inquiring about the unusual stones that had strange animals carved on them. These reports verify that the stones were in existence long before those discovered by Dr. Darquea. Since that time, other investigators have had the opportunity to observe stones in Nasca tombs, as well as to inspect the entire Darquea collection.

Interestingly, several *Diplodocus*-like dinosaurs on the stones have what appear to be dermal frills–something never previously reported by scientists. In 1992, however, dermal frills were found during an examination of fossilized remains of sauropods. In an article titled "New Look for Sauropod Dinosaurs," paleontologist Stephen Czerkas noted:

> Recent discovery of fossilized sauropod (diplodocid) skin impressions reveals a significantly different appearance for these dinosaurs. The fossilized skin demonstrates that a median row of [dermal] spines was present.... Some are quite narrow, and others are broader and more conical (1992, 20:1068).

Also, the skin of many of the carved dinosaurs resembled bumpy rosettes. For many years, scientists pointed to this as proof that these stones were not scientifically accurate. However, more recent discoveries of fossilized dinosaur skin and embryos have silenced the critics. In more than one report, these bumpy rosettes have been identified and discussed. In fact, one of the discoveries comes from the same continent as the Ica burial stones. Luis Chiappe and colleagues discussed sauropod dinosaur embryos, noting:

> The general skin pattern consists of round, non-overlapping, tubercle-like scales.... A rosette pattern of scales is present in PVPH-130 [designation for one of the specimens–BT/BH] (Chiappe, et al., 1998, 396: 259).

Again, we must ask: How could the Incas have drawn such accurate pictures of dinosaurs if they never had seen the animals (or had them described by someone who had seen them)? [For a discussion of Dr. Darquea's research, see Swift, 1997].

Natural Bridges National Monument Petroglyph

Natural Bridges National Monument is located in a desolate area in southeastern Utah. Visitors to this site will see where the White River has carved meandering paths through the sandstone rock. Three natural bridges have formed where these wandering streams have undercut the above rock formations: Sipapu Bridge (the second largest natural bridge in the world); Kachina Bridge; and Owachomo Bridge. It is at Kachina Bridge where an Indian petroglyph depicting a dinosaur was discovered. In fact, visitors to the site can see three or four drawings that appear to be dinosaur-like creatures.

Francis Barnes, an evolutionist and widely recognized authority on rock art of the American Southwest, had this to say about this find just outside of Blanding, Utah:

> There is a petroglyph in Natural Bridges National Monument that bears a startling resemblance to a dinosaur, specifically a *Brontosaurus*, with long tail and neck, small head and all. In the San Rafael Swell, there is a pictograph that looks very much like a pterosaur, a Cretaceous flying reptile. The artists who created this "pterosaur," and the "dinosaur," could of course, have been trying to portray some other real or imagined creatures. But what about other animals seen on rock art panels, such as "impalas," "ostriches," "mammoths" and others that either are long extinct in the western hemisphere or were never here

> at all? Such anomalous rock art figures can be explained away, but they still tend to cast doubt upon the admittedly flimsy relative-time age-dating schemes used by archaeologists (Barnes and Pendleton, 1979, pp. 201-202).

If *National Geographic* is correct in stating that "no human being has ever seen a live dinosaur," then whence came the models for these petroglyphs?

The Acambaro Figurines

On a bright and sunny morning in July 1944, Waldemar Julsrud, a German merchant in Acambaro, Mexico, found himself riding on horseback on the lower slope of El Toro (The Bull) Mountain. From his elevated vantage point, Mr. Julsrud spotted some partially exposed, hewn stones and a

Image courtesy of www.bible.ca

ceramic object half buried in the dirt. After climbing off his horse, he dug the stones (and a few ceramic pieces) out of the ground. Being somewhat archaeologically astute, Julsrud immediately realized that these artifacts were unlike anything that he had ever seen. The objects he held in his hand seemed distinctively different than those from other known Indian cultures. He eventually worked out a deal with a local farmer to excavate these precious pieces.

Eventually, over 33,500 figurines and artifacts of ceramic and stone (including some in jade) were uncovered. A key feature of this discovery was the fact that many of the artifacts were highly detailed **dinosaur** figurines. Charles Hapgood, a professor of history and anthropology at Keene State College (of the University of New Hampshire), became interested in the figurines and decided to investigate firsthand. Initially, Hapgood was a self-confessed (but open-minded) skeptic. However, after witnessing the excavations (even going so far as to dictate specific locations for the workers doing the digging), and after examining the figurines personally, he became a believer. He made his first visit to Acambaro in 1955, returned on numerous occasions, and eventually authored a book about his eighteen years of research into the figurines (see Hapgood, 2000). Consider the following measures, enacted to establish the authenticity of the Acambaro collection:

> When Teledynes Isotopes laboratories performed dating tests on the carbon deposited during firing on ceramic samples submitted by Hapgood, dates of up to 4530 B.C. obtained. Arthur M. Young, the inventor of the Bell Helicopter, who had sponsored Hapgood's investigation along with [Erle Stanley] Gardner [author of the Perry Mason mysteries–BT/BH], submitted Julsrud artifact samples [i.e., the Acambaro figurines–BT/BH] to the University of Pennsylvania for dating. Radiocarbon dating performed by Dr. Froelich Rainey in the laboratories of the University indicated that this culture may have been developed between 6,400 and 3,500 years ago. Additional tests using thermoluminescence method of dating pottery were performed. They produced dates of up to 4,500 B.P. (Before Present), or 2500 B.C., which upset the professional archaeologists and set off within the scientific and museum world a controversy over the ac-

> curacy of thermoluminescence dating. Retesting was done, and it was announced that because of anomalous factors in the clays it was impossible to determine an accurate date (Hapgood, p. 17).

According to David Childress, who penned the foreword to Hapgood's book, the most recent thermoluminescence testing done on Acambaro pottery fragments (taken by Bill Cote and John H. Tierney during the filming of the video, *Jurassic Art*, in the early 1990s) obtained results of 3,975±55 B.P. (Hapgood, p. 18). Consider also the fact that teeth from an extinct ice-age horse, the skeleton of a woolly mammoth, and a number of human skulls also were found at the same site as the ceramic artifacts. Hapgood noted: "I later took these teeth to Dr. George Gaylord Simpson, America's leading paleontologist, at the Museum of Natural History. He identified them as the teeth of *Equus conversidans owen*, an extinct horse of the ice age" (p. 82). Thus, the collection had evidence of extinct animals, human skulls, and dinosaur carvings from the same culture of people. But how could this be?

In 1999, Dennis Swift (who also was personally acquainted with Javier Darquea of Peru) made a trip to view the figurines. After receiving permission from the local authorities, he began to unwrap the ceramic figures. Dr. Swift noted:

> There was an absolutely astonishing moment of breathless magnitude as one object was unwrapped and there before us was an *Iguanodon* dinosaur figurine. In the 1940s and 1950s, the *Iguanodon* was completely unknown. No hoaxer could have known of the *Iguanodon's* existence, much less made a model, for it wasn't until 1978 or 1979 that skeletons of adult *Iguanodons* were found with nests and babies (Swift, no date). [For documentation on the *Iguanodon* discovery to which Swift alluded, see *The Dinosaur Encyclopedia* (Michael Benton, 1992, New York: Simon & Schuster, p. 80).]

Childress went on to note in an article titled "In Search of Sea Monsters":

> Adding to the mind-boggling aspects of this controversy is the fact that the Instituto Nacional de Antropologia e Historia through the late Director of Prehispanic Monuments, Dr. Eduardo Noguera, admitted "the apparent scientific legality with which these objects were found." Despite evidence of their own eyes, however, officials declared that because of the objects' "fantastic" nature, they had to have been a hoax! (no date).

This archaeological "hoax" presents insoluble problems for evolutionists. As Childress put it, "Most 'respectable' archaeologists will walk around the Acambaro mystery as if it were a land mine. The very existence of the figurines threatens the ivory tower of the current paradigm of history" (as quoted in Hapgood, 2000, p. 20).

Dinosaur Bones Only Thousands of Years Old?

In 1990, samples of various dinosaur bones were submitted for Carbon-14 dating to the University of Arizona's department of geosciences' laboratory of isotope geochemistry. Bones from an *Allosaurus* and an *Acrocanthosaurus* were among those sent to the university's testing facilities to undergo a "blind" dating procedure (which means that the technicians performing the tests did not know that the bones had come from dinosaurs). Not knowing this, prevented "evolutionary bias," and helped ensure that the results were accurate (within the recognized assumptions and limits of the C-14 dating method). We have in our possession–on the stationery of the University of Arizona–a copy of the test results for the *Allo-*

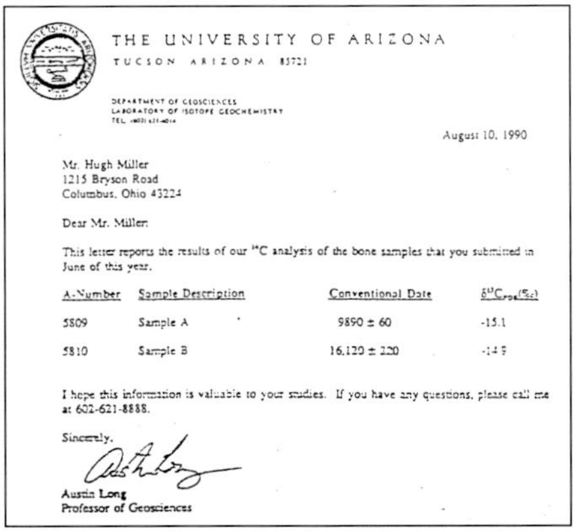
THE UNIVERSITY OF ARIZONA
TUCSON ARIZONA 85721

DEPARTMENT OF GEOSCIENCES
LABORATORY OF ISOTOPE GEOCHEMISTRY
TEL. [illegible]

August 10, 1990

Mr. Hugh Miller
1215 Bryson Road
Columbus, Ohio 43224

Dear Mr. Miller:

This letter reports the results of our ^{14}C analysis of the bone samples that you submitted in June of this year.

A-Number	Sample Description	Conventional Date	$\delta^{13}C_{PDB}$(‰)
5809	Sample A	9890 ± 60	-15.1
5810	Sample B	16,120 ± 220	-14.9

I hope this information is valuable to your studies. If you have any questions, please call me at 602-621-8888.

Sincerely,

Austin Long
Professor of Geosciences

saurus bones (see reproduction on previous page, sample B). Amazingly, the oldest C-14 date assigned to those bones was a mere 16,120 years (and only 23,760 years for the *Acrocanthosaurus* fossils; see Dahmer, et al., 1990). Both dates are a far cry from the millions of years that evolutionists suggest should be assigned to dinosaur fossils.

The Monster of Troy

The February 26, 2000 issue of *Science News* contained an article that diligently attempted to defuse a potential bomb within the evolutionary camp (Hesman, 2000). Sitting inside the Boston Museum of Fine Arts is an ancient Greek vase. This vase is covered by a series of somewhat unusual paintings, including one that is bewildering to both archaeologists and evolutionists. The vase portrays a monster that possesses the head of a **dinosaur**. And, to make matters worse, the images on the vase depict men and dinosaurs as coexisting.

Known as the Hesione vase, this elegant potteryware was created around 550 B.C., and depicts the Greek hero Heracles rescuing Hesione from the monster of Troy. The tale of the monster was first told by Homer in the eighth century B.C. In this legend, a terrifying monster suddenly appeared on the Trojan coast after a flood, and began preying on the farmers in the neighborhood of Sigeum. The king's daughter, Hesione, was sent to be offered as a sacrifice to the monster, but according to the legend, Heracles arrived in time to kill it. The painting on the vase shows Hesione and Heracles battling the monster, with Hesione tossing rocks at it, and Heracles shooting arrows. You can understand the obvious plight of evolutionists when confronted with such imagery. Thus, in an effort to "explain" this artwork in light of evolutionary timescales, the editors of *Science News* concluded that the paintings on this unusual vase simply prove that ancient people dug fossils, too. They believe that this painting was the end result of fossils—possibly of an extinct giraffe—that were dug up thousands of years ago. What's that old saying? If it looks like a duck, walks like a duck, and quacks like a duck, it's probably a–**giraffe**?

Human Footprints with Dinosaur Tracks?

Consider also that in 1983, researchers reported in the science and engineering news section of *The Moscow News* that they had discovered what appeared to be a human footprint in 150-million-year-old Jurassic rock, next to a giant, three-toed dinosaur footprint. The article stated:

> This spring, an expedition from the Institute of Geology of the Turkmen SSR Academy of Sciences found over 1,500 tracks left by dinosaurs in the mountains in the southeast of the Republic [Turkmen Republic–BT/BH]. Impressions resembling in shape a human footprint were discovered next to the tracks of prehistoric animals (see "Tracking Dinosaurs," 1983, 24:10).

Naturally, this report has received precious little attention, given the mindset of evolutionists.

Historical Records of Flying Reptiles

Additional evidence for the coexistence of humans and dinosaurs is derived from various ancient writings. For instance, the largest creature ever known to have soared in the skies above the Earth was a pterosaur identified as *Quetzalcoatlus* (KWET-zal-COAT-lus). The fossil bones of one of these flying reptiles were unearthed in 1972 at Big Bend National Park in Texas. This *Quetzalcoatlus* had a wingspan of 48 feet (which is longer than some small airplanes!). While these giant birds are not classified scientifically as dinosaurs (since they are not strictly land-dwelling creatures, as dinosaurs were, by definition), they often are lumped into a group of animals known as "dinosaur-like" creatures. Notice the following quotation taken from Herodotus, a Greek historian from the fifth century B.C., who wrote:

> There is a place in Arabia...to which I went, on hearing of some winged serpents; and when I arrived there, I saw bones and spines of serpents, in such quantities as it would be impossible to describe. The form of the serpent is like that of a water-snake; but he has wings without feathers, and as like as possible to the wings of a bat (1850, pp. 75-76, emp. added).

Pteranodon

Herodotus knew of flying reptiles, and recognized that these creatures were neither birds, mammals, nor insects–but reptiles with wings. Notice also what the Jewish historian Josephus wrote 2,000 years ago about Moses and his army having a difficult time passing through a particular region because of the presence of flying serpents.

> When the ground was difficult to be passed over, because of the multitude of serpents (which it produces in vast numbers...some of which ascend out of the ground unseen, and **also fly in the air**, and do come upon men at unawares, and do them a mischief)....
>
> [Moses] made baskets like unto arks, of sedge, and filled them with ibes [i.e., birds], and carried them along with them; which animal is the greatest enemy to serpents imaginable, for they fly from them when they come near them; and as they fly they are caught and devoured by them (n.d., 2:10:2, emp. added).

Although these two historians do not mention the extremely large flying reptiles, they do record that snake-like winged creatures, which could fly, did live in the distant past. These reports are consistent with findings that A.H. Verrill reported in 1954 in his book, *Strange Prehistoric Animals and Their Stories.*

> Primitive man, finding a fossil pterodactyl, might assume that the skeleton was that of some strange winged monster which still existed. Being totally ignorant of fossils and geology, an Indian or any other savage or semi-savage human being would never suspect that the bones had been reserved in rock for millions of years. Neither would it be possible for such primitive men to reconstruct mentally the creature as they appeared in life.... It is of course, inconceivable that the Cocle potter had first-hand knowledge of a living pterodactyl, ancient as the pottery is; yet had he been as familiar with the flying monsters as he was with pelicans and jaguars, he could not have depicted them more strikingly and accurately. Not only do the drawings show beak-like jaws armed with sharp teeth, but in addition the wings with two curved claws are depicted. Included also are the short, pointed tail, the reptilian head crest or appendages, and the strong hind feet with five-clawed toes on each (1954, pp. 55,57-58).

Obviously, the scientific evidence for the coexistence of dinosaurs and man speaks loudly, and yet it continues to fall on deaf ears within the evolutionary community. That silence, however, does little to change the documented facts, as we now know them.

DINOSAURS AND THE BIBLE

The question often is asked, "If dinosaurs are so important, why doesn't the Bible mention them?" There are several ways to respond to such an inquiry. First, the word "dinosaur" was not invented until 1842, while the Bible was translated into English much earlier. One hardly would expect to find a word in a book that preceded the word's invention by several centuries!

Second, it should be noted that numerous organisms are not mentioned by name in the Bible, yet such an omission casts no doubt on either their creation or their existence. The

Bible does not mention cats, kangaroos, or bacteria. Yet, just like the things that **are** mentioned by name, it is obvious that these things were created by God. While the Bible speaks accurately on all topics with which it deals, it was not intended to be a taxonomy textbook. The Bible is not a zoology text; its purpose is no more to catalog every species of animal than it is to list every human who has lived or ever will live. When we read that "all things were made by Him, and without Him nothing was made that was made" (John 1:3), we are told by implication that the Creation week included cats, kangaroos—and dinosaurs!

Third, while the word "dinosaur(s)" is not mentioned in the Bible, there is compelling evidence that dinosaurs, and dinosaur-like creatures, **are** described, directly or indirectly, in God's Word. Among the passages which may be considered are Job 40:15-24 and Job 41:1-34. Does the Bible mention specifically the creatures that we today classify as "dinosaurs"?

To answer this question, we need to study three Hebrew words: *behemoth*, *tannim*, and *leviathan*. These terms often are used to describe unusual creatures in the Bible. There can be only three possible explanations for the identity of these creatures: (1) they were mythological creatures that had no true existence in reality; (2) they were non-dinosaurian creatures (living or extinct) that can be identified in the ecosystem of the ancient world; or (3) they were now-extinct creatures that are classified as dinosaurs (and dinosaur-like creatures). The first option fails to satisfy the conservative student who accepts the Bible as the inspired Word of God. To such a person, the Bible does not contain the fabrications of heathen imagination. The second option is acceptable when one finds such creatures that fit the biblical description. The third option, although often unpopular in some religious circles, fits the data best in certain passages, as this study will show. In order to arrive at this conclusion, these three words must be considered in their appropriate contexts.

First, the word *behemoth* occurs with certainty one time in the Hebrew text (Harris, et al., 1980, p. 93). In form, *behemoth* is the same as the plural of *behema*–the Hebrew word for "beast." However, *behemoth* is used as a singular word in Job 40:15, indicating that a specific animal is being described. Some writers suggest that the word appears in two other passages (Brown, et. al., 1979, p. 97). In Psalm 73:22, the psalmist called himself foolish, ignorant, and "as a beast [*behemoth*] before Jehovah." Isaiah 30:6 speaks of "the burden of the beasts [*behemoth*] of the south." If these verses indeed refer to *behemoth*, neither is specific enough to reveal the nature of the animal mentioned.

However, Job 40:15-24 is very explicit in its description of *behemoth*. A particular animal obviously is in focus. The creature thus described was herbivorous, massive in size (with extremely strong muscles and bones), had a noteworthy tail, dwelt near water, and was fearless. Note the description:

> Behold now, *behemoth*, which I made as well as thee; he eateth grass as an ox. Lo now, his strength is in his loins, and his force is in the muscles of his belly. He moveth his tail like a cedar: the sinews of his thighs are knit together. His bones are as tubes of brass; his limbs are like bars of iron. He is the chief of the ways of God: He only that made him giveth him his sword. Surely the mountains bring him forth food, where all the beasts of the field do play. He lieth under the lotus trees, in the covert of the reed, and the fen. The lotus trees cover him with their shade; the willows of the brook compass him about. Behold, if a river overflow, he trembleth not; he is confident, though a Jordan swell even to his mouth. Shall any take him when he is on the watch, or pierce through his nose with a snare.

What is this *behemoth*? Some have argued that it is an elephant or hippopotamus. While the habitat may be fitting, there are some difficulties with this view. First, and perhaps most obvious, neither of these creatures possesses a noteworthy tail. Second, the *behemoth* is said to be "chief of the ways of God." If this phrase is taken to indicate size (which certainly is reasonable), it would rule out the hippo since at his full size he is but seven feet high. Although an elephant may be twice as tall as a hippo, he still is dwarfed by the dinosaurs (some of which reached heights of up to 3 stories and weights of over 100 tons). While it is inappropriate to be dogmatic, it does seem that a dinosaur (such as *Brachiosaurus* or *Apatosaurus*) could be under consideration in Job 40.

The second word that sheds light upon this topic is *tannin* (and its plural form *tannim*), which has been translated in various ways in English versions. Of the sixteen times that the word occurs in the Hebrew scriptures, the King James Version (KJV) renders *tannin* as "whale(s)" three times, "dragon(s)" nine times, "serpent(s)" three times, and "sea monsters" one time. The American Standard Version (ASV) employs the terms "serpent(s)" five times, "sea-monster(s)" six times, "monster" three times, and "jackals" two times in its translations of *tannin*. This seems to indicate that either the word is of a generic character so as to include these variations of meaning, or else the word is too obscure to confidently assign it a consistent definition.

Of these two, the first option is to be preferred when one considers the contexts that surround the word. Representative of these is Genesis 1:21: "And God created the great sea-monsters [*tannim*], and every living creature that moveth, wherewith the waters swarmed, after their kind" (ASV). This verse clearly is a listing of the broad categories of sea life that were created on day five, rather than a listing of particular sea creatures. This fact alone shows the KJV rendering of "whales" in this verse to be inappropriate. Similarly, other passages use *tannin* in a general sense to refer to a sea creature of perhaps enormous and frightful dimensions (Job 7:12; Psalm 74:13; 148:7; et al.).

Specific creatures of somewhat smaller dimensions apparently are indicated in other passages. For example, the parallelism in Psalm 91:13 shows that *tannin* could be used to refer to some sort of serpent: "Thou shalt tread upon the lion and adder: the young lion and the serpent [*tannin*] shalt thou trample under foot." In other passages, *tannin* is used representatively of great powers over which Jehovah has mastery (cf. Isaiah 27:1; 51:9; et al.). In a familiar passage, Aaron's rod was cast to the floor in Pharaoh's court and was transformed into a *tannin*. The English versions call it a serpent, which likely is correct.

Interestingly, Henry Morris has suggested: "If one will simply translate *tannim* by 'dinosaurs,' every one of the...uses of the word becomes perfectly clear and appropriate" (1984, p. 352). While this view likely goes too far, there may be some validity to it. It seems more probable that tannin refers to a general category of reptiles of various sizes, some of which may have been dinosaurs and/or dinosaur-like creatures. [NOTE: The plural form of "jackal" apparently was confused with *tannim* about twelve times in the KJV. Hence, the translators used the word "dragons" when they should have used the word "jackals."]

The third word to consider is *leviathan*. Of its six occurrences in the Hebrew text, the KJV transliterates the word five times as "leviathan" (Job 41:1; Psalm 74:14; 104:26; Isaiah 27:1), and renders it "mourning" one time (Job 3:8). The ASV uses the transliteration every time. In Job 3:8, the patriarch decries the day of his birth and says: "Let them curse it that curse the day, who are ready to rouse up leviathan" (Job 3:8). Job's meaning is unclear. It may be that he (speaking in hyperbole) was suggesting that if aroused, *leviathan* may have blackened the day of his birth—thereby eliminating its occurrence. Regardless, this passage tells little of *leviathan's* nature.

In Psalm 74:13-15 the writer describes the majestic strength of Jehovah by ascribing these accomplishments to Him:

> Thou didst divide the sea by thy strength: Thou brakest the heads of the sea-monsters [*tannin*] in the waters. Thou brakest the heads of *leviathan* in pieces; Thou gavest him to be food to the people inhabiting the wilderness. Thou didst cleave fountain and flood: Thou driedst up the mighty rivers.

In this context, *leviathan* is considered as a creature on the same fearful scale as the ocean and sea-monsters; in fact, it probably is an inhabitant of the seas. Psalm 104:26 confirms this habitat, and portrays *leviathan* on a scale with ships. Added to these sparse facts is the very descriptive text of *leviathan* in Job 41. Many scholars have supposed that the *leviathan* of Job 41 was a crocodile; even the chapter title in the ASV is "God's power in the crocodile depicted." There are some possible similarities between the *leviathan* and the crocodile, but the differences are so numerous and significant that they cannot be ignored. Consider these dissimilarities:

1. "His [the *leviathan's*] sneezings flash forth light... out of his mouth go burning torches, and sparks of fire leap forth out of his nostrils a smoke goeth ...his breath kindleth coals, and a flame goeth forth from his mouth" (verses 18-21).

Crocodiles do not have capacity to breathe fire. If one suggests that this is highly figurative, then to what do the words fire, smoke, and flame refer as concerns the crocodile?

2. "When he raiseth himself up, the mighty are afraid: by reason of consternation they are beside themselves.... He beholdeth everything that is high: he is king over all the sons of pride" (verses 25, 34).

The crocodile is not much more frightening when he stands than when he sits, since his legs are so short. How could it be said of the crocodile "he beholdeth every thing that is high"?

3. "If one lay at him with the sword, it cannot avail; nor the spear, the dart, nor the pointed shaft.... Clubs are counted as stubble: he laugheth at the rushing of the javelin. His underparts are like sharp potsherds" (verses 26,29-30).

Although the hide that covers the crocodile's back is extremely thick and difficult to penetrate, this is not true of his belly. The crocodile is most vulnerable to spears and javelins on his underside; hence, it could not be said of him that, "his underparts are like sharp potsherds."

> 4. "He maketh the deep to boil like a pot.... He maketh a path to shine after him; one would think the deep to be hoary" (verses 31-32).

The *leviathan* causes such commotion in the water that he leaves behind a churning wake; contrastingly, the crocodile is a stealthy swimmer.

> 5. "Canst thou draw out leviathan with a fishhook? Or press down his tongue with a cord? Canst thou put a rope into his nose? Or pierce his jaw through with a hook?... If one lay at him with the sword, it cannot avail; Nor the spear, the dart, nor the pointed shaft" (41:1-2,26).

Since the leviathan is unapproachable and too mighty to be apprehended by men, it is obvious that the creature is represented as "too powerful and ferocious for mere man to dare to come to grips with it" (Pope, 1965, p. 268). He is "beyond the power of men to capture" (Driver and Gray, 1964, p. 353). Leviathan is "peerless and fearless" (Strauss, 1976, p. 437). On the other hand, the crocodile–like the hippopotamus–was hunted and captured by Egyptians. Herodotus described in his writings exactly how they captured crocodiles (Rowley, 1980, p. 259), and how that, after being seized, some even were tamed (Jackson, 1983, p. 87). Hartley says that a baited hook often was used for hunting crocodiles.

> When the bait was swallowed and the hook lodged inside the mouth, the tongue was pressed down by the rope tied to the hook. After the animal was dragged alongside the shore, the hunter smeared its eyes with mud in order to subdue it for the fatal blow (1988, pp. 530-531).

Such a scene hardly depicts the animal being described in such vivid language in Job 40:15ff.

These are just a few incongruities that remove the crocodile as a possible candidate for the *leviathan*. Regardless of the similarities that one might find (and they are indeed difficult to discover), these dissimilarities are incontrovertible. Although it may not be possible to single out the one creature that alone could be called *leviathan*, the possibility that it was a dinosaur-like, sea-dwelling reptile cannot be dismissed.

Some scholars have suggested that perhaps the behemoth described in Job 40 represents a species of dinosaur, and that the leviathan discussed in Job 41 represents a dinosaur-like, water-living reptile. [Dinosaurs, by definition, lived only on land, and therefore leviathan could not have been a dinosaur. However, there was a group of animals that lived in watery environments and that, to the casual observer, looked like dinosaurs. These animals are referred to scientifically as "dinosaur-like, water-living reptiles."] However, this view has not been popular among certain Bible scholars, in large part because so many of them accept the evolutionary theory that dinosaurs became extinct millions of years before man arrived on the planet (see Jackson, 1983, p. 86). As Henry Morris observed:

> Modern Bible scholars, for the most part, have become so conditioned to think in terms of the long ages of evolutionary geology that it never occurs to them that mankind once lived in the same world with the great animals that are now found only as fossils (1988, p. 115).

Even though we are taught continually through books, magazines, movies, and cartoons that dinosaurs existed millions of years ago, we know that dinosaurs and man lived as contemporaries on Earth. Moses wrote by inspiration: "For in six days Jehovah made heaven and earth, the sea, and **all** that in them is" (Exodus 20.11, emp. added). If God created everything in six days, then **everything** created was created in those six days. According to the Genesis record, no animals were created before day five, at which time God created sea-dwelling creatures and birds (Genesis 1:20-23). On day six (Genesis 1:24-25), God created the "creeping things" and "beasts of the earth"–descriptions that certainly would include dinosaurs. Since man likewise was created on day six (Genesis 1: 26-27), the inescapable conclusion is that men and dinosaurs lived on the Earth as contemporaries.

So, while the Bible does speak indirectly (Exodus 20:11) of dinosaurs, it also is possible that direct references are made to these creatures (e.g., Job 40-41). Regardless, Bible teaching is plain. Men and dinosaurs lived upon the Earth at the same time. No other view complements the verbal, plenary inspiration of God's Word.

CONCLUSION

Contrary to popular opinion, dinosaurs do not present a problem for creationists. In fact, quite the opposite is true. It is evolutionists who have a problem. While they continue to maintain, as the late paleontologist Roland T. Bird of the American Museum of Natural History once put it, that "no man had ever existed in the age of the reptiles" (1939, 43[5]:257), the evidence documents exactly the opposite.

The Mosaic record of the Creation is inexhaustively sublime. In it, we learn of the creation of the heavens and the Earth by an Almighty God. By divine fiat, light was formed and atmosphere was wrapped around this planet. Great seas were gathered together, and separated from dry land. The world of botany miraculously bloomed, and lights burst forth in the heavens. The waters swarmed with living creatures, and birds soared through the pristine air. Varieties of domestic animals and beasts were created and finally, man, the zenith of God's creation, stood proudly upon the Earth's bosom.

The dinosaur–one of the most majestic of God's creatures–stood with man. No doubt they pondered each other's existence. Today, we still stand amazed at these awesome giants. And as we do, their presence in the past should remind us of the magnificence of the God Who was able to speak them into existence by "the word of His power" (Hebrews 1:3). Awesome creatures–from the hand of an awesome Creator.

DISCUSSION QUESTIONS

1. Why is it important to have some basic knowledge on dinosaurs? Describe some places you have observed material on dinosaurs. Generally speaking, what is the target audience for this material, and why?
2. What evidence exists that dinosaurs really lived? Regarding timelines, approximately when do evolutionists say that dinosaurs lived? According to the Bible, when did dinosaurs live? Why is it important to know when dinosaurs lived?
3. Discuss some of the evidence that proves humans coexisted with dinosaurs. How would the theory of evolution be affected if dinosaurs and humans coexisted? Why do you think this material is not taught in public schools?
5. What are some of the physical characteristics of the behemoth and leviathan mentioned in Job 40-41? Discuss some clues found in the text that allow us to know recognize the behemoth and leviathan were actual creatures.
6. Discuss the significance of other historical documents that make reference to flying reptiles. Give specific examples.

EVOLUTIONARY ARGUMENTS ANSWERED [PART I]

There are two different, totally opposite explanations for the origin of the Universe and the origin of life in the Universe. Each of these explanations is an entire world view, or philosophy, of origins and destinies, of life and meaning.

One of these world views is the concept of **evolution**. According to the theory of evolution, the Universe is **self-contained**, which means that everything in the Universe has come into being through random processes without any kind of supernatural involvement. This view says that the origin and development of the Universe (and all life in it) can be explained by time, chance, and continuing natural processes. According to evolutionary theory, all living things have arisen from a single-celled organism, which in turn had arisen from something nonliving (such as an amino acid or a protein).

The second world view is the concept of **creation**. According to the theory of creation, the Universe is **not self-contained**. Everything in the Universe has come into being through the design, purpose, and deliberate acts of a supernatural Creator Who, using processes that are not continuing today, created the Universe, the Earth, and all life on the Earth (including all basic types of plants and animals, as well as humans).

There are two and only two possibilities concerning origins. One or the other of them must be true. That is to say, all things either can, or cannot, be explained in terms of ongoing natural processes in a self-contained Universe. If they can, then evolution is true. If they cannot, then they must be explained by a process of creation.

Both evolution and creation may be called scientific models, since both may be used to explain and predict scientific facts. Obviously the one that does the better job of explaining/predicting is the better scientific model.

In order to examine properly the two models, they must be defined in general terms, and then each must be compared to the available facts. **Evolution** includes the evidence for a gradual appearance of present life over eons of time, with complex kinds of life emerging from "simpler" kinds, and ultimately from nonliving matter. **Creation** includes the evidence for a sudden appearance of complex life. The creation model denies "vertical" evolution (also called "macroevolution"–the emergence of complex organisms from simple organisms), and change between kinds (such as an amoeba gradually changing into a man), but does not challenge "horizontal" evolution (also called "microevolution"–the formation of species or subspecies within created kinds, or genetic variation such as a species of birds gradually getting a smaller beak or a species of moth changing its colors over time).

IS EVOLUTION A "FACT OF SCIENCE"?

When we talk about the origin of the Universe and those things in it, we cannot speak as eyewitnesses or firsthand observers since **none of us was present**. Thus, any scientific discussion must be based on certain assumptions, hypotheses, or theories put in place after the fact. An **assumption** is something taken for granted, and represents a legitimate starting point for an investigation. A **hypothesis** is merely an educated guess or tentative assumption. A **theory** is a plausible general principle or set of principles that may be used to explain certain phenomena, and that is supported by at least some documented facts.

Many evolutionists claim that evolution has been proven, and therefore must be spoken of not as a theory, but rather as a fact. Most people today, for example, know the names of Francis Crick and James Watson, the two scientists who shared the

Nobel Prize for their discovery of the structure of DNA (the molecule within each living cell that carries the genetic information). Several years after their discovery, Dr. Watson wrote a book titled *The Molecular Biology of the Gene*, in which he stated: "Today the theory of evolution is an accepted fact…" (1987, p. 2). A few years later, in the August 23, 1999 issue of *Time* magazine, the famous Harvard evolutionist Stephen Jay Gould said that "evolution is as well documented as any phenomenon in science, as strongly as the earth's revolution around the sun rather than vice versa. In this sense, we can call evolution a 'fact'" (1999, 154[8]:59).

Is evolution a "fact" of science? No, it is not. A fact is defined as "an actual occurrence" or "something that has actual existence." With that standard-usage definition in mind, consider the following.

Evolution cannot be considered a fact because it is based on a number of **non-provable assumptions**. Several years ago, George Kerkut, a well-known evolutionist from Great Britain, listed no less than **seven** such assumptions in his classic text, *The Implications of Evolution* (1960). The first two assumptions were: (1) spontaneous generation **must** have occurred; and (2) spontaneous generation must have occurred **only once**.

Spontaneous generation is the idea that something nonliving gave rise to something living–without any outside assistance. This concept is the very basis of organic evolution, since evolutionists believe that when the Universe first began it was composed solely of hydrogen (with perhaps a few atoms of helium). In order to get life started, they are forced to conclude that those nonliving, inorganic chemicals "somehow" turned into something living. But that "somehow" is an extremely difficult problem for the concept of evolution. Scientists have tried for centuries to document that spontaneous generation can occur. Yet every single attempt not only has failed, but failed miserably. No one ever has been able to prove that something **nonliving** can produce something **living**. Therefore, evolutionists simply "assume" that it happened.

Furthermore, they assume that it happened **only once**. But why? All of life is composed of a singular genetic code (the DNA of which we spoke earlier). Because that code is so extremely complicated, and because it is virtually the same throughout all living things (with only minor variations), evolutionists are forced to concede that the events that produced it must have occurred just once. To suggest that it could have happened more than once–and that it produced exactly the same code each time–would be ridiculous. No one would believe such–not even evolutionists.

There are two serious problems with all of this. First, something based upon an assumption **never** can be considered a "fact." At best, **any** idea based on an **assumption** forever remains just that–an assumption. It is not possible, logically, to build a concept upon an assumption and then assert that it is a fact. Since spontaneous generation is the basis of all of evolution (obviously, you cannot get something to evolve if you cannot get it to live in the first place!), and since spontaneous generation is nothing more than an assumption (because it never has been documented scientifically, and all available evidence points against it), then evolution cannot be a fact.

Second, as all scientists know, one-time events cannot be studied by using the scientific method. Biologist Paul Weisz, in his textbook, *Elements of Biology*, stated that "one-time events on earth are outside of science" (1965, p. 4). Why is this the case? Science uses the five senses (touch, smell, sight, taste, and hearing) to study those things that are universal, dependable, and reproducible. This simply means that a scientist working in Hong Kong can do an experiment exactly like a scientist in New York City. If both use the same methods, both will get the same results–today, tomorrow, next year, or ten years from now. And their results can be repeated over and over again. But one-time events are neither universal nor dependable. And, by definition, they cannot be repeated.

Evolutionists admit that two of the seven **non-provable assumptions** upon which evolution is based center on the idea that spontaneous generation must have occurred, and that it must have occurred only once. This means that evolution cannot be a scientific fact. Dr. Kerkut admitted:

> ...[T]he attempt to explain all living forms in terms of evolution from a unique source...is premature and **not satisfactorily supported by present-day evidence**.... The supporting evidence remains to be discovered.... We can, if we like, believe that such an evolutionary system has taken place, but I for one do not think that "it has been proven beyond all reasonable doubt" (1960, pp. vii,viii, emp. added).

Then, after discussing the various aspects of each of the seven **non-provable assumptions** upon which evolution is based, he observed:

> The first point that I should like to make is that these seven assumptions by their nature **are not capable of experimental verification**.... The evidence that supports it is not sufficiently strong to allow us to consider it anything more than a working hypothesis (p. 157, emp. added).

Again, the standard-usage definition of a fact is something that is "an actual occurrence"or "something that has actual existence." Can any process be called "an actual occurrence" when the knowledge of how, when, where, what, and why is missing? If someone suggested that a certain skyscraper had merely "happened," but that the how, when, where, what, and why were complete unknowns, would you be likely to call it a fact, or an "unproven assertion"? To ask is to answer. When the best that evolutionists can offer is an insufficient explanation for life's origin in the first place, an equally inadequate mechanism for the evolution of that life once it "somehow" began by naturalistic processes, and a fossil record full of "missing links" to document its supposed course through time, we will continue to call their "fact" simply a theory (or, better yet, a hypothesis). Twisting the definition of the word "fact" is a poor attempt on the part of evolutionists to add credibility to a theory that lacks any factual merit whatsoever.

And it is not just creationists who have made this point. The well-known Australian molecular biologist and evolutionist, Michael Denton, addressed this very point in his 1985 book, *Evolution: A Theory in Crisis.* After admitting that no one ever has documented any evidence for the supposed evolutionary "chain of life" leading from one type of creature to another, Dr. Denton wrote: "The concept of the continuity of nature has existed in the mind of man, **never** in the facts of nature" (p. 353, emp. in orig.). Thirteen years later, in his 1998 book, *Nature's Destiny*, Dr. Denton shocked everyone when he stated:

> Whether one accepts or rejects the design hypothesis...there is no avoiding the conclusion that the world **looks** as if it has been tailored for life; it **appears to have been designed**. All reality **appears** to be a vast, coherent, teleological whole with life and mankind as its purpose and goal (p. 387, emp. in orig.).

We agree with both of Dr. Denton's statements. The "facts of nature" certainly do **not** support evolution. And the world most assuredly "**appears to have been designed**."

Even evolutionists admit (although somewhat reluctantly at times) that design implies a Designer. The question then becomes: **Who designed the Universe?** It certainly was not those mythical parents, "Father Time" and "Mother Nature." They do not possess the ability to "design" anything. Yet everywhere we look in the world around us, we see evidence of the most intricate kind of design–from our massive Universe to the tiny cells of which we are made. God–not evolution–is responsible. That is the most impressive "fact" we know.

EVOLUTIONARY ARGUMENTS ANSWERED

Genetic Mutations

At the end of the nineteenth century, just as Darwin's dogma of natural selection was beginning to fall on hard times, the science of genetics was born. The concepts that had been published in 1865 in a little-known journal by the Moravian monk Gregor Mendel, but which had lain quietly forgotten on dusty library shelves for thirty-five years, were "rediscovered" with an attendant flourish. Some who began to study this fledgling science felt for the first time that they had in their possession the actual mechanism of evolution–genetic mutations. Their suggestion was that species arose by mutations that then somehow were incorporated into the system by natural selection. Today, the alleged mechanism of evolution, therefore, is not merely natural selection, but rather **natural selection plus genetic mutations**. Hitching wrote in this regard:

> The theory is that a chance favorable mutation gradually spreads through a population of plants or animals by a process of natural selection of the fittest; and over geological periods of time, a new species emerges. Genetics provides the mechanism that supports Darwin's original insight (1982, p. 34).

Writing almost twenty years earlier, Ernst Mayr of Harvard agreed: "The proponents of the synthetic theory maintain that all evolution is due to the accumulation of small genetic changes, guided by natural selection" (1963, p. 586). In their high school biology textbook, *Life: An Introduction to Biology*, Simpson and Beck likewise agreed: "Mutations are the ultimate raw materials for evolution" (1965, p. 430). Evolutionist Theodosius Dobzhansky of the Rockefeller University commented that "the process of mutation is the only known source of the new materials of genetic variability, and hence of evolution" (1957, p. 385).

Through the years, not much has changed in this regard. In a chapter on the role of mutations in evolution for the 1997 book *Evolution* edited by Mark Ridley, evolutionary biologist Sewall Wright observed:

> The observed properties of gene mutation–fortuitous in origin, infrequent in occurrence and deleterious when not negligible in effect–seem about as unfavourable as possible for an evolutionary process. Un-

> der biparental reproduction, however, a limited number of **mutations** which are not too injurious to be carried by the species **furnish an almost infinite field of possible variations through which the species may work its way under natural selection** (pp. 32-33, emp. added).

In his book, *The Way of the Cell*, Franklin M. Harold suggested: "Any alteration in the sequence of DNA, once replicated, is inherited henceforth; that is the chemical basis of mutation, and therefore of much of the genetic variation within populations" (2001, p. 47). Donald Goldsmith noted:

> During the process of DNA replication, small changes called **mutations** can occur.... Some mutational changes tell the organism to do something additional that proves useful its quest to survive and to reproduce. In that case, provided that the mutation can be passed from ancestors to descendants, the organisms carrying the mutation may come to dominate the local scene, and can eventually produce new types of organisms (1997, p. 125, emp. in orig.).

In his 2000 volume, *Quantum Evolution: The New Science of Life*, Johnjoe McFadden wrote: "Mutations are therefore the elusive source of the variation that Darwin needed to complete his theory of evolution. They provide the raw material for all evolutionary change" (p. 65). That same year, evolutionist Paul R. Ehrlich penned the following statement in his book, *Human Natures: Genes, Cultures, and the Human Prospect*: "The ultimate source of variation in the DNA–that is, the creation of different kinds of genes–is mutation: the accidental alteration of DNA that changes genes.... In short, genetic variation has its basic source in mutation" (2000, pp. 20-21). Also that same year, renowned evolutionary geneticist of Stanford University, Luigi Cavalli-Sforza, head of the International Human Genome Diversity Project, remarked in his book, *Genes, Peoples, and Languages*:

> Evolution also results from the accumulation of new information. In the case of a biological mutation, new information is provided by an error of genetic transmission (i.e., a change in the DNA during its transmission from parent to child).... Natural selection makes it possible to accept the good ones and eliminate the bad ones (2000, p. 176, parenthetical item in orig.).

Perhaps this would be a good time to ask, "What, exactly, is a mutation?" Simply put, a mutation is an error made when cells copy DNA–usually the loss, insertion, or change of a nucleotide in a DNA molecule (see Wise, 2002, p. 163). As Ariel Roth put it in his book, *Origins*: "A mutation can refer to a variety of genetic changes, such as: a change in a nucleotide base on the DNA chain, an altered gene position, the loss of a gene, duplication of gene, or insertion of a foreign genetic sequence" (1998, p. 85). In his text, *Biology*, A.O. Wasserman defined a mutation as "a change in the form, qualities, or nature of the offspring from their parent type brought about by a change in the hereditary material from the parents" (1973, p. 803).

There are certain other basic facts about genetic mutations that come into play here. Consider, for example, the following.

Mutations are random. C.H. Waddington, an evolutionary geneticist, once noted: "It remains true to say that we know of no other way other than **random** mutations by which hereditary variation comes into being..." (1962, p. 98, emp. added). Thirty-eight years later, Ehrlich wrote: "A key axiom of modern evolutionary theory is that mutations do not occur in response to the needs of the organism.... Mutations are random" (2000, p. 21). Creationists concur. Henry Morris, for example, observed: "There is no way to control mutations to make them produce characteristics which might be needed. Natural selection must simply take what comes" (1974b, p. 54). In other words, nature is not "selecting" at all. Rather, nature is pressed into accepting whatever appears. The obvious question, then, is this: What appears?

Mutations are rare, not common. How often do random mutations occur? Evolutionists themselves frankly and candidly admit what every research biologist knows–mutations occur rarely. Geneticist Francisco J. Ayala of the University of California once remarked: "It is probably fair to estimate the frequency of a majority of mutations in higher organisms between one in ten thousand and one in a million per gene per generation" (1970, p. 3). In their book, *The Natural Limits to Biological Change*, Lane Lester and Raymond Bohlin commented: "Considering a host of both eukaryotic and prokaryotic organisms, the chances of a single gamete containing a new mutation for a particular gene range from 1/2,000 to 1/1,00,000,000" (1984, p. 59).

Mutations may be good, bad, or neutral. There are, theoretically speaking, at least three types of mutations: good, bad, and neutral. Obviously, the bad mutations (those that cause various diseases such as hemophilia, Duchenne dystrophy, phenylketonuria, galactosemia, etc.) are of no use to evolutionary theory. Neutral mutations likewise are of little use to the evolutionist (see Hitching, 1982, pp. 62-63) because they, then, are dependent on still more mutations in order to be fully expressed and "useful" (in an evolutionary sense). Thus, another obvious question becomes: How often do **good** mutations occur–i.e., "good" in the sense that they can "push evolution forward"?

Good mutations are very, very rare. The late Hermann J. Muller, Nobel laureate in genetics, said: "Accordingly, the great majority of mutations, certainly well over 99%, are **harmful** in some way, as is to be expected of the effects of accidental occurrences" (1950, 38:35, emp. added). Evolutionary geneticist Theodosius Dobzhansky candidly admitted that favorable mutations amount to less than 1% of all mutations that occur (see Davidheiser, 1969, p. 209). Dr. Dobzhansky even remarked that "most mutants which arise in any organism are more or less **disadvantageous** to their possessors..." (1955, p. 105). C.P. Martin, also an evolutionist, wrote in the

American Scientist: "Accordingly, mutations are more than just sudden changes in heredity; **they also affect viability, and, to the best of our knowledge, invariably affect it adversely**. Does not this fact show that mutations are really assaults on the organism's central being, its basic capacity to be a living thing?" (1953, p. 102, emp. added). Almost twenty-five years later, in addressing the rarity of these "good" mutations, one researcher commented: "From the standpoint of population genetics, positive Darwinian selection represents a process whereby advantageous mutants spread through the species. Considering their great importance in evolution, it is perhaps surprising that well-established cases are so scarce" (Kimura, 1976, 138[6]:260). And twenty-five years after that, Harvard's eminent taxonomist, Ernst Mayr, remarked that "...the occurrence of new beneficial mutations is rather rare" (2001, p. 98). Numerous researchers through the years have written in agreement (Winchester, 1951, p. 228; Martin, 1953, p. 100; Ayala, 1968, p. 1436; Morris, 1984, p. 203; Klotz, 1985, p. 181; Margulis and Sagan, 2002, pp. 11-12).

Furthermore, those animals or plants that ought to show the most mutants apparently show the least—which is not an insignificant problem for the population geneticist. France's preeminent zoologist, Pierre-Paul Grassé, lamented:

> Bacteria, the study of which has formed a great part of the foundation of genetics and molecular biology, are the organisms which, because of their huge numbers, produce the most mutants.... Bacteria, despite their great production of intra-specific varieties, exhibit a great fidelity to their species. The bacillus, *Escherichia coli*, whose mutants have been studied very carefully, is the best example. The reader will agree that it is surprising, to say the least, to want to prove evolution and to discover its mechanisms and then to choose as a material for this study a being which practically stabilized a billion years ago (1977, p. 87).

Interestingly, the same is true of other species. Consider the lowly fruit fly. "The fruit fly (*Drosophila melanogaster*), the favorite pet insect of the geneticists, whose geographical, bio-

tropical, urban, and rural genotypes are now known inside out, seems not to have changed since the remotest times" (Grassé, p. 130). Dr. Grassé has provided an insightful evaluation, and is absolutely correct in his assessment. We are being asked to believe that organisms that have been in a period of **stasis** (i.e., no change) "somehow" provide the proof of evolution (vast amounts of change). As Roth put it:

> ...[T]housands of laboratory experiments with bacteria, plants, and animals witness to the fact that the changes that a species can tolerate have definite limits. There appears to be a tight cohesion of interacting systems that will accept only limited change without inviting disaster. After decades or centuries of experimentation, fruit flies retain their basic body plan as fruit flies, and wool-producing sheep remain basically sheep. Aberrant types tend to be inferior, usually do not survive in nature, and, given a chance, tend to breed back to their original types. Scientists sometimes call this phenomenon genetic inertia (genetic homeostasis) [1998, pp. 85-86, parenthetical item in orig.].

Two other points bear mentioning here as well. First, as Wise observed:

> **Of carefully studied mutations, most have been found to be harmful to organisms**, and most of the remainder seem to have neither positive nor negative effect. Mutations that are actually beneficial are extraordinarily rare and involve insignificant changes. **Mutations seem to be much more degenerative than constructive**... (2002, p. 163, emp. added).

Favorable mutations are indeed "extraordinarily rare." It also is a well-known fact that "most mutations are recessive–that is, they will not manifest themselves unless present in both parents. Furthermore, while mutations producing minor changes may survive, **those causing significant modification are especially detrimental and unlikely to persist**" (Roth, p. 86, emp. added). Lester and Bohlin also addressed this point:

> Overall, however, mutations would primarily be a constant source of genetic noise and degeneration.... Mutations occur in organisms that are already adapted to their environment. Any large-scale, rapid alteration to the organism will not only be deleterious but most likely lethal (1984, pp. 171,68).

Second, as David DeWitt of Liberty University observed: "Successful macroevolution requires the addition of **new** information and **new** genes that produce **new** proteins that are found in **new** organs and systems" (2002, emp. in orig.). And therein lies the problem. Mutations do not add new information. When Luigi Cavalli-Sforza (quoted earlier) remarked that "new information is provided by an error of genetic transmission," he could not have been more wrong. It most certainly is not! Jonathan Sarfati correctly commented:

> The issue is not **new traits**, but new genetic information.... If evolution from goo to you were true, we should expect to find **countless** information-adding mutations. But we have not even found one (2002a, emp. in orig.).

Mutations do **not** result in **new** information! And this is what evolution is all about. Lester and Bohlin noted:

> The usual answer given to the dilemma of new genetic information is that as a gene continues to mutate, eventually something different will arise. But immediately, several questions come to our minds. What function, for example, is this protein performing while all this mutating is going on? Is its function slowly changing? If so, is its former function still needed? If not, why not? And if so, then how is the former function being handled? (p. 87).

Good points, these. Mutations in bacteria, to use just one example, may result in antibiotic resistance. But in the end, the resistant microorganisms are still the same species of microorganisms they were **before** the mutations occurred. Alan Hayward was right on target when he wrote that

> ...mutations do not appear to bring progressive changes. Genes seem to be built so as to allow changes to occur within certain narrow limits, and to prevent those limits from being crossed. To oversimplify a little: mutations very easily produce new varieties within a species, and might occasionally produce a new (though similar) species, but–despite enormous efforts by experimenters and breeders–**mutations seem unable to produce entirely new forms of life** (1985, p. 55, emp. added, parenthetical item in orig.).

In the end, after mutations have occurred, no macroevolution has taken place. Evolutionary theory requires that mutations occur–in order to add the information needed to push evolution "uphill." But the mutations that we observe, generally are neutral (i.e., they do not alter the information or the "message" of the DNA code), or else they go "downhill" (from an informational standpoint), which results in the loss or corruption of information. In addition, the rare "beneficial" mutations that do occur and that do confer some type of survival advantage, still result in the loss of information, and thus are headed in the wrong direction, from an evolutionary vantage point.

Evolutionists Lynn Margulis and Dorion Sagan, in their 2002 book, *Acquiring Genomes: A Theory of the Origins of Species*, expressed their strong disagreement with genetic mutations as the alleged mechanism of evolution.

> We certainly agree that random heritable changes, or gene mutations, occur. We also concur that these random mutations are expressed in the chemistry of the living organism.... The major difference between our view and the standard neodarwinist doctrine today concerns the importance of random mutation in evolution. **We believe random mutation is wildly overemphasized as a source of hereditary variation**. Mutations, genetic changes in living organisms, are inducible; this can be done by X-ray radiation or by addition of mutagenic chemicals to food. Many ways to induce mutations are known but none leads

> to new organisms. **Mutation accumulation does not lead to new species or even to new organs or new tissues.** If the egg and a batch of sperm of a mammal is subjected to mutation, yes, hereditary changes occur, but as was pointed out very early by Hermann J. Muller (1890-1967), the Nobel prizewinner who showed X-rays to be mutagenic in fruit flies, 99.9 percent of the mutations are deleterious. **Even professional evolutionary biologists are hard put to find mutations, experimentally induced or spontaneous, that lead in a positive way to evolutionary change** (pp. 11-12, emp. added).

They went on to say:

> We agree that very few potential offspring ever survive to reproduce and that populations do change through time, and that therefore natural selection is of critical importance to the evolutionary progress. **But this Darwinian claim to explain all of evolution is a popular half-truth whose lack of explicative power is compensated for only by the religious ferocity of its rhetoric. Although random mutations influenced the course of evolution, their influence was mainly by loss, alteration, and refinement.... Never, however, did that one mutation make a wing, a fruit, a woody stem, or a claw appear. Mutations, in summary, tend to induce sickness, death, or deficiencies. No evidence in the vast literature of hereditary change shows unambiguous evidence that random mutation itself, even with geographical isolation of populations, leads to speciation** (pp. 28-29, emp. added).

Adding their combined weight to the testimony of Margulis and Sagan are such eminent evolutionists as the late Pierre-Paul Grassé, who held the position of the Chair of Evolution at the Sorbonne in Paris for over 30 years, and the late Stephen Jay Gould of Harvard. Dr. Grassé remarked:

> The opportune appearance of mutations permitting animals and plants to meet their needs seems hard to believe. Yet the Darwinian theory is even more demanding: a single plant, a single animal would require thousands and thousands of lucky, appropriate events. Thus, miracles would become the rule: events with an infinitesimal probability could not fail to occur.... There is no law against day-dreaming, but science must not indulge in it.
>
> Some contemporary biologists, as soon as they observe a mutation, talk about evolution. They are implicitly supporting the following syllogism: mutations are the only evolutionary variations, all living beings undergo mutations, therefore all living things evolve. This logical scheme, is, however, unacceptable: first, because its major premise is neither obvious nor general; second, because its conclusion does not agree with the facts. No matter how numerous they may be, **mutations do not produce any kind of evolution** (1977, p. 103, emp. added).

Gould's testimony is no less weighty. In a speech titled, "Is a New and General Theory of Evolution Emerging?," presented at Hobart College on February 14, 1980, Dr. Gould went on record as stating: "A mutation doesn't produce major new raw material. You don't make a new species by mutating the species.... That's a common idea people have; that evolution is due to random mutations. A mutation is not the cause of evolutionary change" (as quoted in Sunderland, 1984, p. 106). Or, as Lester and Bohlin put it:

> Mutations are mistakes, errors in the precise machinery of DNA replication. Combine this with the rarity and randomness of mutations, and one has a major reason why Neo-Darwinists perceive evolutionary change as being gradual and slow. **Since any specific mutation is rare, and most are deleterious, a mutation that somehow enhances survival is admittedly highly unlikely**... (1984, p. 67, emp. added).

Nobel laureate Sir Ernest Chain (credited with purifying penicillin in a way that made it possible to employ it as an antibiotic) wrote in agreement.

> **To postulate that the development and survival of the fittest is entirely a consequence of chance mutations seems to me a hypothesis based on no evidence and irreconcilable with the facts.** These classical evolutionary theories are a gross oversimplification of an immensely complex and intricate mass of facts, and it amazes me that they are swallowed so uncritically and readily, and for such a long time, by so many scientists without a murmur of protest (1970, p. 1, emp. added).

Writing in the *Proceedings of the National Academy of Sciences*, D.H. Erwin and J.W. Valentine remarked:

> Viable mutations with major morphological or physiological effects are exceedingly rare and usually infertile; the chance of two identical rare mutant individuals arising in sufficient propinquity to produce offspring seems too small to consider as a significant evolutionary event (1984, 81:5482-5483).

"Chances" that are "too small to consider as a significant evolutionary event"? What is **that** all about? It has to do with the mathematical probability of having random mutations account for all we see around us–a probability that is, well, infinitesimal. It would require **many** non-harmful mutations to produce the characteristics of just one useful structure. The problem is how to get such extremely rare events to occur **simultaneously** in an organism, in order to produce a functional structure that possessed survival value. Evolutionist E.J. Ambrose outlined the problem as follows:

> The frequency with which a single non-harmful mutation is known to occur is about 1 in 1,000. The probability that two favourable mutations will occur is $1 \times 10^3 \times 10^3 = 1 \times 10^6$, 1 in a million. Studies of *Drosophila* [the fruit fly–BT/BH] have revealed that large numbers of genes are involved in the formation of separate

> structural elements. There are as many as 30-40 involved in a single wing structure. It is most unlikely that fewer than five genes could ever be involved in the formation of even the simplest new structure previously unknown to the organism. The probability now becomes one in one thousand million million. We already know that mutations in living cells appear once in ten million to once in one hundred thousand million. It is evident that the probability of five favourable mutations occurring within a single life cycle of an organism is effectively zero (1982, p. 120).

What is the conclusion to be drawn from these facts? Simpson admitted that if there was an effective breeding population of **100 million** individuals, and they produced a new generation **every day**, the likelihood of obtaining good evolutionary results from mutations could be expected only about once every **274 billion years**! He was forced to conclude: "Unless there is an unknown factor tremendously increasing the chance of simultaneous mutations, such a process has played no part whatever in evolution" (1953, p. 96). Little wonder Grassé concluded: "No matter how numerous they may be, **mutations do not produce any kind of evolution**" (1977, p. 103, emp. added).

If evolution does not occur by natural selection, and if it does not occur by mutation, how, then, does it occur? Even evolutionists have admitted that both of the alleged mechanisms for evolution are impotent in this regard. Creationists have been stressing these points for years by noting that mutations either are harmful or neutral (neither of which provides the forward thrust for evolution), and that since mutations are unpredictable, random changes in an extremely complex system, any change represents a **mistake**, not an improvement. The practical end result of mutations has been noted time and again by those within the scientific community. The Environmental Mutagenic Society, in a report published in *Science*, warned that "being an error process, mutation consists of all possible changes in the genetic material (excluding recombination and segregation)" and that "most mutations producing effects large enough to be observed are deleterious." Further, the Society stated in its report that "since the vast majority of detectable mutations are deleterious, an artificially increased human mutation rate would be expected to be harmful in proportion to the increase" (1975, 187:503-504).

Mutations, as much as evolutionists hate to have to admit it, **presuppose creation**. After all, mutations are changes in **already-existing genes**. A gene must be present before it can mutate, and the end result of such mutations is merely a varied form of an already existing gene (i.e., variation within a type, which is consistent with the creation model). Mutations represent an undesirable departure from the original. We do not know of mutations that can cause one kind of animal to give rise to another kind of animal or one kind of plant to give rise to another kind of plant. What we **do** know, and **have** documented, are mutations that damage or destroy what already is present. The creation model predicts a built-in variation within the gene pool. If living things were created, variation within types certainly is good design. Mutations militate **against** evolution. The story confirmed by the actual scientific facts is much more in accord with the creation model than with the evolution model.

Comparative Arguments and the Case from Homology

Undoubtedly, one of the most impressive arguments for the theory of evolution is provided by the comparative sciences such comparative anatomy, comparative embryology, comparative physiology, comparative cytology, comparative biochemistry, etc. As scientists have worked in these related fields, and have learned to compare one organism with another, basic similarities have arisen among, and between, various groups. When making comparisons of parts of organisms, scientists commonly speak of **homologous** structures, suggesting that these particular structures go through similar stages of development, have similar attachments, etc. In discussing these comparative arguments and homology, R.L. Wysong noted:

> Much of the case for amoeba to man evolution is built upon arguments from similarity. Evolutionists argue that if similarity can be shown between organisms through comparative anatomy, embryology, vestigial organs, cytology, blood chemistry, protein and DNA biochemistry, then evolutionary relationship can be proven (1976, p. 393).

Michael Denton, in his text, *Evolution: A Theory in Crisis*, devoted a large portion of the book to such arguments and wrote: "Since 1859 the phenomenon of homology has been traditionally cited by evolutionary biologists as providing one of the most powerful lines of evidence for the concept of organic evolution" (1985, p. 143). Denton is correct in his assessment. Charles Darwin himself thought of the argument from homology as one of the greatest single proofs of his theory. Denton commented that "homology provided Darwin with apparently positive evidence that organisms had undergone descent from a common ancestor" (p. 143). Darwin himself stated as much in *The Origin of Species* when he wrote:

> We have seen that the members of the same class, independently of their habits of life, resemble each other in the general plan of their organization.... Is it not powerfully suggestive of true relationship, of inheritance from a common ancestor? (1962, pp. 434-435).

Denton therefore observed: "The phenomenon of homology has remained the mainstay of the argument for evolution right down to the present day" (p. 144). Strausburg and Weimer, in their text, *General Biology*, suggested: "The greater the similarity of structure, the closer the relationship, and, wherever close relationship is found, a common ancestry is indicated" (1947, p. 629).

That statement was made in 1947. Decades later, the same kind of thinking is still standard fare. For example, the 1981 edition of the respected *Encyclopaedia Britannica* gave pride of place to the argument from homology in discussing the evidence for evolution:

> The indirect evidence for evolution is based primarily on the significance of similarities found in different organisms.... The similarity of plan is easily explicable if all descended with modification from a common ancestor, by evolution, and the term homologous is used to denote corresponding structures formed in this way.... Invertebrate animals, the skeleton of the forelimb is a splendid example of homology, in the bones of the upper arm, forearm, wrist, hand, and fingers, all of which can be matched, bone for bone, in rat, dog, horse, bat, mole, porpoise, or man. The example is all the more telling because the bones have become modified in adaptation to different modes of life but have retained the same fundamental plan of structure, inherited from a common ancestor (1981, 7:8).

Denton acknowledged the importance of such thinking within the evolutionary camp, and showed why such thinking is so necessary, when he observed that "without underlying homologous resemblance in the fundamental design of dissimilar organisms and organ systems then evolution would have nothing to explain and comparative anatomy nothing to contribute to evolutionary theory" (1985, p. 145). The late biochemist, Isaac Asimov, one of America's most prolific science writers, suggested that our ability to classify plants and animals on a groups-within-groups hierarchical basis virtually forces scientists to treat evolution as a "fact" (1981, 89[9]: 85-87).

At first glance, descent from a common ancestor appears to be a "logical" argument because it seems to make so much sense. After all, isn't that how we explain such similarities as brothers and sisters looking more alike than, say, cousins?

They have parents closer in common. And evolutionists have an impressive array of data at their disposal. They are quick to point out that the wing of the bat, the forefoot of the turtle, the forefoot of the frog, and the arm of the man all have the same general structure. They also note, correctly, that the forefoot of the dog, the flipper of the whale, and the hand of the man contain essentially the same bones and muscles. As Michael Pitman observed:

> To the evolutionist, homologous structures are clear evidence of common ancestry and a family tree of life. Bat wings, bird wings, flippers, and human arms are similar because the ancestors common to birds, bats and humans had just such a structure–a forelimb built on the pattern that biologists identify as "pentadactyl" or "five-fingered" (1984, p. 40).

In more recent times, this argument even has been carried to the molecular level as scientists begin to compare similarities in blood groups, cytochrome C composition, enzymes, cellular DNA, and a myriad of other molecular entities. For example, it has been suggested that the chimpanzee and the human have DNA that is similar 95% of the time (Britten, 2002). The conclusion we are supposed to draw, of course, is that evolution must be true because we can trace our ancestral lineages to a common ancestor who lived millions of years ago. That, in fact, is exactly what the late scientist of Cornell University, Carl Sagan, suggested: "The inner workings of terrestrial organisms–from microbes to men–are so similar in their biochemical details as to make it highly likely that all organisms on the Earth have evolved from a single instance of the origin of life" (Shklovskii and Sagan, 1966, p. 183).

The Creationist Response to Homology

What is the creationist's response to all of this? Do similarities exist? And if so, is the evolutionist's explanation the correct, or the only, explanation that fits the facts of the case?

First, let us note how the creationist does **not** respond to this argument. Creationists do not deny the existing similarities; similarities **do** exist. Creationists are not ignorant of the existence of such facts of science. It is here, however, that we can learn an extremely valuable lesson in the creation/evolution controversy. That lesson is this: **rarely is it the data that are in dispute–it is the interpretation placed on the data that is in dispute**. In the cases of basic similarities, whether at the anatomical or biochemical level, denying that such similarities exist serves no good purpose. Creationists and evolutionists both have access to the same data. The evolutionist, however, looks at the data and says that similarity is proof of **common ancestry**. The creationist, on the other hand, examines the exact same data and suggests that similarity is evidence of **creation according to a common design**. In essence, a stalemate exists. Both sides have an answer to the data at hand. And in many instances, either explanation might appear legitimate.

However, the evolutionists' argument works only if certain portions of the data on homology are presented. If **all** the available data are allowed full exposure, then the evidence from homology fails. Many years ago, T.H. Morgan of Columbia University, himself a committed evolutionist, candidly admitted what many evolutionists do not want to become common knowledge: "If, then, it can be established beyond dispute that similarity or even identity of the same character in different species is not always to be interpreted that both have arisen from a common ancestor, the whole argument from comparative anatomy seems to tumble in ruins" (1923, p. 246). Or, as Wysong wrote: "If the law of similarity can be used to show evolutionary relationships, then dissimilarities can be used to show a lack of relationship" (1976, pp. 393-394).

Ferenco Kiss, as dean of the medical faculties at the University of Budapest, once stated that "...it is necessary for the evolutionists–in order to maintain their theory–to collect only the similarities and to neglect the numerous differences" (1949, p. 3). Evolution is a complete cosmogony. It must explain both similarities **and** differences within its own framework. It is not the similarities that present the problem; it is the numerous differences. As Sir Alistair Hardy, former professor of zoology at Oxford University, wrote: "The concept of homology is fundamental to what we are talking about when we speak of evolution, yet in truth we cannot explain it all in terms of present-day biological theory" (1965, p. 211).

What did Dr. Hardy mean when he said, more than thirty-five years ago, that "we cannot explain it all in terms of present-day biological theory"? He meant simply this: only when evolutionists are allowed to "pick and choose" similarities that fit their theory, can the argument from homology be made to work. When evolutionists are forced to use **all** the data–including those documenting dissimilarity–the argument from homology utterly fails.

His point is well taken–even today. It is a documented fact that evolutionists are guilty of filtering the data to make it appear as if homology supports evolutionary theory. Now, however, that "picking and choosing" method has been exposed, as Lester and Bohlin have observed.

> Another problem is that from the raw data alone, not one single phylogeny emerges, but several. The one that agrees most closely with the traditional phylogeny is **assumed** to be the most "correct." This hardly demonstrates the independent confirmation of evolutionary relationships. The combining of several phylogenies from different proteins combines not only strengths but also weaknesses (1984, p. 173, emp. in orig.).

Vincent Demoulin likewise pointed out the fallacy inherent in this kind of "pick and choose" game when he noted that "the composite evolutionary tree encompasses all the weaknesses of the individual trees" (1979). That is to say, adding up **all** the available data from homology studies makes for an even weaker argument than already is present when examining just a few of the data on this topic.

Homology and the "Rest of the Story"

But there is no need to take any creationist's word on the subject. Evolutionist Michael Denton stated quite succinctly just how valuable all this "proof" from similarity studies really is.

> Invariably, as biological knowledge has grown, common geneology as an explanation for similarity has tended to grow ever more tenuous. Clearly, such a trend carried to the extreme would hold calamitous consequences for evolution, as homologous resemblance is the very *raison d'être* of evolution theory. Without the phenomenon of homology–the modification of similar structures to different ends–there would be little need for a theory of descent with modification....
>
> Like so much of the other circumstantial "evidence" for evolution, that drawn from homology is not convincing because it entails too many anomalies, too many counter-instances, far too many phenomena which simply do not fit easily into the orthodox picture. The failure of homology to substantiate evolutionary claims has not been as widely publicized as have the problems in paleontology.
>
> The discussion in the past three chapters indicates that the facts of comparative anatomy and the pattern of nature they reveal provide nothing like the overwhelming testimony to the Darwinian model of evolution that is often claimed. Simpson's claim that "the facts simply do not make sense unless evolution is true," or Dobzhansky's that "nothing in biology makes sense except in the light of evolution" are simply not true if by the term evolution we mean a gradual process of biological change directed by natural selection....
>
> In the last analysis the facts of comparative anatomy provide no evidence for evolution in the way conceived by Darwin, and even if we were to construe with the eye of faith some "evidence" in the pattern of diversity for the Darwinian model of evolution, this could only be seen, at best, as indirect or circumstantial....

> ...the same hierarchic pattern which may be explained in terms of a theory of common descent, also, by its very nature, implies the existence of deep divisions in the order of nature. The same facts of comparative anatomy which proclaim unity also proclaim division; while resemblance suggests evolution, division, especially where it appears profound, is counter-evidence against the whole notion of transmutation (1985, pp. 154-155).

What did Denton mean when he said that the "evidence" for evolution from homology studies "entails too many anomalies, too many counter-instances, far too many phenomena which simply do not fit easily into the orthodox picture"? The answer to that lies in an examination of the data that have become available during the past several years. For example, Wysong provided an extensive list of such data, among which are the following examples:

1. The octopus eye, pig heart, Pekingese dog's face, milk of the ass, and the pronator quadratus muscle of the Japanese salamander are all very similar to analogous human structures. Do these similarities show evolutionary relationships?

2. The weight of the brain in proportion to body weight is greater in the dwarf monkey of South America, the marmoset, than in man. Since this proportion is used to show relationship between primates and man, is the marmoset, therefore, more evolved than man?

3. The plague bacterium (*Pasteurella pestis* [now designated as *Yersinia pestis*–BT/BH]) afflicts only man and rodent. Does this similarity show close relationship?

4. Plant nettle stings contain acetylcholine, 5-hydroxytryptamine and histamine. These chemicals are also found in man. Are man and plant closely related?

5. The root nodules of certain leguminous plants and the crustacean, Daphnia, contain hemoglobin, the blood pigment found in man. Are these organisms closely related to man?
6. If certain specific gravity tests are run on the blood of various animals, the frog and snake are found to be more similar to man than the monkey is to man.
7. If the concentration of red blood cells in animals is compared (millions per cubic millimeter of blood), man is more similar to frogs, fish, and birds than he is to sheep.
8. Since bones are often used to show relationships, bone chemistry should be useful in this regard. If the calcium/phosphorus ratio is plotted against bone carbonate, man proves to be close to the turtle and elephant, the monkey close to the goose, and the dog close to the horse but distant from the cat.
9. The tetrapyrole chemical ring is found in plant chlorophyll, in hemoglobin and other animal respiratory pigments, sporadically as a coloring pigment in molluscan shells, and also in the feathers of some bird species. How does tetrapyrole similarity speak for relationships (1976, pp. 394-395).

After examining examples such as these, it is easy to understand what Dr. Denton meant when he said that there are too many "anomalies," too many "counter-instances," and "too many phenomena which simply do not fit easily into the orthodox picture." Other writers, both evolutionists and creationists, have documented this same problem. Michael Pitman, for example, remarked:

> Consider reptilian scales, bird feathers, and fur. The evolutionist holds that feathers and fur have evolved, divergently, from scales. But can such different skin coverings be called "homologous"? For example, a feather and a scale develop from different layers of

> skin and follow different development paths; the feather's greater structural complexity must reflect a more complex genetic background. Yet the first known feather is entirely featherlike, not at all scale-like. The genes coding for each type of skin-covering must contain a sequence (subroutine) for keratin, because each is made primarily of a form of keratin. Yet this subroutine could well be integrated into quite a different overall set of genes. If so, how could we explain their origin in terms of simple inheritance from a common ancestor (1984, p. 42)?

Such anomalies have caused evolutionists to search for a way to salvage the argument from homology. Some evolutionary scientists have suggested that evidence now is available that can perform such a "salvage operation." Bernard Davis of the Bacterial Physiology Unit at Harvard Medical School explained:

> In most of its development evolutionary biology has depended on morphological homologies, both in the fossil record and among living species; but this approach has not revealed the continuum of transition forms between species that Darwin predicted. Moreover, while he expected further research in paleontology to fill in the gaps, we no longer entertain that hope. But now, at least, molecular genetics has provided a direct, radically different kind of evidence for such continuity.... Not only does molecular genetics provide the most convincing evidence for evolutionary continuity, but this evidence should impress a public that is well aware of the power of this science in other areas (1985, 28:252-253).

Notice two important points in Davis' statement. First, he admits that the approach from morphological homologies "has not revealed the continuum of transition forms that Darwin predicted." In other words, if you look at the data from morphological homologies (i.e., the kind of data examined above), then the result is a dismal failure for evolutionary theory. The required "continuum" simply does not exist. Second, however, Dr. Davis believes that something better, something more powerful as a proof from homology, has been found–evidence from molecular (as opposed to morphological) homology. His point is: now that the "proofs" from morphological homologies have failed, the hope is that the "proofs" from molecular homologies will not. Dr. Davis obviously is optimistic that such proofs **will** succeed. His optimism, however, proved to be short lived.

Despite the bright promise that molecular evidences are so strong as to provide almost undeniable proof for evolution, several puzzles have emerged from studies in molecular homologies. In 1981, Colin Patterson (senior paleontologist at the British Museum of Natural History) came to America to speak to several scientific societies. During his various speeches, Dr. Patterson suggested that he had "experienced a shift from evolution as knowledge to evolution as faith." He then presented numerous specific examples documenting the failure of the evolutionary hypothesis of common ancestry. He said that the hypothesis acted as an "anti-theory" and conveyed nothing but "anti-knowledge." Dr. Patterson presented data on amino acid sequences for the alpha hemoglobins of a viper, crocodile, and chicken. Evolutionists "know" (since evolution is assumed to be true) that vipers and crocodiles (two reptiles) should be much more closely related than either is to a bird. But the crocodile and the chicken showed the greatest similarity (17.5% of their amino acids in common) with the viper and the chicken the next most similar (10.5%), and the two reptiles with the **least** similarity (5.6%).

An examination of the amino acids in myoglobin showed that crocodiles and lizards (two reptiles) shared 10.5%, but that a lizard and a chicken (reptile/bird) also shared the same percentage (10.5%). Dr. Patterson then described studies of mitochondrial DNA performed on man and on various primates. He acknowledged that where there should have been a high percentage of similarities, there was a very low percentage. After all his data were presented, Dr. Patterson remarked that "the theory makes a prediction, we've tested it, and the prediction is falsified precisely" (as quoted in Sunderland, 1982).

Homology, Genes, and Chromosomes

Additional molecular studies over the past few years have yielded no better results. For example, within cells of living organisms are found chromosomes that carry the genes responsible for the individual organism's genetic make-up. If there has been a gradual evolution of all creatures–from the simple to the complex, as evolution demands–then the evolutionary scheme would predict that there likewise would be an increase in chromosome number and quality as one moves up the evolutionary scale. Today, however, advanced molecular technology has caused the evolutionary prediction to fall on hard times. Note the following chart comparing the actual chromosome numbers of several organisms with the evolutionary prediction.

PREDICTION	**FACTS**
Simple to Complex	**Chromosome Counts**
Man	Fern–512
Dog	Crayfish–200
Bat	Dog–78
Herring Gull	Herring Gull–68
Reptiles	Reptiles–48
Fern	Man–46
Crayfish	Bat–32

The chromosome count does not "fit" what one would predict based upon the theory of evolution. Evolutionist Ashley Montagu thus was forced to admit: "The number of chromosomes does not appear to be associated with the degree of complexity of an organism" (1960, p. 24), and that would most assuredly include the chromosomes, since they are the carriers of the genetic material.

Furthermore, it would make sense that, if humans and chimpanzees (our alleged closest evolutionary ancestor) were 95% genetically the same, then the manner in which they store DNA also would be similar. Yet it is not. DNA, the fundamental blueprint of life, is tightly compacted into chromosomes. All cells that possess a nucleus contain a specific number of chromosomes. Common sense would seem to necessitate that organisms that share a common ancestry would possess the same number of chromosomes. However, chromosome numbers in living organisms vary from 308 in the black mulberry (*Morus nigra*) to six in animals such as the mosquito (*Culex pipiens*) or nematode worm (*Caenorhabditis elegans*) [see Sinnot, et al., 1958]. Additionally, complexity does not appear to affect the chromosomal number. The radiolaria (a simple protozoon) has over 800, while humans possess 46. Chimpanzees, on the other hand, have 48 chromosomes. A strict comparison of chromosome numbers would indicate that we are more closely related to the Chinese muntjac (a small deer found in Taiwan's mountainous regions), which also has 46 chromosomes.

This hurdle of differing numbers of chromosomes may appear trivial, but we must remember that chromosomes contain genes, which themselves are composed of DNA spirals. If the blueprint of DNA locked inside the chromosomes codes for only 46 chromosomes, then how can evolution account for the **loss** of two entire chromosomes? The task of DNA is to continually reproduce itself. If we infer that this change in chromosome number occurred through evolution, then we are asserting that the DNA locked in the original number of chromosomes did not do its job correctly or efficiently. Considering that each chromosome carries a number of genes, **losing** chromosomes does not make sense physiologically, and probably would prove deadly for new species. No respectable biologist would suggest that by removing one chromosome (or more), a new species likely would be produced. To remove even **one** chromosome would potentially remove the DNA codes for millions of vital body factors. Eldon Gardner summed it up as follows: "Chromosome number is probably more constant, however, than any other single morphological characteristic that is available for species identification" (1968, p. 211). To put it another way, humans always have had 46 chromosomes, and chimps always have had 48.

Other such "anomalies" abound. Wysong pointed out that human cells contain 7 picograms of DNA/cell, whereas the frog contains more, and the African lungfish contains 100 picograms of DNA/cell. According to evolutionary predictions, should the frog and lungfish contain more DNA than a man? Or what about amino acid sequences? Cytochrome C, for example, is a coenzyme found in the mitochondria of all aerobic cells and therefore is found in most organisms. As evolutionists have studied amino acid sequences among organisms, they have found many similarities. But what about the many differences? One hears a lot these days about the similarities among organisms in regard to their cytochrome C content, yet numerous dissimilarities exist as well (but rarely are mentioned by evolutionists). Frair and Davis, in their book *A Case for Creation*, pointed out that 104 amino acids are strung together in building cytochrome C. On the basis of the number of differences in these units, the gray whale has more in common with the duck than with another mammal, the monkey; the bullfrog has more in common with the fruit fly than with the rattlesnake; and the tuna has more in common with the rabbit than with the dogfish (1983, pp. 45-53). Lester and Bohlin, in their discussion of cytochrome C and many of the dissimilarities associated with it, noted:

> The most well-known phylogeny is that of cytochrome C, which appears to agree very well with the accepted phylogeny. However, there are exceptions and procedural difficulties of interpretation. There are often large discrepancies between the protein phylogeny

> and the traditional one. In cytochrome C chickens are more closely related to penguins than to ducks and pigeons, turtles are closer to birds than to snakes (fellow reptiles), and people and monkeys diverge from the mammals before marsupial kangaroos separate from the rest of the mammals (1984, pp. 172-173).

The facts simply do not fit the predictions. And perhaps no one has done a more outstanding job of providing the evidence for that statement than evolutionist Michael Denton. Evolutionists suggest that as one ascends the "tree of life," organisms should become increasingly separated by differences in biochemistry from the "earliest" and most "primitive" organisms. In fact, no evolutionary trend can be observed in the biochemical data–at least none that can be adequately defended. Denton showed that bacteria are as divergent from yeast (69%) as they are from wheat (66%), silkmoths (65%), tuna (65%), pigeons (64%), horses (64%), or humans (65%). There is no gradation from one group to another that would show any kind of evolutionary sequence. Denton's conclusion was that "at a molecular level there is no trace of the evolutionary transition from fish to amphibian to reptile to mammal" (1985, p. 285). He then added: "To those well acquainted with the traditional picture of vertebrate evolution, the result is truly astonishing" (p. 285). Dr. Denton went on to state that "at a molecular level, no organism is 'ancestral' or 'primitive' or 'advanced' compared with its relatives" (p. 290). "Yet," he said, "in the face of this extraordinary discovery the biological community seems content to offer explanations which are no more than apologetic tautologies" (p. 306).

Homology does not prove common ancestry. The entire genome of the tiny nematode, *Caenorhabditis elegans*, also has been sequenced as a tangential study to the human genome project. Of the 5,000 best-known human genes, 75% have matches in the worm (see "A Tiny Worm Challenges Evolution"). Does this mean that humans are 75% identical to a nematode worm? Just because living creatures share some genes with humans does not mean there is a linear ancestry. Biologist John Randall admitted this when he wrote:

> The older textbooks on evolution make much of the idea of homology, pointing out the obvious resemblances between the skeletons of the limbs of different animals. Thus the "pentadactyl" [five bone–BT/BH] limb pattern is found in the arm of a man, the wing of a bird, and flipper of a whale–and this is held to indicate their common origin. Now if these various structures were transmitted by the same gene couples, varied from time to time by mutations and acted upon by environmental selection, the theory would make good sense. Unfortunately this is not the case. Homologous organs are now known to be produced by totally different gene complexes in the different species. The concept of homology in terms of similar genes handed on from a common ancestor has broken down... (as quoted in Fix, 1984, p. 189).

Yet textbooks and teachers still continue to proclaim that humans and chimps are 95-98% genetically identical. The evidence clearly demonstrates vast molecular differences–differences that can be attributed to the fact that humans, unlike animals, were created in the image and likeness of God (Genesis 1:26-27; see Lyons and Thompson, 2002a, 2002b). Elaine Morgan commented on this difference.

> Considering the very close genetic relationship that has been established by comparison of biochemical properties of blood proteins, protein structure and DNA and immunological responses, the differences between a man and a chimpanzee are more astonishing than the resemblances. They include structural differences in the skeleton, the muscles, the skin, and the brain; differences in posture associated with a unique method of locomotion; differences in social organization; and finally the acquisition of speech and tool-using, together with the dramatic increase in intellectual ability which has led scientists to name their own species *Homo sapiens sapiens*–wise wise man. During the period when these remarkable evolutionary changes were taking place, other closely related apelike species changed only very slowly, and with far

> less remarkable results. **It is hard to resist the conclusion that something must have happened to the ancestors of *Homo sapiens* which did not happen to the ancestors of gorillas and chimpanzees** (1989, pp. 17-18, emp. added).

That "something" actually is "Someone"–the Creator.

A Word about Comparative Embryology

Embryology, as its name implies, is the study of the embryo. In *The Origin of Species* (1859), Darwin asserted (in a discussion occupying 12 pages) that similarity among the various embryos of animals and man was a primary proof of the theory of evolution. In fact, he called it "second to none" in importance. In *The Descent of Man* (1871), Darwin devoted the entire first chapter to this line of evidence, stressing how critical it was to the success of his theory.

Ernst Heinrich Haeckel (1834-1919) was a German biologist who was such a devoted follower of Darwin that he was dubbed "the apostle of Darwinism in Germany." He taught at the University of Jena, and became famous for his popularization of the so-called "theory of embryonic recapitulation" (or, as he referred to it, the great "Biogenetic Law"). [NOTE: Haeckel's "Biogenetic Law" should not be confused with the Law of Biogenesis, which correctly states that all life comes from previous life of its kind.] Haeckel suggested that the successive stages of human embryonic development repeat the evolutionary stages of our animal ancestry. The catch-phrase he developed to popularize this idea was that "ontogeny [the development of one] recapitulates [repeats] phylogeny [the development of the race]." In other words, the human embryo passes through all stages representing its ancestors–from the one-celled stage to the human. Seeing a human embryo grow would therefore be like watching a silent, moving picture of all our ancestral history.

Today, we recognize that this argument is specious, and those who keep up with the scientific literature no longer use it. Why? To quote the late George Gaylord Simpson of Harvard: "It is now firmly established that ontogeny does not repeat phylogeny" (1965, p. 352). Over seventy years ago, Sir Arthur Keith bluntly stated:

> It was expected that the embryo would recapitulate the features of its ancestors from the lowest to the highest forms in the animal kingdom. Now that the appearances of the embryo at all stages are known, the general feeling is one of disappointment; the human embryo at no stage is anthropoid in appearance. The embryo of the mammal never resembles the worm, the fish, or the reptile. **Embryology provides no support whatsoever for the evolutionary hypothesis** (1932, p. 94, emp. added).

A word of explanation is in order. Haeckel was an accomplished artist who used his artistic talent to falsify certain of the drawings that accompanied his scientific articles. One writer summarized the matter as follows:

> To support his theory, however, Haeckel, whose knowledge of embryology was self-taught, faked some of his evidence. He not only altered his illustrations of embryos, but also printed the same plate of an embryo three times, and labeled one a human, the second a dog and the third a rabbit to show their similarity (Bowden, 1977, p. 128).

Haeckel even went so far as to alter the drawings of some of his colleagues, including the famous embryologist, professor L. Rutimeyer of Basel University, and professor Arnold Bass. The two university professors, after realizing what Haeckel had done, publicly condemned his actions. In the end, as H.H. Newman of the University of Chicago put it, Haeckel's works "did more harm than good to Darwinism" (1932, p. 30).

Haeckel's falsified drawings were published around 1866. One of the major points stressed by Haeckel in his "research"—and one of the items that has remained ensconced in the evolutionary literature to this very day—is the idea that the human embryo possesses gill slits that are leftovers from its past fish-like ancestor stage. Evolutionist Irvin Adler, in his book, *How Life Began*, wrote:

> The embryo of each species seems to repeat the main steps by which the species developed from the common ancestor of all living things. All mammal embryos, for example, pass through a stage in which they have gills like a fish, showing that mammals are descended from fishlike ancestors (1957, p. 22).

Fast-forward almost fifty years to the twenty-first century. In an educational program produced in 2001 by the University of Chicago for its Newton Electronic Community division, the following statement appeared: "All mammals have gill slits in their very early fetal development" (Myron, 2001, p. 1).

We have known for almost 150 years that the "Biogenetic Law" is not correct, and that human embryos do not possess gill slits (see Assmuth and Hull, 1915; Grigg, 1996, 1998; Pennisi, 1997; Richardson, 1997a, 1997b; Youngson, 1998). Even though it was common knowledge by the end of the 1920s that Haeckel's concepts, to use Stephen Jay Gould's words, had "utterly collapsed" (1977a, p. 216), Haeckel's drawings and ideas still continue to turn up in modern biology texts and instructional tools as a "proof" of evolution. Modern editions of most high school and college textbooks rarely present the latest evolutionary ideas on embryology, but instead remain content to rest their case on century-old woodcuts and misnamed "gill slits." Unfortunately, even today the "Biogenetic Law" still is being taught as a scientific fact in many public schools and universities. Of fifteen high school biology textbooks being considered for adoption by the Indiana State Board of Education as late as 1980, nine offered embryonic recapitulation as evidence for evolution. In a letter to the editor in the August 28, 1998 issue of *Science*, Michael Richardson lamented: "Sadly, it is the discredited 1874 drawings that are used in so many British and American biology textbooks" (281:1289). Yes, sadly, it is. The question is: Why?

Evolutionists themselves have conceded that the idea of embryonic recapitulation has become so deeply rooted in evolutionary dogma that it cannot be "weeded out." Paul

Ehrlich observed: "Its shortcomings have been almost universally pointed out by modern authors, but the idea still has a prominent place in biological mythology" (1963, p. 66). The evidence of such an assessment is obvious when one looks at just how far-reaching Haeckel's drawings have become. America's famous "baby doctor," Benjamin Spock, perpetuated Haeckel's recapitulation myth in his well-known book, *Baby and Child Care.* Spock confidently assured expectant mothers that

> each child as he develops is retracing the whole history of mankind, physically and spiritually, step by step. A baby starts off in the womb as a single tiny cell, just the way the first living thing appeared in the ocean. Weeks later, as he lies in the amniotic fluid of the womb, he has gills like a fish (1998, p. 223).

Such imagery persists in the popular media, too. As an example, consider the position of the late atheist Carl Sagan and his third wife, Ann Druyan. In an article on "The Question of Abortion" that they co-authored for *Parade* magazine, these two humanists contended for the ethical permissibility of human abortion on the grounds that the fetus, growing within a woman's body for several months following conception, is not a human being. Sagan and Druyan stated that the embryo begins as "a kind of parasite" that eventually looks like a "segmented worm." Further alterations, they wrote, reveal "gill arches" like that of a "fish or amphibian." Supposedly, "reptilian" features emerge, which later give rise to "mammalian...pig-like" traits. By the end of two months, according to these two authors, the creature resembles a "primate but is still not quite human" (Sagan and Druyan, 1990, p. 6). Although they never mentioned Haeckel by name, their point was clear: abortion in the first few months of pregnancy is acceptable because the embryo or fetus is a lower form of life during this period. Their conclusion, therefore, was that the killing of this tiny creature is not murder. And what was the basis for this assertion? Sagan and Druyan argued their case by subtly employing the concept known as "embryonic recapitulation." When, three years later, *USA Today* published an article on genetic similarities as proof for evolution, the author's analogy and sole illustration invoked the icons of comparative embryology (Friend, 1993).

The cover story of the November 11, 2002 issue of *Time* magazine detailed what were at the time the latest findings in human fetal development. Juxtaposed between the illustrations and the article were photo-captions that contained throwbacks to the outdated concept of embryonic recapitulation theory: "32 days: ...The brain is a labyrinth of cell-lined cavities, while the emerging arms and legs still resemble flipper-like paddles. 40 days: At this point, a human embryo looks no different from that of a pig, chick or elephant. All have a tail, a yolk sac and rudimentary gills" (Nash, 2002, 160[20]:71). The article itself presented a "marvelous," seemingly "miraculous," and "vastly complicated" embryonic process. But the glossy pictures that accompanied the article–the ones that people tend to remember–had captions that painted an entirely different picture.

The scientific community has known for decades that Ernst Haeckel–the man responsible for conjuring up this theory and then falsifying drawings to support it–purposely misled the public during the late 1800s. Embryologist Erich Blechschmidt regarded Haeckel's "Great Biogenetic Law" as one of the most egregious errors in the history of biology. In his book, *The Beginnings of Human Life*, he minced no words in repudiating Haeckel's fraudulent forgeries: "The so-called basic law of biogenetics is wrong. No buts or ifs can mitigate this fact. It is not even a tiny bit correct or correct in a different form. It is totally wrong" (1977, p. 32). Biologist James W. Leach of Ohio State University bluntly commented:

> The undeniable tendency of a complex animal to pass through some developmental stages reminiscent of the adult conditions of a selected and graduated series of lower forms has long been described as the "Biogenetic Law." But as "law" inscribed by nature it is perhaps more full of "loopholes" and "bypasses" than any law thus far inscribed by man (1961, p. 44).

In their widely used high school biology textbook, *Life: An Introduction to Biology*, George Gaylord Simpson and William Beck included a footnote to their student readers on this point. They wrote: "The human embryo does not have any differentiated gill tissue, and the gill-like pouches do not have open gill slits as in fishes. Fins are lacking. The tail is not at all like any fish's tail. Indeed, the resemblance to an adult fish is vague and superficial" (1965, p. 240). Simpson and Beck went on to conclude: "It is now firmly established that ontogeny does **not** recapitulate phylogeny" (p. 241, emp. in orig.).

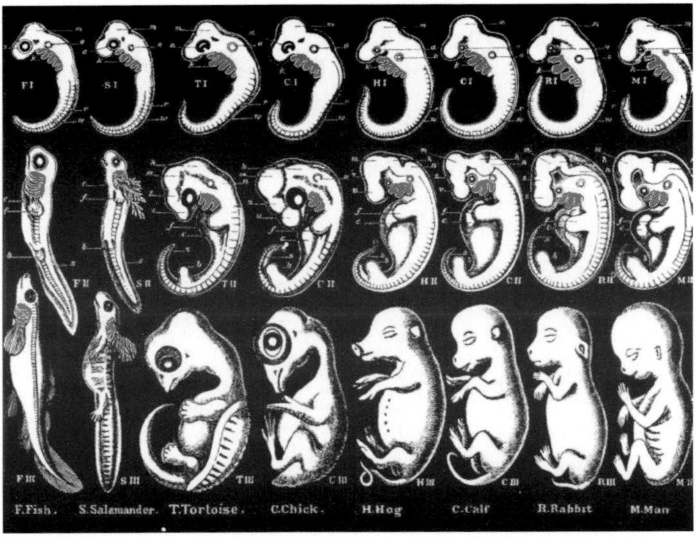

Haeckel's drawings of embryos at three different stages for (from left to right): fish, salamander, tortoise, chick, hog, calf, rabbit and man (from 1876, Plates VI-VII). The alleged "gill-slits" are shown in gray.

Why, then, does the concept of embryonic recapitulation persist? Perhaps John Tyler Bonner, former head of the biology department at Princeton University, explained it best when he admitted: "We may have known for almost a hundred years that Haeckel's blastaea-gastraea theory of the origin of the metazoa is probably nonsense, but it is so clear-cut, so simple, so easy to hand full-blown to the student" (1961, p. 240). Yes, it is. But is it **right**? No, it is not. In fact, recognition of Haeckel's falsehoods still appears in scientific journals from time to time, as was evident in a letter to the editor in the May 15, 1998 issue of *Science.* The seven authors of the letter pointed out (correctly) that Haeckel was overzealous and purposely gave incorrect details in his embryonic drawings (Richardson, et al., 1998). In her book, *Essays in the History of Embryology and Biology*, Jane Oppenheimer observed that Haeckel's work "was the culmination of the extremes of exaggeration which followed Darwin," (1967, p. 150). She lamented: "Haeckel's doctrines were blindly and uncritically accepted," and "delayed the course of embryological progress." Almost thirty years earlier, W.D. Matthew, former chairman of the geology department at the University of California, had acknowledged the fact that, sadly, some doctrines are "blindly and uncritically accepted." He wrote: "Many a false theory gets crystallized by time and absorbed into the body of scientific doctrine through lack of adequate criticism when it is formulated" (1939, p. 159). Never was there a more blatant case of such, than Haeckel's "Biogenetic Law" with its catch-phrase of "ontogeny recapitulates phylogeny."

What should be the creationist's response to embryology as an alleged "proof" of evolution? Our response–if, indeed, any is needed in light of the startling facts presented above–is exactly the same as that offered by the eminent Canadian biologist, W.R. Thompson, in the "Introduction" he authored for the 1956 edition of Darwin's *Origin of Species.* He wrote: "The 'Biogenetic Law' as a proof of evolution is valueless" (1956, p. xvi). Biologist Aaron Wasserman observed that the mammalian embryo "can in no sense be called a fish; it never actually develops functional gills and is at all times a mammal" (1973, p. 497). Jonathan Sarfati noted: "A human embryo never looks reptilian or pig-like. A human embryo is always a human embryo, from the moment of conception; it is never anything else. It does not **become** human sometime after eight weeks" (2002b, p. 202, emp. in orig.). Indeed, embryology no longer can be offered as a legitimate proof of evolution.

Although Haeckel's theory has fallen into disfavor, embryonic recapitulation has survived in a modified form. In its current version, evolutionists argue that similar patterns of embryo development in different animals prove their common descent. For example, the neck folds in human embryos (which Haeckel labeled as "gill slits") eventually give rise to the jaw. These folds develop from a similar area of the vertebrate column, and are controlled by similar gene sequences, as the gill arches of fish embryos (e.g., Gould, 1990, p. 16). The evolutionist concludes from this that fish and humans had a common ancestor.

However, this similarity also is evidence of common design. Mice, men, and pigs have four appendages and a head, and therefore it is not surprising that embryos should follow a similar path of development. Indeed, the ability of embryos to form in such perfection demands something more than evolution. Natural selection works primarily on organisms exposed to the environment or competition. Yet the embryo is isolated from the outside world. Evolutionary processes are at a loss to explain the origin of the mechanism that causes a fertilized egg to develop into a young version of the adult. Life's startling complexity–complete with DNA-coded instruction causing each embryo to be totally different from all others–is compelling evidence of a masterful plan of design inherent in the system. As one writer put it:

> ...in terms of DNA and protein, right at conception each of these types of life is as totally different chemically as each will ever be structurally.... Embryonic development is not even analogous to evolution, which is meant to indicate a progressive increase in potential. The right Greek word instead would be *entelechy*, which means an unfolding of potential present right from the beginning. That's the kind of development that so clearly requires creative design (Morris, 1982, p. 34).

What could be clearer? From DNA to the organs of the body, evidence of design is everywhere, while gradualistic development is countered by the perpetual discontinuity seen in nature. There is nothing–either in the proposed mechanisms, or by direct observation–to show that Darwin's theory of general evolution is a "fact" of science. The "miracle" that we know as "life" cannot be explained by random acts of natural selection coupled with genetic mutations. The evolution model, to use the words of geneticist T.H. Morgan, does indeed "tumble in ruins."

DISCUSSION QUESTIONS

1. How can Christians account for so many colors of skin and four different blood types if we all originated from Adam and Eve?
2. Discuss the impact of Ernst Haeckel's work, and the reasons why he would fake scientific drawings.
3. Scientists (and the media) would like everyone to believe that "all reputable scientists" believe in organic evolution. Is this true? How do we know otherwise?
4. What is the difference between a hypothesis, theory, and fact? Why are evolutionists so quick to describe evolution as a fact? Are they justified in doing so?
5. Discuss some of the assumptions upon which evolutionary theory is built. What part do genetic mutations play? What do we now know regarding genetic mutations that does not favor evolution?

Chapter 11

EVOLUTIONARY ARGUMENTS ANSWERED [PART II]

Both evolution and creation are concepts that may be explored as scientific models, since both may be used to explore and explain certain scientific facts. Obviously, the one that ultimately does the better job of explaining is the better scientific model. In order to examine properly the two models, each must be compared to the available facts. In this chapter, we would like to continue our examination of some of that evidence–in particular, evidence that relates to the geologic timetable, evidence from the fossil record that pertains to the creation/evolution controversy in general, and evidence from the fossil record that relates specifically to the matter of human origins.

The Fossil Record

As we consider the evidence, it is essential to know exactly what the evolution and creation models predict, so that the predictions can be compared to the actual data. When it comes to the fossil record, the evolution model predicts that: (a) the "oldest" rocks would contain evidence of the most "primitive" forms of life capable of fossilization; (b) "younger" rocks would exhibit more "complex" forms of life; (c) a gradual change in organisms from "simple-to-complex" would be apparent; and (d) transitional forms should be present. Charles Darwin himself stated in *The Origin of Species* that "the number of intermediate varieties, which have formerly existed, must be truly enormous." However, he went on to note: "Geology assuredly does not reveal any such finely graduated organic chain; and this, perhaps, is the most obvious and serious objection which can be argued against this theory. The explanation lies, I believe, in the extreme imperfection of the geological record" (1956, pp. 292-293). While Darwin predicted that the fossil record should show numerous transitional fossils, almost a century and a half later, the best that evolutionists are able to produce is a handful of dubious and disputable candidates.

This was a problem for Darwin's theory in 1859, and remains a problem for the modern version of evolution, even today. After all, isn't it a bit ridiculous to expect people to accept a scientific theory as truth when its advocates have to explain why much of the critical evidence is missing? It would be somewhat like a prosecuting attorney trying a murder case, and saying in his opening speech: "We know that the defendant is guilty of murder, although we cannot find a motive, the weapon, the body, or any witnesses."

It is true, of course, that the fossil record is imperfect. Darwin suggested a reason for that imperfection–insufficient searching. In 1859 (when Darwin wrote his book), most fossil collecting had been done in Europe and the United States. However, after more than 140 years of additional paleontological work, Darwin's defense no longer can be upheld. In fact, one evolutionary geologist, T.N. George of Great Britain, stated over forty years ago: "There is no need to apologize any longer for the poverty of the fossil record. In some ways it has become almost unmanageably rich" (1960, 48[1]:1-5).

The creation model, on the other hand, predicts that: (a) the "oldest" rocks would not always contain evidence of the most "primitive" forms of life, and "younger" rocks would not always contain evidence of more "complex" forms of life; (b) a "simple-to-complex" progression of life forms would not always appear; instead, there would be a sudden "explosion" of diverse and highly complex forms of life; and (c) there would be a regular and obvious absence of transitional fossils, since there were no transitional forms.

Evolutionists and creationists do agree on one thing: If there is ever to be any **physical evidence** for evolution, by necessity it will have to come from the fossil record, for it is only here that the actual historical evidence of evolution can be located. One well-known evolutionist, LeGros Clark, commented on this very point when he wrote:

> That evolution actually did occur can only be scientifically established by the discovery of the fossilized remains of representative samples of those intermediate types which have been postulated on the basis of the indirect evidence. In other words, the really crucial evidence for evolution must be provided by the paleontologist whose business it is to study the evidence of the fossil record (1955, p. 7).

Indeed, in the past, some mistakenly thought that it was within the record of the rocks—"nature's museum"—that evolution finally would be documented. As more and more finds were discovered, however, it became plainly obvious that the evidence from the fossil record strongly **opposes** evolution, and strongly **supports** creation.

First, consider the prediction of the evolution model that the fossil record should reveal a simple-to-complex progression of life forms. Until fairly recently, an examination of the Precambrian strata of the geologic timetable showed no undisputed evidence of multicellular fossil forms, while the Cambrian layer (the next layer in succession) exhibited a sudden "explosion" of life forms. In years gone by, this was a serious and fundamental problem in evolutionary theory. Today, evolutionists suggest that they have found, in the Precambrian era, multicellular animals that had neither shells nor skeletons. Labeled the "Ediacaran fossil complex," these finds include animals resembling jellyfishes, segmented worms, and possible relatives of corals, according to evolutionists. But even with these new finds, the serious, fundamental problem for evolution still remains. Geneticist John Klotz has explained why:

> All of the animal phyla are represented in the Cambrian period except two minor soft-bodied phyla (which may have been present without leaving any fossil evidence), and the chordates. Even the chordates may have been present, since an object which looks like a fish has been discovered in Cambrian rock. It is hardly conceivable that all these forms should have originated in this period; and yet there is no evidence for the existence of many of them prior to the Cambrian period (1972, pp. 193-194).

Since Klotz's book was published, the chordates have, in fact, been found in Cambrian rocks (see Repetski, 1978). Writing in *Science News*, Richard Monastersky detailed one such find.

> Paleontologists have long regarded vertebrates as latecomers who straggled into evolutionary history after much of the initial sound and fury had fizzled. Chinese paleontologists, however, have discovered fossils of two fish that push the origin of vertebrates back to the riotous biological bash when almost all other animal groups emerged in the geologic record.
>
> Preserved in 530-million-year-old rocks from Yunnan province, the paper clip-size impressions record the earliest known fish, which predate the next-oldest vertebrates by at least 30 million years. The fossil finds, while not totally unexpected, thrill paleontologists who despaired of ever uncovering such evidence from Earth's dim past. "It's important because up to now the vertebrates were absent from the big bang of life, as we call it–that is, the great early Cambrian explosion, where all the major animal groups appeared suddenly in the fossil record," comments Philippe Janvier, a paleontologist at the National Museum of Natural History in Paris (1999, 156:292).

The problem of the "missing ancestors" in Precambrian rocks is as severe as it ever was. As one science text commented:

> Even theoretically, to make the vast biological leap from primitive organisms to the Cambrian fauna poses enormous problems. A remarkable series of transformations is required to change a single-celled

> protozoan into a complex animal such as a lobster, crab, or shrimp. The new life-forms appearing in the Cambrian were not simply a cluster of similar cells; they were complex, fully formed animals with many specialized types of cells.... The new Cambrian animals represented an astonishing leap to a higher level of specialization, organization, and integration (see *Teaching Science*..., 1986, pp. 35,37).

We are asked by evolutionists to believe that from such "ancestors" as those found in the Ediacaran complex, **all** of the major animal phyla "evolved" in the period represented by a jump between the Precambrian and the Cambrian periods. Such is not only impossible, but also unreasonable.

Writing under the title of "When Earth Tipped, Life Went Wild," Monastersky remarked:

> Before the Cambrian period, almost all life was microscopic, except for some enigmatic soft-bodied organisms. At the start of the Cambrian, about 544 million years ago, animals burst forth in a rash of evolutionary activity never since equaled. Ocean creatures acquired the ability to grow hard shells, and a broad range of new body plans emerged within the geologically short span of 10 million years. Paleontologists have proposed many theories to explain this revolution but have agreed on none (1997, 152:52).

Stefan Bengtson, of the Institute of Paleontology at Uppsala University in Sweden, suggested:

> If any event in life's history resembles man's creation myths, it is this sudden diversification of marine life when multicellular organisms took over as the dominant actors in ecology and evolution. Baffling (and embarrassing) to Darwin, this event still dazzles us and stands as a major biological revolution on a par with the invention of self-replication and the origin of the eukaryotic cell. **The animal phyla emerged out of the Precambrian mists with most of the attributes of their modern descendants** (1990, 345: 765, parenthetical item in orig., emp. added).

Evolutionist Richard Dawkins of Oxford University, wrote:

> The Cambrian strata of rocks, vintage about 600 million years [evolutionists are now dating the beginning of the Cambrian at about 530 million years], are the oldest in which we find most of the major invertebrate groups. **And we find many of them already in an advanced state of evolution, the very first time they appear. It is as though they were just planted there, without any evolutionary history.** Needless to say, this appearance of sudden planting has delighted creationists (1986, p. 229, bracketed comment in orig., emp. added).

Indeed, this "sudden planting" has delighted creationists, because the evidence it provides fits perfectly with the creation model. In an article appearing in *American Scientist* on "The Origin of Animal Body Plans," Erwin Douglas and his colleagues discussed what Dawkins referred to as an "advanced state of evolution."

> **All of the basic architectures of animals were apparently established by the close of the Cambrian explosion**; subsequent evolutionary changes, even those that allowed animals to move out of the sea onto land, involved only modifications of those basic body plans. About 37 distinct body architectures are recognized among present-day animals and from the basis of the taxonomic classification level of phyla.... Clearly many difficult questions remain about the early radiation of animals. Why did so many unusual morphologies appear when they did, and not earlier or later? The trigger of the Cambrian explosion is still uncertain, although ideas abound (1997, 85:126, 127, emp. added).

As Stephen Jay Gould once observed: "Even the most cautious opinion holds that 500 million subsequent years of opportunity have not expanded the Cambrian range, achieved in just five million years. **The Cambrian explosion was the most remarkable and puzzling event in the history of life**" (1994, 271:86, emp. added). Or, as Andy Knoll noted three years earlier: "We now know that the Ediacaran radiation was indeed abrupt and that the geologic floor to the animal fossil record is both real and sharp" (1991, 265:64). This explosion of life that is found in the fossil record all over the world is a serious stumbling block for evolutionists, while for creationists it makes logical sense–God created all living things during the Creation week. Once again, it is creationists who have built a logical scientific theory on the actual evidence (the sudden appearance of fully formed, completely functional, well-designed organisms), while evolutionists have been forced to invent theory after theory due to a complete **lack** of available evidence.

Second, if the fossil record is to offer support for evolution, it must demonstrate a clear-cut sequence of fully functional intermediate forms, by which we mean that certain conditions must be met before an organism (fossil or living) may be considered a true intermediate form. That means we should see transitional body parts such as half scales/half feathers, or animals that are something like half reptile/half mammal. Yet the fossil record does not satisfy the conditions for any such transitional forms. For instance, mammals take many forms, but all are equally mammalian; birds vary greatly, but all are avian.

The late Harvard paleontologist Stephen Jay Gould once remarked that the absence of fossil intermediary stages has remained a "persistent and nagging problem for gradualistic accounts of evolution" (1980, p. 127). Indeed it has. But why is this the case? Gould had answered that question some three years earlier when he wrote: **The extreme rarity of transitional forms in the fossil record persists as the trade secret of paleontology**" (1977b, 86[5]:14, emp. added). This is a fascinating admission. We were not aware that science–by all accounts, a very public enterprise–was supposed to have "trade secrets."

George Gaylord Simpson (also of Harvard, and one of Gould's mentors) wrote as far back as 1944:

> This **regular absence of transitional forms** is not confined to mammals, but is an almost universal phenomenon, as has long been noted by paleontologists. It is true of almost all orders of all classes of animals, both vertebrate and invertebrate. *A fortiori*, it is also true of the classes, and of the major animal phyla, and it is apparently also true of analogous categories of plants (p. 105, emp. added).

Thirty years later, University of Oklahoma paleontologist Dave Kitts acknowledged:

> Despite the bright promise that paleontology provides a means of "seeing" evolution, it has presented some nasty difficulties for evolutionists, the most notorious of which is the presence of "gaps" in the fossil record. **Evolution requires intermediate forms between species and paleontology does not provide them**... (1974, 28:467, emp. added).

Gould thus lamented:

> Paleontologists have paid an exorbitant price for Darwin's argument. We fancy ourselves as the only true students of life's history, yet to preserve our favored account of evolution by natural selection, we view our data as so bad that we never see the very process we profess to study (1977b, 86[5]:14).

As late as 2001, Ernst Mayr of Harvard admitted: "Nothing has more impressed the paleontologists than the discontinuous nature of the fossil record. This is the reason so many of them were supporters of saltational [by "leaps" or "jumps"–BT/BH] theories of evolution" (p. 163).

When one examines the various "candidates" for actual transitional forms, it quickly becomes clear how desperate evolutionists are to find such forms. One of the most famous "missing links" of the past has been the supposed half-reptile/half-bird, *Archaeopteryx*. We have dealt with this at great length elsewhere, and so will not repeat that refutation here (see Harrub and Thompson, 2001; 2002). *Archaeopteryx* is not now, nor has it ever been, a missing link between reptiles and birds. It is just an extinct bird–period. And it is not just creationists who have offered such an assessment. Evolutionists have chimed in to agree as well. Evolutionary ornithologist Allan Feduccia wrote in *Science* a decade ago:

> I conclude that *Archaeopteryx* was arboreal and volant [i.e., possessing extended wings for flight–BT/BH], considerably advanced aerodynamically, and probably capable of flapping, powered flight to at least some degree. ***Archaeopteryx*...was, in the modern sense, a bird** (1993, 259:792, emp. added).

Plus, the fossil remains of two crow-sized birds 75 million years **older** than *Archaeopteryx* (i.e., approximately 225 million years old according to evolutionary dating schemes) were found in 1986 near Post, Texas, by Sankar Chatterjee and colleagues from Texas Tech University in Lubbock, Texas (see Beardsley, 1986; Chatterjee, 1991). Chatterjee has named the find *Protoavis texensis* (first bird from Texas). In 1997, he authored a beautifully illustrated book on the evolution of birds (*The Rise of Birds*), in which *Protoavis* was displayed prominently as being the forerunner of modern birds. All of this, needless to say, has caused evolutionists severe problems because *Protoavis* appeared at the time of the earliest dinosaurs, which means that if it is accepted as genuine, then birds certainly could not have evolved from dinosaurs and *Archaeopteryx* could not be the ancestor of modern birds. After looking at the evidence for *Protoavis*, Kansas University paleontologist Larry Martin suggested: "There's going to be a lot of people with *Archaeopteryx* eggs on their face" (as quoted in Anderson, 1991, 253:35).

On occasion, evolutionists still trot out the so-called horse lineage as evidence of transitional fossils, beginning with the tiny *Eohippus* and going all the way up to our modern *Equus* (see, for example, Rennie, 2002). Many evolutionists, however, no longer consider horse evolution to be a good example of transitional forms, since they do not believe it represents anything like a straightforward progression, but instead a bush with many varying branches. Heribert Nilsson correctly pointed out as long ago as 1954:

> The family tree of the horse is beautiful and continuous only in the textbooks. In the reality provided by the results of research it is put together from three parts, of which only the last can be described as including horses. The forms of the first part are just as much little horses as the present day damans are horses. The construction of the horse is therefore a very artificial one, since it is put together from non-equivalent parts, and cannot therefore be a continuous transformation series (pp. 551-552).

Thus, as far back as the 1950s, scientists already had cast aside the false notion of horse evolution in North America via classic Darwinian changes. Paleontologist David Raup acknowledged:

> Well, we are now about 120 years after Darwin, and knowledge of the fossil record has been greatly expanded.... Ironically, we have even fewer examples of evolutionary transition than we had in Darwin's time. By this I mean that some of the classic cases of Darwinian change in the fossil record, such as the evolution of the horse in North America, have had to be discarded or modified as a result of more detailed information–what appeared to be a nice, simple progression when relatively few data were available now appears to be much more complex and much less gradualistic (1979, pp. 24,25).

Simpson summed it up well when he wrote: "The uniform, continuous transformation of *Hyracotherium* into *Equus*, so dear to the hearts of generations of textbook writers, **never happened in nature**" (1953, p. 125, emp. added). Creationist Jonathan Sarfati wrote along these lines:

> Even informed evolutionists regard horse evolution as a bush rather than a sequence. But the so-called *Eohippus* is properly called *Hyracotherium*, and has little that could connect it with horses at all. The other animals in the "sequence" actually show hardly any more variation between them than that within horses today. One non-horse and many varieties of the true horse kind does not a sequence make (2002a).

In fact, the fossil record does not demonstrate a sequence of transitional fossils **for any** species. As *Newsweek* reporter Jerry Adler accurately noted:

> In the fossil record, missing links are the rule: the story of life is as disjointed as a silent newsreel, in which species succeed one another as abruptly as Balkan prime ministers. The more scientists have searched for the transitional forms between species, the more they have been frustrated.... Evidence from fossils now points overwhelmingly away from the classical Darwinism which most Americans learned in high school: that new species evolve out of existing ones by the gradual accumulation of small changes, each of which helps the organism survive and compete in the environment (1980, 96[18]:95).

Evolutionists continue to set forth various candidates–from whales, to reptiles turning into feathered birds. But when all is said and done, the story ends the same way it has for centuries–with a lot of wishful thinking, and no reputable transitional form candidates that can be used to document the long and perilous journey from an amoeba-like creature to a human.

Certainly many authentic fossils do exist. However, as paleontologist Colin Patterson admitted in his 1999 book, *Evolution*: "Fossils may tell us many things, but one thing they can never disclose is whether they were ancestors of anything else" (p. 109). Henry Gee, the chief science writer for *Nature*, reiterated that point in his 1999 book, *In Search of Deep Time*, when he stated:

> We know that it is impossible when confronted with a fossil, to be certain whether it is your ancestor, or the ancestor of anything else, even another fossil. We also know that adaptive scenarios are simply justifications for particular arrangements of fossils made after the fact, and which rely for their justification on authority rather than on testable hypotheses (p. 127).

Thus, even if legitimate transitional fossils had been found (and they have not), that still would not prove "descent from common ancestry." That is something the fossil record is not equipped to prove.

In an article ("A Theory Evolves") in the July 29, 2002 issue of *U.S. News & World Report*, staff writer Thomas Hayden correctly observed that Darwin held that new species evolve slowly, "the result of countless small changes over many generations" (133[4]:44). Hayden also correctly noted, however, that "many creatures still appear quite suddenly in the fossil record." He went on to admit that the first animals appearing in the fossil record are "complex animals, including worms, mollusks, and shrimplike arthropods" that "show up some 545 million years ago." "Paleontologists," Hayden continued, "have searched far and wide for fossil evidence of gradual progress toward these advanced creatures but have come up empty" (pp. 44-45). He then quoted paleontologist Whitey Hagadorn of Amherst College, who sheepishly confessed: "Paleontologists have the best eyes in the world. If we can't find the fossils, sometimes you have to think that they just weren't there" (p. 45).

While at first glance the average reader might view this as an amazing, first-of-a-kind admission of defeat, history shows otherwise. The fact of the matter is, this statement–made in 2002–is little more than a dim echo of an identical admission made more than half a century ago by the eminent evolutionary paleontologist George Gaylord Simpson, who wrote:

> Possibility for such dispute exists because transitions between major grades of organization are seldom well recorded by fossils. There is in this respect a tendency toward systematic deficiency in the record of the history of life. **It is thus possible to claim that such transitions are not recorded because they did not exist**... (1949, p. 231, emp. added).

Creationists–adhering to the concept that scientific theories should be based upon the actual **presence** of evidence, rather than on the **absence** of evidence–have long taken exactly such a stance, and have suggested that such **transitional forms are not recorded for the simple reason that they did not exist!**

The creation model, of course, predicts a sudden "explosion" of life–with fully formed plants and animals. The creation model predicts a mixture of life forms. The creation model predicts a systematic absence of transitional forms. The evidence from the fossil record clearly shows: (a) fully formed life appearing suddenly; (b) a mixture of life forms (for example, almost all, if not all, of the phyla in the Cambrian period); and (c) an obvious lack of reputable transitional forms.

Evolutionists today certainly are in an embarrassing position. They can find neither the transitional forms their theory demands, nor the mechanism to explain how the evolutionary process supposedly occurred. The facts, however, fit the creation model perfectly.

Creationists and evolutionists both agree that fossils occur, and that they represent the environments in which they once lived. However, it is not the fossils themselves that creationists question, but rather the **interpretation** placed on those fossils by evolutionists. And nowhere is this more evident (or more critically important) than in the fossils that relate to human evolution–an area we would like to investigate further in this chapter.

The Fossil Record and Human Evolution

Let's be blunt about one thing. Of all the branches to be found on that infamous "evolutionary tree of life," the one leading to man should be the best documented. After all, as the most recent evolutionary arrival, pre-human fossils supposedly would have been exposed to natural decay processes for the shortest length of time, and thus should be better preserved and easier to find than any others. [Consider, for example, how many dinosaur fossils we possess, and those animals were supposed to have existed over a hundred million years before man!] In addition, since hominid fossils are of the greatest interest to man (because they are supposed to represent his past), it is safe to say that more people have been searching for them longer than for any other type of fossils. If there are any real transitional forms anywhere in the world, they should be documented most abundantly in the line leading from the first primate to modern man. Certainly, the fossils in this field have received more publicity than in any other. But exactly what does the human fossil record reveal? What is its central message?

Lyall Watson, writing in *Science Digest*, put it bluntly: "The fossils that decorate our family tree are so scarce that there are still more scientists than specimens. The remarkable fact is that all the physical evidence we have for human evolution can still be placed, with room to spare, inside a single coffin" (1982, p. 44). And relatively few "family tree" fossils have been found since that statement was made.

The public, of course, generally has no idea just how scarce, and how fragmentary (literally!), the "evidence" for human evolution actually is. Furthermore, it is practically impossible to determine which "family tree" one should accept. Richard Leakey (of the famed fossil-hunting family in Africa) has proposed one. His late mother, Mary Leakey, proposed another. Donald Johanson (now of the University of Arizona) has proposed yet another. And Meave Leakey (Richard's wife) has proposed still another. At an annual meeting of the American Association for the Advancement of Science, anthropologists from all over the world descended on New York City to view hominid fossils exhibited by the American Museum of Natural History. Reporting on this exhibit, *Science News* had this to say:

> One sometimes wonders whether orangutans, chimps and gorillas ever sit around the tree, contemplating which is the closest relative of man. (And would they want to be?) Maybe they even chuckle at human scientists' machinations as they race to draw the definitive map of evolution on earth. If placed on top of

> one another, all these competing versions of our evolutionary highways would make the Los Angeles freeway system look like County Road 41 in Elkhart, Indiana (see "Whose Ape Is It, Anyway?," 1984, p. 361).

How, in light of such admissions, can evolutionary scientists possibly defend the idea of ape/human evolution as a "scientifically proven fact"?

The primate family (hominidae) supposedly consists of two commonly accepted genera: *Australopithecus* and *Homo.* While it is impossible to present **any** scenario of human evolution upon which even the evolutionists themselves would agree, currently the alleged scenario (gleaned from evolutionists' own writings) might appear like this:

Aegyptopithecus zeuxis (28 million years ago) ➔ *Dryopithecus africanus* (20 million) ➔ *Ramapithecus brevirostris* (12-15 million) ➔ *Orrorin tugenensis* (6 million) ➔ *Ardipithecus ramidus* (5.8-4.4 million) ➔ *Kenyanthropus platyops* (3.8 million years) ➔ *Australopithecus anamensis* (3.5 million) ➔ *Australopithecus afarensis* (3.4 million) ➔ *Homo habilis* (1.5 million) ➔ *Homo erectus* (2-0.4 million) ➔ *Homo sapiens* (0.3 million-present).

Here, now, is what is wrong with all of this. *Aegyptopithecus zeuxis* has been called by Richard Leakey "the first ape to emerge from the Old World monkey stock" (1978, p. 52). No controversy there; the animal is admittedly an ape. *Dryopithecus africanus* is (according to Leakey) "the stock from which all modern apes evolved" (p. 56). But, as evolutionists David Pilbeam and Elwyn Simons have pointed out, *Dryopithecus* already was "too committed to ape-dom" to be the progenitor of man (1971, p. 23). No controversy there; the animal is admittedly an ape. What about *Ramapithecus*? Thanks to additional work by Pilbeam, we now know that *Ramapithecus* was not a hominid at all, but merely another ape (1982, 295: 232). No controversy there; the animal is admittedly an ape. What, then, shall we say of these three "ancestors" that form the taproot of man's family tree? We simply will say the same thing evolutionists have said: all three were nothing but apes.

The 13 fossil fragments that form *Orrorin tugenensis* (broken femurs, bits of lower jaw, and several teeth) were found in the Tugen Hills of Kenya in the fall of 2000 by Martin Pickford and Brigitte Senut of France, and have been controversial ever since. If *Orrorin* were considered to be a human ancestor, it would predate other candidates by around 2 million years. Pickford and Senut, however, in an even more drastic scenario, have suggested that **all the australopithecines**—even those considered to be our direct ancestors—should be relegated to a dead-end side branch in favor of *Orrorin*. Yet paleontologist David Begun of the University of Toronto has stated that scientists can't tell whether *Orrorin* was "on the line to humans, on the line to chimps, a common ancestor to both, or just an extinct side branch" (2001).

In 1994, Tim White and his coworkers described a new species known as *Australopithecus ramidus* (renamed a year later as *Ardipithecus ramidus*), which was dated at 4.4 million years. The August 1999 issue of *Time* contained a feature article, "Up From the Apes," about the creature. When first found (and while still considered an australopithecine), morphologically this was the earliest, most ape-like australopithecine yet discovered, and thus seemed to be a good candidate for the most distant common ancestor of the hominids. Dr. White eventually admitted, however, that *A. ramidus* was not a missing link, but instead had numerous "chimp-like features." A year later, Meave Leakey and colleagues described the 3.5-4.2 million-year-old *Australopithecus anamensis*, a taxon that bears striking similarities to *Ardipithecus* (an admitted chimp) and *Pan* (the actual genus of the chimpanzees). In 1997, researchers discovered another *Ardipithecus*—*A. ramidus kadabba*—which was dated at 5.8-5.2 million years old. [The original *Ardipithecus ramidus* then was renamed *A. ramidus ramidus*.] Once again, *Time* ran a cover story on this alleged "missing link" (in its July 23, 2001 issue). What was it that convinced evolutionists that *kadabba* walked upright and was on the road to becoming man? A single toe bone!

Then, in the March 22, 2001 issue of *Nature*, Meave Leakey and her co-authors announced the discovery of *Kenyanthropus platyops* ("flat-faced man of Kenya"). The authors described their finds as "a well-preserved temporal bone, two partial maxillae, isolated teeth, and most importantly a largely complete, **although distorted**, cranium" (410:433, emp. added). Leakey placed a tremendous amount of importance on the flatness of the facial features of this find, due to the widely acknowledged fact that more modern creatures supposedly possessed an admittedly flatter facial structure than their older, more ape-like alleged ancestors. This is no small problem, however, because creatures younger than *K. platyops*, and therefore closer to *Homo sapiens*, have much more pronounced, ape-like facial features. *K. platyops* was dated at 3.8 million years, and yet has a much flatter face than any other hominid that old. Thus, the evolutionary scenario seems to be moving in the wrong direction.

Some have argued that *K. platyops* belongs more properly in the genus *Australopithecus*. In fact, in the March 28, 2003 issue of *Science*, paleontologist Tim White of the University of California, Berkeley, published an article titled "Early Hominids–Diversity or Distortion?," in which he took strong exception to Meave Leakey's creation of a new genus (*Kenyanthropus*), and in which he argued that *Kenyanthropus* is nothing more than another *Australopithecus afarensis* (2003, 299:1994-1995,1997). White has suggested that the fossil that Leakey and her colleagues found had undergone what is known as "expanding matrix distortion." In short, this means that the shape of the fossil had been distorted by the geological formation in which it was found. Rex Dalton addressed the controversy that Tim White's article caused when he offered the following assessment on *Nature's* Web site on March 28, 2003: "Geology, not genes, gave the Flat-faced Man his distinctive looks, White reckons. Over time, he explains, fine-grained rock invaded tiny cracks in the skull and distorted its shape in an irregular way" (2003). Or, to quote White directly: "The most insidious aspect of EMB [expanding matrix distortion–

BT/BH] is its ability to radically alter morphology in a nonlinear manner. Because matrix expansion does not enlarge all dimensions equally, it often causes highly complex distortion such as that seen in *Kenyanthropus*" (2003, 299:1995). In the end, it appears that Leakey's *Kenyanthropus* is nothing but another australopithecine, rather than some new "missing link."

Australopithecus afarensis was discovered by Donald Johanson in 1974 at Hadar, Ethiopia. Dr. Johanson contends that this creature (known as "Lucy") is the direct ancestor of man (see Johanson and Edey, 1981). Other evolutionists strongly disagree. Lord Solly Zuckerman, the famous British anatomist, published his views in his book, *Beyond the Ivory Tower*. He studied the australopithecines for more than 15 years, and concluded that if man descended from an apelike ancestor, he did so without leaving a single trace in the fossil record (1970, p. 64). Some might say, "But Zuckerman's work was done before Lucy was discovered." True, but that misses the point. Zuckerman's research–which established conclusively that the australopithecines were nothing but knuckle-walking apes–was performed on fossils **younger** (i.e., closer to man) than Lucy! If more recent finds are nothing but apes, how could an **older** specimen be "more human"? Charles Oxnard, while at the University of Chicago, reported on his multivariate computer analysis, which documented that the australopithecines were nothing but knuckle-walking apes (1975, pp. 389-395). Then, in the April 1979 issue of *National Geographic*, Mary Leakey reported finding footprints–dated even older than Lucy at 3.6-3.8 million years–that she admitted were "remarkably similar to those of modern man" (p. 446). If Lucy gave rise to humans, how, then, could humans have existed for more than 500,000 years before her in order to make such footprints? [See Lubenow, 1992, pp. 45-58, and Harrub and Thompson, 2003, for a detailed refutation of Lucy.]

What of *Homo habilis*? J.T. Robinson and David Pilbeam have long argued that *H. habilis* is the same as *A. africanus*. Louis Leakey (Richard's father) even stated: "I submit that morphologically it is almost impossible to regard *Homo habilis* as representing a stage between *Australopithecus africanus* and *Homo erectus*" (1966, 209:1280-1281). Dr. Leakey later reported the contemporaneous existence of *Australopithecus*, *Homo habilis*, and *H. erectus* fossils at Olduvai Gorge (see Mary Leakey, 1971, 3:272). Even more startling was Mary Leakey's discovery of the remains of a circular stone hut at the bottom of Bed I at Olduvai Gorge–**beneath** fossils of *H. habilis*! Evolutionists have long attributed the deliberate manufacture of shelter only to *Homo sapiens*, yet Dr. Leakey discovered the australopithecines and *H. habilis* together with manufactured housing. As Duane Gish asked: "If *Australopithecus*, *Homo habilis*, and *Homo erectus* existed contemporaneously, how could one have been ancestral to another? And how could any of these creatures be ancestral to Man, when Man's artifacts are found at a lower stratigraphic level, directly underneath, and thus earlier in time to these supposed ancestors of Man?" (1995, p. 271). Good question!

And what about *Homo erectus*? Examine a copy of the November 1985 issue of *National Geographic* and see if you can detect any differences between the pictures of *Homo erectus* and *Homo sapiens* (pp. 576-577). The fact is, there are no recognizable differences. As Ernst Mayr, the famed evolutionary taxonomist of Harvard remarked: "The *Homo erectus* stage is characterized by a body skeleton which, so far as we know, does not differ from that of modern man in any essential point" (1965, p. 632). The fossil evidence for evolution (human or otherwise) simply is not there. Apes always have been apes, and humans always have been humans.

The Geologic Timetable and the Age of the Earth

The Grand Canyon frequently is described as one of the most awe-inspiring and spectacular natural features on the face of the Earth. Listed as one of the Seven Natural Wonders of the World, it became a national park in 1919, and in 1979 was named a World Heritage Site–a designation reserved only for those places that are considered to have universal value

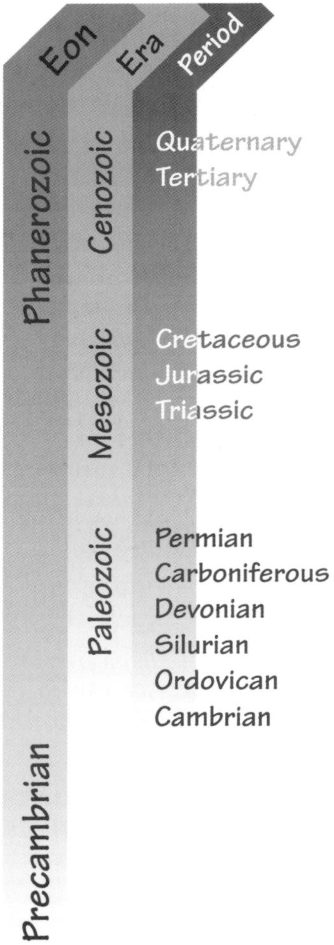

for all humankind. Because of its sheer size, the origin of this natural beauty has been the object of a great deal of speculation. Theories regarding the geological events that possibly led to the present canyon are as abundant as visitors to the South Rim.

To the "man on the street," one of the most impressive arguments for an ancient Earth is the testimony of sedimentary-rock layers (many of which are thousands of feet thick) strewn around the planet. Scientists (and park rangers) subject us to examples like the Grand Canyon, and present their spiel so effectively that —as we observe those layers of sedimentary rocks piled one on top of another—the only logical explanation seems to be that vast amounts of time must have been involved. Each section of the rocks, we are told, represents a time eons ago and an ancient world that long since has ceased to exist.

Evolutionists contend that the Earth is 4.6 billion years old. Further, they allege that for the past three billion years or so, life has evolved gradually from simple organisms to those that are increasingly complex. One of the methods of presenting this idea is by means of the so-called "geologic timetable." While it may sound surprising, the standard geologic column actually was devised prior to 1860 by catastrophists who considered themselves creationists (Ritland, 1982). The timetable is a common feature in most textbooks dealing with geology, biology, paleontology, etc., and proposes to show the development of living creatures, in ascending order from the simple to the complex, from the ancient past to the present. While it certainly looks good on paper, the actual evidence tells a completely different story.

Old Earth/Young Earth

Much of the controversy today between creationists and evolutionists centers on the age of the Earth. A large part of that controversy has to do with the fact that there is no compromise that will permit the old-Earth/young-Earth scenarios to coexist; the gulf separating the biblical and evolutionary views on the topic of the age of the Earth is just too large. Marshall and Sandra Hall recognized this fact when they observed: "It is not easy to overthrow a belief, however absurd and harmful it may be, which your civilization has promulgated as the scientific truth for the better part of a century." The Halls continued by saying:

> Time, as poets and insurance salesmen remind us, is the enemy of life. But time has its friends, too. Without great, incomprehensible, immeasurable stretches of time to fall back on, the evolutionists would be sitting ducks for the barbed queries of even high school students. **Time** is the evolutionists' refuge from the slings and arrows of logic, scientific evidence, common sense, and the multiplication table (1974, pp. 74, 69,71,75, emp. in orig.).

The point is well made. It **is** difficult to overthrow a belief that has been taught as the "scientific truth" for so long. And it is especially difficult to overthrow such a concept when an entire world view is based upon it. Yet when **all** the evidence is considered, it does not bode well for the evolutionists' claims of an ancient Earth/Universe. The actual evidence, however, firmly supports the concept of a young Earth. We would like to consider some of that evidence here.

Evolutionists have divided the geologic column into a hierarchical system of eons, eras, periods, and epochs. The two major eon divisions are the Precambrian (590 million to 4.5 billion years ago) and the Phanerozoic (590 million years to the present). The three major eras of the Phanerozoic are the Paleozoic–referred to as the age of the trilobites (which includes the Cambrian, Ordovician, Silurian, Devonian, Carboniferous, and Permian periods), the Mesozoic–referred to as the age of the dinosaurs–(which includes the Triassic, Jurassic, and Cretaceous periods), and Cenozoic–referred to as the age of the mammals–(which includes the Tertiary and Quaternary periods). Many of us have been taught that the geologic column "proves" that evolution is true and that the Earth is extremely old. Actually, the geologic column provides extraordinary evidence which demonstrates that evolution is not true and that the Earth is not ancient. Consider the following.

Out-of-Place Fossils

According to the evolutionary hypothesis, man (*Homo sapiens*) appears near the top of the geologic column. Man's history, therefore, represents but a tiny fraction (approximately 1/1000th) of the geologic record. To an evolutionist, it is inconceivable that evidence of human habitation could exist in earlier periods. Yet there are many such examples of "out-of-place" fossils that undermine the theory of evolution.

For example, several years ago, evolutionist Albert G. Ingalls (the state geologist of Kentucky) was working in the coal veins in Kentucky and nearby states. Dr. Ingalls stumbled across "human-like" footprints embedded in the coal veins of those states. Coal, of course, is supposed to have been laid down during the so-called Carboniferous period, which allegedly is separated from mankind by 250 million years according to the standard geologic timetable. How, then, could human footprints possibly occur in coal? Dr. Ingalls did not discover these footprints just in Kentucky. He also found them in Missouri, Illinois, Pennsylvania, Virginia, West Virginia, and even westward toward the Rocky Mountains. Dr. Ingalls was invited by the editors of *Scientific American* to write an article about this unusual find. He accepted, and in the January 1940 issue (under the title of "The Carboniferous Mystery"), he included photographs of the prints (see reproductions below) and wrote:

> On sites reaching from Virginia and Pennsylvania, through Kentucky, Illinois, Missouri and westward toward the Rocky Mountains, prints similar to those shown above, and from 5 to 10 inches long, have from time to time been found on the surface of exposed rocks, and more and more keep turning up as the years go by. What made these prints? As yet the answer is unknown to science. **They look like human footprints** and it often has been said, though not by scientists, that they really are human footprints made in the soft mud before it became rock (162:14).

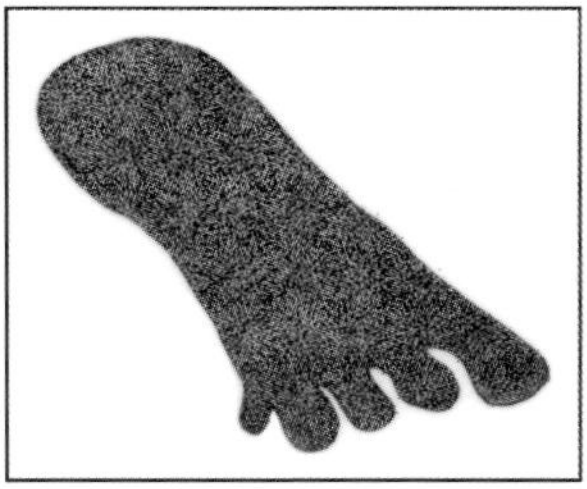

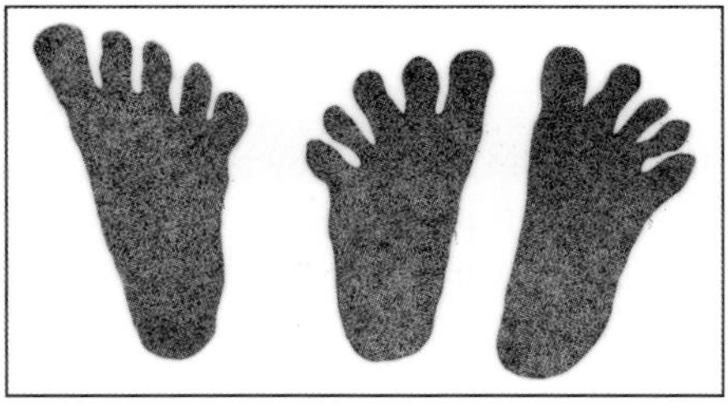

Ingalls was not the only person to investigate the tracks, however. A.E. Wilder-Smith, of the United Nations, also examined the tracks, and reported as follows:

> The tracks are in formations considered to be in Upper Carboniferous (250 million years old) and show five toes and an arch which is unquestionably human. The tracks are 9½ inches long and 4.1 inches broad at the heel. The width at the forward end of the track by the toes was 6 inches. The being that left the tracks was a biped that walked uprightly like a human. *Antiquities* published photographs of the tracks and said

> that similar ones had been found in Carboniferous formats in Pennsylvania and Missouri. The Missouri tracks look exceedingly human and resemble those of Southeast Asian aborigines (1975, p. 300).

Some evolutionists have suggested that a few of the pictures reproduced in Ingalls' *Scientific American* article do not look like "human" footprints, because they are too "splayed" (spread out). However, for a human to have a splayed foot is not unusual, especially for people who routinely walk without shoes. Examine the pictures below of splayed human feet, and compare them to the pictures published along with Ingalls' *Scientific American* article, and we think you will be able to see for yourself the point we are making.

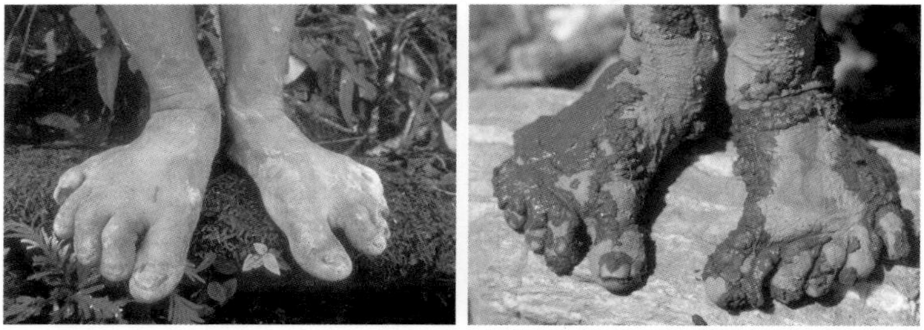

The feet on the left belong to an unnamed native who lives in a tropical rain forest; the feet at the right belong to José Maria Roa of Ecuador, who was 87 years old at the time the photograph was taken. Photographs courtesy of Frans Lanting (left) and Black Star Publishing (right). Used by permission.

How did Dr. Ingalls "explain away" the tracks that he, himself, admitted "look like human footprints"? He wrote:

> If man, or even his ape ancestor, or even the ape ancestor's early mammal ancestor, existed as far back as in the carboniferous period in any shape, then the whole science of geology is so completely wrong that all geologists will resign their jobs and take up truck driving. Hence, for the present at least, science rejects the attractive explanation that man made these mysterious prints in the mud of the carboniferous period with his feet (162:14).

"Science rejects the attractive explanation"–**since when**? Science is systematized knowledge derived from observation, collection, and interpretation of data. Scientists do not "reject" the **data** simply because they do not fit the currently reigning theory. Rather, they reject the theory and abandon it, or modify it so it fits with the new, incoming data. And it works like that in every area of science except one–where evolution is concerned.

Furthermore, the tracks that Ingalls reported were not the only ones that have been discovered. In an article titled "Human-Like Tracks in Stone are Riddle to Scientists" that appeared in the October 29, 1938 issue of *Science News Letter*, the following pictures appeared.

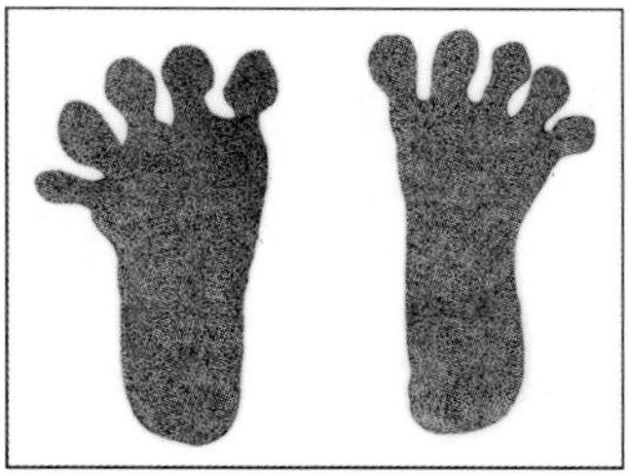

Interestingly, underneath the picture you see at the left, was the following caption: "These aren't human. But they look enough that way to fool almost everybody. They are footprints made ages ago by a still unknown animal in the late Coal Age."

In the article accompanying the footprints, the editors of the journal offered the following "explanation."

> The footprints are exceedingly curious things. They are the right size to be human–nine or ten inches in length–and they are almost the right shape. **Practically everyone who sees them thinks at first they were made by human feet and it is almost impossible to persuade some people that they were not**....
>
> **A further puzzling fact is the absence of any tracks of front feet.** The tracks, apparently all of the hind feet of biped animals, are turned in all kinds of random directions. At Berea [Kentucky], two of them are side by side, as though one of the creatures had stood still for a moment (see "Human-Like Tracks...," pp. 278-279, emp. added).

And so, we are asked to believe that what are obvious human footprints–**aren't**! Rather, even though they are the "right size to be human," and even though "everyone who sees them thinks at first they were made by human feet," according to evolutionists, the tracks were made by some "unknown animal" that walked in upright fashion but left only tracks from its "hind feet." Is this not incredible?! We cannot help but be reminded of what G.K. Chesterton once said: "When men stop believing in God, they don't believe in nothing; they believe in anything." This particular scenario is the perfect example of the truthfulness of that statement.

However, there is additional evidence to be considered along these lines. In 1936, a metal hammer with a wooden handle was dug out of Cretaceous limestone (dated by evolutionists at 135 million years old) in the area near London, Texas. The hammer's broken handle is 6¾ inches long, and the hammer itself is made of a very strong metal. When the surface oxidation was removed, the metal was still shiny. [Details of this remarkable discovery (including photographs) may be found in Helfinstine and Roth (1994, pp. 83,91-92), and the February 1984 issue of *Creation Ex Nihilo* magazine (see "Ordovician Hammer Report," 2[3]:16-17).]

Equally as fascinating are the various items that have been discovered in coal veins around the globe. Ivan Sanderson reported on one such find that was reported in the Morrisonville, Illinois, newspaper, the *Illinois Times*, on June 11, 1891.

> A much greater enigma is presented by the items that have been found in coal. This substance has been deposited on the surface of this earth at various times but most notably in what is called the Carboniferous (and specifically the Upper Carboniferous, so-called, or Pennsylvanian of America) which is calculated to be from 270 to 230 millions of years old; and from the Miocene of the Tertiary Era estimated to be from 26 to 12 million years of age. From it several items have appeared that confound just about everything we believe. For instance, it has been reported that in

> 1891 a Mrs. Culp of Morrisonville, Illinois dropped a shovelful of coal in transferring it to her cooking range, and a large lump broke in two, disclosing a lovely little gold chain of intricate workmanship neatly coiled and embedded (1967, pp. 195-196, parenthetical comments in orig.; cf. also Wysong, 1976, p. 370).

Upon examination, it was determined that the chain was ten inches long and made out of 8-karat gold. Who–according to evolutionary timescales–was around 250 million years ago to be making "little gold chains of intricate workmanship"?

J.Q. Adams, writing in the *American Antiquarian* (1883, 5: 331-332), documented the discovery of a woman's sewing thimble in a lump of coal that was said by evolutionists to have been formed in the period between the Tertiary and Cretaceous periods. In 1915, an iron pot also was discovered in coal deposits that were dated at 300 million years (see Rusch, 1970, 7: 201-213).

In 1889, while boring a well at Nampa, Idaho, workmen struck artesian water contained in rocks over 300 feet deep, underneath a "Tertiary" lava sheet that would be approximately 12 million years old according to evolutionary dating schemes. Pumped up from the 300-foot depth was a tiny baked clay figurine with one of its legs missing–something that obviously had been made by humans (see Bird, 1934, pp. 17-26; Velikovsky, 1955, p. 90). Again, we are constrained to ask, what human was around twelve million years ago who had the ability to fashion (and bake) a clay figurine?

The trilobite, a small, marine arthropod with a hard exoskeleton, is considered so important as to be classified as an "index fossil" for the earliest period of the Paleozoic Era, the Cambrian. Evolutionist J.E. O'Rourke, in a paper in the *American Journal of Science* titled "Pragmatism versus Materialism in Stratigraphy," discussed the use of index fossils to determine the geologic age of a formation. He noted that the methodology involved starts

> ...**from a chronology of index fossils, and imposes them on the rocks**. Each taxon represents a definite time unit and so provides an accurate, even "infallible" date. If you doubt it, bring in a suite of good index fossils, and the specialist without asking where or in what order they were collected, will lay them out on the table in chronological order (1976, 276:51, emp. added).

In other words, the assumption that evolution is true is used to place the index fossils in the appropriate order from simple to complex. The index fossils then are used to "date" the layers in order to "prove" that evolution is true. If this sounds like "circular reasoning" to you, congratulations. It most certainly is! As O'Rourke went on to admit:

> **The intelligent layman has long suspected circular reasoning in the use of rocks to date fossils and fossils to date rocks**. The geologist has never bothered to think of a good reply, feeling the explanations are not worth the trouble as long as the work brings results. This is supposed to be hardheaded pragmatism.... The rocks do date the fossils, but the fossils date the rocks more accurately. Stratigraphy cannot avoid this kind of reasoning if it insists on using only temporal concepts, because circularity is inherent in the derivation of time scales (276:47,53, emp. added).

As one scientist noted: "The dating of the rocks depends on the evolutionary sequence of the fossils, but the evolutionary interpretation of the fossils depends on the dating of the rocks. No wonder the evolutionary system, to outsiders, implies circular reasoning" (Morris, 1977, p. ii). No wonder indeed!

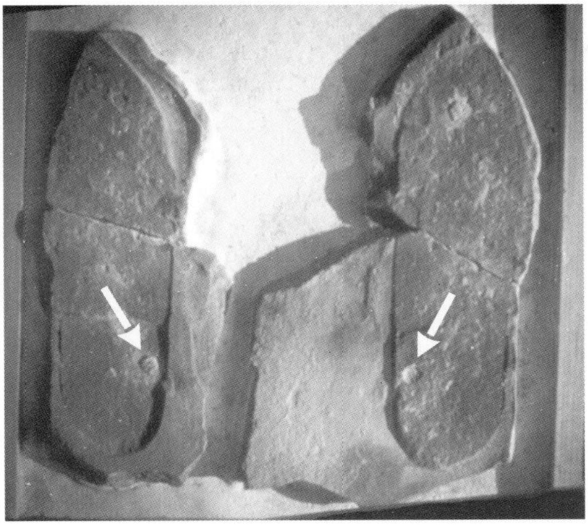

Photograph of human sandalprint with trilobite fossils in the heel and toe areas. Left and right sides are mirror images of each other. Line of demarcation between heel and sole is evident, as is wearing of sandal at heel area.

Trilobites supposedly flourished a half-billion years before humans arrived on the scene. On June 1, 1968, however, evolutionist William J. Meister, an amateur fossilologist, was working near Antelope Springs, Utah, and made a discovery that was destined to dispel that incorrect evolutionary supposition. Working his way up the side of a mountain some 2,000+ feet (to a ledge above), he broke open a slab of rock with his hammer to investigate it for fossils. Imagine his astonishment when he "saw on one side the footprint of a human with trilobites right in the footprint itself. The other half of the rock slab showed an almost perfect mold of the footprint and fossils. Amazingly the human was wearing a sandal" (as quoted in Lammerts, 1976, pp. 186-187). Numerous other fossilized human footprints, from both adults and children, have since been found in the area, as well as dinosaur prints. The contemporaneousness of man and the trilobite effectively collapses a half-billion years of the geologic column.

Additionally, fossilized animals, including chordate fish, appear in the fossil record fully formed and distinct. No ancestral forms can be found in deeper layers for animals such as the protozoans, arthropods, brachiopods, mollusks, bryozoans, coelenterates, sponges, annelids, echinoderms, or chordates—suggesting an abrupt beginning (creation) rather than descent from a common ancestor (evolution). If space permitted, we could present much additional information on such "anomalies" to show that much of the geologic column is a figment of the evolutionists' imagination. Consider, if you will, the following abbreviated listing of such contradictions composed by Erich von Fange (1974, 11:19ff.).

(a) Fossil leather sole imprint, with a double line of sewed stitches found in "Triassic" rock estimated to be 225 million years old.

(b) Fossil sole imprint with visible sewn thread in coal estimated at 15 million years old.

(c) Flint carvings on extinct saurian (reptilian) bones estimated to be 180 million years old.

Polystrate Fossils

Embedded in sedimentary rocks all over the globe are what are known as "polystrate" fossils. Polystrate means "many layers," and refers to fossils that cut through at least two sedimentary-rock layers. Probably the most widely recognized of the polystrate fossils are tree trunks that extend vertically through two, three, or more sections of rock that supposedly were laid down in epochs covering millions of years. However, organic material (such as wood) that is exposed to the elements will rot, not fossilize. Thus, the entire length of these tree trunks must have been preserved quickly, which suggests that the sedimentary layers surrounding them must have been deposited rapidly—possibly (and likely) during a single catastrophe. As Paul Ackerman has suggested: "They constitute a sort of frozen time clock from the past, indicating that terrible things occurred—not over millions of years but very quickly" (1986, p. 84).

Further, tree trunks are not the only representatives of polystrate fossils. In the state of Oklahoma, geologist John Morris studied limestone layers containing fossilized reed-like creatures known as Calamites that ranged from one to six inches in diameter. Dr. Morris noted: "These segmented 'stems' were evidently quite fragile once dead, for they are usually found in tiny fragments. Obviously, the limestones couldn't have accumulated slowly and gradually around a still-growing organism, but must have been quite rapidly deposited in a series of underwater events" (1994, p. 101).

At times, even animals' bodies form polystrate fossils (like catfish in the Green River Formation in Wyoming–see Morris, 1994, p. 102). Probably the most famous is the fossilized skeleton of a whale discovered in 1976 near Lompoc, California. The whale is covered in "diatomaceous earth." Diatoms are microscopic algae. As they die, their skeletons form deposits–a process that evolutionists say is extremely slow. But the whale (which is more than 75 feet long) is standing almost on its tail at an angle and is completely covered by the diatomaceous earth. There simply is no way a whale could have stood upright for millions of years while diatoms covered it, because it would have decayed or been eaten by scavengers. [For a complete discussion of the baleen whale fossil, see Snelling, 1995.]

Trees, reeds, catfish, and the other organisms with which the fossil record abounds did not die and lie around for hundreds, thousands, or millions of years while slowly being turned into polystrate fossils. Truth be told, polystrate fossils testify loudly to a young Earth whose layers formed rapidly–and not very long ago!

The Bible and the Age of the Earth

The question frequently is asked, "Does the Bible offer any evidence regarding the age of the Earth?" Yes, it does. An investigation of that evidence makes for a fascinating and profitable study. We would like to examine it here briefly.

In chapter 8, we dealt with attempts on the part of some to compromise the literal, historical nature of Genesis 1-11. In their attempts to do accommodate God's Word to evolution-based time schemes, some have suggested that the Bible does not place any restrictions on the age of the Earth, and therefore a Christian is free to believe whatever he or she desires regarding the age of the Earth. Not only is such a statement untrue, but those who make such comments generally have an ulterior motive in doing so—defending an ancient Earth.

In order to accommodate the Bible to an evolutionary timetable, billions of years somehow must be inserted into the biblical record. But where, exactly, can this vast amount of time be placed to guarantee such antiquity? There are only three possible options. The time needed to guarantee an old Earth might be placed: (a) **before** the Creation week; (b) **during** the Creation week; or (c) **after** the Creation week. Let us explore each of these options.

Time *Before* the Creation Week: The Gap Theory

Those who attempt to place the billions of years necessary for evolution **before** the creation week generally advocate what has come to be known as the Gap Theory. This theory suggests that a vast "gap" of time (of billions of years) should be inserted between Genesis 1:1 and Genesis 1:2. During this time, God supposedly created a fully functional Earth complete with animals, plants, and even humans who lived before Adam. That creation, the theory suggests, was destroyed as the result of a rebellion fomented on Earth by Satan. The raging war between Satan and God supposedly left this planet "without form and void" (Genesis 1:2), which, it is claimed, accounts for the myriad of fossils present in the Earth. Then, starting in Genesis 1:2, God "re-created" (or "restored") the Earth in six literal, 24-hour days. Thus, Genesis 1 is the story of an original, perfect creation, a judgment and ruination (the Earth in its "without form and void" state), and a re-creation.

While at first glance this may appear to be an alluring theory, it cannot possibly be true if the biblical record is taken at face value. First, the Gap Theory blatantly contradicts Exodus 20:11: "For in six days the Lord made the heavens and the earth, the sea, and all that is in them, and rested the seventh day." If God made **everything** in six days, how many things did He make before those days? The answer, of course, is none.

Second, there is no biblical evidence whatsoever to substantiate the claim that Satan's rebellion against God took place on the Earth. The idea of a so-called cataclysm that destroyed the initial Earth is not supported by an appeal to Scripture, but instead is a concept that has been imposed on Scripture from outside sources by those attempting to defend the necessity and validity of the Gap Theory.

Finally, the Gap Theory is false because it implies that humans died before Adam and Eve. The inspired apostle Paul observed that death entered this world as a result of Adam's sin (1 Corinthians 15:21; Romans 5:12; 8:20-22). Paul also stated that Adam was **the first man** (1 Corinthians 15:45). Yet, if the Gap Theory is correct, there existed a band of sinful people who lived many years before Adam. Additionally, Moses recorded in Genesis 1:31 that everything God had created was "very good"—a very strained interpretation if the Earth and its inhabitants already had been destroyed. The simple fact of the matter is that Paul and the Gap Theory cannot both be right.

A word of caution is in order here, however. In their attempts to oppose evolution and to make the case for the biblical account of origins, some creationists (who no doubt are well intentioned) have misinterpreted, and thus misapplied, the teachings of two important New Testament passages. The first of those passages is Romans 5:12-14.

> Therefore, just **as through one man sin entered the world, and death through sin**, and thus death spread to all men, because all sinned. For until the law, sin was in the world, but sin is not imputed when there is no law. Nevertheless death reigned from Adam to Moses, even over those who had not sinned according to the likeness of the transgression of Adam, who is a type of Him who was to come.

The second passage is 1 Corinthians 15:20-22:

> But now Christ is risen from the dead, and has become the firstfruits of those who have fallen asleep. For since **by man came death**, by Man also came the resurrection of the dead. For as in Adam all die, even so in Christ all shall be made alive.

The portions of these two verses (shown in bold type) that are emphasized by certain creationists stress the fact that **death entered the world as a result of man's sin**. The argument set forth, therefore, is as follows. Gap theorists suggest that there were billions of years of happenstance, contingency, incredible waste, **death**, pain, and horror after God's initial creation. The Bible states quite specifically, however, that human death did not exist until Adam and Eve sinned against God. The Gap theorist's scenario, therefore, is apodictically impossible, because it requires the death of untold thousands of species of plants, animals, and humans.

But is it correct to say that there was **absolutely no death of any kind** prior to Adam and Eve's sin? No, it is not. To say that there was no **human** death prior to the fall of man is to make a perfectly biblical statement. The passages in Romans 5 and 1 Corinthians 15 make that crystal clear. However, using those same scriptures to suggest that not even plants or animals could die ignores the specific context of each of the passages and is a serious abuse of the texts under consideration. Paul's presentation in Romans 5:12-14 and 1 Corinthians 15:20-22 had nothing whatsoever to do with the death of either plants or animals. Rather, an examination of the two passages reveals that, **in the context**, he was discussing **only the death of humans**–a death which resulted from the tragic events that transpired in the Garden of Eden after Adam and Eve's willful sin.

Time *During* the Creation Week: The Day-Age Theory

Because of the dismal failure of the Gap Theory to provide an adequate means of inserting billions of years into the Genesis record, some have suggested that perhaps the days discussed in Genesis 1 were not literal 24-hour periods, but instead were long eons of times during which evolution could have taken place (a concept known as the Day-Age Theory). After all, we are told, the word translated "day" in Genesis can have up to seven different meanings and, on rare occasions, even can refer to a long period of time. Thus, according to proponents of the Day-Age Theory, the Creation week was seven long spans of time that consisted of millions or billions of years each. Is that the case? How long were the days of the Creation week, really?

A straightforward reading of the text in Genesis 1 indicates that Moses wanted his readers to understand, in no uncertain terms, that the six days of creation were literal 24-hour periods. The available evidence reveals several reasons why we can know that these days were not millions or billions of years, but rather were approximately the same kind of days we experience currently. First, whenever the Hebrew word translated as "day" (*yom*) is preceded by a numeral (in non-prophetical passages such as Genesis 1), it **always** carries the meaning of a 24-hour day. Second, whenever the word "day" appears in the plural form (*yamim*) in non-prophetical literature, it **always** means a literal day. In fact, the Old Testament uses *yamim* in this manner more than 700 times, and it always means a literal day in its non-prophetic usage. Therefore, when Exodus 20:11 states: "For in six **days** (*yamim*) the Lord made the heavens and the earth," there can be absolutely no doubt that the text means six literal days.

Third, *yom* is both used and defined in Genesis 1:5. "God called the light Day, and the darkness he called Night. So the **evening** and the **morning** were the first day" (emp. added). The word *yom* accompanies the words "evening" and "morning" over 100 times in non-prophetical passages in the Old Testament, and each time it refers to an obvious 24-hour day.

Fourth, if the "days" of Genesis were not days at all, but long geological periods, then a problem of no little consequence arises in the field of botany. Plants came into existence on the third day (Genesis 1:9-13). If the days of Genesis 1 were long geological ages, how did the plant life survive millions of years of total darkness? Also, how would the plants that depend on insects for pollination have survived the supposed millions or billions of years between "day" three and "day" five (when insects were created).

Fifth, while Jesus was on the Earth He taught that man and woman were here "from the beginning of creation" (Mark 10:6; cf. Matthew 19:4). Paul affirmed this same sentiment in Romans 1:20-21, where he stated that man and woman have been here "from the beginning of the creation" when they were "perceiving the things that were made." The Day-Age Theory, on the other hand, places man at the end of billions of years of geologic time. Both cannot be true!

Sixth, in Genesis 1:14, Moses stated regarding the Sun, Moon, and stars: "Then God said, 'Let there be lights in the heavens to divide the day from the night; and let them be for signs and for seasons, for days and for years.'" If the "days" were millions or billions of years, then, pray tell, what would the "years" have been?

Finally, we need to ask the question: If God had wanted us to know that He created the world in six literal days, what other words could He have used than the ones He did? Or if we wanted to explain to someone else that God created everything in a literal six days, what words would we use? The answer, of course, is that both God and we would use the exact words that appear in Genesis 1. The writer of Genesis had other ways to say that the periods were long eons of time. He could have employed the Hebrew word *dôr*, which means a long period of time. But he did not; instead he used the word day, modified it with the phrase "evening and morning," put numerals before it, and in Exodus 20:11 made it plural. He used practically every means at his disposal to show that the days were not long periods of time but were literal 24-hour periods. Thus, the idea that the billions of years needed for evolution occurred during creation week simply cannot be defended. You can trust your Bible when it records: "For in six **days** [not six billion years–BT/BH] the Lord made the heavens and the earth, the sea, and all that is in them, and rested the seventh day" (Exodus 20:11).

But what about 2 Peter 3:8? Doesn't it indicate that "with the Lord one day is as a thousand years and a thousand years as one day." Isn't this New Testament passage teaching that the days of Genesis could have been very long periods of time? No, it is not. Let us consider the passage in its appropriate context. In 2 Peter 3:8, the apostle's discussion has nothing to do with the length of the days in Genesis 1. Rather, he is discussing the "last days" (3:3; i.e., the Christian dispensation) and Christ's Second Coming. Some, said Peter, would suggest that since Christ had not returned already, then He was not going to return–ever! But Peter reminded his readers that God is not bound by time. He can do more in one day than humans can do in a thousand years, or, conversely, He may wait a thousand years to do what humans wish He would do in a day. Nevertheless, God keeps His promises (3:9). It is interesting to note, is it not, that from a reading of the text, God Himself recognizes the difference between an earthly day and an earthly thousand years. It also is interesting to note that Peter did not say that a day **is** a thousand years or a thousand years **is** a day, but that a day is "**as**" a thousand years and a thousand years is "**as**" a day. God always has recognized the difference between an earthly day, month, and year. The passage in 2 Peter 3:8 proves that He is able to communicate the difference to human beings. What did He say the time periods in Genesis 1 were? Days!

Time *After* the Creation Week

We have seen that the time needed for evolution to take place cannot be placed **before** the Creation week because the Bible says that God created everything in six days. We also have seen that vast amounts of time cannot be placed **during** the six days of creation because they were literal, 24-hour periods. The only possible place left for the eons of time, then, is **after** the Creation week.

Those who wish to place the billions of years needed to accommodate evolutionary geology **after** the Creation week are few and far between, because the Bible contains lengthy and extensive genealogies that extend all the way back to Adam. And one of the messages of those genealogies is that **man has been on the Earth since the beginning, and that beginning was not very long ago**.

In one sense, the Bible tells us exactly how old the Earth is. In Mark 10:6, Jesus stated that "from the beginning of the creation, God made them male and female." How long have humans been on this Earth? Jesus said "from the beginning of the creation." Genesis 1:26-31 explains that God chose the sixth day of the Creation week to form mankind from the dust of the ground. He chose the first day to construct the Earth. Thus, the Earth is exactly five days older than humanity!

So, in order to determine the age of the Earth, we must determine how long man has been here–which is not as difficult as it may seem. Speaking in round figures, how long has it been since Jesus Christ visited the Earth? Answer: about 2,000 years. Secular history volunteers that piece of information via its designation of dates as "A.D." (i.e., *anno Domini*, meaning "in the year of the Lord"). Next, we must determine how many years came between Jesus and Abraham. Fortunately, secular history also volunteers that figure, which turns out to be around 2,000 years. These two figures can be obtained from practically any secular history book.

The final number we must uncover is the number of years between Abraham and Adam. Once we know this figure, simple addition of the three will give us the approximate age of the Earth. Note, however, that the figure representing the period between Abraham and Adam cannot be retrieved from secular history (nor should we expect it to be!), since the Great Flood during Noah's day destroyed most, if not all, of the records pertaining to that time period. Then how can the figure be obtained?

In Luke 3, the physician/writer listed 55 generations between Jesus and Abraham–a time frame archaeology has determined to be approximately 2,000 years. In that same chapter, Luke documented that there were only 20 generations between Abraham and Adam. But how much time, total, do those twenty generations cover? Since Genesis 5 and 11 list the ages of the fathers at the time of the births of their sons between Abraham and Adam, it is a simple matter to calculate the approximate number of years involved–a figure that turns out to be around 2,000. In chart form the information appears as follows:

Present time to Jesus	2,000 years
Jesus to Abraham	2,000 years (55 generations)
Abraham to Adam	2,000 years (20 generations)

The fact that the 55 generations between Jesus and Abraham cover 2,000 years, while only 20 generations between Abraham and Adam cover the same amount of time, is explained quite easily on the basis of the vast ages of the patriarchs (like Methuselah, for example, who lived 969 years).

Some have argued that the genealogies in Genesis 5 cannot be used to demonstrate the approximate age of the Earth because they are riddled with huge gaps. But in Jude 14, the writer noted that Enoch was "the seventh from Adam" (he is listed exactly seventh in Genesis 5:21). Therefore, we know that there are no gaps between the first seven patriarchs, because Jude confirmed the accuracy of the Old Testament in this regard. That leaves only 13 generations with potential gaps between them. But in order to accommodate the evolutionary scenario which suggests that man has been on the Earth (in one form or another) approximately 3.5 million years, you would need to insert over 290,000 years between **each** of the 13 generations. It does not take a wealth of either Bible knowledge or common sense to see that this quickly becomes ludicrous. Who could believe that the first seven of these generations are so exact, while the remaining 13 contain "gaps" of over a quarter of a million years? What type of biblical exegesis is that?

While it may be true on the one hand to say that an **exact** age of the Earth is unobtainable from the information contained within the genealogies, at the same time it is important to note that–using the best information available to us from Scripture–the genealogies hardly can be extended to anything much beyond 6,000 to 7,000 years. For someone to suggest that the genealogies do not contain legitimate chronological information, or that the genealogies somehow are so full of gaps as to render them useless, is to misrepresent the case and distort the facts.

Numerous theories have been concocted to entice Christians to believe in an ancient Earth, while supposedly allowing them to maintain their belief in the Bible as God's Word. It soon becomes clear, however, that if biblical instruction is taken at face value, an ancient Earth is an impossibility. Scientific theories change, and estimates of the age of the Earth come and go. "The Word of the Lord," however, "endures forever" (1 Peter 1:25; cf. Isaiah 40:8).

CONCLUSION

Some time long ago, our office received a heart-rending letter from a young Christian who was a graduate student in the applied sciences at a state university. His major professor was a man he termed "a giant in his field... rocket-scientist intelligent...and a devout evolutionist." In his letter, the student went on to say:

> Working this closely with one who thinks as he does is beginning to cause not a small amount of cognitive dissonance in my own mind. Hundreds of thousands of scientists can't be wrong, can they? Consensual validation cannot be pushed aside in science. How can that many people be following a flag with no carrier, and someone not find out? **I do not want to be a fool!**

This young writer expressed what many people experience, yet are unable to enunciate so eloquently. It is not an enjoyable experience to be exposed to the slings and barbs of infidelity. Nor is it pleasant to be labeled as dumb, stupid, or ignorant because you hold to a belief different than your opponent's. Yet it is those very labels that have been applied to those of us who are willing to defend the existence of God or the concept of creation. Several years ago, the famous atheist/evolutionist of Oxford University, Richard Dawkins wrote: "It is absolutely safe to say that if you meet somebody who claims not to believe in evolution, that person is **ignorant**, **stupid**, or **insane** (or **wicked**, but I'd rather not consider that)" (1989, p. 34, parenthetical item in orig., emp. added).

The "cognitive dissonance" mentioned by the young man is the label for the internal struggle one experiences when presented with new information that contradicts what he believes to be true. As the student struggled for consistency, he realized that he had only two choices. He either had to: (1) alter what he previously believed; or (2) disregard the new information being presented to him by "a rocket-scientist intelligent" professor whom he respected. This young Christian—like so many before and after him—once knew what he believed, and why. But by the time his letter arrived in our office, he no longer knew either. He pleaded: "I am a confused young man with some serious questions about my mind, my faith, and my God. Please help me."

That agonizing plea—"please help me"—has been echoed countless times through the centuries by those who languish in the "cognitive dissonance" that results from replacing the wisdom of God with the wisdom of man. The young graduate student asked: "Hundreds of thousands of scientists can't be wrong, can they?" This question may be addressed as follows. First, any argument based on "counting heads" is fallacious. Philosophy professors instruct their students on the various fallacies of human thought, one of which is the "fallacy of consensus." In his book, *Fundamentals of Critical Thinking*, atheistic philosopher Paul Ricci discussed the "argument from consensus," and explained in detail its errors (1986, p. 175). Interestingly, however, in the pages prior to his discussion, Ricci had offered the following as a "proof" of evolution: "The reliability of evolution not only as a theory but as a principle of understanding is not contested by **the vast majority** of biologists, geologists, astronomers, and other scientists" (1986, p. 172, emp. added).

Mr. Ricci thus fell victim to the very fallacy about which he tried to warn his readers—i.e., **truth is not determined by popular opinion or majority vote**. A thing may be, and often is, true even when accepted only by a small minority. The history of science is replete with such examples. British medical doctor, Edward Jenner (1749-1823), was scorned when he suggested smallpox could be prevented by infecting people with a less-virulent strain of the disease-causing organism. Yet his vaccine has helped eradicate smallpox. Dr. Ignaz Semmelweis (1818-1865) of Austria is another interesting case study. He noticed the high mortality rate among surgical patients and suggested that the deaths resulted from surgeons washing neither their hands nor their instruments between patients. Dr. Semmelweis asked them to do both, but they ridiculed him and refused to comply (thereby endangering the lives of thousands of patients). Today, the solutions posed by this gentle doctor are the basis of antiseptic techniques in surgery.

Scientific successes often have occurred **because** researchers rebelled against the status quo. Sometimes "consensual validation" must be set aside–**for the sake of truth**. The cases of Jenner and Semmelweis document all too well the fact that "the intellectuals," although in the majority, may be wrong. Just because "hundreds of thousands of scientists" believe something does not make it right. As Darrell Huff observed: "People can be wrong in the mass, just as they can individually" (1959, p. 122). If something is true, stating it a million times does not make it any truer. Similarly, if something is false, stating it a million times does not make it true.

Second, the prestige of a position's advocates has nothing to do with whether that position is true or false. Newspaper magnate William Randolph Hurst Jr. once wrote about pressures from "fashionable ideas...which are advanced with such force that common sense itself becomes the victim." He observed that a person under such pressure then may act "with an irrationality which is almost beyond belief" (1971, p. A-4). Consider, as proof of his point, the suggestion by renowned scientist and Nobel laureate W.B. Shockley that highly intelligent women be artificially inseminated using spermatozoa from Nobel Prize winners to produce super-intelligent offspring. There can be no doubt that Shockley happened to be "a giant in his field" with "rocket scientist" intelligence. If the intellect or prestige of a person is enough to guarantee the validity of the positions he (or she) espouses, then perhaps humanity should have taken Dr. Shockley up on his suggestion.

But intellectual prowess or prestige does **not** confer veracity on a person's position(s). Shockley's idea, for example, was based on nothing more than the narcissism of an over-inflated ego. As Taylor has commented: "Status in the field of science is no guarantee of the truth" (1984, p. 226). The soundness or strength of a claim is not based on: (a) the number of people supporting the claim; or (b) the intellect or prestige of the one(s) making that claim.

Third, the idea of strict objectivity in intellectual circles is a myth. While most scholars like to think of themselves as broad-minded, unprejudiced paragons of virtue, the fact is that they, too, on occasion, suffer from bouts of bias, bigotry, and presuppositionalism. Nobel laureate James Watson remarked rather bluntly: "In contrast to the popular conception supported by newspapers and mothers of scientists, a goodly number of scientists are not only narrow-minded and dull, but also just stupid" (1968, p. 14). Phillip Abelson, one-time editor of *Science*, wrote: "One of the most astonishing characteristics of scientists is that some of them are plain, old-fashioned bigots. Their zeal has a fanatical, egocentric quality characterized by disdain and intolerance for anyone or any value not associated with a special area of intellectual activity" (1964, 144:373). No doubt the same could be said of intellectuals in other fields as well (e.g., philosophy, business, the arts, etc.).

Fourth, on occasion it has been the "intellectuals" who have championed what can only be called "crazy" concepts. Bales addressed this fact when he wrote:

> There is no unreasonable position, there is no weird idea, which has not been propagated by some brilliant man who has a number of degrees after his name.

> Some have argued that everything is an illusion, others have maintained that they are nothing but a mess of matter or just a living mass of meat, others maintain that there is no realm of the rational and thus the very concept of an intellectual is an illusion... (1976, p. 91).

Space would fail us if we were to try to provide a comprehensive listing of the "weird" ideas proposed by those esteemed as "intellectuals." For example, the eminent astrophysicist of Great Britain, Sir Fred Hoyle, proposed in his book, *Evolution from Space*, that life was planted here by creatures from outer space, and that insects are their representatives here on Earth (1981, p. 127). The celebrated philosopher René Descartes, in his *Meditations on First Philosophy* (1641), propounded the view that it is impossible to **know** anything (which makes one want to ask, "How does he **know** that it is impossible to **know**?"). And so on.

The majority ultimately will abandon God's wisdom in favor of their own. But the wisdom with which we **are** impressed is not always the wisdom with which we **should be** impressed. Christ, in His Sermon on the Mount, warned that "narrow is the gate and difficult is the way which leads to life, and there are few who find it" (Matthew 7:14). Moses commanded the Israelites: "Thou shalt not follow a multitude to do evil" (Exodus 23:2). Guy N. Woods observed that this injunction

> ...was designed to guard the Lord's people from the corrupting influences of an evil environment, as well as from the powerful appeals of mob psychology to which so many in every generation succumb.... Man, by nature, is a social and gregarious being, tending to flock or gather together with others of his kind.... Man may, and often does, imbibe the evil characteristics of those about him as readily, and often more so, than the good ones (1982, 124[1]:2).

It should not surprise us that many "intelligent" people view belief in God as the fool's way out. Paul commented that

> not many wise after the flesh, not many mighty, not many noble, are called: but God chose the foolish things of the world, that he might put to shame them that are wise; and God chose the weak things of the world, that he might put to shame the things that are strong (1 Corinthians 1:26-27).

The most intelligent often are the least spiritual because "the god of this world" (2 Corinthians 4:3-4) has blinded their minds.

We must not fall prey to mob psychology which suggests because "everyone is doing it," that somehow makes it right. The graduate student said, "I do not want to be a fool." It was a joy to tell him that he does not have to bear that stigma because "the fool hath said in his heart, there is no God" (Psalm 14:1). We need not be intimidated by the pseudo-intellectualism of those who esteem themselves with higher regard than they do their Creator. Lucy, the character in the *Peanuts* cartoon strip, was correct when she told Charlie Brown, "You're not right; you just **sound** right!"

DISCUSSION QUESTIONS

1. Use the genealogies provided in Genesis 5 to calculate how many years there were between Adam and the Flood. Then discuss what happened to mankind in that short period of time.
2. Discuss types of fossils that appear and how they appear in the fossil record. Why does a sudden appearance of a complex life form cause problems for evolutionists?
3. Human population statistics and polystrate fossils are legitimate scientific methods which suggest that the Earth is relatively young. Why do you think that this type of information is not in the average public school science textbook? Is it any less scientific than the other information that is included in such books?
4. Why are archaeology and secular history valuable tools when talking to a skeptic? How can these secular tools help determine the age of the Earth? What are some of the limitations of these tools that do not apply to the Bible? What are some definite problems with the fossil record?
5. The verses in the Bible that provide information about the Earth's age must be "pieced together" from several places within the text. List several good reasons that might explain why God arranged it this way. Fit into your answer verses such as Matthew 7: 7-11 and 2 Timothy 2:15.
6. If humans did evolve from ape-like creatures, at what point did we acquire our consciousness and the human soul? Discuss why this poses a problem for theistic evolutionists.

Chapter 12

WHAT MUST ONE DO TO BE SAVED?

> And Jehovah God formed man of the dust of the ground, and breathed into his nostrils the breath of life; and man became a living soul (Genesis 2:7).

Of all the living beings that dwell on planet Earth, one solitary creature was made "in the image of God." On day six of His creative activity, God said: "Let us make man in our image, after our likeness. And God created man in his own image, in the image of God created he him; male and female created he them" (Genesis 1:26-27).

Mankind was not created in the physical image of God, of course, because God, as a Spirit Being, has no physical image (John 4:24; Luke 24:39; Matthew 16:17). Rather, mankind was fashioned in the spiritual, rational, emotional, and volitional image of God (Ephesians 4:24; John 5:39-40; 7:17; Joshua 24:15; Isaiah 7:15). Humans are superior to all other creatures. No other living being was given the faculties, the capacities, the capabilities, the potential, or the dignity that God instilled in each man and woman. Indeed, humankind is the peak, the apex, the pinnacle of God's creation.

In its lofty position as the zenith of God's creative genius, mankind was endowed with certain responsibilities. Men and women were to be the stewards of the entire Earth (Genesis 1:28). They were to glorify God in their daily existence (Isaiah 43:7). And, they were to consider it their "whole duty" to serve the Creator faithfully throughout their brief sojourn on the Earth (Ecclesiastes 12:13).

MAN'S PREDICAMENT: DISOBEDIENCE AND DEATH

Unfortunately, the first man and woman used their volitional powers–and the free moral agency based on those powers–to rebel against their Maker. Finite man made some horribly evil choices, and so entered the spiritual state biblically designated as "sin." The Old Testament not only presents in vivid fashion the entrance of sin into the world through Adam and Eve (Genesis 3), but also alludes to the ubiquity of sin within the human race when it says: "There is no man that sinneth not" (1 Kings 8:46). Throughout its thirty-nine books, the Old Covenant discusses time and again both sin's presence amidst humanity and its destructive consequences. The great prophet Isaiah reminded God's people: "Behold, Jehovah's hand is not shortened that it cannot save; neither his ear heavy that it cannot hear: but your iniquities have separated between you and your God, and your sins have hid his face from you, so that he will not hear" (59:1-2).

The New Testament is no less clear in its assessment. The apostle John wrote: "Every one that doeth sin doeth also lawlessness; and sin is lawlessness" (1 John 3:4). Thus, sin is defined as the act of transgressing God's law. In fact, Paul observed that "where there is no law, neither is there transgression" (Romans 4:15). Had there been no law, there would have been no sin. But God **had** instituted divine law. And mankind freely chose to transgress that law. Paul reaffirmed the Old Testament concept of the universality of sin (1 Kings 8:46) when he stated that "all have sinned, and fall short of the glory of God" (Romans 3:23).

As a result, mankind's predicament became serious indeed. Ezekiel lamented: "The soul that sinneth, it shall die" (18:20a). Once again, the New Testament writers reaffirmed such a concept. Paul wrote: "Therefore, as through one man sin entered into the world, and death through sin; and so death passed unto all men, for that all sinned" (Romans 5:12). He then added that "the wages of sin is death" (Romans 6:23). Years later,

James would write: "But each man is tempted, when he is drawn away by his own lust, and enticed. Then the lust, when it hath conceived, beareth sin: and the sin, when it is full-grown, bringeth forth death" (1:15-16).

As a result of mankind's sin, God placed the curse of death on the human race. While all men and women must die physically as a result of Adam and Eve's sin, each person dies spiritually for his or her own sins. Each person is responsible for himself, spiritually speaking. The theological position which states that we inherit the guilt of Adam's sin is false. We do not inherit the **guilt**; we inherit the **consequences**. And there is a great difference between the two.

Consider, as an illustration of this point, the family in which a drunken father arrives home late one evening, and in an alcoholic stupor severely beats his wife and children. His spouse and offspring suffer the consequences of his drunkenness, to be sure. But it would be absurd to suggest that they are guilty of it! The same concept applies in the spiritual realm. People die **physically** because of Adam's sin, but they die **spiritually** because of their own personal transgression of God's law. In Ezekiel 18:20, quoted earlier, the prophet went on to say: "The son shall not bear the iniquity of the father, neither shall the father bear the iniquity of the son: the righteousness of the righteous shall be upon him, and the wickedness of the wicked shall be upon him."

THE REALITY OF SIN

The reality of sin is all around us, is it not? Consider the ways in which mankind has been affected by sin.

Physically–Disease and death were introduced into this world as a direct consequence of man's sin (Genesis 2:17; Romans 5:12).

Geophysically–Many features of the Earth's surface that allow for tragedies such as earthquakes, tornadoes, hurricanes, etc. can be traced directly to the Great Flood of Noah's day (which was the result of man's sin, Genesis 6:5ff.).

Culturally–The numerous communication problems that man experiences, due to the multiplicity of human languages, are traceable to ambitious rebellion on the part of our ancestors (Genesis 11:1-9).

Psychologically–Man generally is without the peace of mind for which his heart longs (look at the number of psychiatrists in the Yellow Pages of any telephone book!). Isaiah opined: "They have made them crooked paths; whosoever goeth therein doth not know peace" (59:8; cf. 57:21).

Spiritually–By sinning, man created a chasm between himself and God (Isaiah 59:2). Unless remedied, this condition will result in man's being unable to escape the "judgment of hell" (Matthew 23:33), and in his being separated from God throughout all eternity (Revelation 21:8; 22:18-19).

The key phrase in the discussion above is that man's sin will result in an eternal separation from God **unless remedied**. The question then becomes: Has God provided such a remedy? Fortunately, He has.

GOD'S REMEDY FOR SIN

Regardless of how desperate, or how pitiful, man's condition has become, one thing is certain: God had no **obligation** to provide a means of salvation for the ungrateful creature who so haughtily turned away from Him, His law, and His beneficence. The Scriptures make this apparent when they discuss the fact that angels sinned (2 Peter 2:4; Jude 6), and yet "not to angels doth he give help, but he giveth help to the seed of Abraham" (Hebrews 2:16). The rebellious creatures that once inhabited the heavenly portals were not provided a redemptive plan. But man was! Little wonder the psalmist inquired: "What is **man**, that thou art mindful of **him**?" (Psalm 8:4, emp. added).

Why would God go to such great lengths for mankind, when His mercy was not even extended to the angels that once surrounded His throne? Whatever answers may be proffered, there can be little doubt that the Creator's efforts on behalf of sinful man are the direct result of pure love. As a loving God

(1 John 4:8), He acted out of a genuine concern, not for His own desires, but instead for those of His creation. And let us be forthright in acknowledging that Jehovah's love for mankind was completely **undeserved**. The Scriptures make it clear that God decided to offer salvation–our "way home"–even though we were ungodly, sinners, and enemies (note the specific use of those terms in Romans 5:6-10). The apostle John rejoiced in the fact that: "Herein is love, not that we loved God, but that He loved us" (1 John 4:10).

God's love is universal, and thus not discriminatory in any fashion (John 3:16). He would have **all men** to be saved (1 Timothy 2:4)–**if they would be** (John 5:40)–for He is not willing that **any** should perish (2 Peter 3:9). And, Deity's love is unquenchable. Read Romans 8:35-39 and be thrilled! Only man's wanton rejection of God's love can put him beyond the practical appropriation of heaven's offer of mercy and grace.

God's Plan in Preparation

Did God understand that man would rebel, and stand in eventual need of salvation from the perilous state of his own sinful condition? The Scriptures make it clear that He did. Inspiration speaks of a divine plan set in place even "before the foundation of the world" (Ephesians 1:4; 1 Peter 1:20). After the initial fall of man, humankind dredged itself deeper and deeper into wickedness. When approximately a century of preaching by the righteous Noah failed to bring mankind back to God, Jehovah sent a worldwide flood to purge the Earth (Genesis 6-8). From the faithful Noah, several generations later, the renowned Abraham was descended, and, through him, eventually the Hebrew nation would be established. From that nation, the Messiah–God incarnate–would come.

Some four centuries following Abraham, the Lord, through His servant Moses, gave to the Hebrews the written revelation that came to be known as the Law of Moses. Basically, this law-system had three distinct purposes. First, its intent was to define sin and sharpen Israel's awareness of it. To use Paul's expression in the New Testament, the Law made "sin exceeding sinful" (Romans 7:7,13). Second, the law was designed to show man that he could not, by his own merit or efforts, save himself. For example, the Law demanded perfect obedience, and since no mere man could keep it perfectly, all stood condemned (Galatians 3:10-11). Thus, the Law underscored the need for a **Savior**–Someone Who could do for us what we were unable to do for ourselves. Third, in harmony with that need, the Old Testament pointed the way toward the coming of the Messiah. He was to be Immanuel–"God with us" (Matthew 1:23).

Mankind was prepared for the coming of the Messiah in several ways. **Theophanies** were temporary appearances of God in various forms (see Genesis 16:7ff.; 18:1ff.; 22:11ff., et al.). A careful examination of the facts leads to the conclusion that many of these manifestations were of the preincarnate Christ. In addition, the Old Testament contains **types** (pictorial previews) of the coming Messiah. For example, every bloody sacrifice was a symbol of the "Lamb of God that taketh away the sin of the world" (John 1:29). Finally, there are more than 300 **prophecies** containing countless minute details that speak of the coming Prince of Peace. These prophecies name the city in which He was to be born, the purpose of His earthly sojourn, and even the exact manner of His death.

The simple fact is, Jehovah left no stone unturned in preparing the world for the coming of the One Who would save mankind. Through a variety of avenues, He alerted Earth's inhabitants to the importance of Him Who was yet to come, and to the urgency of complete belief in Him.

God's Plan in Action

One of God's attributes, as expressed within Scripture, is that He is an absolutely **holy** Being (see Revelation 4:8; Isaiah 6:3). As such, He cannot, and will not, ignore the fact of sin. The prophet Habakkuk wrote: "Thou that art of purer eyes than to behold evil, and thou canst not look on perverseness" (1:13). Yet another of God's attributes is that He is absolutely **just**. Righteousness and justice are the very foundation of His throne (Psalm 89:14). The irresistible truth arising from the fact that God is both holy and just is **that sin must be punished!**

If Jehovah were a cold, vengeful Creator (as some infidels wrongly assert), He simply could have banished humankind from His divine presence forever, and that would have been the end of the matter. But the truth is, He is not that kind of God! Our Creator is loving (1 John 4:8), and "rich in mercy" (Ephesians 2:4). Thus, the problem became: How could a loving, merciful God pardon rebellious humanity?

Paul addressed this very matter in Romans 3. How could God be just, and yet a justifier of sinful man? The answer: He would find someone to stand in for us–someone to receive His retribution, and to bear our punishment. That "someone" would be Jesus Christ, the Son of God. He would become a substitutionary sacrifice, and personally would pay the price for human salvation. In one of the most moving tributes ever written to the Son of God, Isaiah summarized the situation like this:

> But he was wounded for our transgressions, he was bruised for our iniquities; the chastisement of our peace was upon him; and with his stripes we are healed. All we like sheep have gone astray; we have turned every one to his own way; and Jehovah hath laid on Him the iniquity of us all (53:5-6).

Jehovah's intent was to extend grace and mercy freely–through the redemptive life and death of His Son (Romans 3:24ff.). As a member of the Godhead, Christ took upon Himself the form of a man. He came to Earth as a human being (John 1:1-4,14; Philippians 2:5-11; 1 Timothy 3:16), and thus shared our full nature and life-experiences. He even was tempted in all points, just we are, yet He never yielded to that temptation (Hebrews 4:15).

But what has this to do with us? Since Christ was tried (Isaiah 28:16), and yet found perfect (2 Corinthians 5:21; 1 Peter 2:22), He alone could satisfy heaven's requirement for justice. He alone could serve as the "propitiation" (atoning sacrifice) for our sins. Just as the lamb without blemish that was used in Old Testament sacrifices could be the (temporary) propitiation for the Israelites' sins, so the "Lamb of God" (John 1:29) could be the (permanent) propitiation for mankind's sins.

In the gift of Christ, Heaven's mercy was extended; in the death of the Lamb of God, divine justice was satisfied; and, in the resurrection of Christ, God's plan was documented and sealed historically forever!

MANKIND'S APPROPRIATION OF GOD'S GIFT OF SALVATION

As wonderful as God's gift of salvation is, there is one thing it is not. It is not **unconditional**. Mankind has a part to play in this process. While the gift of salvation itself is free (in the sense that the price levied already has been paid by Christ), God will not **force** salvation on anyone. Rather, man must–by the exercise of his personal volition and free moral agency–do something to accept the pardon that heaven offers. What is that "something"?

In His manifold dealings with mankind, Jehovah has stressed repeatedly the principle that man, if he would be justified, must live "by faith" (see Habakkuk 2:4; Romans 1:17; Galatians 3:11; Hebrews 10:38). Salvation has been available across the centuries, conditioned upon God's foreknowledge of the atoning death of Christ upon the Cross at Calvary (see Galatians 4:4-5; Hebrews 9:15-17; 10:1ff.). Yet "living by faith" never denoted a mere "mental ascent" of certain facts. Instead, "living by faith" denoted **active obedience**.

Faith consists of three elements: (1) an acknowledgment of historical facts; (2) a willingness to trust the Lord; and (3) a wholehearted submission (obedience) to the divine will. Further, it should be remembered that faith has not always–for all men, in all circumstances–required the same things. It always has required obedience, but obedience itself has not always demanded the same response.

For example, in God's earliest dealings with men, obedient faith required that those men offer animal sacrifices at the family altar (Genesis 4:4). Later, God dealt with the nation of Israel, giving them the Law at Mount Sinai (Exodus 20). Under that Law, animal sacrifices continued, along with the observance of certain feast days and festivals. Acceptable faith, under whatever law that was then in force, demanded obedience to the will of God.

The Scriptures are clear that "obedience of faith" (Romans 1:5; 16:26) is based on the Word of God (Romans 10:13), and that both the faith and the obedience are demonstrated by **action**. Hebrews 11, in fact, devotes itself to an examination of that very concept. "By faith" Abel **offered**. "By faith" Noah **prepared**. "By faith" Abraham **obeyed**. "By faith," Moses **refused**. And so on. Even the casual reader cannot help but be impressed with the heroes of faith listed in Hebrews 11:32-40, and the **action** they took **because of their faith**. Writing by inspiration, James observed that faith, divorced from obedience, is dead (James 2:26). What, then, is involved in this "obedience of faith" in regard to salvation? What must a person **do** to be saved?

Several critically important questions need to be asked here. First, where is salvation found? Paul told Timothy: "Therefore I endure all things for the elect's sake, that they also may obtain **the salvation which is in Christ Jesus** with eternal glory" (2 Timothy 2:10, emp. added).

Second, where are all spiritual blessings found? They are found only "in Christ." Paul wrote in Ephesians 1:3: "Blessed be the God and Father of our Lord Jesus Christ, who hath blessed us with every spiritual blessing in the heavenly places **in Christ**" (emp. added).

Third, and most important, how, then, does one get "into Christ"? In other words, how does the alien sinner rid himself of his soul-damning sin? What "obedience of faith" is required to appropriate the free gift of salvation that places him "in Christ"?

THE ROAD HOME: SALVATION THROUGH "OBEDIENCE OF FAITH"

The only way to find the "road home" to heaven is to follow God's directions **exactly**. There are numerous things God has commanded that a person **do** in order to enjoin the "obedience of faith" and thereby receive the free gift of salvation. According to God's Word, in order to be saved a person must do the following.

First, the sinner must **hear** God's Word (Romans 10:17). Obviously, one cannot follow God's commands if he has not heard them, so God commanded that people hear what He has said regarding salvation.

Second, one who is lost cannot be saved if he does not **believe** what he hears. So, God commanded that belief ensue (John 3:16; Acts 16:31).

Third, one who is lost cannot obtain salvation if he is unwilling to **repent** of his sins and seek forgiveness (Luke 13:3). Without repentance he will continue in sin; thus, God commanded repentance.

Fourth, since Christ is the basis of our salvation, God commanded the penitent sinner to **confess** Him before men as the Son of God (Romans 10:9-10).

However, this is not all that God commanded. Hearing, believing, repentance, and confession will not rid one of his sin. The overriding question is: **How does one get rid of sin**? Numerous times within the pages of the New Testament, that question is asked and answered. The Jews who had murdered Christ, and to whom Peter spoke on the Day of Pentecost when he ushered in the Christian age, asked that question. Peter's sermon had convicted them. They were convinced that they were sinners and, as such, desperately in need of salvation at the hand of an almighty God. Their question then became: "Brethren, what shall we do?" (Acts 2:37). Peter's response could not have been any clearer. He told them: "Repent ye, and **be baptized** every one of you in the name of Jesus Christ **unto the remission of your sins**" (Acts 2:38, emp. added). Saul, who later would be known as Paul, the famous apostle to the Gentiles, needed an answer to that same question. While on a trip to Damascus for the explicit purpose of persecuting Christians, Saul was blinded (see Acts 22). Realizing his plight, he asked: "What shall I do, Lord?" (Acts 22:10). When God's servant, Ananias, appeared to Saul in the city, he answered Saul's question by commanding: "And now why tarriest thou? Arise, and **be baptized, and wash away thy sins**" (Acts 22:16, emp. added).

What, then, is the correct biblical answer regarding how one rids himself of soul-damning sin? The biblical solution is that the person who has heard the Gospel, who has believed its message, who has repented of past sins, and who has confessed Christ as Lord must then–in order to receive remission (forgiveness) of sins–be baptized. [The English word "baptize" is a transliteration of the Greek word *baptizo*, meaning to immerse, dip, plunge beneath, or submerge (Thayer, 1958, p. 94).]

Further, it is baptism that puts a person "in Christ." Paul told the first-century Christians in Rome:

> Or are ye ignorant that all we who were baptized into Christ Jesus were baptized into his death? We were buried therefore with him through baptism into death: that like as Christ was raised from the dead through the glory of the Father, so we also might walk in newness of life (Romans 6:3-4).

Paul told the Galatians: "For as many of you as were **baptized into Christ** did put on Christ" (3:37, emp. added). Little wonder, then, that Peter spoke of baptism as that which saves (1 Peter 3:21).

Numerous New Testament writers made the point that it is only when we come into contact with Christ's blood that our sins can be washed away (Ephesians 1:7-8; Revelation 5:9; Romans 5:8-9; Hebrews 9:12-14). The question arises: **When** did Jesus shed His blood? The answer, of course, is that He shed His blood on the Cross at His death (John 19:31-34). Where, and how, does one come into contact with Christ's blood to obtain the forgiveness of sin that such contact ensures? Paul answered that question when he wrote to the Christians in Rome. It is only in baptism that contact with the blood, and the death, of Christ is made (Romans 6:3-11). Further, the ultimate hope of our resurrection (to live with Him in heaven) is linked to baptism. Paul wrote of "having been buried with him in baptism, wherein ye were raised with him through faith in the working of God, who raised him from the dead" (Colossians 2:12). If we are not baptized, we remain in sin. If we are not baptized, we have no hope of the resurrection that leads to heaven.

Baptism, of course, is no less, nor more, important than any other of God's commands regarding what to do to be saved (see Jackson, 1997c). But it is **essential**, and one cannot be saved without it. Is baptism a command of God? Yes (Acts 10:48). Is baptism where the remission of sins occurs? Yes (Acts 2:38; Acts 22:16; 1 Peter 3:21).

Some, who no doubt mean well, teach that a person is saved by "faith only." That is, people are taught simply to "pray and ask Jesus to come into their hearts" so that they might be saved from their sins. This teaching, though widespread, is completely at odds with the Bible's specific instructions regarding what one must do to be saved.

First, the Scriptures teach clearly that God does not hear (i.e., hear to respond with forgiveness) the prayer of an alien sinner (Psalm 34:15-16; Proverbs 15:29; Proverbs 28:9). Thus, the sinner can pray as long and as hard as he wants, but God has stated plainly how a person is to be saved. This makes perfect sense, since in John 14:6 Christ taught: "I am the way, and the truth, and the life; no one cometh to the Father but by me." The alien sinner cannot approach God on his own, and, as an alien sinner, has no advocate to do so on his behalf. That is one of the spiritual blessings reserved for Christians (Ephesians 1:3). Thus, it is fruitless for an alien sinner to pray to God to "send Jesus into his heart." God does not hear (i.e., hear to respond to) such a request (see Bass, et. al., 2001).

Second, the Scriptures plainly teach that man **cannot be saved by faith alone**. James, in his epistle, remarked that indeed, a man may be justified (i.e., saved), but "not only by faith" (James 2:24). This, too, makes perfectly good sense. As James had observed only a few verses earlier: "Thou believest that God is one; thou doest well; the demons also believe, and shudder" (James 2:19). It is not enough merely to believe. Even the demons who inhabit the eternal regions of hell believe. But they hardly are saved (see 2 Peter 2:4). It is obvious, therefore, that mere faith **alone** is insufficient to save mankind.

Also, where, exactly, in the Scriptures does it teach that, in order to be saved, one should "pray to ask Jesus to come into his heart"? Over the years, we have asked numerous people within various religious groups this important question. But we have yet to find anyone who could provide a single biblical reference to substantiate such a claim.

Salvation is not conditioned on prayer; it is conditioned on the "obedience of faith." The case of Saul provides a good example. As Christ's enemy-turned-penitent, he prayed earnestly while living in his blind state in the city of Damascus. Yet the fact remains that his sins were removed ("washed away") only when he obeyed God's command (as verbalized by Ananias) to be baptized. Prayer could not wash away Saul's sins. But the Lord's blood could–at the point of baptism (Hebrews 9:22; Ephesians 5:26).

OBJECTIONS TO GOD'S PLAN OF SALVATION

When the topic of salvation is discussed, it is not unusual to hear certain objections to God's designated plan. At times, such objections result from a misunderstanding of the steps involved in the salvation process (or the reasons for those steps). On occasion, however, the objections result from a stubborn refusal to acquiesce to God's commands regarding what constitutes salvation. We would like to consider three such objections here.

Is Salvation the Result of "Baptismal Regeneration"?

Is the forgiveness of sins (that results from being baptized) due to some special power within the water? No. "Baptismal regeneration" is the idea that there is a miraculous power in the water that produces salvation (i.e., regeneration). As Wayne Jackson has noted: "...the notion that baptism is a 'sacrament' which has a sort of mysterious, innate power to remove the contamination of sin–independent of personal faith and a volitional submission to God's plan of redemption"–is plainly at odds with biblical teaching (1997b, 32:45). An examination of the Old Testament (which serves as our "tutor" [Galatians 3:24] and contains things "for our learning" [Romans 15:4]) provides important instruction regarding this principle. When Naaman the leper was told by Elisha to dip seven times in the Jordan River, at first he refused, but eventually obeyed–and was healed. However, there was no meritorious power in the muddy waters of the Jordan. Naaman was healed because He did exactly what God commanded him to do, in exactly the way God commanded him to do it.

This was true of the Israelites' salvation as well. On one occasion when they sinned, and God began to slay them for their unrighteousness, those who wished to repent and be spared were commanded to look upon a brass serpent on a pole in the midst of the camp (Numbers 21:1-9). There was no meritorious power in the serpent. Rather, the Israelites were saved from destruction because they did exactly what God commanded them to do, in exactly the way God commanded them to do it.

The New Testament presents the same principle. Jesus once encountered a man born blind (John 9). Then Lord spat on the ground, made a spittle/clay potion, and placed it over the man's eyes. He then instructed the man to "go, wash in the pool of Siloam" (John 9:7). Was there medicinal power in Siloam's waters? No. It was the man's obedient faith that produced the end-result, not some miraculous power in the water.

What would have happened if the man had refused to obey Christ, or had altered the Lord's command? Suppose the man had reasoned: "If I wash in Siloam, some may think I am trusting in the **water** to be healed. Others may think that I am attempting to perform some kind of 'work' to 'merit' regaining my sight. Therefore I simply will 'have faith in' Christ, but I will **not** dip in the pool of Siloam." Would the man have been healed? Most certainly not!

What if Noah, during the construction of the ark, had followed God's instructions to the letter, except for the fact that he decided to build the ark out of a material other than the gopher wood that God had commanded? Would Noah and his family have been saved? Most certainly not! Noah would have been guilty of violating God's commandments, since he had not done **exactly** as God commanded him. Did not Jesus Himself say: "If ye love me, ye will **keep My commandments**" (John 14:15, emp. added)?

Peter used the case of Noah to discuss the relationship of baptism to salvation. He stated unequivocally that baptism is involved in salvation when he noted that, just as Noah and his family were transported from a polluted environment of corruption into a realm of deliverance, so in baptism we are moved from the polluted environment of defilement into a realm of redemption. It is by baptism that one enters "into Christ" (Romans 6:4; Galatians 3:27), wherein salvation is found (2 Timothy 2:10). In Ephesians 5:26 and Titus 3:5, Paul described baptism as a "washing of water" or a "washing of regeneration" wherein the sinner is "cleansed" or "saved." [Baptist theologian A.T. Robertson admitted that both of these passages refer specifically to water baptism (1931, 4:607).]

The power of baptism to remove sin lies not in the water, but in the God Who commanded the sinner to be baptized in the first place.

Is Baptism a Human Work?

Is baptism a meritorious human work? No. But is it required for a person to be saved? Yes. How is this possible? The Bible clearly teaches that we are **not** saved by works (Titus 3:4-7; Ephesians 2:9). Yet the Bible clearly teaches we **are** saved by works (James 2:14-24). Since inspiration guarantees that the Scriptures never will contradict themselves, it is obvious that **two different kinds of works** are under consideration in these passages.

The New Testament mentions at least four kinds of works: (1) works of the Law of Moses (Galatians 2:16; Romans 3:20); (2) works of the flesh (Galatians 5:19-21); (3) works of merit (Titus 3:4-7); and (4) works resulting from obedience of faith (James 2:14-24). This last category often is referred to as "works of God." This phrase does not mean works **performed by** God; rather, the intent is "works **required and approved by** God" (Thayer, 1958, p. 248; cf. Jackson, 1997c, 32:47). Consider the following example from Jesus' statements in John 6: 27-29:

> Work not for the food which perisheth, but for the food which abideth unto eternal life.... They said therefore unto him, What must we do, that we may work the **works of God**? Jesus answered and said unto them, This is the **work of God**, that ye believe on him whom he hath sent.

Within this context, Christ made it clear that there are works which humans must do to receive eternal life. Moreover, the passage affirms that believing itself is a work ("This is the **work** of God, that ye **believe** on him whom he hath sent"). It therefore follows that if one is saved **without any type of works**, then he is saved **without faith**, because **faith is a work**. Such a conclusion would throw the Bible into hopeless confusion!

In addition, it should be noted that repentance from sin is a divinely appointed work for man to perform prior to his reception of salvation. The people of ancient Nineveh "repented" at Jonah's preaching (Matthew 12:41), yet the Old Testament record relates that "God saw their **works**, that they turned from their evil way" (Jonah 3:10). Thus, if one can be saved without **any kind** of works, he can be saved **without repentance**. Yet Jesus Himself declared that without repentance, one will surely perish (Luke 13:3,5).

But what about baptism? The New Testament **specifically excludes** baptism from the class of human meritorious works unrelated to redemption. The context of Titus 3:4-7 reveals the following information. (1) We **are not saved** by works of righteousness that we do by ourselves (i.e., according to any plan or course of action that we devised–see Thayer, p. 526). (2) We **are saved** by the "washing of regeneration" (i.e., baptism), exactly as 1 Peter 3:21 states. (3) Thus, baptism is excluded from all works of human righteousness that men contrive, but is itself a "work of God" (i.e., required and approved by God) necessary for salvation. When one is raised from the watery grave of baptism, it is according to the "working of God" (Colossians 2:12), and not any manmade plan. No one can suggest (justifiably) that baptism is a meritorious work of human design. When we are baptized, we are completely passive, and thus hardly can have performed any kind of "work." Instead, we have obeyed God through saving faith. Our "works of God" were belief, repentance, confession, and baptism–all commanded by the Scriptures of one who would receive salvation as the free gift of God (Romans 6:23).

Is the Baptism Associated with Salvation Holy Spirit Baptism?

To circumvent the connection between water baptism and salvation, some have suggested that the baptism discussed in passages such as Acts 2:38, Acts 22:16, and 1 Peter 3:21 is Holy Spirit baptism. But such a position cannot be correct. Christ commanded His followers–after His death and ascension–

to go into all the world and "make disciples of all the nations, baptizing them into the name of the Father and of the Son and of the Holy Spirit" (Matthew 28:18-20). That same command applies no less to Christians today.

During the early parts of the first century, we know there was more than one baptism in existence (e.g., John's baptism, Holy Spirit baptism, Christ's baptism, etc.). But by the time Paul wrote his epistle to the Christians who lived in Ephesus, **only one** of those baptisms remained. He stated specifically in Ephesians 4:4-5: "There is one body, and one Spirit, even as also ye were called in one hope of your calling; one Lord, one faith, **one baptism**." Which **one** baptism remained? One thing we know for certain: Christ never would give His disciples a command that they could not carry out.

The Scriptures, however, teach that Jesus administers baptism of the Holy Spirit (Matthew 3:11; Luke 3:15-17). Yet Christians were commanded to baptize those whom they taught, and who believed (John 3:16), repented of their sins (Luke 13:3), and confessed Christ as the Son of God (Matthew 10:32). It is clear, then, that the baptism commanded by Christ was not Holy Spirit baptism. If it were, Christ would be put in the untenable position of having commanded His disciples to do something they could not do–baptize in the Holy Spirit. However, they **could** baptize in **water**, which is exactly what they did. And that is exactly what we still are doing today. Baptism in the Holy Spirit no longer is available; only water baptism remains, and is the one true baptism commanded by Christ for salvation (Ephesians 4:4-5; Mark 16:16; Acts 2:38).

When a person does precisely what the Lord has commanded, he has not "merited" or "earned" salvation. Rather, his obedience is evidence of his faith (James 2:18). Are we saved by God's grace? Indeed we are (Ephesians 2:8-9). But the fact that we are saved by grace does not negate human responsibility in obeying God's commands. Every person who wishes to be saved must exhibit the "obedience of faith" commanded within God's Word (Romans 1:5; 16:26). A part of that obedience is adhering to God's command to be baptized.

CONCLUSION

The biblical message–from Genesis 1 to Revelation 22–is that mankind is in a woefully sinful condition, and desperately in need of help in order to find his way "back home." A corollary to that message is that God takes no pleasure in the death of the wicked (Ezekiel 18:23; 33:11), and genuinely desires that all should be saved (John 3:16). But in order to be saved, one must do **exactly** what God commanded, in **exactly** the way God commanded it. When a person hears, believes, repents, confesses, and is baptized for the forgiveness of his sins, that person becomes a Christian–nothing more, and nothing less. God Himself then adds that Christian to His Son's one true body–the church. The child of God who remains faithful even unto death (Revelation 2:10) is promised a crown of life and eternity in heaven as a result of his faith, his obedience, God's mercy, and God's grace (John 14:15; Ephesians 2:8-9; Romans 1:5). What a joyous thought–to live the "abundant life" (John 10:10b) with a "peace that passes understanding" (Philippians 4:7) here and now, and then to be rewarded with a home in heaven in the hereafter (John 14:2-3). What a joyous thought indeed!

DISCUSSION QUESTIONS

1. Discuss some biblical truths regarding God's love for mankind.
2. Why is simply "accepting Jesus into your heart" not enough?
3. Why do humans need a spotless sacrifice, and how do we come into contact with the blood of that sacrifice today to receive forgiveness of sins?
4. When was God's New Testament plan of salvation put into effect? Discuss how we know this, and give scriptural references to each part.
5. How do we know God had a plan for man's salvation from the beginning? What role did Abraham and the Jewish nation play in that plan?

THE ESSENTIALITY AND SINGULARITY OF CHRIST'S CHURCH

"But when the fulness of the time came," the apostle Paul wrote, "God sent forth his Son, born of a woman, born under the law, that he might redeem them that were under the law, that we might receive the adoption of sons" (Galatians 4:4-5). God incarnate had come to Earth, bringing the "good news" about the last and final covenant that Heaven would make with man. The series of events that began with the birth of Christ in Bethlehem, and culminated in His death, burial, and resurrection outside Jerusalem approximately thirty-three years later, stirred a whirlwind of controversy in the first century. Twenty centuries later, it still does.

To the Christian, there is little of more importance than the proclamation and defense of the Old Jerusalem Gospel that is able to save men's souls. Christianity did not come into the world with a whimper, but a bang. It was not in the first century, neither is it intended to be in the twentieth, something "done in a corner." Instead, it arrived like a trumpet's clarion call.

Christ spent three-and-a-half years teaching in order to make disciples. When He finally was ready to call them to action, it was not for a quiet retreat into the peaceful, nearby hills. He never intended that they be "holy men" who set themselves apart to spend each hour of every day in serene meditation. Rather, they were to be soldiers–fit for a spiritual battle against forces of evil (Ephesians 6:10-17). Jesus called for action, self-denial, uncompromising love for truth, and zeal coupled with knowledge. His words to those who would follow Him were: "If any man would come after me, let him deny himself, and take up his cross, and follow me" (Mark 8: 34). And many did.

The teaching did not stop when Christ left to return to His home in heaven. He had trained others–apostles and disciples–to continue the task He had begun. They were sent to the uttermost parts of the world with the mandate to proclaim the Gospel boldly through preaching and teaching (Matthew 28: 18-20). This they did daily (Acts 5:42). The result was additional, new disciples. They too, then, were instructed and grounded in the fundamentals of God's Word (Acts 2:42) and sent on their way to teach still others.

The results were extraordinary indeed. In a single day, in a single city, over 3,000 constituted the original church as a result of the teaching they had heard from Christ's apostles (see Acts 2:41). In fact, so effective was this kind of instruction that the enemies of Christianity attempted to prohibit any further public teaching (Acts 4:18; 5:28), yet to no avail. Two millennia later, the theme of the Cross still is alive, vibrant, and forceful. Christianity's central message, the manner in which that message was taught, and the dedication of those into whose hands it had been placed, were too powerful for even its bitterest foes to abate or defeat. That Christianity continues to be taught, and to thrive, is evidence aplenty of this fact.

While it may be true to say that some religions flourish best in secrecy, such is not the case with Christianity. It is intended both to be presented, and to be defended, in the marketplace of ideas. In addition, while some religions eschew open investigation and critical evaluation, Christianity welcomes both. Of all the major religions based upon an individual rather than a mere ideology, it is the only one that claims, and can document, an empty tomb for its Founder.

Furthermore, Christians, unlike adherents to some other religions, do not have an option regarding the distribution and/or dissemination of their faith. The efficacy of God's saving grace–as made possible through His Son, Jesus Christ–is a message that all accountable people need to hear, and one that Christians are commanded to proclaim (John 3:16; Matthew 28:18-20; cf. Ezekiel 33:7-9).

CHRIST'S CHURCH–HIS SINGULAR, UNIQUE BODY OF SAVED BELIEVERS

At Caesarea Philippi, situated at the base of Mount Hermon that rises over seven thousand feet above it, Jesus asked His disciples how the public viewed Him. "Who do men say that the Son of man is?," He inquired (Matthew 16:13). The reply of the disciples was: "Some say, John the Baptist; some, Elijah; and others, Jeremiah, or one of the prophets" (16:14). But Jesus delved deeper when He asked the disciples: "But who say ye that I am?" (16:15). Ever the impulsive one, Simon Peter quickly answered: "Thou art the Christ, the Son of the living God" (16:16). Jesus' response to Peter was this:

> Blessed art thou, Simon Bar-Jonah: for flesh and blood hath not revealed it unto thee, but my Father who is in heaven. And I also say unto thee, that thou art Peter, and upon this rock I will build my church; and the gates of Hades shall not prevail against it (16:17-18).

Jesus had come "in the fulness of time" to bring the one thing that all the Earth's inhabitants needed. From Cain, the first murderer, to the lawless men who eventually would put Him to death on the cross, mankind desperately needed the salvation that the heavenly plan would provide. In writing to the young evangelist Timothy, Paul observed that it had been God's plan to save men through Christ even before the foundation of the world. He wrote of God, "who saved us, and called us with a holy calling, not according to our works, but according to his own purpose and grace, which was given us in Christ Jesus before times eternal" (2 Timothy 1:9). Through His foreknowledge, God knew that man one day would need redemption from sin. In fact, throughout the history of Israel, God made both promises and prophecies concerning a coming kingdom and its King. The promise was that from David's seed, God would build a "house" and "kingdom" (2 Samuel 7:11-17–a promise, incidentally, that was reaffirmed in Psalm 132:11 and preached as reality by Peter in Acts 2:29-34 when the church began). Seven hundred years before Christ's arrival, the prophet Isaiah foretold:

> For unto us a child is born, unto us a son is given; and the government shall be upon his shoulder: and his name shall be called Wonderful, Counsellor, Mighty God, Everlasting Father, Prince of Peace. Of the increase of his government and of peace there shall be no end, upon the throne of David, and upon his kingdom, to establish it, and to uphold it with justice and with righteousness from henceforth even for ever. The zeal of Jehovah of hosts will perform this (Isaiah 9:6-7).

Thus, Christ's exclamation to Peter that the building of His church would be upon a "rock" was nothing more than what the Old Testament prophets had foretold hundreds of years before. Isaiah prophesied: "Therefore, thus saith the Lord Jehovah, Behold, I lay in Zion for a foundation a stone, a tried stone, a precious corner-stone of sure foundation: he that believeth shall not be in haste" (Isaiah 28:16). Later, Peter himself–through inspiration, and no doubt with the events of Caesarea Philippi still fresh on his mind–would make reference to this very rock foundation when he wrote about the "living stone, rejected indeed of men.... The stone which the builders rejected, the same was made the head of the corner" (1 Peter 2:4,7). In fact, even Jesus Himself mentioned the "rejected stone" of Old Testament allusion. In Matthew 21:42, Mark 12:10, and Luke 20:17, He made reference to the psalmist's statement about "the stone which the builders rejected is become the head of the corner" (Psalm 118:22), and applied the rejection of the stone by the builders to the Sanhedrin's rejection and repudiation of Him.

Sadly, some today erroneously teach that Christ's church was established out of desperation as an "emergency measure" set in motion when the Jews rejected Him as Savior. The basis for such a view is the idea that Jesus presented Himself to the Jewish nation as its Messiah but was rebuffed–a rejection that came as an unexpected surprise to Him and His Father. Christ's failure to convince the Jews of His rightful place as their King forced Him to have to re-evaluate, and eventually delay, His plans–His intention being to re-establish His kingdom at some distant point in the future. In the meantime, the story goes, He established the church to allay temporarily the complete failure of His mission.

However, such a view ignores the inspired writers' observations that "before times eternal" God had set in motion His plan for man's salvation as His Son's church. [The Greek word *ekklesia*, translated "church" in the English, denotes God's "called out."] It ignores the Old Testament prophecies that specifically predicted Christ's rejection by the Jews. And, it ignores Christ's own allusions to those prophecies during His earthly ministry. But worst of all, it impeaches the omniscience of both God and His Son by suggesting that they were "caught off guard" by the Jews' rejection of Christ as the Messiah, thus causing Heaven's emissary to have to rethink His plans. What an offensive and unscriptural view this is!

Jesus was a man with a mission–and He completed successfully what He had come to accomplish. Deity had come to Earth, taking the form of a servant (Philippians 2:7) to communicate to man the truth (John 8:32) about the lost state in which man now found himself (Romans 3:23; 6:23), and to pay the ransom for man (Matthew 20:28), thereby extricating him from a situation from which he could not extricate himself (Jeremiah 10:23).

When Christ died upon the cross, it was not for any sin that He had committed. Though He was tempted in all points like as we are, He did not sin (Hebrews 4:15). When Peter wrote that Jesus "did not sin," he employed a verbal tense which suggests that the Lord **never** sinned–not even once (1 Peter 2:22). Isaiah emphasized the substitutionary nature of the Lord's death when he wrote: "But he was wounded for our transgressions, he was bruised for our iniquities; the chastisement of our peace was upon him; and with his stripes we are healed.... Jehovah hath laid on him the iniquity of us all" (Isaiah 53:5-6). When the prophet declared that our "iniquity" was laid upon the Son of God, he employed a figure of speech referred to as metonymy (wherein one thing is used to designate another). In this case, the cause is being used for the effect. In other words, God did not actually put our **sins** upon Christ; He put the **penalty** of our wrongs upon His Son at Calvary. Yet, in spite of the fact that all sinners deserve to be lost, God provided a way to "escape the judgment of hell" (Matthew 23:33).

Jesus made it clear that He would provide this way of escape through a plan that would result in the establishment of His church–i.e., His body of "the called out." The first messianic prophecy was to be fulfilled: Satan would bruise the Lord's heel, but the Lord would overcome, and bruise Satan's head (Genesis 3:15). Against the building of Christ's church, not even the Gates of Hades could prevail (Matthew 16:18).

Further, there would be one and only one church. Paul wrote that Christ "is the head of **the body, the church**" (Colossians 1:18, emp. added). In Ephesians 1:22, he stated concerning Christ that God "gave him to be head over all things to the church, **which is his body**." Thus, Paul clearly identified the body as the church. Three chapters later, however, in Ephesians 4:4, Paul stated: "There is **one body**." Expressed logically, one might reason as follows:

> There is one body (Ephesians 4:4).
> But Christ is the Savior of the body (Ephesians 5:22).
> Thus, Christ is the Savior of **one body.**

And,

> Christ is the Savior of one body.
> But the body is the church (Ephesians 1:22-23; Colossians 1:18,24).
> Thus, Christ is the Savior of **one** church.

The body, Christ's church, would be known as "the church of the Lord" (Acts 20:28), "the church of God" (1 Corinthians 1:2; Galatians 1:13), "the house of God" (1 Timothy 3:15), "the household of faith" (Galatians 6:10), and "the kingdom of God" (Acts 28:23,31). The Lord's people were to wear Christ's name (Acts 11:26; 26:28; 1 Peter 4:16). The church would be His bride (Revelation 21:2), His wife (Revelation 19:7-8), and His kingdom (Revelation 1:9). Those in it would be victorious over Satan and death forever (1 Corinthians 15: 26,54-56; 2 Timothy 1:9-10).

Unfortunately, men sought to alter the divine plan, and to infuse it with their own personal belief systems. Thus, the concept of denominationalism was born. Denominationalism, however, is unknown to, and unauthorized by, the Word of God. A denomination is defined as: "a class or kind having a specific name or value...." We speak of various monetary denominations–a five-dollar bill, a ten-dollar bill, etc. They all are different. The same is true of religious denominations. They all are different.

Denominationalism ignores the singularity and uniqueness of the true church, and establishes various groups teaching conflicting doctrines that are antagonistic both to the Bible and to each other. It also ignores the church's relationship to Christ, described so beautifully in Ephesians 5 where Paul reminded first-century Christians that "the husband is the head of the wife, as Christ also is the head of the church" (5: 23). The apostle's point was this: In a physical context, the wife is the bride and the husband is the bridegroom; in a spiritual context, the church is the bride and Christ is the bridegroom (the same point reiterated by John in Revelation 21: 9). In Acts, Peter discussed Christ's relationship to His church when he observed that "neither is there any other name under heaven, that is given among men, wherein we must be saved" (Acts 4:12).

Denominations are manmade institutions that are neither recognized in, nor sanctioned by, the Word of God. The simple truth of the matter is that John the Baptist–while a marvelous harbinger of the Messiah–did not die to establish the church. Why, then, be a member of a denomination bearing his name? As great a reformer as Martin Luther was, the fact remains that he did not die to establish the church. Why, then, be a member of a denomination bearing his name? The early church's presbyters (i.e., elders, bishops, overseers) did not give their lives on a cross to establish the church. Why, then, be a member of a denomination named after such men? The Bible–although it prophesies the coming of the church and documents its arrival–did not make possible the church. Why, then, be a member of a "Bible church"? Instead, should not Christians seek to be simply a member of the singular church that honors Christ's authority, and that He purchased with His blood? It is His bride; He is its bridegroom. His congregations are called the "churches of Christ" (Romans 16:16).

Those who are true New Testament Christians are those who have done exactly what God has commanded them to do to be saved, in exactly the way God has commanded that it be done. In so doing, they have not "joined" some manmade religious denomination that, like a five-dollar bill is one denomination among many others, is simply one religious group among many others. If the church is the body, and if there is only one body, then there is only one church. Further, one does not "join" the church. The Scriptures teach that as a person is saved, God Himself "adds" that person to the one true church (Acts 2:41) that bears His Son's name.

CHRIST'S CHURCH–HIS DIVINELY DESIGNED, BLOOD-BOUGHT, SPIRIT-FILLED KINGDOM

During His earthly ministry, Jesus taught: "All authority hath been given unto me in heaven and on earth" (Matthew 28:18). Having such authority from His Father, He alone possessed the right to be Head of the church, His singular body of believers (Ephesians 1:22-23; Colossians 1:18). Recognizing

Christ's position as authoritative Head of the church, Paul was constrained to remind Christians: "And whatsoever ye do, in word or in deed, do all in the name of [by the authority of–BT/BH] the Lord Jesus" (Colossians 3:17).

Christ announced while on Earth that He would build His church (Matthew 16:18). It would be divinely designed (John 10:25; Acts 2:23), blood bought (Acts 20:28), and Spirit filled (1 Corinthians 6:19-20; Romans 8:9-10). On Pentecost following the Lord's death, burial, and resurrection, Peter rebuked the Jews for their duplicity in killing God's Son, and convicted them of their sin of murder (Acts 2:22-23). Luke recorded that they were "pricked in their heart" and sought to make restitution and be forgiven (Acts 2:27). On that fateful day, at least 3,000 people were added together by God to constitute Christ's church (Acts 2:41). Later, Luke noted that great fear fell upon the **whole church** as a result of God's having disciplined sinners within it (Acts 5:11). There is no doubt that the church was established in Christ's generation.

The Bible speaks of the church as Christ's kingdom. Jesus said the time for its coming had been "fulfilled" (Mark 1:15) and that the kingdom was as near as the generation of people to whom He spoke, since some of them would not taste of death before they saw the kingdom of heaven come (Mark 9:1). Paul taught that the church is constituted of saints (1 Corinthians 1:1-2). But when he wrote his epistle to the Colossians (c. A.D. 62), he specifically stated that by that time the saints in the church at Colossae were subjects in "the kingdom of the Son of his love" (Colossians 1:13).

If the kingdom had not been established, then Paul erred in saying that the Colossians already were in it. [Those who teach that the church and the kingdom are separate, and that the kingdom has yet to arrive, must contend that there are living on the Earth today some of the very people to whom Jesus spoke nearly 2,000 years ago–since He stated that some who heard Him **would not die until the kingdom had come** (Mark 9:1).]

The New Testament teaches that the **church** is composed of individuals purchased with the blood of Christ (Acts 20:28), and that those so purchased were made to be a **kingdom** (Revelation 1:5-6; 5:9-10). Since the church and the kingdom both are composed of blood-purchased individuals, the church and the kingdom must be the same. And since the Christians that constitute the church were themselves translated into the kingdom, it is conclusive that the church and the kingdom **are** the same. The establishment of the kingdom coincided with the establishment of the church. Not only did the Lord foretell both the establishment of the kingdom and the church in His generation, but the New Testament writers spoke of both the church and the kingdom as being in existence during the very generation of His arrival (i.e., the first century).

CHRIST'S TRIUMPHANT CHURCH

From the first to the last of His earthly ministry, Jesus admonished those who would be His disciples that they would be both controversial and persecuted. He warned them:

> Think not that I came to send peace on the earth: I came not to send peace, but a sword. For I came to set a man at variance against his father and the daughter against her mother, and the daughter in law against her mother in law: and a man's foes shall be they of his own household (Matthew 10:34-36).

Jesus wanted no misunderstanding about the trials and tribulations His followers would endure. He constantly reminded them of such (Matthew 10:16,39; 16:24; 24:9; John 15:2,18, 20; 16:1-2; 21:18-19). While He desired that men be at peace with men, His primary goal was to bring men to a peaceful, covenant relationship with God. In addressing the Christians at Rome, Paul wrote:

> Who shall separate us from the love of Christ? shall tribulation, or anguish, or persecution, or famine, or nakedness, or peril, or sword?... Nay, in all these things

> we are more than conquerors through him that loved us. For I am persuaded that neither death, nor life, nor angels, nor principalities, nor things present, nor things to come, nor powers, nor height, nor depth, nor any other creature, shall be able to separate us from the love of God, which is in Christ Jesus our Lord (Romans 8:35,37-39).

Christ alerted His followers to the pressure yet to be brought upon them by other religions (Matthew 10:17), by civil governments (Matthew 10:18), and sadly, by some of their own (2 Thessalonians 4:1ff.). He said: "And ye shall be hated of all men for my name's sake" (Matthew 10:22). History records that Christ's words accurately depicted what was to befall those early saints. As James O. Baird has noted: "In actuality, Christianity was opposed more vigorously than any other religion in the long history of Rome" (1978, p. 29).

Persecution against the church was, and is, rooted in the nature and work of Christ: "But me it hateth, because I testify of it, that its works are evil" (John 7:7). The world hated Christ because of the judgment He brought against what the world is, does, and loves. It will hate those in the church who remind it–by word and by deed–of this judgment. Jesus lamented: "If the world hateth you, ye know that it hath hated me before it hated you" (John 15:18). Hatred often results in persecution. The church, if true to its mission, will be opposed. But Jesus also said:

> Blessed are ye when men shall reproach you, and persecute you, and say all manner of evil against you falsely, for my sake. Rejoice, and be exceeding glad: for great is your reward in heaven: for so persecuted they the prophets that were before you (Matthew 5: 11-12).

One thing, however, was beyond doubt. Those saints who remained faithful–even unto death if necessary–would be triumphant (Revelation 2:10). As the great Restorationist, F.G. Allen, so beautifully wrote:

> One by one will we lay our armor down at the feet of the Captain of our salvation. One by one will we be laid away by tender hands and aching hearts to rest on the bosom of Jesus. One by one will our ranks be thus thinned, till erelong we shall all pass over to the other side. But our cause will live. Eternal truth shall never perish. God will look down from His habitation on high, watch over it in His providence, and encircle it in the arms of His love. God will raise up others to take our places; and may we transmit the cause to them in its purity! Though dead, we shall thus speak for generations yet to come, and God grant that we shall give no uncertain sound! Then may we from our blissful home on high, watch the growth of the cause we love, till it shall cover the whole earth as the waters cover the face of the great deep (1949, pp. 176-177).

CONCLUSION: HOW HUMANITY SHOULD SERVE GOD

In His manifold dealings with mankind, God consistently has reiterated the fact that, as Sovereign of the Universe, He alone is worthy to be worshipped. When He provided the Israelites with their cherished ten commandments, for example, He reminded them in no uncertain terms:

> I am Jehovah thy God, who brought thee out of the land of Egypt, out of the house of bondage. Thou shalt have no other gods before me. Thou shalt not make unto thee a graven image, nor any likeness of anything that is in heaven above, or that is in the earth beneath, or that is in the water under the earth; thou shalt not bow down thyself unto them; for I Jehovah thy God am a jealous God (Exodus 20:2-5).

It was not enough, however, for man merely to worship God. Through the millennia, God provided specific instructions concerning not only the fact that He was to be worshipped, but the **manner** in which He was to be worshipped. A straightforward reading of the Scriptures reveals that apparently these instructions were set forth very early in human history. The writer of the Book of Hebrews substantiated this when he commented on events that transpired shortly after Adam and Eve's expulsion from the Garden of Eden, and the subsequent birth of two of their children, Cain and Abel. The inspired writer observed that "by faith Abel offered unto God a more excellent sacrifice than Cain, through which he had witness borne to him that he was righteous, God bearing witness in respect of his gifts" (Hebrews 11:4).

Whatever else might be gleaned from the Bible's statements about these two brothers, one thing is certain: Abel's worship to God was acceptable; Cain's was not. The conclusion, therefore, is inescapable: Abel had obeyed whatever instructions God had given the first family regarding their worship of Him, while Cain had ignored those same instructions.

These two brothers are not the only siblings from whom such a lesson can be drawn. In the Old Testament Book of Leviticus, the story is told of two of Aaron's sons, Nadab, his firstborn, and Abihu. Leviticus 10 presents a chilling commentary on the two boys' ill-fated attempt to worship God according to their own desires, and not as God had commanded.

> And Nadab and Abihu, the sons of Aaron, took each of them his censer, and put fire therein, and laid incense thereon, and offered strange fire before Jehovah, which he had not commanded them. And there came forth fire from before Jehovah, and devoured them and they died before Jehovah (Leviticus 10:1-2).

The key to understanding the account, of course, is in the fact that they offered "strange fire" that God "had not commanded." Aaron's two sons suffered a horrible death because they ignored Jehovah's specific commands relating to **how** He was to be worshipped.

In referring to the Old Testament, the apostle Paul commented: "For whatsoever things were written aforetime were written for our learning, that through patience and through comfort of the scriptures we might have hope" (Romans 15:4). From the accounts of Cain and Abel, and Nadab and Abihu, we can learn a critically important lesson regarding how God views man's worship of Him. That lesson is this: **God places a premium on foundational knowledge, proper understanding, correct mental attitude, contrite spirit, and reverent obedience** in matters relating to worship offered to Him!

A New Testament example not only bears this out, but also brings the matter more clearly into focus. In Matthew 6:1ff., Jesus condemned the Pharisees for their public display of ritualistic religion when He said:

> Take heed that ye do not your righteousness before men, to be seen of them: else ye have no reward with your Father who is in heaven. When therefore thou doest alms, sound not a trumpet before thee, as the hypocrites do in the synagogues and in the streets, that they may have glory of men. Verily I say unto you, They have received their reward.... And when ye pray, ye shall not be as the hypocrites: for they love to stand and pray in the synagogues and in the corners of the streets, that they may be seen of men. Verily I say unto you, They have received their reward.... Moreover, when ye fast, be not, as the hypocrites, of a sad countenance: for they disfigure their faces, that they may be seen of men. Verily I say unto you, They have received their reward (Matthew 6:1-2, 5,16).

Consider the Pharisees that Christ used as an example of how **not** to worship God. They gave alms; they prayed; they fasted. Under normal circumstances, would each of these acts be acceptable to God? Indeed they would. But the Pharisees performed them for the wrong reason–"to be seen of men." In other words, although the act itself was correct, the **purpose** for which they did it, and the **attitude** with which they did it, were wrong. Hence, **God would not accept their worship!**

Consider also additional New Testament passages that bear on this issue. In 2 Corinthians 9:7, Paul discussed a person's giving of his financial means to the Lord, and stated that "each man" was to "do according as he hath purposed in his heart; not grudgingly, or of necessity: for God loveth a cheerful giver." Both the purpose of the act, as well as the understanding and attitude of the worshiper, were critical. Further, in Luke 22: 19, in speaking of the memorial supper that He was instituting, Christ commanded: "This do in remembrance of me." The Scriptures make it clear, however, that it is possible to partake of the Lord's supper in an incorrect way (see 1 Corinthians 11:27-29), thus making it null and void in its effects. In other words, foundational knowledge, proper understanding, correct mental attitude, contrite spirit, and reverent obedience are all vitally important. And when they are missing, the act of worship is vain.

An additional point needs to be examined as well. Sincerity alone is not enough to make an act pleasing and acceptable to God. In 2 Samuel 6, the story is told of a man by the name of Uzzah who was accompanying the Ark of the Covenant of God as it was being moved from one location to another at the command of King David. The Ark had been placed on an ox cart, and the text says simply that "the oxen stumbled" (2 Samuel 6:6). Uzzah–no doubt believing that the precious cargo was about to be tumble from its perch on the cart and be damaged or destroyed–reached up to steady the Ark (2 Samuel 6:6). But Jehovah had commanded that no man (except the High Priest as he entered into the Holy of Holies in the Tabernacle once a year) was to touch the holy things of God (Numbers 4:15). And so, the moment Uzzah touched the Ark, God struck him dead (2 Samuel 6:7).

Was Uzzah sincere in what he did? Undoubtedly. But his sincerity counted for nothing because he disobeyed. Note specifically the Bible's statement that "God smote him there for his **error**" (2 Samuel 6:7b, emp. added). God does not want just sincerity; He wants obedience. Jesus Himself said: "If ye love me, ye will keep my commandments" (John 14:15). Furthermore, the way of the Lord is both restrictive and narrow, as Jesus made clear in His beautiful sermon on the mount (read specifically Matthew 7:13-14). In fact, Christ observed: "Not everyone that saith unto me, Lord, Lord, shall enter into the kingdom of heaven; but he that doeth the will of my Father who is in heaven" (Matthew 7:21). Jesus later commented on the attitude of the people of His day when He said: "This people honoreth me with their lips, but their heart is far from me. But in vain do they worship me, teaching as their doctrines the precepts of men" (Matthew 15:8-9).

These people of whom Jesus spoke did not have the foundational knowledge, proper understanding, correct mental attitude, contrite spirit, or reverent obedience God demands of those who would worship and serve Him as He has commanded. There is a valuable lesson in each of these accounts for those of us today who seek to worship and serve God. That lesson is this: we must do **exactly** what God has commanded, in **exactly** the way He has commanded that we do it. Nothing can take the place of simple obedience to the law of God. Neither sincerity nor good intentions will suffice. Only the person who reverently obeys because of adequate foundational knowledge, a proper understanding, a correct mental attitude, and a contrite spirit will be acceptable to God. That being the case, let us all strive not only to worship and serve God, but also to worship and serve Him in a scriptural fashion.

DISCUSSION QUESTIONS

1. How does one become a member of Christ's church?
2. Is everyone who professes to be a Christian a member of that blood-bought church? Why, or why not?
3. If Christ established only one church, then what is the fate of those who sincerely believe in Jesus, but regularly attend manmade denominations?
4. Discuss the fate of those who have never heard the Gospel. Will they be saved, or are they lost eternally?
5. When Christ told Peter that He would establish His church "upon this rock," to what was He referring?

REFERENCES

Abelson, Phillip (1964), "Bigotry in Science," *Science*, April 24.

Ackerman, Paul D. (1986), *It's A Young World After All* (Grand Rapids, MI: Baker).

Adams, J.Q. (1883), *American Antiquarian*, 5:331-332.

Adler, Irvin (1957), *How Life Began* (New York: John Day).

Adler, Jerry (1980), "Is Man a Subtle Accident?," *Newsweek*, 96[18]:95, November 3.

"Age of the Dinosaurs" (1993), *National Geographic*, 183[1]: 142, January.

Albright, William F. (1953), *Archaeology and the Religion of Israel* (Baltimore, MD: Johns Hopkins University Press).

Allan, John (1989), *The Human Difference* (Oxford, England: Lion).

Allen, F.G. (1949), "The Principles and Objects of the Current Reformation," *Foundation Facts and Primary Principles*, ed. G.C. Brewer (Kansas City, MO: Old Paths Book Club).

Ambrose, E.J. (1982), *The Nature and Origin of the Biological World* (New York: John Wiley & Sons).

Anderson, Alan (1991), "Early Bird Threatens *Archaeopteryx's* Perch," *Science*, 253:35, July 5.

Anderson, Bruce L. (1980), *Let Us Make Man* (Plainfield, NJ: Logos International).

Andrews, E.H. (1978), *From Nothing to Nature* (Welwyn, Hertfordshire, England: Evangelical Press).

Asimov, Isaac (1970), "In the Game of Energy and Thermodynamics You Can't Even Break Even," *Smithsonian Institute Journal*, pp. 4-10, June.

Asimov, Isaac (1975), *The Intelligent Man's Guide to Science* (London: Pelican).

Asimov, Isaac (1981), "The Genesis War," *Science Digest,* 89 [9]:82-87, October. [NOTE: This is a written debate with creationist Duane Gish.]

Assmuth, J. and E.R. Hull (1915), *Haeckel's Frauds and Forgeries* (New York: Abelard-Schuman).

Avraham, Regina (1989), *The Circulatory System* (New York: Chelsea House).

Ayala, Francisco J. (1968), "Genotype, Environment, and Population Numbers," *Science,* 162:1436.

Ayala, Francisco J. (1970), *Philosophy of Science,* March.

Baird, James O. (1978), "The Trials and Tribulations of the Church from the Beginning," *The Future of the Church,* ed. William Woodson (Henderson, TN: Freed-Hardeman College).

Bakker, Robert T. (1986), *The Dinosaur Heresies* (New York: William Morrow).

Baldi, Pierre (2001), *The Shattered Self: The End of Natural Evolution* (Cambridge, MA: MIT Press).

Bales, James D. (1976), *How Can Ye Believe?* (Shreveport, LA: Lambert).

Bales, James D. and Woolsey Teller (1947), *The Existence of God–A Debate* (Shreveport, LA: Lambert).

Ball, Philip (2002), "Is Physics Watching Over Us?," *Nature,* [On-line], URL: www.nature.com/nsu/020812/020812-2.html, August.

Barlow, Nora, ed. (1959), *The Autobiography of Charles Darwin 1809-1882 with Original Omissions Restored* (New York: Harcourt, Brace, and World).

Barnes F.A., and Michaelene Pendleton (1979), *Canyon Country Prehistoric Indians: Their Cultures, Ruins, Artifacts and Rock Art* (Salt Lake City, NV: Wasatch Publishers).

Barnett, Lincoln (1959), *The Universe and Dr. Einstein* (New York: Mentor).

Barrow, John D. (2000), *The Book of Nothing: Vacuums, Voids, and the Latest Ideas about the Origins of the Universe* (New York: Pantheon).

Bartelmez, George W. (1926), "Human Structure and Development," *The Nature and the World of Man*, ed. H.H. Newman (Garden City, NY: Garden City Publishing), pp. 440-470.

Bass, Alden, Bert Thompson, and Brad Harrub (2001), "Does God Hear and Respond to the Prayer of an Alien Sinner?," *Reason & Revelation*, 21:81-87, November.

Bass, Thomas (1990), "Interview with Richard Dawkins," *Omni*, 12[4]:58-60,84,86-89, January.

Beardsley, Tim (1986), "Fossil Bird Shakes Evolutionary Hypothesis," *Nature*, 322:677, August 21.

Beck, William (1971), *Human Design* (New York: Harcourt, Brace, Jovanovich).

Begun, David (2001), "Early Hominid Sows Division," [Online], URL: http:// bric.postech.ac.kr/science/97now/01_2now/010222c.html.

Behe, Michael J. (1998), "Intelligent Design Theory as a Tool for Analyzing Biochemical Systems," *Mere Creation*, ed. William A. Dembski (Downers Grove, IL: InterVarsity Press).

Bengtson, Stefan (1990), "The Solution to a Jigsaw Puzzle," *Nature*, 345:765-766, June 28.

Benton, Michael (1992), *The Dinosaur Encyclopedia* (New York: Simon & Schuster).

Berlinski, David (1998), "Was There a Big Bang?," *Commentary*, pp. 28-38, February.

Bird, A. (1934), *Boise: The Peace Valley* (Boise, ID: Caxton Publishers).

Bird, Roland T. (1939), "Thunder in His Footsteps," *Natural History*, 43[5]:254-261, May.

Birdsell, J.B. (1972), *Human Evolution* (Chicago, IL: Rand McNally).

Blanchard, John (2000), *Does God Believe in Atheists?* (Auburn, MA: Evangelical Press).

Blechschmidt, Erich (1977), *The Beginnings of Human Life* (New York: Springer-Verlag).

Block, Irvin (1980), "The Worlds Within You," *Science Digest*, special edition, pp. 49-53,118, September/October.

Bonner, John Tyler (1961), "Review of *The Implications of Evolution*," *American Scientist*, 49:240, June. [See Kerkut (1960) for the publication data of the book Dr. Bonner was reviewing.]

Borek, Ernest (1973), *The Sculpture of Life* (New York: Columbia University Press).

Boslough, J. (1985), *Stephen Hawking's Universe* (New York: William Morrow).

Bowden, Malcolm (1977), *Ape-Men: Fact or Fallacy?* (Bromley, England: Sovereign Publications).

Brand, Paul and Phillip Yancey (1980), *Fearfully and Wonderfully Made* (Grand Rapids, MI: Zondervan).

Britten, Roy J. (2002), "Divergence between Samples of Chimpanzee and Human DNA Sequences is 5%, Counting Intels," *Proceedings of the National Academy of Sciences*, 99:13633-13635, October 15.

Bromling, Brad T. (1989), "Jesus–My Lord and My God," *Reasoning from Revelation*, 1[9]:1-2, September.

Bromling, Brad T. (1991a), "Jesus and Jehovah–An Undeniable Link," *Reasoning from Revelation*, 3[2]:3, February.

Bromling, Brad T. (1991b), "The Prophets' Portrait of Christ," *Reason & Revelation*, 11:45-47, December.

Bromling, Brad T. (1995), "Jesus: Truly God and Truly Human," *Reason & Revelation*, 15:17-20, March.

Brown, F., S.R. Driver, and C.A. Briggs (1979), *The New Brown-Driver-Briggs-Gesenius Hebrew and English Lexicon* (Peabody, MA: Hendrickson).

Buffaloe, Neal D. and N. Patrick Murray (1981), *Creationism and Evolution* (Little Rock, AR: The Bookmark).

Burnett, Allison L. (1961), *Natural History*, November.

Burns, George W. (1973), *The Science of Genetics: An Introduction to Heredity* (New York: MacMillan), third edition.

Butt, Kyle (2000), "The Historical Christ–Fact or Fiction,?" *Reason & Revelation*, 20:1-6, January.

Cahill, George F. (1981), *Science Digest*, 89[3]:105, April.

Cairns-Smith, A.G. (1985), *Seven Clues to the Origin of Life* (Cambridge: Cambridge University Press).

Cardoso, Silvia H. (1997-1998), "What is Mind?," *Brain & Mind*, [On-line], URL: http://www.epub.org.br/cm/n04/editori4_i.htm, No. 4, December (1997)-February (1998).

Carnell, Edward John (1948), *An Introduction to Christian Apologetics* (Grand Rapids, MI: Eerdmans).

Cavalli-Sforza, Luigi Luca (2000), *Genes, Peoples, and Languages* (New York: North Point Press).

Chain, Ernest (1970), *Responsibility and the Scientist in Modern Western Society* (London: Council of Christians and Jews).

Chatterjee, Sankar (1991), "Cranial Anatomy and Relationships of a New Triassic Bird from Texas," *Philosophical Transactions of the Royal Society of London* (biology), 332:277-346.

Chiappe, Luis M., Rodolfo Coria, et al. (1998), "Sauropod Dinosaur Embryos from the Late Cretaceous of Patagonia," *Nature*, 396:258-261, November 19.

Childress, David H. (no date), "In Search of Sea Monsters," *World Explorer*, vol. 1 no. 7, [On-line], URL: http://www.wexclub.com/BackIssues/WEX7.html.

Clark, W. LeGros (1955), *Discovery*, January.

Clarke, William N. (1912), *An Outline of Christian Theology* (New York: Charles Scribner's Sons).

Clayton, John N. (1968a), "The History of Man on Planet Earth," *Does God Exist? Correspondence Course*, Lesson 8.

Clayton, John N. (1968b), Teacher's Manual, *Does God Exist? Correspondence Course.*

Clayton, John N. (1976), " 'Flat Earth' Bible Study Techniques," *Does God Exist?*, 3[10]:2-7, October.

Clayton, John N. (1977), "Dinosaurs and the Bible," *Evidences of God, Volume I* (South Bend, IN: Privately published by the author), pp. 149-151.

Clayton, John N. (1979), "Letter to the Editor," *Rocky Mountain Christian*, 7[4]:3, March.

Clayton, John N. (1982), "Where Are the Dinosaurs?," *Does God Exist?*, 9[10]:2-6, October.

Cosgrove, Mark P. (1987), *The Amazing Body Human* (Grand Rapids, MI: Baker).

Cousins, Norman (1985), "Commentary," in *Nobel Prize Conversations* (Dallas, TX: Saybrook). [This book is a record of conversations that occurred in November, 1982 at the Isthmus Institute in Dallas, Texas, among four Nobel laureates: Sir John Eccles, Ilya Prigogine, Roger Sperry, and Brian Josephson.]

Cramer, John G. (1999), "Before the Big Bang," *Analog Science Fiction & Fact Magazine*, [On-line], URL: http://www.npl.washington.edu/ AV/altvw94/html, March.

Culp, G. Richard (1975), *Remember Thy Creator* (Grand Rapids, MI: Baker).

Czerkas, Stephen (1992), "New Look for Sauropod Dinosaurs," *Geology*, 20:1068-1070.

Dahmer, Lionel, D. Kouznetsov, et al. (1990), "Report on Chemical Analysis and Further Dating of Dinosaur Bones and Dinosaur Petroglyphs," *Proceedings of the Second International Conference on Creationism*, ed. Robert E. Walsh and Christopher L. Brooks (Pittsburgh, PA: Creation Science Fellowship), pp. 371-374.

Dalton, Rex (2003), "Flat-faced Man in Family Feud," [On-line], URL: www.nature.com/nsu/030324/030324-10. html, March 28.

Darwin, Charles (1859), *On the Origin of Species* (Cambridge, MA: Harvard University Press; a facsimile of the first edition).

Darwin, Charles (1956 edition), *The Origin of Species* (London: J.M. Dent & Sons).

Darwin, Charles (1962 reprint), *The Origin of Species* (New York: Collier Books, sixth edition).

Darwin, Francis (1898), *The Life and Letters of Charles Darwin* (New York: D. Appleton).

Davidheiser, Bolton (1969), *Evolution and Christian Faith* (Phillipsburg, NJ: Presbyterian and Reformed).

Davidheiser, Bolton (1973), "Theistic Evolution," *And God Created*, ed. Kelly L. Segraves (San Diego, CA: Creation-Science Research Center), 3:49-53.

Davies, Paul (1984), *Superforce: The Search for a Grand Unified Theory* (New York: Simon and Schuster).

Davies, Paul (1988), *The Cosmic Blueprint: New Discoveries in Nature's Creative Ability to Order the Universe* (New York: Simon & Schuster).

Davies, Paul (1992a), *The Mind of God* (New York: Simon & Schuster).

Davies, Paul (1992b), "The Mind of God," *Omni*, 14[5]:4, February.

Davis, Bernard (1985), "Molecular Genetics and the Foundations of Evolution," *Perspectives in Biology and Medicine*, Winter.

Davis, George E. (1958), "Scientific Revelations Point to a God," *The Evidence of God in an Expanding Universe*, ed. John C. Monsma (New York: G.P. Putnam's Sons).

Davis, John D. (1944), *Westminster Dictionary of the Bible* (Philadelphia, PA: Westminster).

Dawkins, Richard (1982), "The Necessity of Darwinism," *New Scientist*, 94:130-132, April 15.

Dawkins, Richard (1986), *The Blind Watchmaker* (New York: W.W. Norton).

Dawkins, Richard, (1989), "Book Review" (of Donald Johanson and Maitland Edey's *Blueprint*), *The New York Times*, section 7, p. 34, April 9.

DeBakey, Michael E. (1984), in *World Book Encyclopedia* (Chicago, IL: World Book/Childcraft International).

Denton, Michael (1985), *Evolution: A Theory in Crisis* (London: Burnett Books).

Denton, Michael (1998), *Nature's Destiny: How the Laws of Biology Reveal Purpose in the Universe* (New York: Simon & Schuster).

Desmond, Adrian (1997), *Huxley* (Reading, MA: Addison-Wesley).

Desmond, Adrian and James Moore (1991), *Darwin* (New York: Warner).

DeWitt, David A. (2002), "Hox Hype," [On-line], URL: http://www.answersingenesis.org/docs2002/0215hox_hype.asp.

Diamond, Jared (1992), *The Third Chimpanzee* (New York: HarperCollins).

Dobzhansky, Theodosius (1955), *Evolution, Genetics and Man* (New York: John Wiley & Sons).

Dobzhansky, Theodosius (1957), *American Scientist,* December.

Douglas, Erwin, James W. Valentine, and David Jablonski (1997), "The Origin of Animal Body Plans," *American Scientist,* 85:126-137, March/April.

Driver, S.R. and G.B. Gray (1964), *A Critical and Exegetical Commentary on the Book of Job* (Edinburgh: T. & T. Clark).

Dyson, Lisa, Matthew Kleban, and Leonard Susskind (2002), "Disturbing Implications of a Cosmological Constant," *Journal of High Energy Physics,* 10:011-037, November 12. [Also available on-line at: http://xxx.1an1.gov/abs/hep-th/0208013.]

Eaves, Thomas F. (1980), "The Inspired Word," *Great Doctrines of the Bible,* ed. M.H. Tucker (Knoxville, TN: East Tennessee School of Preaching).

Eccles, John C. (1958), *Scientific American,* September.

Eccles, John C. (1973), *The Understanding of the Brain* (New York: McGraw-Hill).

Eccles, John C. (1984), "Modern Biology and the Turn to Belief in God," *The Intellectuals Speak Out About God,* ed. Roy A. Varghese (Chicago, IL: Regnery Gateway), pp. 47-50.

Ehrlich, Paul R. (2000), *Human Natures: Genes, Cultures, and the Human Prospect* (Washington, D.C.: Island Press).

Ehrlich, Paul R. and Richard W. Holm (1963), *The Process of Evolution* (New York: McGraw-Hill).

Eiseley, Loren (1961), *Darwin's Century* (Garden City, NY: Anchor Books).

Encyclopaedia Britannica (1981), (Chicago, IL: Encyclopaedia Britannica, Inc.), fifteenth edition.

Encyclopaedia Britannica (1989), s.v. "Bionics," (Chicago, IL: Encyclopaedia Britannica, Inc.).

England, Donald (1983), *A Scientist Examines Faith and Evidence*, (Delight, AR: Gospel Light).

Environmental Mutagenic Society, The (1975), *Science,* 187: 503-504, February 14.

Erwin, D.H. and J.W. Valentine (1984), "'Hopeful Monsters,' Transposons, and Metazoan Radiation," *Proceedings of the National Academy of Sciences*, 81:5482-5483, September.

Estling, Ralph (1995), "Letter to the Editor," *Skeptical Inquirer*, 19[1]:69-70, January/February.

Feduccia, Allan (1993), "Evidence from Claw Geometry Indicating Arboreal Habits of *Archaeopteryx*," *Science,* 259:790-793, February 5.

Felix, Charles (1988), "Geology and Paleontology," *Evolution and Faith*, ed. J.D. Thomas (Abilene, TX: ACU Press).

Ferguson, Kitty (1994), *The Fire in the Equations: Science, Religion, and the Search for God* (Grand Rapids, MI: Eerdmans).

Fix, William (1984), *The Bone Peddlers* (New York: Macmillan).

Fortey, Richard (1997), *Life: A Natural History of the First Four Billion Years of Life on Earth* (New York: Knopf).

Foster, R.C. (1971), *Studies in the Life of Christ* (Grand Rapids, MI: Baker).

Frair, Wayne A. and Percival Davis (1983), *A Case for Creation* (Chicago, IL: Moody).

Friend, Tim (1993), "Clues to Human Development Float in Nature's Gene Pool," *USA Today*, p. 5-D, July 27.

Fukuyama, Francis (2002), *Our Posthuman Future* (New York: Farrar, Straus and Giroux).

Gardner, Eldon J. (1968), *Principles of Genetics* (New York: John Wiley and Sons).

Gardner, Lynn (1994), *Christianity Stands True* (Joplin, MO: College Press).

Gardner, Martin (1988), *The New Age: Notes of a Fringe Watcher* (Buffalo, NY: Prometheus).

Gardner, Martin (2000), *Did Adam and Eve Have Navels?* (New York: W.W. Norton).

Gee, Henry (1999), *In Search of Deep Time* (New York: Free Press).

Geisler, Norman L. (1976), *Christian Apologetics* (Grand Rapids, MI: Baker).

Geisler, Norman L. (1984), "The Collapse of Modern Atheism," *The Intellectuals Speak Out About God*, ed. Roy A. Varghese (Chicago, IL: Regnery), pp. 129-152.

Geisler, Norman L. and William E. Nix (1986), *A General Introduction to the Bible* (Chicago, IL: Moody), revised edition.

Geisler, Norman L. and Winfried Corduan (1988), *Philosophy of Religion* (Grand Rapids, MI: Baker).

George, T.N. (1960), *Science Progress*, 48[1]:1-5, January.

Gillen, Alan L. (2001), *Body By Design* (Green Forest, AR: Master Books).

Gish, Duane T. (1995), *Evolution: The Fossils Still Say No!* (El Cajon, CA: Institute for Creation Research).

Gitt, Werner (1999), *The Wonder of Man* (Bielefeld, Germany: Christliche Literatur-Verbreitung E.V.).

Gliedman, John (1982), "Scientists in Search of the Soul," *Science Digest*, 90[7]:77-79,105, July.

Glueck, Nelson (1959), *Rivers in the Desert: A History of the Negev* (New York: Farrar, Strauss, and Cudahy).

Goldsmith, Donald (1997), *The Hunt for Life on Mars* (New York: Dutton).

Goodpasture, B.C. (1970), "Inspiration of the Bible," *The Church Faces Liberalism*, ed. T.B. Warren (Henderson, TN: Freed-Hardeman College).

Gould, Stephen Jay (1977a), *Ever Since Darwin* (New York: W. W. Norton).

Gould, Stephen Jay (1977b), "Evolution's Erratic Pace," *Natural History*, 86[5]:12-14, May.

Gould, Stephen Jay (1980), "Is a New and General Theory of Evolution Emerging?," *Paleobiology*, 6:119-130, Winter.

Gould, Stephen Jay (1989), *Wonderful Life: The Burgess Shale and the Nature of History* (New York: W.W. Norton).

Gould, Stephen Jay (1990), "An Earful of Jaw," *Natural History*, 99[3]:12-23, March.

Gould, Stephen Jay (1994), "The Evolution of Life on Earth," *Scientific American*, 271:85-91, October.

Gould, Stephen Jay (1999), "Dorothy, It's Really Oz," *Time*, 154[8]:59, August 23.

Grassé, Pierre-Paul (1977), *The Evolution of Living Organisms* (New York: Academic Press).

Gribbin, John (1983), "Earth's Lucky Break," *Science Digest*, 91[5]:36-37,40,102, May.

Gribbin, John (1986), "Cosmologists Move Beyond the Big Bang," *New Scientist*, 110[1511]:30.

Grigg, Russell (1996), "Ernst Haeckel: Evangelist for Evolution and Apostle of Deceit," *Creation Ex Nihilo*, 18[2]:33-36.

Grigg, Russell (1998), "Fraud Rediscovered," *Creation Ex Nihilo*, 20[2]:49–51, March-May.

Guinness, Alma E., ed. (1987), *ABC's of the Human Body* (Pleasantville, NY: Reader's Digest).

Guth, Alan (1981), "Inflationary Universe: A Possible Solution to the Horizon and Flatness Problems," *Physical Review D*, 23:347-356.

Guth, Alan (1988), *Interview in Omni*, 11[2]:75-76,78-79,94,96-99, November.

Guth, Alan and Paul Steinhardt (1984), "The Inflationary Universe," *Scientific American*, 250:116-128, May.

Haeckel, Ernst (1876), *The Evolution of Man* (Akron, OH: Werner, translated from the German third edition).

Haeckel, Ernst (1905), *The Wonders of Life*, trans. J. McCabe (London: Watts).

Hager, Dorsey (1957), "Fifty Years of Progress in Geology," *Geotimes*, August.

Hall, Marshall and Sandra (1974), *The Truth: God or Evolution?* (Grand Rapids, MI: Baker).

Halley, H.H. *Halley's Bible Handbook* (Grand Rapids, MI: Zondervan).

Hapgood, Charles (2000), *Mystery in Acambaro* (Kempton, IL: Adventures Unlimited Press).

Hardy, Alistair (1965), *The Living Stream* (New York: Collins).

Harold, Franklin M. (2001), *The Way of the Cell* (Oxford, England: Oxford University Press).

Harris, R.L., G.L. Archer, and B.K. Waltke (1980), *Theological Wordbook of the Old Testament* (Chicago, IL: Moody).

Harrub, Brad and Bert Thompson (2001), "*Archaeopteryx*, *Archaeoraptor*, and the 'Dinosaurs to Birds' Theory" [Parts I&II], *Reason & Revelation*, 21:25-31,33-39, April and May.

Harrub, Brad and Bert Thompson (2002), "Creationists Fight Back: A Review of *U.S. News & World Report's* Cover Story on Evolution," *Reason & Revelation*, 22:65-71, September.

Harrub, Brad and Bert Thompson (2003), *The Truth About Human Origins* (Montgomery, AL: Apologetics Press).

Hartley, John E (1988), *The Book of Job* (Grand Rapids, MI: Eerdmans).

Havron, Dean (1981), "Curious Cure-Alls," *Science Digest*, 89 [8]:62, September.

Hawking, Stephen W. (1988), *A Brief History of Time* (New York: Bantam).

Hayden, Thomas (2002), "A Theory Evolves," *U.S. News & World Report*, 133[4]:42-50, July 29.

Hayward, Alan (1985), *Creation or Evolution: The Facts and the Fallacies* (London: Triangle Books).

Heeren, Fred (1995), *Show Me God* (Wheeling, IL: Searchlight Publications).

Helfinstine, Robert F. and Jerry D. Roth (1994), *Texas Tracks and Artifacts* (Anoka, MN: Privately published by authors).

Herodotus, (1850 reprint), *Historiae*, trans. Henry Clay (London: Henry G. Bohn).

Hesman, T. (2000), "Vase Shows that Ancients Dug Fossils, Too," *Science News*, 157:133, February 26.

Hitching, Francis (1982), *The Neck of the Giraffe* (New York: Ticknor and Fields).

Holt, L.E. and R. McIntosh (1953), *Holt Pediatrics* (New York: Appleton-Century-Crofts), twelfth edition.

Horne, Thomas H. (1970 reprint), *An Introduction to the Critical Study and Knowledge of the Holy Scriptures* (Grand Rapids, MI: Baker).

Hoyle, Fred (1982), "The Universe: Past and Present Reflections," *Annual Review of Astronomy and Astrophysics*, 20:1-35.

Hoyle, Fred and Chandra Wickramasinghe (1981), *Evolution from Space* (London: J.M. Dent & Sons).

Hubbard, Samuel (1925), *Discoveries Relating to Prehistoric Man by the Doheny Scientific Expedition* (Oakland, CA: Oakland Museum of Natural History).

Huff, Darrell (1959), *How to Take a Chance* (New York: W.W. Norton).

Hull, David (1974), *Philosophy of Biological Science* (Englewood Cliffs, NJ: Prentice-Hall).

Hull, David (1991), "The God of the Galapagos," *Nature*, 352: 486, August 8. [Dr. Hull, of the philosophy department at Northwestern University, was reviewing Philip Johnson's 1991 book, *Darwin on Trial* (Washington, D.C.: Regnery Gateway).]

Humanist Manifestos I & II (1933/1973), (Buffalo, NY: Prometheus).

"Human-Like Tracks in Stone are Riddle to Scientists" (1938), *Science News Letter*, pp. 278-279, October 29.

Hurst, William R. Jr. (1971), "Editor's Report," *The [Los Angeles] Herald-Examiner*, section A, p. 4, November 14.

Huxley, Julian (1960), "The Evolutionary Vision," *Issues in Evolution* [Volume 3 of *Evolution After Darwin*], ed. Sol Tax (Chicago, IL: University of Chicago Press).

Huxley, Leonard (1900), *Life and Letters of Thomas Henry Huxley* (New York: Macmillan).

"The Inflationary Universe" (2001), [On-line], URL: http://astsun.astro.virginia.edu/~jh8h/Foundations/chapter 15.html.

Ingalls, Albert G. (1940), "The Carboniferous Mystery," *Scientific American*, 162:14, January.

Jackson, Wayne (1974), *Fortify Your Faith in an Age of Doubt* (Stockton, CA: Courier Publications).

Jackson, Wayne (1979), "Isaiah 53: The Messiah," *Great Chapters of the Bible*, ed. Thomas F. Eaves (Knoxville, TN: East Tennessee School of Preaching and Missions).

Jackson, Wayne (1983), *The Book of Job* (Abilene, TX: Quality).

Jackson, Wayne (1984), "Rules by Which Men Live," *Reason & Revelation*, 4:21-224, May.

Jackson, Wayne (1987), "Does the Genesis Account of Creation Allow for Theistic Evolution?," *Questions Men Ask about God*, ed. Eddie Whitten (Bedford, TX: Christian Supply Center), pp. 125-133.

Jackson, Wayne (1988), "The Earth: A Planet Plagued with Evil," *Reason and Revelation*, 8:49-52, December.

Jackson, Wayne (1991), "Bible Unity–An Argument for Inspiration," *Reason & Revelation*, 11:1-3, January.

Jackson, Wayne (1993), *The Human Body: Accident or Design?* (Stockton, CA: Courier Publications).

Jackson, Wayne (1997a), "Daniel's Prophecy of the Seventy Weeks," *Reason & Revelation*, 17:49-53, July.

Jackson, Wayne (1997b), "The Matter of 'Baptismal Regeneration,' " *Christian Courier*, 32:45-46, April.

Jackson, Wayne (1997c), "The Role of 'Works' in the Plan of Salvation," *Christian Courier*, 32:47, April.

Jastrow, Robert (1977), *Until the Sun Dies* (New York: W.W. Norton).

Jastrow, Robert (1978), *God and the Astronomers* (New York: W.W. Norton).

Jastrow, Robert (1981), *The Enchanted Loom: Mind in the Universe* (New York: Simon and Schuster).

Jastrow, Robert (1982), "A Scientist Caught Between Two Faiths," interview with Bill Durbin in *Christianity Today*, August 6.

Jeans, James (1929), *The Universe Around Us* (New York: MacMillan.

Johanson, Donald C. and Maitland Edey (1981), *Lucy: The Beginnings of Humankind* (New York: Simon & Schuster).

Johanson, Donald C. and Blake Edgar (1996), *From Lucy to Language* (New York: Nevraumont).

Johanson, Donald C., Lenora Johanson, and Blake Edgar (1994), *Ancestors* (New York: Villard).

Josephus, Flavius (no date), *Antiquities of the Jews* (Grand Rapids, MI: Baker, reprint).

Kandel, Eric R. (1991), "Nerve Cells and Behavior," *Principles of Neural Science,* ed. Eric R. Kandel, James H. Schwartz, and Thomas M. Jessell (New York: Elsevier), third edition.

Kautz, Darrel (1988), *The Origin of Living Things* (Milwaukee, WI: Privately published by the author).

Keith, Arthur (1932), *The Human Body* (London: Butterworth).

Kenny, Anthony (1980), *The Five Ways: St. Thomas Aquinas' Proofs of God's Existence* (South Bend, IN: University of Notre Dame Press).

Kerkut, George A. (1960), *The Implications of Evolution* (London: Pergamon Press,).

Kimura, Motoo (1976), "Population Genetics and Molecular Evolution," *The Johns Hopkins Medical Journal,* 138[6]:253-261, June.

Kiss, Ferenco (1949), *History,* April.

Kitts, David G. (1974), "Paleontology and Evolutionary Theory," *Evolution,* 28:458-472, September.

Klotz, John (1972), *Genes, Genesis and Evolution* (St. Louis, MO: Concordia).

Klotz, John (1985), *Studies in Creation* (St. Louis, MO: Concordia).

Knoll, Andy H. (1991), "End of the Proterozoic Eon," *Scientific American*, 265:64-73, October.

Koch, Christof (1997), "Computation and the Single Neuron," *Nature*, 385:207-210, January 16.

Kolb, Rocky (1998), "Planting Primordial Seeds," *Astronomy*, 1998, 26[2]:42-43.

Lammerts, Walter, ed. (1976), *Why Not Creation?* (Grand Rapids, MI: Baker), pp. 185-193.

Lawton, April (1981), "From Here to Infinity," *Science Digest*, 89[1]:98-105, January/February.

Leach, James W. (1961), *Functional Anatomy–Mammalian and Comparative* (New York: McGraw-Hill).

Leakey, Louis S.B. (1966), "*Homo habilis*, *Homo erectus*, and *Australopithecus*," *Nature*, 209:1280-1281.

Leakey, Mary D. (1971), *Olduvai Gorge* (Cambridge, England: Cambridge University Press).

Leakey, Mary D. (1979), "Footprints in the Ashes of Time," *National Geographic*, 155[4]:446-457, April.

Leakey, Meave, et al. (2001), "New Hominin Genus from Eastern Africa Shows Diverse Middle Pliocene Lineages," *Nature*, 410:433-440, March 22.

Leakey, Richard (1978), *People of the Lake* (New York: E.P. Dutton).

Leakey, Richard and Roger Lewin (1977), *Origins* (New York: E. P. Dutton).

Lemonick, Michael D. (2001), "The End," *Time*, 157[25]:48-56, June 25.

Lemonick, Michael D. (2003), "The Power of Mood," *Time*, 161[3]:64-69, January 20.

Lenihan, John (1974), *Human Engineering* (New York: John Braziller).

Lester, Lane P. and James C. Hefley (1998), *Human Cloning* (Grand Rapids, MI: Revell).

Lester, Lane P. and Raymond Bohlin (1984), *The Natural Limits of Biological Change* (Grand Rapids, MI: Zondervan).

Lewin, Roger (1992), *Complexity: Life at the Edge of Chaos* (New York: Macmillan).

Lewis, C.S. (1952), *Mere Christianity* (New York: MacMillan).

Lewontin, Richard (1978), "Adaptation," *Scientific American*, 239[3]:212-218,220,222,228,230, September.

Linde, Andrei (1994), "The Self-Reproducing Inflationary Universe," *Scientific American*, 271[5]:48-55, November.

Lindsell, Harold (1977), *Christianity Today*, pp. 17-18, June.

Lipe, David (1987), "The Foundations of Morality," *Reason and Revelation*, 7:25-27, July.

Lipson, H.S. (1980), "A Physicist Looks at Evolution," *Physics Bulletin*, 31:138, May.

Livio, Mario (2000), *The Accelerating Universe* (New York: John Wiley).

Lockerbie, D. Bruce (1998), *Dismissing God* (Grand Rapids, MI: Baker).

Lockyer, Herbert (1973), *All the Messianic Prophecies of the Bible* (Grand Rapids, MI: Zondervan).

Lubenow, Marvin (1992), *Bones of Contention* (Grand Rapids, MI: Baker).

Lyons, Eric and Bert Thompson (2002a), "In the 'Image and Likeness of God' [Part I]," *Reason & Revelation*, 22:17-23, March.

Lyons, Eric and Bert Thompson (2002b), "In the 'Image and Likeness of God' [Part II]," *Reason & Revelation*, 22:25-31, April.

Macalister, Alexander (1886), "Man Physiologically Considered," *Living Papers* (Cincinnati, OH: Cranston and Stowe).

Major, Trevor J. (1998), "The Problem of Suffering," *Reason and Revelation*, 18:49-55, July.

Margenau, Henry and Abraham Varghese, eds. (1992), *Cosmos, Bios, and Theos* (La Salle, IL: Open Court Publishers).

Margulis, Lynn and Dorion Sagan (2002), *Acquiring Genomes: A Theory of the Origins of Species* (New York: Basic Books).

Marlin, George J., Richard P. Rabatin, and John L. Swan, eds. (1986), *The Quotable Chesterton: A Topical Compilation of the Wit, Wisdom, and Satire of G.K. Chesterton* (San Francisco, CA: Ignatius Press).

Martin, C.P. (1953), "A Non-Geneticist Looks at Evolution," *American Scientist.*

Mather, Kirtley F. (1960), *Science Ponders Religion*, ed. Harlow Shapley (New York: Appleton-Century-Croft).

Matthew, William D. (1939), *Climate and Evolution* (New York: New York Academy of Sciences), second edition.

Mayberry, Thomas C. (1970), "God and Moral Authority," *The Monist*, January.

Mayr, Ernst (1963), *Animal Species and Evolution* (Boston, MA: Belknap Press of Harvard University).

Mayr, Ernst (1965), *Animal Species and Evolution* (Boston: Harvard University Press).

Mayr, Ernst (2001), *What Evolution Is* (New York: Basic Books).

McDowell, Josh (1972), *Evidence that Demands a Verdict* (San Bernardino, CA: Campus Crusade for Christ).

McFadden, Johnjoe (2000), *Quantum Evolution: The New Science of Life* (New York: W.W. Norton).

McGarvey, J.W. (1875), *The New Testament Commentary: Matthew and Mark* (Delight, AR: Gospel Light).

McGarvey, J.W. (1881), *Lands of the Bible* (Philadelphia, PA: Lippincott).

McGrath, Alister E. (1993), *Intellectuals Don't Need God* (Grand Rapids, MI: Zondervan).

McKenzie, John L. (1959), "Myth and the Old Testament," *The Catholic Biblical Quarterly*.

McMillen, S.I. (1963), *None of These Diseases* (Old Tappan, NJ: Revell).

Meiklejohn, J.M.D., trans. (1878), Immanuel Kant, *Critique of Pure Reason* (London).

Meyer, Stephen C. (1998), "The Explanatory Power of Design: DNA and the Origin of Information," *Mere Creation*, ed. William A. Dembski (Downers Grove, IL: InterVarsity Press).

Miethe, Terry L. and Gary R. Habermas (1993), *Why Believe? God Exists!* (Joplin, MO: College Press).

Miller, Benjamin and Goode, Ruth (1960), *Man and His Body* (New York: Simon and Schuster).

Monastersky, Richard (1997), "When Earth Tipped, Life Went Wild," *Science News*, 152:52, July 26.

Monastersky, Richard (1999), "Waking Up to the Dawn of Vertebrates," *Science News*, 156:292, November 6.

Montagu, Ashley (1960), *Human Heredity* (New York: Mentor Books).

Morgan, Elaine (1989), *The Aquatic Ape: A Theory of Human Evolution* (London: Souvenir Press).

Morgan, T.H. (1923), "The Bearing of Mendelism on the Origin of Species," *Scientific Monthly*, March.

Morris, Henry M. (1966), *Studies in the Bible and Science* (Grand Rapids, MI: Baker).

Morris, Henry M. (1967), *Evolution and the Modern Christian* (Grand Rapids, MI: Baker).

Morris, Henry M. (1969), *The Bible and Modern Science* (Chicago, IL: Moody).

Morris, Henry M. (1974a), *Many Infallible Proofs* (San Diego, CA: Creation-Life Publishers).

Morris, Henry M. (1974b), *Scientific Creationism* (San Diego, CA: Creation-Life Publishers).

Morris, Henry M. (1977), *Circular Reasoning in Evolutionary Geology*, Impact #48 (El Cajon, CA: Institute for Creation Research), June.

Morris, Henry M. (1982), *Evolution in Turmoil* (San Diego, CA: Creation-Life Publishers).

Morris, Henry M. (1984), *The Biblical Basis for Modern Science* (Grand Rapids, MI: Baker).

Morris, Henry M. (1988), *The Remarkable Record of Job* (Grand Rapids, MI: Baker).

Morris, John D. (1994), *The Young Earth* (Green Forest, AR: Master Books).

Morrison, Philip and Phylis (2001), "The Big Bang: Wit or Wisdom?," *Scientific American*, 284[2]:93,95, February.

Morton, Jean S. (1978), *Science in the Bible* (Chicago, IL: Moody).

Muller, Hermann J. (1950), "Radiation Damage to the Genetic Material," *American Scientist*, 38:33-50,126, January.

Murphy, Nancey and George F.R. Ellis (1996), *On the Moral Nature of the Universe* (Minneapolis, MN: Fortress).

Murray, I. MacKay (1969), *Human Anatomy Made Simple* (Garden City, NY: Doubleday).

Murray, Michael J. (1999), *Reason for the Hope Within* (Grand Rapids, MI: Eerdmans).

Myron, Harold (2001), "Gill Slits in Humans," [On-line], URL: http://Newton.dep.anl.gov/askasci/zoo00/zoo00105.htm.

Nash, J. Madeleine (2002), "Inside the Womb," *Time*, 160[20]: 68-78, November 11.

Newman, H.H. (1932), *Evolution Yesterday and Today* (Baltimore, MD: William & Wilkins).

Newman, John Henry (1887), *An Essay in Aid of a Grammar of Assent* (London: Longmans, Green and Co.).

Nichols, Gus (1972), "The Scheme of Redemption," *The Bible Versus Liberalism*, ed. Thomas B. Warren (Henderson, TN: Freed-Hardeman University).

Nielsen, Kai (1973), *Ethics Without God* (London: Pemberton).

Niessen, Richard (1980), "Significant Discrepancies Between Theistic Evolution and the Bible," *UFO's, Satan, and Evolution*, ed. Sidney J. Jansma Sr. (Privately published by editor).

Nilsson, Heribert (1954), *Synthetische Artbildung* (Lund, Sweden: Vertag CWE Gleenrup).

Nourse, Alan E., ed. (1964), *The Body* (New York: Time, Inc.).

Nuland, Sherwin B. (1997), *The Wisdom of the Body* (New York: Knopf).

Oppenheimer, Jane (1967), *Essays in the History of Embryology and Biology* (Boston, MA: MIT Press).

"Ordovician Hammer Report" (1984), *Creation Ex Nihilo*, 2[3]: 16-17, February.

Ornstein, Robert (1991), *The Evolution of Consciousness* (New York: Prentice Hall Press).

Ornstein, Robert and Richard F. Thompson (1984), *The Amazing Brain* (Boston, MA: Houghton Mifflin).

O'Rourke, J.E. (1976), "Pragmatism Versus Materialism in Stratigraphy," *American Journal of Science*, 276:51, January.

Overbye, Dennis (2001), "Before the Big Bang, There Was… What?," *The New York Times* [On-line], URL: http://www.nytimes.com/2001/05/22/science/22BANG.html.

Overton, Basil (1981), *Evolution in the Light of Scripture, Science, and Sense* (Winona, MS: Choate).

Oxnard, Charles E. (1975), "The Place of the Australopithecines in Human Evolution: Grounds for Doubt?," *Nature*, 258:389-395, December.

Patterson, Colin (1999), *Evolution* (Ithaca, NY: Cornell University Press), second edition.

Pennisi, Elizabeth (1997), "Haeckel's Embryos: Fraud Rediscovered," *Science*, 277:1435, month/day.

Perutz, H.F. (1964), *Scientific American*, pp. 64-65, November.

Pfeiffer, Charles F. (1966), *The Biblical World* (Grand Rapids, MI: Baker).

Pfeiffer, John (1961), *The Human Brain* (New York: Harper and Brothers).

Pfeiffer, John (1964), *The Cell* (New York: Time).

Pilbeam, David (1982), "New Hominoid Skull Material from the Miocene of Pakistan," *Nature*, 295:232-234, January.

Pilbeam, David and Elwyn Simons (1971), "A Gorilla-Sized Ape from the Miocene of India," *Science*, 173:23, July.

Pines, Maya (1986), in *The Incredible Machine* (Washington, D.C., National Geographic Society).

Pinker, Steven (1997), "Why They Kill Their Newborns," *New York Times Magazine*, November 2.

Pitman, Michael (1984), *Adam and Evolution* (London: Rider).

Pope, Marvin H. (1965), *Job* (Garden City, NY: Doubleday).

Popper, Karl R. and John C. Eccles (1977), *The Self and Its Brain* (New York: Springer International).

Pratchett, Terry (1994), *Lords and Ladies* (New York: HarperPrism).

Price, Ira (1907), *The Monuments and the Old Testament* (Philadelphia, PA: American Baptist Publication Society).

"Primate Ancestor Lived with Dinos" (2002), [On-line], URL: http://news.bbc.co.uk/hi/english/sci/tech/newsid_1935000/1935558.stm.

Raup, D. (1979), "Conflicts Between Darwin and Paleontology," *Field Museum of Natural History Bulletin*, 50[1]:24-25.

Rennie, John (2002), "15 Answers to Creationist Nonsense," *Scientific American*, 287[1]:78-85, July.

Repetski, John E. (1978), "A Fish from the Upper Cambrian of North America," *Science*, 200:529-531, May 5.

Ricci, Paul (1986), *Fundamentals of Critical Thinking* (Lexington, MA: Ginn Press).

Richardson, Michael (1997a), "Embryonic Fraud Lives On," *New Scientist*, 155[2098]:23.

Richardson, Michael (1997b), "Heterochrony and the Phylotypic Period," *Developmental Biology*, 172:412-421.

Richardson, Michael (1998), "Haeckel's Embryos, Continued," *Science*, 281:1289, August 28.

Richardson, M., J. Hanken, L. Selwood, G.M. Wright, R.J. Richards, C. Pieau, A. Raynaud (1998), "Haeckel, Embryos, and Evolution," *Science*, 280:983-984, May 15.

Ridenour, Fritz (1967), *Who Says God Created?* (Glendale, CA: Gospel Light).

Ridley, Mark, ed. (1997), *Evolution* (Oxford, England: Oxford University Press).

Ridley, Matt (1999), *Genome: Autobiography of a Species in 23 Chapters* (New York: HarperCollins).

Ritland, R. (1982), "Historical Development of the Current Understanding of the Geologic Column: Part II," *Origins*, 9:28-47.

Robertson, A.T. (1931), *Word Pictures in the New Testament* (Nashville, TN: Broadman).

Roth, Ariel A. (1998), *Origins: Linking Science and Scripture* (Hagerstown, MD: Review and Herald Publishing Association).

Rowley, Harold Henry (1980), *Job* (Grand Rapids, MI: Eerdmans).

Rusch, W.H. Sr. (1970), "Human Footprints in Rocks," *Creation Research Society Quarterly*, 7:201-213.

Russell, Bertrand (1961), *Religion and Science* (London: Oxford University Press).

Sagan, Carl (1974), "Life on Earth," *Encyclopaedia Britannica* (New York: Encyclopaedia Britannica, Inc.), 10:894ff.

Sagan, Carl (1980), *Cosmos* (New York: Random House).

Sagan, Carl (1997), "Life," *Encyclopaedia Britannica* (New York: Encyclopaedia Britannica, Inc.), 22:964-981.

Sagan, Carl and Ann Druyan (1990), "The Question of Abortion," *Parade*, pp. 4-8, April 22.

Sanderson, Ivan T. (1967), *Uninvited Visitors* (New York: Cowles Education Corporation).

Sarfati, Jonathan D. (1998), "If God Created the Universe, then Who Created God?," *Creation Ex Nihilo Technical Journal*, 12[1]:21.

Sarfati, Jonathan D. (2002a), "15 Ways to Refute Materialistic Bigotry," [On-line], URL: http://www.answersingenesis.org/news/scientific_american.asp.

Sarfati, Jonathan (2002b), *Refuting Evolution 2* (Green Forest, AR: Master Books).

Schaff, Philip (1910), *History of the Christian Church* (Grand Rapids, MI: Eerdmans).

Schaff, Philip (1913), *The Person of Christ* (New York: American Tract Society).

Schiefelbein, Susan (1986), in *The Incredible Machine* (Washington, D.C.: National Geographic Society).

Schonfield, Hugh J. (1965), *The Passover Plot* (New York: Bantam).

Science Digest (1981), 89[1]:124, January/February.

Sedeen, Margaret (1986), in *The Incredible Machine* (Washington, D.C.: National Geographic Society).

Shklovskii, I.S. and Carl Sagan (1966), *Intelligent Life in the Universe* (New York: Dell).

Shryock, Harold (1968), "Your Bones Are Alive!," *Signs of the Times*, January.

Simpson, George Gaylord (1944) *Tempo and Mode in Evolution* (New York: Columbia University Press).

Simpson, George Gaylord (1949), *The Meaning of Evolution* (New Haven, CT: Yale University Press).

Simpson, George Gaylord (1953), *Life of the Past* (New Haven, CT: Yale University Press).

Simpson, George Gaylord (1967), *The Meaning of Evolution* (New Haven, CT: Yale University Press), revised edition.

Simpson, George Gaylord, C.S. Pittendrigh, and L.H. Tiffany (1957), *Life: An Introduction to Biology* (New York: Harcourt, Brace and Company).

Simpson, George Gaylord and William S. Beck (1965), *Life: An Introduction to Biology* (New York: Harcourt, Brace & World).

Sinnot, E.W., L.C. Dunn, and T. Dobzhansky (1958), *Principles of Genetics* (Columbus, OH: McGraw Hill) fifth edition.

Snelling, Andrew A. (1995), "The Whale Fossil in Diatomite, Lompoc, California," *Creation Ex Nihilo Technical Journal*, 9[2]:244-258.

Solomon, David (1972), "Procurator," *Encyclopaedia Judaica*, ed. Cecil Roth (Jerusalem: Keter Publishing).

Sperry, Roger W. (1966), "Mind, Brain, and Humanist Values," *Bulletin of the Atomic Scientists*, September.

Spetner, Lee M. (1997), *Not By Chance* (Brooklyn, NY: Judaica Press).

Spock, Benjamin (1998), *Baby and Child Care* (New York: Pocket Books).

Sproul, R.C. (1992), *Essential Truths of the Christian Faith* (Wheaton, IL: Tyndale House).

Sproul, R.C. (1994), *Not A Chance* (Grand Rapids, MI: Baker).

Stace, W.T. (1934), *A Critical History of Greek Philosophy* (London).

Stenger, Victor J. (1987), "Was the Universe Created?," *Free Inquiry*, 7[3]:26-30, Summer.

Stoner, Peter W. and Robert C. Newman (1976), *Science Speaks* (Chicago, IL: Moody), revised edition.

Strausburg and Weimer, (1947), *General Biology* (New York: John Wiley & Sons).

Strauss, James D. (1976), *The Shattering of Silence* (Joplin, MO: College Press).

Sunderland, Luther D. (1982), "Evolution? Prominent Scientist Reconsiders," *Impact* Article #108, June (San Diego, CA: Institute for Creation Research).

Sunderland, Luther D. (1984), *Darwin's Enigma* (El Cajon, CA: Master Books).

Swift, Dennis (no date), "The Dinosaurs of Acambaro," [Online], URL: http://www.omniology.com/3-Ceramic-Dinos.html.

Swift, Dennis (1997), "Messages on Stone," *Creation Ex Nihilo*, 19[2]:20-23, March-May.

Tait, Katherine (1975), *My Father Bertrand Russell* (New York: Harcourt, Brace, & Jovanovich).

Tattersall, Ian (1998), *Becoming Human* (San Diego, CA: Harcourt Brace).

Tavaré, Simon, C.R. Marshall, et al. (2002), "Using the Fossil Record to Estimate the Age of the Last Common Ancestor of Extant Primates," *Nature*, 416:726-729, April 18.

Taylor, Ian (1984), *In the Minds of Men* (Toronto, Canada: TFE Publishing).

Taylor, Robert R. Jr. (1974), "More Problems for Theistic Evolutionists," *Gospel Advocate*, 116[1]2,6-7, January 3.

Teaching Science in a Climate of Controversy (1986), (Ipswich, MA: American Scientific Affiliation).

Templeton, Charles B. (1996), *Farewell to God* (Toronto, Ontario, Canada: McClelland and Stewart).

Thaxton, Charles B., Walter L. Bradley, and Roger L. Olsen (1984), *The Mystery of Life's Origin* (New York: Philosophical Library).

Thayer, Joseph H. (1958 reprint), *Greek-English Lexicon of the New Testament* (Edinburgh, Scotland: T. & T. Clark).

Thompson, Bert (1977), *Theistic Evolution* (Shreveport, LA: Lambert).

Thompson, Bert (1990), "Does Human Suffering Disprove the Existence of a Benevolent God?," *Giving a Reason for Our Hope*, ed. Winford Claiborne (Henderson, TN: Freed-Hardeman College), pp. 280-285.

Thompson, Bert (1993), "Do Natural Disasters Negate Divine Benevolence?," *Reason and Revelation*, 13:65-69, September.

Thompson, Bert (2000a), *Creation Compromises* (Montgomery, AL: Apologetics Press), second edition.

Thompson, Bert (2000b), "The Origin, Nature, and Destiny of the Soul–Parts I-V," *Reason & Revelation*, 20:9-15,17-20,33-39,41-47,49-55, February-March, May-July.

Thompson, Bert (2000c), *Rock-Solid Faith: How to Build It* (Montgomery, AL: Apologetics Press).

Thompson, Bert and Wayne Jackson (1992), *A Study Course in Christian Evidences* (Montgomery, AL: Apologetics Press).

Thompson, W.R. (1956), "Introduction," *The Origin of Species* (New York: E.P. Dutton & Sons), pp. vii-xxv.

Thornhill, Randy and Craig T. Palmer (2000), *A Natural History of Rape* (Cambridge, MA: MIT Press).

Thornhill, Randy (2001), "A Natural History of Rape," Lecture delivered at Simon Fraser University. See full transcript [On-line], URL: http://www.harbour.sfu.ca/general-info/psa/psych/Thornhill_on_rape.pdf.

"A Tiny Worm Challenges Evolution" (no date), [On-line], URL: http://www.cs.unc.edu/plaisted/ce/worm.html.

Tipler, Frank (1994), *The Physics of Immortality* (New York: Doubleday).

"Tracking Dinosaurs" (1983), *Moscow News*, 24:10.

Trefil, James (1996), *101 Things You Don't Know about Science and No One Else Does Either* (Boston, MA: Houghton Mifflin).

Tryon, Edward P. (1973), "Is the Universe a Vacuum Fluctuation?," *Nature*, 246:396-397, December 14. [NOTE: Tryon's article was reprinted in *Modern Cosmology and Philosophy* (1998), ed. John Leslie (New York: Prometheus), pp. 222-225.]

Tryon, Edward P. (1984), "What Made the World?," *New Scientist*, 101:14-16, March 8.

(The) United Church Herald (1961), March 9.

Velikovsky, Immanuel (1955), *Earth in Upheaval* (New York: Dell).

Verrill, A.H. (1954), S*trange Prehistoric Animals and Their History* (Boston, MA: L.C. Page).

von Fange, Erich A. (1974), "Time Upside Down," *Creation Research Society Quarterly*, 11:19, June.

von Mises, Richard (1968), *Positivism* (New York: Dover).

Waddington, C.H. (1962), *The Nature of Life* (New York: Atheneum Press).

Wasserman, Aaron O. (1973), *Biology* (New York: Appleton-Century-Crofts).

Watson, James D. (1968), *The Double Helix* (New York: Atheneum).

Watson, James D. (1987), *Molecular Biology of the Gene* (New York: W.A. Benjamin).

Watson, James D. (2003), *DNA* (New York: Alfred A. Knopf).

Watson, Lyall (1982), "The Water People," *Science Digest*, 90[5]: 44, May.

Weinberg, Steven (1993), *Dreams of a Final Theory* (New York: Vintage Books).

Weiss, Joseph (1990), "Unconscious Mental Functioning," *Scientific American*, March.

Weisz, Paul (1965), *Elements of Biology* (New York: McGraw-Hill).

Wharton, Ed (1972), *Redemption is Planned, Needed, Provided* (West Monroe, LA: Howard).

Whitcomb, John C. (1972), *The Early Earth* (Grand Rapids, MI: Baker).

White, Robert (1978), *Reader's Digest*, September.

White, Tim (2003), "Early Hominids–Diversity or Distortion?," *Science*, 299:1994-1995,1997, March 28.

Whitelaw, Thomas (no date), "Genesis," *The Pulpit Commentary* (Grand Rapids, MI: Eerdmans).

"Whose Ape Is It, Anyway?" (1984), *Science News*, 125[23]: 361, June 9.

Wilder-Smith, A.E. (1975), *Man 's Origin: Man 's Destiny* (Minneapolis, MN: Bethany Fellowship).

Wilder-Smith, A.E. (1976), *A Basis for a New Biology* (Einigen: Telos International).

Wilder-Smith, A.E. (1987), *The Scientific Alternative to Neo-Darwinian Evolutionary Theory* (Costa Mesa, CA: TWFT Publishers).

Wile, Jay L. (2000), *Exploring Creation with General Science* (Anderson, IN: Apologia Educational Ministries).

Wilson, Edward O. (1982), "Toward a Humanistic Biology," *The Humanist*, September/October.

Wilson, Edward O. (1998), *Consilience* (New York: Knopf).

Winchester, A.M. (1951), *Genetics* (Boston, MA: Houghton-Mifflin).

Wise, Kurt (2002), *Faith, Form, and Time* (Nashville, TN: Broadman & Holman).

Woods, Guy N. (1976), "Man Created in God's Image," *Gospel Advocate*, 118[33]:514,518, August 12.

Woods, Guy N. (1982), "'And be not Conformed to this World,'" *Gospel Advocate*, 124[1]:2, January 7.

Wright, Sewall (1997), "The Role of Mutation, Inbreeding, and Selection in Evolution," *Evolution*, ed. Mark Ridley (Oxford, England: Oxford University Press), pp. 32-40.

Wylie, Evan M. (1962), *Today's Health*, July.

Wysong, R.L. (1976), *The Creation-Evolution Controversy* (East Lansing, MI: Inquiry Press).

Young, Edward J. (1975), *Studies in Genesis One* (Grand Rapids, MI: Baker).

Youngson, Robert (1998), *Scientific Blunders: A Brief History of How Wrong Scientists Can Sometimes Be* (New York: Carroll and Graf).

Zehavi, Idit and Avishal Dekel (1999), "Evidence for a Positive Cosmological Constant from Flows of Galaxies and Distant Supernovae," *Nature,* 401:252-254, September 16.

Zuckerman, Solly (1970), *Beyond the Ivory Tower* (New York: Taplinger).

SUBJECT INDEX

A

B

C

D

E

F

G

H

I

J

K

L

M

N

O

P

Q

R

S

T

U

NAME INDEX

E

F

G

H

I

J

K

L

M

V

W

Y

Z